Brides, Inc.

American Weddings and the Business of Tradition

Vicki Howard

UNIVERSITY OF PENNSYLVANIA PRESS

Philadelphia

Copyright © 2006 University of Pennsylvania Press
All rights reserved
Printed in the United States of America on acid-free paper

10 9 8 7 6 5 4 3 2 1

Published by
University of Pennsylvania Press
Philadelphia, Pennsylvania 19104-4112

Library of Congress Cataloging-in-Publication Data

Howard, Vicki.
    Brides, Inc. : American weddings and the business of tradition / Vicki Howard.
        p.   cm.
    Includes bibliographical references and index.
    ISBN-13: 978-0-8122-3945-4
    ISBN-10: 0-8122-3945-8 (alk. paper)
    1. Wedding supplies and services industry—United States.   2. Bridal shops—United
States.   3. Weddings—Economic aspects—United States.   I. Title.
HD9999.W373 U646   2006
338.4′739250973 22

2006041845

To Sean

Contents

Introduction

At the beginning of the twenty-first century, more people are choosing to have big weddings, which are more expensive than ever before. In 2005, the average cost of a wedding neared $30,000. For most families, this represented the most significant payout they would ever make, after purchasing a home and paying for college. Weddings today are a $70 billion industry and have become an important part of the economy.[1] They give business to florists, caterers, bridal consultants, photographers, and limousine firms, as well as the jewelry, wedding apparel, and honeymoon tourism industries, not to mention the enterprises that provide ceremony and reception venues and the retailers that support the lucrative wedding gift tradition. Although the rise of the big wedding was likely responsible for some of Americans' massive consumer debt at the turn of the century, it was good news for the many businesses that supported major advertising magazines like *Bride's*, whose 1,271-page spring 2000 issue is in the *Guinness Book of World Records* as the largest magazine ever produced.[2] If size is a measure of success, then the American wedding industry has been very successful.

The extent of the bridal market today and the wide range of businesses that cater to this market suggest that consumers readily agree to the commercialization of their marriage rituals. Simply put, Americans love big weddings. The rise in wedding-related consumption has been accompanied by a seemingly endless appetite for weddings in popular culture—on reality television shows, in magazine and newspaper features on the nuptials of Hollywood and television stars, in popular fiction for women, and in a host of wedding-themed movies and toys for young girls.[3] However, as we will see, the big white wedding was not always widespread. For most men and women from the colonial period through the nineteenth century, a wedding was not a consumer rite but rather a communal celebration of marriage embedded in a system of reciprocity. By the last quarter of the nineteenth century, a range of businesses were providing services and goods for the celebration of middle-class or elite nuptials. Brides could shop at new luxurious department stores or specialty jewelers, employ dressmakers or purchase ready-made clothing, hire florists and caterers, have a wedding portrait taken at a professional studio, and take a honeymoon trip to Niagara Falls. Etiquette books began including sections on weddings, giving advice on wedding invitations and thank-you letters, wedding gifts, the bridal gown, and the trousseau. A wedding industry catering to a mass market, however, still did not exist at this point. For most people, weddings did not revolve around the singular display of goods and special once-in-a-lifetime consumption as they would later in the twentieth century. Wedding ring customs, for example, were still modest and not linked to particular brand names or advertising campaigns that shaped their meaning. Bridal gowns, if they were even white, were not yet meant to be used only once in a display of conspicuous consumption, but could be worn again. Catering services and commercial reception venues existed, but family members continued to provide homemade wedding cakes and hold receptions at home.

As the twentieth century progressed, weddings were increasingly surrounded by consumer rites—invented traditions or elaborations of older customs that grew out of business's need for new and dependable markets. Just as consumer capitalism touched almost every aspect of American culture by the 1920s, the rite of marriage also began to enter mass consumer society. By the 1930s, in spite of, and in some cases because of, the Depression, businesses invented new ritual goods and services and offered up an alternate mass consumer ideal to replace earlier communal or ethnic wedding practices. Composed of many different types of businesses, from mass retailers and publishers to smaller firms and even kitchen capitalists who worked out of their homes providing services for the bride, this wedding industry also provided economic opportunities for a broad range of women and for African American entrepreneurs who found a niche in catering to a disfranchised bridal market. As this industry evolved, these individuals and firms were increasingly positioned to transform the practice of ordinary people. Introducing new services, such as the gift registry and the bridal salon, the wedding industry set higher standards of consumption and naturalized the lavish formal white wedding. As cultural producers, these businesses and entrepreneurs wielded immense authority on issues of taste and etiquette, and established a cultural ideal against which all weddings would be judged.

As the industry sought to "trade on tradition," it faced deep cultural ambivalence about the nature of its enterprise.[4] Indeed, suspicions of bridal consumption (and women) run amok developed side by side with the new consumer rites. Around the turn of the twentieth century, a host of cultural critics opposed lavish nuptials and those who "spent beyond their means." As celebrations of the institution of marriage and the culmination of romantic love, weddings were not supposed to be commercial ventures. A bride was supposed to be innocent and pure, not a slave to fashion or a status seeker. Wedding tradition, moreover, was something that was supposed to be handed down from generation to generation, following the dictates of custom, religion, and culture. Given the special nature of a wedding, businesses faced a fundamental dilemma: how to persuade consumers to accept new goods and services in connection with a ritual that was ostensibly "traditional" and noncommercial.

Deeply invested in the potentially problematic invention of wedding tradition, jewelers, department stores, fashion designers, bridal consultants, and many others became experts on inventing tradition, creating their own versions of the past to legitimize new rituals and help overcome cultural resistance to the lavish affair. According to historian Eric Hobsbawm's well-known formulation, invented traditions were the "set of practices, normally governed by overtly or tacitly accepted rules and of a ritual or symbolic nature, which seek to inculcate certain values and norms of behavior by repetition, which automatically implies continuity with the past."[5] In other words, traditions were invented to soothe the discomfort and dislocation of social change, or at least to make some parts of social life appear constant.[6] Indeed, jewelers, bridal magazine editors and etiquette writers, department store window-display artists, bridal consultants, fashion designers, and many others constructed the "traditional wedding" as something timeless and unchanging, even though it was forever adapting to suit the demands of the marketplace. In their writings, visual representations, and merchandising promotions, they used the ideal of the traditional white wedding to sell new goods and professional services and uphold their role as experts. Businesses continued to employ both the idea of tradition and the idea of modernity to fit the formal white wedding into new social contexts created by World War II, the Cold War, and changing women's roles in the 1960s and 1970s. Claiming ties with "ancient customs," the wedding industry promoted new goods and services as traditional, even as it introduced a variety of fashions in wedding apparel and ring customs, and modern services, such as gift registries that rationalized gift customs, bridal salons that saved time and made wedding planning more efficient, and wedding packages that standardized ceremonies and reception celebrations. Through the efforts of the wedding industry, the "traditional" white wedding, ironically, became associated with the "Modern Bride" by the postwar period.

This emphasis on wedding tradition served a wider social function. By the 1950s, a new cult of marriage was working its way into the culture. The wedding industry was one facet of this "homeward bound" movement.[7] Even corporations like DuPont, with no direct connection to the wedding industry, celebrated the early marriage and the rising marriage rates of their employees as a validation of the American way of life. Businesses took advantage of growing household needs created by the marriage boom, but they also capitalized on the consumer ethic in which this demographic shift was couched. The formal white wedding emerged as a cultural ideal by the 1950s in part because it embodied postwar liberal values in an era of affluence.[8] It was connected to historian Lizabeth Cohen's concept of the consumers' republic, "a strategy that emerged after the Second World War for reconstructing the nation's economy and reaffirming its democratic values through promoting the expansion of mass consumption." It was also connected to a renewed celebration of women's domesticity. In film, on television, and in magazine advertising, housewives embraced their traditional role and the goods that went with it for the most part, though reality was much more complicated.[9] At the same time, masculine ideals shifted slightly, as men were supposed to become more equal partners in this domestic scene, something that new wedding rituals reflected. Bridal magazines, retailers' promotions, and advertisements echoed changing gender ideologies, turning the double-ring ceremony and the formal white wedding into a "right" of all American brides and grooms. In the context of postwar fears of communism and other threats to the "American way of life," such consumer rites became a symbol of the nation's economic prosperity and social stability—of the "better living" provided by capitalism. While not everyone had equal access to the traditional white wedding, in the early postwar era businesses reached outside the white middle class for the first time to create a truly national bridal market.

* * *

Although the wedding industry is big business today and weddings are ubiquitous in American society, no full-length historical study of this phenomenon has emerged to date. In recent years, several treatments of the meaning of the white wedding in American culture have been published, perhaps mirroring the national obsession with weddings. Weighted more toward the contemporary period than my work here, these studies provide fascinating insights into the reasons why consumers embrace the formal white wedding ideal, but do not focus on the historical role of business in transforming the way people married.[10] Uncovering the origins of the wedding industry, *Brides, Inc.* goes behind the scenes to show how entrepreneurs and various industries helped create the wedding culture that dominates today in the United States. *Brides, Inc.* demonstrates how the commercial became the cultural—how the rise of consumer capitalism transformed one of life's most significant, intimate moments.

More broadly, I use the wedding industry to explore the ways in which consumer capitalism has shaped social relationships and produced meaning in the twentieth century. The wedding industry came to wield immense power over the course of the twentieth century. Although businesses like Marshall Field's department store claimed to "Give the Lady What She Wants," it is important to remember that these social institutions helped define these wants in the first place.[11] To this end, *Brides, Inc.* focuses on the producers of the white wedding, a story that has not been told fully and needs to be. However, I also attempt to shed light on the ways in which consumers participated in social and economic transformations.[12] Those who married helped define American wedding culture and made it a meaningful part of their lives.[13] Consumers planning and shopping for their nuptials and future homes certainly had a degree of autonomy. Women, who were understood to be the main consumers of wedding-related goods and services, were not mere victims of advertising and merchandising campaigns, nor did they simply accept wedding industry advice uncritically. As this study of the wedding industry shows, moreover, at different points in time those about to marry made choices that went against the commercial ideal promoted by the business of brides. Women followed other dictates besides those offered up by etiquette writers, bridal magazine editors, department-store bridal consultants, and the other wedding entrepreneurs and professionals they encountered when planning their ceremonies and receptions and shopping for their future homes. Ethnic and religious custom, family tradition, class identity, regional practice, and individual tastes and preferences certainly all played a role in shaping wedding consumption, though to do justice to each would require another book.[14] For the most part, however, the wedding industry was extraordinarily successful in introducing new traditions and elaborating upon old ones, as in the case of the groom's ring or the white wedding dress. Yet, when invented traditions like the male engagement ring did not resonate with consumers, they failed.

A book about the wedding industry should say something about the relation between the invented tradition of the big white wedding and the institution of marriage. Dramatic demographic shifts surrounding marriage took place in the twentieth century. These changes, which included an increase in premarital pregnancy and cohabitation before marriage, gave greater symbolic weight to the institution and have also been political fodder in the culture wars between traditionalists, or the "family values" camp, and those who espouse more liberal views about sexuality and marriage. On the surface of things, a formal white wedding, held in a religious setting amidst family and members of one's community, would seem to accommodate the former view. The cost of the wedding, its ritualistic aspects and apparent timelessness, and its public nature suggest a seriousness of purpose, a dedication perhaps to a traditional conception of marriage based on monogamy and citizenship.[15]

While the notion of the white wedding elevated and idealized marriage, however, other factors made married life a different reality. Throughout the twentieth century, married white women increasingly entered the workforce while upholding a "second shift" at home. Divorce became more accessible and less stigmatized during this period as well. As marriage became a more flexible institution, and as women experienced a transformation in their social and economic roles, it might be expected that weddings would reflect these changes and become less "traditional." In fact, the opposite occurred. New gender roles and less traditional marital behavior paralleled an elaboration of consumer rites—weddings got bigger. By the 1980s, living together before marriage, premarital pregnancy, or a second marriage did not preclude a traditional white wedding as it once had.[16] Premarital history of the couple aside, other factors also contributed to the escalation of consumer rites. On a practical level, standards of living and increased prosperity after the Depression and World War II allowed for bigger, more expensive weddings for larger numbers of people. While these sociological and economic explanations for changing practices are convincing, I focus instead on the role that experts, entrepreneurs, and businesses played in popularizing the white wedding ideal and transforming marriage rites into consumer rites by the postwar period.

The wedding industry consists of numerous types of businesses, each with its own historical trajectory and set of issues. In general, each was affected by the rise of mass production and mass distribution in the nineteenth century, followed by the consolidation of corporate power in the twentieth century. Each industry, however, experienced these transformations in a variety of ways and with different results. Several industries were in direct competition with each other, such as specialty jewelers and department stores. Department stores employed new merchandising techniques to attract the wedding trade and transferred their nineteenth-century emphasis on service and amenities to the luxurious new bridal salons that began appearing in the 1920s. Bridal magazines grew out of a new interest in market segmentation in the 1930s and growing reliance on advertising. Custom-made bridal gowns gave way to ready-to-wear dresses during this period as well. And businesses that supplied the venue for the wedding reception took different forms in various regions of the nation. While businesses had to deal with varying economic, institutional, and regional concerns, in the end, each envisioned the bridal market along similar lines during roughly the same time period. Many entrepreneurs, experts, and businesses developed similar merchandising methods. In the 1930s, these businesses rallied around the idea that "love knows no depression," promoting new bridal services. A variety of businesses began keeping track of marriage rates and the favored months of marriage; by the 1940s, many began formally studying brides' consumer habits. With marriage rates rising as couples rushed to marry before men went to war, the jewelry industry and others were keen to hear "wedding bells on the cash register."[17] Through the concerted efforts of a host of businesses, by the 1950s those about to marry had become their own market segment. Although locally dispersed, businesses with wedding trade became part of a unified force with a national market through the efforts of bridal magazines and professional organizations.

Because of this diversity of issues, I have devoted a separate chapter to the history of each business or industry with a bridal market. While this organization results in some overlap, it allows for a richer history of each segment of the wedding industry. Certain businesses with significant though not necessarily exclusive wedding trade, such as florists and photographers, are largely omitted for reasons of space. The honeymoon industry, which has received excellent treatment in recent years, is also not covered.[18] After Chapter 1, which examines the initial concerns and critiques of the big wedding when it first appeared, the remaining rituals and their related businesses are introduced in the order that consumers encountered them as they progressed from the engagement to the planning of the wedding to the shopping for the bridal gown and trousseau, and finally, to the marriage ceremony and reception. I set the stage by exploring differing views of wedding consumption around the turn of the twentieth century, before the industry took shape. Chapter 2 looks at the jewelry industry and its role in the invention of ring traditions. Chapter 3 focuses on the way that women's magazines, bridal magazines, and etiquette books linked weddings and consumerism and helped invent the bridal market. Chapter 4 is about the major role department stores played in fashioning the white wedding ideal through new merchandising techniques, such as window display, fashion shows, and gift registry promotions, things that became traditions in their own right. The department-store bridal salon is discussed extensively here, but the field of bridal consulting as a profession for women is examined in Chapter 5, which focuses on the female entrepreneurs in the industry, such as specialty bridal shop owners, wedding consultants, fashion designers, and wedding gown manufacturers. Chapter 6 surveys the history of the catering industry and the diverse venues available for the wedding reception, looking at the evolution of public and private spaces and the cultural debates surrounding each. An epilogue on the postmodern wedding and recent developments in the industry, such as Internet wedding planning, discount bridal apparel, wedding expositions, and the gay wedding market, brings the story up to its multibillion-dollar present.

CHAPTER ONE

The Evil of Elaborate and
Showy Weddings

Think of a big wedding and many images come to mind—the demanding bride and her mother, the reluctant groom, the resigned father of the bride—all going deeper and deeper into debt as the bills mount for rings, flowers, gifts, wedding apparel, a catered affair, limousine service, music, photography, videography, and a honeymoon to an exotic location. These figures have been the subject of humor and satire, but for the most part, a lavish celebration of marriage and the overspending associated with it have become an accepted and expected part of American wedding culture. Such consumerism, however, has not always been considered "good taste." Nor was the commercialized wedding inevitable. In fact, it faced serious impediments in the last quarter of the nineteenth century and first decade of the twentieth century when a variety of fiction writers, etiquette authors, reformers, and religious leaders attacked useless wedding presents, ostentatious gift displays, the excessive accumulation of bridal finery, trousseau fashions, and costly receptions. During this period, a variety of wedding morality tales emerged to tell different stories about the relationship among consumption, taste, and power.

Criticism of wedding excess fit into a larger social critique of consumption that developed in the decades after the Civil War, at which time a new concern for what historian Daniel Horowitz has called the "morality of spending" arose. As the nation became increasingly industrial, urban, and immigrant, new commercial leisure practices came under attack by those who believed a simpler, more traditional way of life was slipping away. Proponents of Victorian genteel culture felt threatened in the face of an expanding world of goods and an emerging mass culture. Like changing leisure and consumption patterns, shifts in wedding practice, or even the older tradition of the big, communal marriage celebration, were now viewed as a sign of social decline or profligacy. To elites, wedding rituals were supposed to be an immutable mark of civilization, something that "belong[ed] to the dawn of history." As more and more people—black and white, native-born and immigrant, middle and working class—appeared able to afford or emulate the trappings of the formal white wedding, the meaning of this celebration changed. Critiques of the big wedding dissipated by the 1920s, just as a nascent wedding industry began introducing a host of invented traditions.[1]

CHANGING PRACTICES

Before the rise of the lavish catered affair, American weddings defied generalization. In the colonial period and early republic, regional differences abounded, the result of religious, social, and geographic factors. Many unions were formed without much ado, and marriages took place without state or church sanction. In the colonial period, informal marriages were widespread among white settlers with limited access to church or state officials. Informal or common-law marriage decreased in northern colonies by the eighteenth century when officiants were more readily on hand, but it persisted in the Anglican southern colonies where the required church clerics were few and far between. Couples made reciprocal promises of marriage and then moved in together, declaring themselves married. Pregnancy or childbirth also served as an indication of marriage.[2]

By the early nineteenth century, informal marriage was much less common, but persisted in the South among poor whites and among slaves. For the millions of enslaved men and women in the United States, marriage was tied to freedom. Slave marriages were not recognized as legal unions. Even so, according to William Wells Brown, it was "very common for slaves to be married." Bondsmen and women marked their unions by "jumping the broom" and by simply setting up housekeeping together after a "Parson Blanket" marriage, in which the future husband brought his blanket and laid it down beside his chosen one. Only on occasion were weddings or religious ceremonies sponsored by paternalistic owners who allowed the material trappings of a wedding while denying its legal status (and on occasion collected a fee for marrying the slave couple). These ceremonies omitted phrases from the ritual like "Till death do you part," and "Those whom God hath joined together, let no man put asunder."[3]

Weddings in pre-industrial America fit into the seasonal rhythm of everyday life. In the country, the celebration of a marriage brought entire neighborhoods together. For some, weddings were big events, characterized by inclusiveness and reciprocity. At communal activities such as barn raisings, apple-paring bees, corn huskings, quilting bees, and sleighing parties, those attending were rewarded by a neighborhood dance. A marriage might mean food, drink, and revelry, or perhaps just a special meal for the family, but mainly it was about the establishment of a new household. The process began with the publication of the banns and ended with the couple "going into housekeeping," a final event that could take place weeks after the couple was joined in matrimony. In the Northeast, it involved communal activities that lasted for weeks as women got together to ready the bride's clothing and help sew quilts and the bride's linens, thus weaving the new couple into the community.[4] Whether large or small, however, in this period the wedding ceremony and "reception" were informal events that provided opportunities for sociability and strengthened family and community ties.

Marriage in most of the United States during the nineteenth century consisted of a panoply of regional and local folk customs. Ceremonies might involve folk customs specific to the couple's background, such as the African American marriage ritual of "jumping the broom," the various money-gathering rituals at German- and Polish-American celebrations, or the white southern "infare," a reception for the community held at the groom's home the day after the ceremony. One of the more common folk customs was the shivaree. When rural couples in the Southwest broke with tradition and did not make their wedding a communal celebration, they were "shivareed" by friends and neighbors. A shivaree involved teasing and sometimes raucous behavior; African Americans also practiced them on "old bachelors" who married.[5] One white Texas rancher who married in 1888 hosted a "big supper" and gave a dance in the courthouse to "keep the boys from shivareeing." Another Texas cowboy was not as lucky: as William Wall reminisced to a Works Progress Administration (WPA) interviewer, he and his bride were woken on their wedding night by an ox bell and "the awfullest racket you ever heard" created by buckets of rocks. The members of his cowboy community then chased Wall on horseback and threatened to throw him in the river if he did not throw them a dance, which he eventually did.[6] The marriage celebrations that Wall observed, however, were simple, marked by feasts of barbequed meat, bread, coffee, and whiskey, as well as fiddle music and out-door dances on a big, flat rock in camp.[7]

Similarly, raucous bedding rituals persisted in less urban settings as late as 1890. The old tradition of bedding the bridal couple lingered on in nineteenth-century rural England and persisted in some areas of Canada until later in the century. One Ohio wedding, recorded in the diary of a young teacher who closed school early to take part in the nuptials of her friends, featured an "elegant supper" at home. After the meal everyone "beheld the bride in bed but were not allowed to see the groom." During the night, as the teacher discreetly wrote in her diary, the newlyweds' bed "accidentally fell down and lots of other things."[8] The viewing of the bride without the groom signaled a shift away from the older custom of a public bedding ritual in which the couple was put to bed together for the night. The teacher's reticence in recording the event perhaps also revealed a growing awareness that marriage "belonged" in the private sphere.

Increasingly, middle-class weddings were celebrated with more elaboration, formality, and regularity—and greater expenditure. As historian Ellen Roth-man has argued, the formal wedding began with northern elites in the early nineteenth century, and later spread to the middle classes. In the early nine-teenth century, most middle-class northern couples married in quiet, informal home ceremonies that required little advance preparation. Invitations were sent on average only a week ahead of time and were often verbal or handwritten. As ceremonies were small, there was little display or pageantry. Bridal atten-dants were uncommon. More well-to-do parents might help the couple get established, giving them money or property as a wedding gift, but gifts were not yet customary. Printed invitations and bridal attendants, however, soon spread beyond the elite to middle-class white northern brides. Lavish wedding receptions were sometimes even accompanied by formal menus (figure 1).[9]

Such weddings fit an emerging middle-class domestic ideal that incorporated new notions of decorum and sexuality. Restrained in their celebration of nup-tial bliss in the private sphere of the home, family affairs were far from the cowboy weddings William Wall observed in Texas. Weddings were more of a

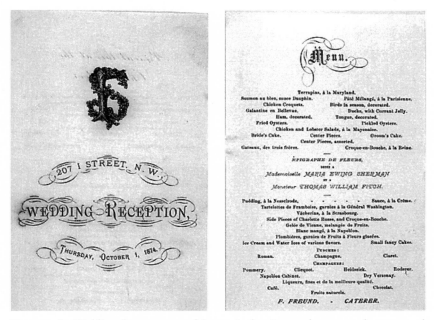

FIGURE 1. Weddings became more elaborate in the nineteenth century, demonstrated by the popularity of engraved invitations and printed menus. Library of Congress, Rare Book and Special Collections Division, Printed Ephemera Collection, Portfolio 206, Folder 40.

private affair characterized by mannered and sedate behavior. For example, many middle-class, northern, white Protestant brides married in their family parlor or in front of a decorated fireplace at home.[10] Still, a home wedding could be a ceremonious affair. Popular Underwood & Underwood stereograph views of "The Wedding Day" showed how banks of palms could transform a plain room into an exotic background for a ceremony. Although a home ceremony was considered highly proper, the church became an increasingly desirable place to marry. Church weddings also fit the domestic ideal, but in a different way. Pious and pure at the altar, the virgin bride in white was a symbol of "True Womanhood." By the mid-nineteenth century, northern middle-class and elite brides typically had a church wedding followed by a reception at home paid for and provided by the bride's family, a pattern that early etiquette writers established as a cultural ideal.[11] While negative examples of the home wedding ceremony appeared in popular culture at this time, the tradition of marrying at home was still an acceptable, and in many cases a desirable, choice. By 1890, religious ceremonies, whether at home, at church, or in another location, accounted for 85 percent of marriages in the famous Middletown study by sociologists Robert and Helen Lynd.[12]

On the surface, middle-class marriage ceremonies and receptions of the late nineteenth century resembled those of later years. Indeed, the nineteenth-century elite Victorian wedding provided a model for the more commercial one of the twentieth century. A ring was purchased, and after the date was set, invitations were sent out. The ceremony usually consisted of the procession of the wedding party, with the bride in a long, formal, white gown, in a religious venue or home decorated with flowers, music, and an exchange of vows and the ring given to the bride. Professionals were hired, such as florists who decorated the church with palms and provided the bouquets.[13] The reception that followed also included all the recognizable elements, such as a white wedding cake, sometimes tiered, sometimes not, a cake-cutting ritual, refreshments, and perhaps music and dancing.

Though weddings in the late nineteenth and twentieth centuries were similar, there were crucial differences. Before the rise of the wedding industry, most weddings took place without extensive use of professionals or commercial services (figure 2). Letters, diaries, oral histories, and literature document how early weddings were the loving product of family labor. Prescriptive literature outlined lavish menus for wedding breakfasts or buffets, assuming the help of servants, though their numbers had been declining since the Civil War.[14] While the middle class and well-to-do hired help, more commonly female relatives of the bride were crucial to the success of the event. At the 1883 wedding of an African American couple in Missouri, the bride's aunt hosted the dinner after the church wedding, furnishing everything but the turkey, which the groom provided. Communal immigrant weddings featured simple fare prepared by female relatives, such as the smoking potatoes, heaps of bologna sausages, and pitchers of beer depicted at the *veselija* in Upton Sinclair's novel *The Jungle*. For women, this was hard, sometimes stressful, labor, but it was also a source of pride and pleasure for those helping. It was also appreciated by women attending the reception. One interested guest at a white southerner's 1906 wedding wrote that the bride's aunt made the wedding cake using "36 eggs, and a fence of icing four inches with a miniature bride and groom

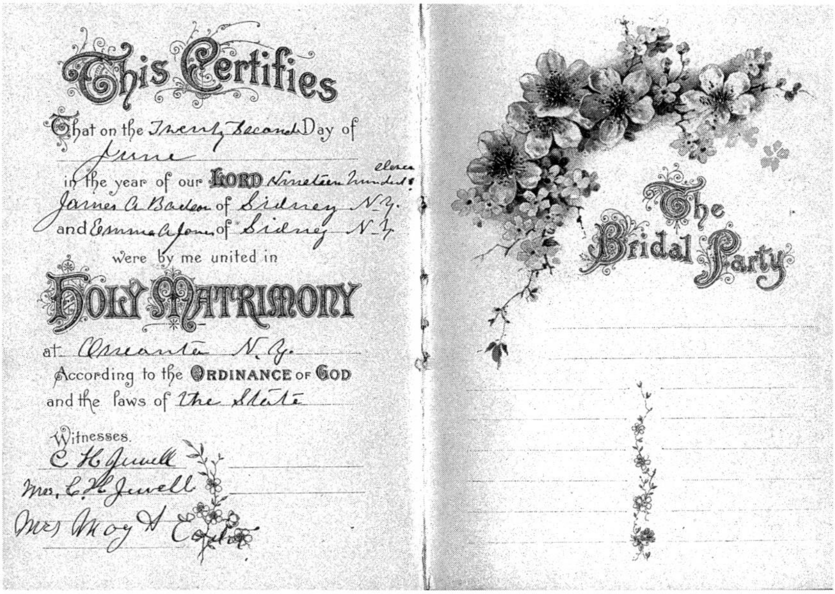

FIGURE 2. Wedding booklets, which later were sponsored by retailers and provided lists for gifts, did not promote consumption in the early twentieth century. This one included poems and biblical passages, as well as decorated pages to list guests and members of the wedding party. *Wedding Chimes* booklet, New York: C. R. Gibson & Company, circa 1911. Collection of the author.

beneath a bell hung from a bunch of orange blossoms." She commented, "don't you know it was pretty."[15] Embedded in the community and the product of family labor, these rituals were nevertheless increasingly connected to the market and thus the subject of a host of cultural anxieties generated by the social and economic transformations of the age. As the country urbanized and as greater segments of the population began participating in American consumer culture, aunts hosted fewer dinners and made fewer wedding cakes for their nieces, receptions began moving out of the home, and the modern wedding began to take shape.

THE "WEDDING BAZAAR"

The commercialization of American weddings began with the rise of the wedding gift tradition, much to the consternation of the apostles of thrift. The custom originated among elites. Society brides compiled huge guest lists and sent out hundreds of engraved invitations that resulted in vast quantities of gifts and many duplicates. One 1908 Tennessee bride invited 1,600 people from all over the South. Though certainly all did not attend, she still received seventy silver gifts, fifty-seven glass and crystal items, thirty-one pieces of china, nine sets of linens, and sixty miscellaneous items. In Boston, the 1899 marriage of William Graves Titcomb and Jessie Watson Shepard resulted in more than 340 gifts, each of which was painstakingly recorded with its sender in their wedding album. Their marriage provided more than enough material trappings to fill a cluttered Victorian parlor. Numerous Doulton and Canton vases, doilies, chair scarves, card receivers, etchings such as *The Steps of Capri* and *The Mandolin Player*, and oil paintings such as *The Cliffs*, as well as a set of white-and-gold furniture from "Mama Shepard" helped the couple decorate a comfortable new home. As was typical, their most frequent gift was silver, something pushed by numerous trade articles at the time, followed by china goods and decorative items.[16] Books were another common gift—they received three complete sets of Shakespeare on the occasion of their marriage.[17]

The new tradition of the obligatory wedding present took hold because it fit mid-nineteenth-century gender roles and social relations. Wedding presents in this sense were distinct from the Jewish *mitgift* or the European tradition of the bride's dowry, intended to signal a social contract and to provide economic support for the new couple. As it emerged in American culture, the wedding present was not part of marriage negotiations between two families, nor was it really supposed to set up a couple in their new home. Wedding presents were not necessarily purchased goods, but could be handmade trifles, items for personal use, as well as objects for the decoration and furnishing of the home. These gifts were directed at the bride's domestic sphere and were sent to her, not the groom, mirroring the increasingly rigid division of labor that emerged in the industrial period.[18] Wedding presents were also a part of women's work, as the organizing, recording, and thanking fell to them.

As women did these tasks, however, they imbued their presents with different meanings. By the time that Mary Paul wrote to her future husband in Maryland in 1905 about their upcoming nuptials, wedding gifts had become an expected part of getting married, and brides like her looked forward to receiving them. Mary Paul wrote: "It is too much fun getting presents—I adore it and they can't come too many or too often for me!" At one point she told her future husband, "We have 200 presents." For some women, particular gifts carried a special meaning related to their marriage. Gifts of Lady Baltimore pattern silver, engraved with the bride's new initial in Old English, and sets of china for entertaining could signify a future life with one's husband, as they did for Pauline Wright on the occasion of her marriage to Irby Nichols in 1918.[19] Presents marked other special relationships as well. For example, hand-made gifts, which persisted into the twentieth century in the South, allowed the giver to make a personal connection with the new bride. As one wedding guest wrote of her handmade gift to Mary Moody Northern in Galveston, Texas, "every stitch was a living thing."[20]

Not everyone liked the practice of giving wedding presents. As it became an obligatory custom, some began to resist the new tradition, spelling out their objections in popular periodicals and in etiquette manuals. The well-known minister Henry Ward Beecher was one of the first to attack this new social obligation in an 1870 article aptly titled "Wedding Bazaars," which appeared in the *New York Ledger* and in *Godey's*, a widely circulated women's periodi-cal.[21] Writing five years before his own infamous adultery trial in which he was charged with seducing a married woman in his congregation, Beecher ironically celebrated the innocence and sentiment of love at the beginning of marriage, heralding its ability to sustain individuals through later hardships of life. "Wedding Bazaars" harkened back to "simpler ages," revealing a yearn-ing for the past and a concern with the perceived hypocrisy and social striving of Victorian life. The minister suggested that presents were supposed to ex-press a deeply felt sentiment, something possible in a communal, face-to-face world where everyone knew the marrying couple and their families. Beecher particularly disapproved of wedding gifts that were connected to social striving or a desire for monetary gain. He envisioned a dangerous competitiveness when "the near neighbor recalls, when his daughter was married, that the bride's father gave her a silver urn, and surely it would not do for him to be less generous." Those who could not afford expensive gifts, moreover, felt pressured to pay "for a gift beyond his means."[22] By the time he was writing, the battle was well on the way to being lost, as more people had begun to follow the script of the formal white wedding, with engraved invitations, pres-ents, a gift display, a church ceremony, and a reception.

Beecher's concerns appeared elsewhere in popular culture in the many etiquette books appearing during this period. Like Beecher, etiquette writers criticized "bold display of wealth and ostentatious generosity."[23] Unlike the minister, however, etiquette writers advised on the proper execution of the custom and upheld elaborate new consumer rites. Writers told wedding guests that gifts were required if one were invited to the reception, but not if only to the ceremony. They discussed when to give the gifts (early was better), suggested appropriate items, and advised on the proper wording of the card. They also reminded brides to write personal thank-you notes for each gift and to display the gifts on long tables, sometimes with cards noting the giver. Etiquette advice was not always followed by the bride or her guests, and in part, this was what offended the defenders of culture. *Godey's* in 1873 quipped that "Wedding cards are now issued with the notice 'No Plated Ware,' printed in one corner. Would it not be as well to add, 'No presents from the Dollar stores put up in Caldwell's or Bailey's boxes'?"[24]

Etiquette advice on presents showed how the new tradition generated social fears among wedding guests. Etiquette books were a decoder for those unsure of middle-class manners and wedding gifts, a potential way up the social ladder. In *Gems of Deportment* (1882), Mrs. M. L. Rayne humorously depicted potential concerns over status: "When we hear of a forthcoming wedding among friends we groan in despair, for it entails the giving of a present, and henceforth the question 'What shall it be?' tortures and vexes our souls." Guests were in danger of revealing their lack of knowledge of correct social form, or at least their lack of good taste. Mrs. Rayne described how guests' fear of offending the couple led to the purchase of standard items that were potentially inferior, such as "a pair of individual salt-cellars, 'solid silver,' as the newspapers report them." In a way that suggested her own doubts about its propriety, she predicted that the custom would "probably pass into oblivion after a few years, and the obligations of giving and receiving wedding presents will have ceased to be a social burden."[25]

Wedding gift customs became more elaborate with the spread of the elite custom of displaying presents. At society weddings, guests perused long cloth-covered tables laden with silver, china, jewels, and even furniture at the bride's family home. Newspaper announcements recounted society gift viewings, noting the designer or manufacturer of gifts, names such as Minton, Dresden, and

Tiffany. Such displays were a symbol of wealth as in Edith Wharton's 1905 novel, *House of Mirth*, where the bridal jewels and presents painfully reminded the heroine, Lily Bart, of the social status and economic security she lacked. The custom suggested the wealth of the guests as well as the future prosperity and comfort of the married couple. At the 1914 Texas wedding of Leonra McCue Norwell and Ernest Fordyce Latta, the newspaper announcement described presents "displayed upon great tables where dazzling and shimmering of glass and flash of silver held the attention of guests before and after the ceremony." A "handsome check," "substantial dividend-bearing stock," lamps, rugs, vases, and many platters and bowls were on view, gifts that the society reporter noted were "indispensable to a present-day wedding."[26]

Like the new tradition of the obligatory wedding present, these gift displays also came under attack. Those who disapproved often used the language of commerce to express their distaste. In a variety of these accounts, consumer culture was at odds with the true meaning of marriage and the gender roles embedded within the institution. The practice, according to Henry Ward Beecher, turned the sacred marriage rite into a marketplace, a bazaar where sentiment was for sale. Using commercial terms from the masculine sphere, Beecher criticized the bride who "does not shrink from calculating the probable gifts" and takes "an account of stock" after the wedding. While the custom was firmly in place by the turn of the century, other writers continued to express disapproval of this linkage between marriage and markets.[27] Critiques of wedding gift customs also revealed a growing ambivalence about female consumption. According to *Gems of Deportment*, women were supposed to marry for love, not money, and lavish wedding gift displays made it seem otherwise.[28] Brides who displayed their gifts risked appearing cold and calculating, as one 1904 etiquette writer implied when she tried subtly to overturn the new custom, noting that a bride might choose not to "exhibit" her gifts "ticketed and labeled with the names of their givers, like dry goods in a shop window."[29] Such connections also challenged a middle-class sense of the separation between the feminine private and the masculine public spheres. Displays put one's private belongings up for public inspection. Images of the wedding gift display depicted the scrutiny and potential criticism that were a part of the custom (figure 3).[30] Men appeared not to like the custom, though advertisements for silverware depicted men paying close attention to the gifts. Beecher

FIGURE 3. By 1915, the tradition of displaying wedding gifts was widespread. This ad used the tradition to show that the "1847 Rogers Bros." silver plate could withstand scrutiny and uphold the status of the giver. N. W. Ayer Advertising Agency Records, Archives Center, National Museum of American History, Behring Center, Smithsonian Institution, Washington, D.C.

himself complained of the "familiar question"—"Have you been up to see the presents?"—and dryly noted that he "seldom [took] pleasure in looking at the wedding treasure chamber." According to a 1909 etiquette publication, "To go through them bores some persons tremendously, and they are not always allowed to skip the process. It delights others."[31]

Some early twentieth-century critics saw gift displays as a symbol of women's unequal position in marriage. In *House of Mirth*, Wharton criticized the money-making aspect of weddings and the unequal system of gender relations that made marriage an economic necessity for women when she described Grace Van Osburgh's envied display as "bridal spoils." Looking back at the nineteenth century from the vantage point of 1912, sociologist Mary Roberts Coolidge condemned the "material phases of marriage" that developed in the nineteenth century, describing them as a distraction intended to divert attention from a woman's impending role as wife. In her interpretation of nineteenth-century wedding customs, setting up the household and other duties before the marriage tired the bride out, leaving her ill prepared to deal with the wedding night. Coolidge also noted how wedding planning marginalized the groom and made him serve the bride, causing him to curse privately "the social traditions which had involved him in so irksome a tangle of splurge and etiquette." Like others at the time, Coolidge opposed an overt display of goods, noting that "when wedding etiquette reached the stage where all the presents must be displayed to the givers and the guests in a room set apart for them, the custom had degenerated into undisguised commercialism."[32]

Around this time, etiquette advice on wedding gifts and fictional accounts of wedding preparation also began to feature a new character—the out-of-control, consuming bride. One morality tale that appeared repeatedly was the story of the bride who invited too many guests out of mercenary motives. For example, a 1904 etiquette writer told the allegedly true story of a bride she knew who "sent her invitations far and near," and when questioned why she sent them to people she barely knew, answered that she was "after the spoils."[33] Readers were supposed to feel horror at this bride's bad taste and keep their own consumer desires in line. Another less elite version of this morality tale emerged in "A Ghetto Wedding," an 1898 short story by Abraham Cahan, the well-known socialist writer and editor of the *Jewish Daily Forward*. The story traced the wedding plans of Goldy, a seamstress, and Nathan, a street peddler of china dishes. Unable to accumulate enough money for both the wedding and a nicely furnished apartment, Goldy pushed Nathan to have a big wedding: "Let us spend all our money on a grand, respectable wedding, and send out a big lot of invitations, and then—well, won't uncle Leiser send us a carpet or a parlor set? And aunt Beile, and cousin Shapiro, (etc) won't each present something or other, as is the custom among respectable people?"[34] After hiring a hall and sending out over a hundred invitations, Goldy and Nathan waited for presents to arrive at their rented rooms. Their marriage, however, came during hard times when many of their invited friends were out of work and without presentable clothes to wear to a big celebration. Unable to buy the required gift, their friends and relatives chose not attend the wedding, rather than risk being seen as not "respectable." Because of Goldy's plan, the couple was financially ruined. More than a story about greed for wedding presents, this morality tale perhaps revealed the ambivalent feelings of those, like Cahan, who witnessed a grand transformation at the end of the nineteenth century.

SPENDING BEYOND ONE'S MEANS

Looking at a world in the midst of great change, Gilded Age and Progressive Era critics and writers like Henry Ward Beecher, Mary Roberts Coolidge, Edith Wharton, Abraham Cahan, Upton Sinclair, and others expressed their ambivalence about modern life. Even as some bemoaned the rise of a more impersonal, striving, competitive society, many were drawn to the pleasures and promises of the new consumer culture.[35] After the Civil War, when aspects of the big white wedding first came under extensive attack, American culture was in the middle of an economic, social, and political transformation. Relations between business and labor, black and white, native-born and immigrant were tense and often explosive. Waves of immigrants from eastern Europe introduced new customs and practices that Americanized immigrants and the native-born scorned. The new corporations welcomed the unskilled immigrants and used them to drive the labor market down, something trade unions resented and resisted. These transformations, however, also created a vibrant city life where one found numerous opportunities to challenge genteel Victorian culture. Small but significant groups of urban middle-class African Americans participated in the growing consumer culture. White working-class women "put on style" using cheap, ready-made fashions and entered the public sphere of dance halls, nickelodeons, theaters, and amusement parks.[36] Increasingly, what were considered luxuries in the past were within reach of the middle class. Between 1909 and 1929, personal consumption almost tripled. Consumer choice seemed to spread to marriage as well, though to many, the institution of marriage appeared to be collapsing as the divorce rate rose 2,000 percent between 1867 and 1929. Even as divorce rates rose, between 1900 and 1920 more people chose to marry and the average marriage age declined for both men and women.[37]

Against this backdrop, debates over proper wedding practice emerged. In the nineteenth century, popular writers and others tied formal marital rites to the idea of civilization. According to one etiquette writer, "no nation was so barbarous as not to solemnize marriage with some rites, ceremonies, and public rejoicings." One French observer in the mid-nineteenth century claimed that Americans were too busy to follow wedding tradition and had quick, informal ceremonies, perhaps signaling their lack of civilization.[38] Certain less-settled areas of the country were known for having "laws of greater laxity," leading to "clandestine marriages" or "marriage runaways."[39] Even so, in the Southwest and the South, white settlers sought to impose their ideas of civilization on marriage patterns. Quick, informal weddings were not what "decent folks" did, according to an Irish woman who allegedly criticized homesteader Royal Jackman in New Mexico when he married his bride on the way to catch a train in 1897. In a similar vein, South Carolina farmer Johnny Haselton remembered the communal celebrations of his youth in the late nineteenth century, noting that when a wedding lasted several days and included the "whole countryside," then it "was really something to talk about." He lamented the decline of such celebrations and blamed the coming of the automobile and new, informal types of courtship, implying that marriage was less permanent as a result.[40]

The formal wedding, then, was more than just a party—it was a highly symbolic event that spoke worlds about those who participated in it. Etiquette and taste were a form of power. Being able to define what constituted proper behavior and good taste allowed one group to assert its vision of things over another. Taste was more than just an expression of aesthetic preference; it signaled one's social identity or class status as well. For example, nineteenth-century ready-to-wear clothing was viewed as "morally suspect" by some. Without the restraint of middle-class good taste, women's desire for cheap ball gowns and other rich-appearing ready-made fashions had the potential to lead them astray.[41] When wedding consumption did not reflect this idea of restraint and "good taste," it too came under attack. For example, in *Age of Innocence*, Wharton's 1920 novel about the Gilded Age, when May Welland was to marry, her grandmother criticized the engagement ring, "a large thick sapphire set in invisible claws." The elderly scion noted that in her time "a cameo set in pearls was thought sufficient."[42]

Critics also charged that the lavish society wedding would inspire others to spend more than they could afford. As early as 1882, etiquette writers noted the "spirit of emulation which belongs to every American heart" and warned of the dangers of big society weddings. These writers implicitly blamed those who allegedly imitated the wealthy. With Thorstein Veblen's *Theory of the Leisure Class*, the debate took a new twist and those with lavish pecuniary habits came under attack. While not specifically addressing weddings, Veblen viewed balls or large entertainments as conspicuous consumption. In his view, leisure-class consumer practices like these spurred imitation and ultimately hurt those who could least afford it.[43] Similar concerns over emulation continued into the early twentieth century. For example, a 1912 *Suburban Life* article by Margaret Woodward on the costliness of weddings warned that the display of luxury by the rich could foment social discord. In this middle-class magazine, Woodward criticized the rich for providing a bad example for the poor, who would copy lavish displays and "squander their hard-won earnings." In a manner that smacked of nativism, Woodward warned of the reaction "when the wretched poverty-stricken father of a numerous family hears that his rich employer has bought five thousand orchids from overseas at a dollar apiece, to grace a banquet."[44]

The emerging ideal of the simple wedding reflected middle-class ambivalence over the rising consumer culture. The "simple wedding" served to bridge these concerns, allowing a bride to have her wedding cake and eat it too. Although the term *simple* here suggests a return to homespun rural values and a rejection of the trappings of consumer society, it was anything but. This wedding ideal was part of a larger elevation of the "simple life" promoted by Edward Bok, editor of the popular *Ladies' Home Journal* from 1889 to 1919, and others. As a moral vision or philosophy, the simple life sought to bring what was good from the past into modern society. On a more basic level, it advocated unadorned styles in fashions, furnishings for the home, and architecture, and also promoted women's role as expert household consumer. Simple, however, did not mean cheap, nor did it entail a rejection of consumer culture. Women's dress reform and the "artistic dress" movement, for example, advocated simple styles, but such clothing was not available ready-made and was out of reach for many women.[45]

Similarly, the simple, tasteful wedding could be quite costly and require the expenditure of cultural capital. The simple wedding, as it took shape during this period, was in keeping with the emerging feminist consciousness of the "New Woman," a term that emerged between 1890 and the 1920s. Brides who were troubled by the inequality of marriage and its expression in the wedding ceremony followed the material outlines of the white wedding even as they tried to escape its larger implications. The New Women sought autonomy and independence in work and in their marriages.[46] Many of them were committed to social causes, higher education, and professional careers. New Womanhood embraced values that challenged the big white wedding, with its conspicuous display and celebration of traditional gender roles in the exchange of vows, the giving away of the bride, and new consumer rites, like the bridal shower, that elevated domesticity. For example, Lucy Sprague Mitchell, a Progressive leader in the education of children, wanted her wedding to be "as simple and informal as possible." She instructed her aunt Nan that the invitations, the music, and the wedding breakfast not be too lavish. Mitchell had a religious ceremony, but put limits on it, telling her aunt that she "would feel a fake with a formal ceremony." Similarly, the "social display" of weddings likely seemed frivolous to another turn-of-the-century bride, Elsie Clews Parson, who would become a prominent feminist and anthropologist. According to her biographer, Desley Deacon, Elsie Clews spent little time on her wedding dress and the event itself was as simple as the mother of the bride would allow.[47]

Early twentieth-century middle-class weddings that did not uphold this ideal of simplicity were the subject of a number of critiques. Morality tales depicted the debt-inducing, lavish white wedding with all the trimmings as the embodiment of all that was wrong with the rising consumer society. Spending beyond one's means was not only believed to be "vulgar," it could also destroy a family, as it did in the 1912 *Suburban Life* article by Margaret Woodward. Condemning the "evil of elaborate and showy weddings," Woodward described a selfish and spoiled bride who drove her family to near ruin with the bills of "dressmakers, milliners, tailors, and tradesmen of different kinds" and a hapless father who went into debt for the wedding, mortgaging his house to renovate and enlarge it for the reception. In a way that harkened back to Henry Ward Beecher, Woodward questioned the "reckless and extravagant use of money" and referred to "our Puritan fathers" to support her point. Condemning the "ostentatious display" that overshadowed the "sacredness of marriage," she tried to draw a line between marriage and commerce, one that the rising consumer culture increasingly tried to erase.[48]

Big, inclusive weddings also offended those Progressive reformers and social critics who were seeking to rework American society. Many Progressives turned their attention to the consumption patterns of working-class and immigrant people.[49] Although less conservative than earlier moralists in their judgments in that they focused on conditions rather than character to explain poverty, they continued to emphasize the "bourgeois virtues of hard work, respectability, and self-restraint." While they began to accept higher levels of comfort than earlier reformers, Progressives continued to believe that thrift was necessary for success. Their studies criticized spending habits that did not fit their middle-class model, such as expenditure on liquor at saloons and cheap fashionable clothing. In this context, a propensity to spend "freely on festive occasions" such as weddings came under scrutiny.[50]

Although critiques of big urban immigrant and working-class weddings emerged during this period, Progressive reformers also saw something of value in the communal wedding. Some Progressives admired elements of working-class and immigrant culture. Reformer Margaret Byington reflected these ambivalent attitudes toward immigrant consumption in her 1910 study of Slavic women in Homestead, Pennsylvania. Byington critically noted the pressure people felt to host a bigger wedding celebration than they could afford. But, she also believed that these social rituals enriched daily life. In her words, Homestead weddings were "the gayest affairs in the life of a community." At either a home or a hall, dancing and drinking started in the afternoon and "by midnight the revel is at its height." Men paid a dollar to dance with the bride, and the money, which served as "their form of a wedding present," helped furnish the home for the couple.[51] Music and dancing, and food and drink, for all who came to celebrate the happiness of the two families of the bride and

FIGURE 4. Typical of nineteenth-century rural marriage celebrations, Paul Hoff and second-generation Norwegian-American Bedille Vogard had a big wedding celebration held at the home of Knute Vogard in Holt Township, Fillmore County, Minnesota, in 1890. Note the bride and her attendants did not wear white. Photo courtesy of Dorothy Melby.

groom were picturesque in Byington's account. Implicitly, communal weddings were a thing apart—a vestige of a traditional past. Such activities were far from the modern restrained bourgeois ideal of the simple wedding favored by the Protestant native-born.

Those who were the objects of reform and study had a different view of wedding consumption. Large celebrations brought the risk of debt, but rituals like money dances at rural Polish and German weddings or Italian money collections were supposed to bring much-needed material aid to the new couple.[52] If everyone contributed, a communal wedding might help the couple get their feet on the ground. As described in WPA oral history accounts, these big celebrations also linked the new couple to their ethnic culture and fulfilled community expectations (figure 4).[53]

For poor urban immigrant brides, an elaborate wedding symbolically claimed a place in the larger society. In Abraham Cahan's short story about Jewish New York, Goldy desired to have a "respectable" rather than a "slipshod wedding." She wanted to be somebody, to stand under the bridal canopy not as a "beggar maid." This feared slipshod wedding was "anything short of

a gown of white satin and slippers to match; two carriages to bring the bride
and bridegroom to the ceremony, and one to take them to their bridal apart-
ments; a wedding band and a band of at least five musicians; a spacious ball-
room crowded with dancers, and a feast of a hundred and fifty covers." On
one level, the failure of Goldy and Nathan's lavish wedding was in keeping
with contemporary Yiddish etiquette manuals' exhortations to "stay within
their means." This type of advice sought to Americanize eastern European
Jewish immigrants along middle-class German-Jewish lines.[54] Cahan's story
does something else as well, however. In the end, he does not condemn or
satirize Goldy's desire for the trappings of middle-class life—here expressed
in terms of wedding consumption. His simple tale ends with the newlyweds
returning to their bare rooms after their pathetic, unattended wedding celebration. Rather than using this as a morality tale to spend within one's means,
Cahan shows the couple forgetting their material woes, happy and in love.
Consumption is not mercenary here, as in other critiques of big weddings;
instead, the material dreams of Goldy represent the immigrant dream for a
better life. When the Jewish community fails to fulfill its obligations to support
the new couple, Cahan does not blame individualism or his characters' Ameri-
canization. Instead, Goldy's plan for lots of gifts to recoup the expenditure on
the wedding does not work because of the economic hardship her guests faced.

Wedding consumption became a multivalent symbol of the promise of the
American way of life as well as its failure to deliver a meaningful existence.
Some writers saw the individualistic American dream destroying the communal customs of urban immigrant groups. Large celebrations created debt that
the young couple could never escape. In the context of the industrial city, new
Americanized ways undermined communal big weddings, as depicted by
Upton Sinclair in *The Jungle*. This best-selling novel opened with the wedding
of two of its main characters. Recent Lithuanian immigrants who worked in
the slaughterhouse industry in Chicago, Jurgis and Ona hosted the traditional
veselija, an inclusive wedding celebration that could cost more than a year's
income. The expenses and risks involved in such an extravagant event were a
key to its meaning. As Sinclair showed, spending a year's income in a single
day proved that one could be "the master of things" and allowed one to "go
back to his toil and live upon the memory all his days." The *vesilija*, however,
was supposed to be "a compact" between members of a village community.[55]

All were supposed to help pay for the festivities by dancing with the bride and giving a donation according to one's ability to pay. The novel shows the custom in decline as guests partake of the plentiful feast of meat, potatoes, buns, and beer, then shirk their duty, sneaking out without dancing with the bride. Sinclair envisioned a selfish individualism destroying the web of obligation and reciprocity that held together village life in Lithuania. Just as Jurgis and Ona must bear the burden of their wedding costs on their own, they stand alone with a makeshift family to face the dehumanizing force of an urban, industrial order.

A CONSPIRACY OF TRADES

At the turn of the century, a few merchants still felt the incongruity of the business of brides. Like etiquette writers and social critics, some expressed ambivalence about linking sentiment and commerce. The professional journal *Dry Goods Economist*, for example, self-consciously noted the appropriateness of a bridal market: "Just now it may not be strictly within correct form to seek business from the prospectives." As if department stores were reluctant to make June brides, in their words, "a fair mark," trade writers encouraged them to target those about to marry. Merchants, however, were concerned with being dignified when selling to brides. Trade writers warned them not to be too squeamish about marketing specifically to brides: "A little sentiment, however, 'is a dangerous thing' in business, and one must up to a certain point shut their eyes and take chances." Just as etiquette writers had counseled good taste and simplicity in gift giving and in personal dress for the bride, trade writers for the industry at the turn of the century exhibited a similar concern for middle-class propriety and good form. They advised the "merchant of refinement" to contact brides unobtrusively through letters. Retailers seemed to be aware that tracking brides by following engagement lists, and writing personal appeals to obtain their business, crossed some fine line of respectability.[56] At the same time, trade articles about marketing wedding silver to the June bride advised New York stores rather cynically not to get "behind in the race," but to "put out their grappling-irons in the shape of windows or ads, for this trade."[57]

By the 1920s, the business climate clearly made it difficult to condemn the "evil of elaborate and showy weddings."[58] The decline of moralistic debates over weddings was connected to broader changes in the American economy.[59] Beginning in the last quarter of the nineteenth century, changes in retailing, distribution, and production began to turn customers into consumers. A mass culture began to take shape with the introduction of branded goods, national advertising campaigns, and new merchandising tactics.[60] Consumers began to let the salesman in the door as older ideas of thrift and saving fell away and it became socially acceptable to purchase goods on installment. Advertising dollars soared in the 1920s, aided by World War I and the rise of national markets. The war effort improved the reputation of advertising though successful Liberty Bond promotions, army recruitment, and food conservation, as well as by the passage of an excess profits tax in 1917 that allowed businesses to deduct advertising expenditures. Advertisers were no longer scorned patent medicine salesmen but "apostles of modernity," like Bruce Barton, founder of the advertising firm BBDO and author of *The Man Nobody Knows*, a best-selling 1926 book that compared Jesus Christ to a successful businessman.[61] New methods of advertising created wants and invented new needs. Technologies like the radio, the movies, and the automobile narrowed the physical and psychological distance between different regions of the country. Increasingly, growing numbers of Americans participated in a national mass culture.[62] Businesses seeking the bridal market could turn to newspapers, magazines, radio, and film by this period. Ambivalence about the bridal market disappeared, and by the 1920s furniture dealers, kitchen-range makers, ice companies, and real estate agents began participating in "congratulatory" selling with letters to brides- and grooms-to-be. By 1930, even radio shows began to consider using weddings as advertising vehicles for goods and services. For example, radio soap operas planned to marry female leads on the air to create an advertising vehicle for companies like Montgomery Ward. One 1930 serial, *Painted Dreams*, was supposed to include "an engagement, a June wedding, the purchasing of a trousseau and household furnishings."[63]

Discussions of wedding spending also changed during this period, entering into the realm of urbane, slightly humorous social commentary. Wedding gift displays appeared in popular culture as a female ritual, one that could be a source of humor.[64] The big wedding itself was now seen in this way as well. For example, a 1925 article in the *Saturday Evening Post*, titled "Purveyors to the Bride," discussed skyrocketing wedding costs in a manner that would not have been possible for someone like Henry Ward Beecher or Edith Wharton. According to the article, written by Jane Grant, who covered society weddings and claimed much experience in the "marriage market" as both a bridesmaid and a bride, weddings cost twice as much as they had in the mid-1910s. Brides were to blame for the rise of the big wedding, though businesses were quick to step in to fill demand. Adopting the peppy language of 1920s business culture, Grant noted that "even with the present-day businesslike viewpoint, all the world loves a lover, and even the trades have joined in the conspiracy for more and bigger weddings."[65] Simplicity remained a value, but by the 1920s, the idea of the tasteful simple wedding had been absorbed by a growing consumer culture (and would later become a very successful market strategy as we will see). According to Grant, in 1925 simplicity often cost $50,000 to achieve. Flowers were chosen for effect, not abundance, and gifts were displayed "with just the right emphasis on a trinket from a powerful personage."[66] The wedding culture that Grant depicted was not the "simple" taste seen earlier at the marriage celebrations of socially committed women and Progressive reformers or of the advocates of the simple life. By the 1920s, it was a simplicity that could be executed only with the help of a staff of professional wedding experts or "purveyors to the bride."

Through the Depression, World War II, and into the postwar period, weddings were celebrated as big business with only murmurs of dissent. This is not to suggest that the big white wedding ceased to generate critical commentary. Critiques of the big white wedding continue to the present day (though they are rare). However, the style and content of these discussions changed. Moralistic attacks on consumption declined by the 1930s and 1940s, as new ideas that spending was healthy for the economy took hold. During this period, costly weddings also gained acceptance, though some nativist critics continued to voice their distaste of immigrant or "ethnic" spending.[67] And, as we will see, with the Cold War, the formal white wedding and all it stood for—consumption, gender norms, and family stability—were seen as necessary for the continuation of democracy. Representations of bridal spending out of control became a stock source of humor and satire, as in the best-selling novel and Hollywood film *Father of the Bride* (1950), though in a way that ultimately upheld rather than transcended the new consumer wedding ideal.

In spite of the ambivalence expressed by a wide assembly of social critics and cultural producers in the late nineteenth and early twentieth centuries, weddings began to be a part of consumer culture, beginning with the engagement and the flurry of presents that arrived after the invitations were sent out. Not surprisingly, the jewelry industry became a cornerstone in the rise of the wedding industry, as did magazine publishers, department stores, bridal consultants, and caterers. As early as 1908, the custom of giving presents to those about to marry generated nearly $9 million. Such figures, while produced by the jewelry industry, suggest that criticism of the obligatory wedding present and the gift display went unheeded and that people embraced or at least went along with new traditions. By the 1920s, the jewelry trade made clear and strong connections between marriage and commerce. According to one 1927 trade writer, "Beginning with the engagement ring, there is a constant string of events taking place that calls for his merchandise that does not end until the last anniversary of the wedding is celebrated."[68] Weddings opened the way for a lifelong business relationship.

CHAPTER TWO

Rings and the Birth of a Tradition

With the help of the jewelry industry, turn-of-the-century opposition to the big wedding faded. The jewelry industry became a key player in the commercialization of the American wedding by the mid-twentieth century. Composed of specialty retail jewelers and manufacturers, it provided rings for marrying, but more important, it helped shape the cultural meaning of these goods and their accompanying rituals. By the 1920s, the jewelry industry portrayed marriage as a consumer rite. Retailers and manufacturers organized national advertising campaigns promoting new ritual goods, such as the male engagement ring, as "ancient customs." Extensive advertising campaigns and promotions appeared in the 1930s and 1940s that pushed elaborations of older, simpler customs in the name of romantic love, introducing brand-name diamond engagement rings, matching bridal sets, and groom's wedding bands. By World War II, in the industry's trade journal, *Jewelers' Circular-Keystone*, it became almost a cliché to advocate the use of "tradition" as a modern selling tool, with writers advising retailers and manufacturers to "trade on tradition" and use sentiment as their "star salesman."[1]

As jewelers sought new ways to increase wedding consumption, they faced a dilemma: unlike their other sales opportunities, a wedding was (ideally) a once-in-a-lifetime event. Brides were also not supposed to be openly consumerist. Weddings were condemned if they were perceived to be "fashion parades" or attempts to accumulate finery and material goods. Wedding tradition by definition was supposed to be unchanging and linked to a long history. Related consumption was supposed to follow long-established customs and rules of etiquette, and not be subject to the changing whims of fashion that were so good to marketers. "Traditional" goods had the potential to run counter to the profit motive and marketers' need to differentiate themselves from competitors. For example, a bride wearing an heirloom ring did not fit the commercial goals of business. With the emergence of the wedding industry, jewelry trade writers, retailers, and manufacturers worked around these contradictions by appropriating the idea of "tradition" as a modern tool.[2] As we will see, advertising and promotions bridged the logical inconsistency of invented ring traditions and depicted elaborate new ritual goods as a necessary part of the traditional wedding.

New ring rituals advocated by the jewelry industry, however, did not always capture the buying public's attention. Why did particular consumer goods become tradition and others not? At different historical moments, invented traditions like the 1920s male engagement ring failed to resonate with consumers, while others, like the bride's diamond engagement ring and the groom's band, became standard by the 1950s, when a new cult of marriage worked its way into the national discourse. Wedding traditions began to embody gendered ideas of consumer democracy and family "togetherness." The bride's diamond engagement ring and the double-ring ceremony became an expected part of the American dream as well as a sign of shifting relations between men and women.

RINGS FOR MARRYING THROUGH THE AGES

The popular belief throughout the twentieth century was that use of rings for marrying was a custom passed down from an ancient Western past, not an "invented" tradition. Early twentieth-century experts observed that the history of ring customs was "somewhat obscure," and that the "true origin of the wedding ring will never be known." Even when noting the difficulty of uncovering the exact source of contemporary wedding ring traditions, these works connected twentieth-century customs with a vast history that included the ancient Egyptians, Romans, Hebrews, Greeks, and Anglo-Saxons. According to one well-known bridal consultant in the 1930s, marriage was the "oldest tradition of civilization."[3] Such accounts linked twentieth-century American wedding customs to a particular idea of civilization. Ideas about national origins said more about contemporary concerns than about the actual history of these ritual objects, reflecting instead late nineteenth- and early twentieth-century social concerns.[4] Tradition did not weave its way across the Atlantic, passing through cultures, continents, and centuries unchanged. Instead, the idea of tradition was continually reworked.

A host of experts—some with ties to the jewelry industry—imagined ancient origins for wedding ring practices. Early twentieth-century popular histories, such as *Customs of Mankind* and *A Short History of Marriage*, and scholarly reference books, such as *Rings for the Finger*, likely influenced later popular ideas about "tradition." In addition, etiquette writers, retailers, bridal magazines, and even scholarly sources repeated these origin stories, further establishing them in tradition, perhaps in the way that accounts of the origin of the wedding cake descended from an early erroneous source.[5] Such works often cited the Romans, the Greeks, and sometimes the early Jews as sources, noting that in these cultures the ring was a pledge of betrothal given to the father of the bride as a payment or as a sign of security or collateral.[6] Industry accounts also described wedding rings as timeless traditions. One 1940s trade writer for the *Department Store Economist* noted that the wedding ring originated during "the time of the Pharaohs." According to *Bride's* magazine in 1942, they were a part of "folklore deep-rooted in our past." And, as recent a wedding commentator as Martha Stewart noted that the components of the wedding, "irrespective of nationality and religion, are legacies from primitive times." In her account, the tradition of wearing the wedding ring on the fourth finger was due to an ancient belief that a vein went directly from it to the heart, an explanation much repeated in wedding lore.[7]

These popular accounts do not reflect the fact that the wedding ring had a complex liturgical history. A few examples of historical practices show how impossible it is to generalize about the origins of contemporary American ring customs. As would be expected, customs varied widely by religion, region, and time period. Rings for the bride were not used at all in the earliest records of Byzantine marriage services. Such rituals did not appear in the Byzantine liturgy in the eighth century, but came in by the tenth century. Two rings became usual in this liturgy by the eleventh century—gold for the bride and silver for the groom. In Italy, rings were not used until the early thirteenth century. In France, two rings appeared for the first time in the sixteenth century. In these early examples, the exchange of rings marked the couple's entry into marriage. Among Jews and Christians in Rome in the fifteenth and sixteenth centuries, after the match was made and consent indicated by a kiss and clasp of hands, gifts of rings and jewelry followed. On a special "ring day," rings were exchanged and troths plighted. This stage married the couple, even though the bride continued to live with her family for a year longer, before being publicly and festively taken to her husband's home.[8]

Conflicts arose over these ring rituals from the medieval period through the Reformation. In fifteenth- and sixteenth-century Christianity, rings "were symbolic of the union of Christ and the Church." The blessing of the ring served as a "reminder of the increasingly indispensable role" of priests in the marital ceremony after the Council of Trent in 1563.[9] The Reformation sought to eliminate the "medievalisms" carrying over from the Sarum, which was the collection of Roman rites that governed the early Church. During the Reformation period in Europe and after, denominations were divided over the custom of ring exchange, which they saw as an example of medievalism. Martin Luther's marriage rite kept the custom of the ring. Similarly, Anglican prayer-book traditions incorporated some medieval customs, such as the ring ritual. Medievalism persisted in the Prayer Book's formula for the ritual, taken from the Sarum: "With this ring I thee wed: This golde and siluer I thee geue: with my body I thee worship: and with al my worldly goodes I thee endow. In the name of the father . . ." With these words, the ring became an active player in the making of the marriage—both a token of bodily devotion and a binding symbol of marital unity. In Reformed marriage ceremonies, however, the ring was not considered a religious object. Martin Luther's marriage service and the Anglican Prayer Book dropped the medieval rite of blessing the ring. By omitting the blessing, the ritual became simply "a token of troth pledged between man and wife." John Calvin went further in his reforms and stripped the marriage service of the ring itself. Popular pressure, however, eventually led Calvinists to reintroduce the ritual use of the ring.[10]

Wedding ring styles themselves, and the manner in which rings were given and worn, also varied widely through the ages. Betrothal or wedding rings of iron, gold, silver, steel, and brass, as well as rings made of rush, leather, and wood, served as marriage tokens or pledges at different points in history. These ritual goods could take the shape of single rings engraved on the inside with poesies, popular during Shakespeare's era, or of linking bands as in the gimmal ring. Of different sizes, from the delicate to the massively architectural, they were worn on the thumb, the index finger, or the "ring finger." The hand where the token was placed also varied. In the medieval Sarum, the ring was placed on the bride's right hand. This became the left hand in Thomas Cranmer's Anglican marriage service. In paintings in the fifteenth and sixteenth centuries, however, Catholic and Jewish brides stood with either the right or left hand outstretched. Rings were also presented to the bride in the ceremony in a variety of ways. For example, in the Reformed service the ring was placed on the book, and the priest then blessed it and sprinkled it with holy water before it was passed to the groom to give to the bride.[11]

Religious variations persisted in the American context. Puritan custom influenced early New England practice. When Puritans gained power in England, they restricted the ring ceremony in the Directory of Public Worship in 1645, which among other things stated that this object could be "a token of malignancy." Reflecting Calvinist beliefs, early Puritan colonists opposed the giving of rings in the service. Marriage was understood to be a civil contract, not a sacrament.[12] In seventeenth-century Massachusetts, for example, magistrates married couples in their home in a simple civil ceremony that did not involve holy vows or wedding bands. As Puritan society grew less orthodox over the generations, wedding practices changed. During the 1692 Salem witchcraft trials, when the estates of several individuals accused or convicted of witchcraft were seized by the sheriff of Essex County court, a wedding ring was among the goods belonging to the accused witch Goodwife Jacobs. (Her ring was returned, after being determined to be the property of her husband.)[13]

In religious marriage ceremonies, rings were customary. For example, the Proposed American Prayer Book of 1786 called for a bride's ring, though the words spoken with the ritual from the Book of Common Prayer were dropped. And, while Methodists in the eighteenth century omitted the ring in their marriage service, popular pressure for a ring was among the forces that led it to reappear in 1846.[14] In the nineteenth century, Presbyterian vows included the ring, but did not make it mandatory. The ring, in this case, was seen as a "token of fidelity to these vows," but was not what actually married the couple. Religious variations continued into the twentieth century. By 1940, the Presbyterian *Book of Common Order* required it, noting that it was given "as a token of the covenant into which you have entered." In the twentieth century, some religious groups, like the Amish and the Seventh Day Adventists, objected to wedding rings.[15] Obviously, religious custom and doctrine shaped wedding practice. Increasingly in the twentieth century, however, businesses and consumers also determined the material and ritual outlines of the American wedding.

THE JEWELRY INDUSTRY AND THE BRIDAL MARKET

Changes in American wedding ring practices were connected to the rise of consumer capitalism. With new mass forms of manufacturing, retailing, and distribution, nineteenth-century jewelers who had operated small family-run businesses faced increased competition and economic uncertainty. In their fight for markets, jewelry manufacturers created an "endless novelty" of goods, to borrow historian Philip Scranton's phrase. Batch production, a flexible manufacturing format characterized by short runs of varied goods, allowed them to meet consumer desire for diverse styles. In contrast, mass producers had to generate demand and thus had less flexibility.[16] Specialty retailers, moreover, had to find ways to compete with the growing numbers of mass marketers that sold luxury goods and their imitations. During the 1890s, mail-order catalogues started selling cheap wedding bands and diamond engagement rings as well. Jewelers competed for the bridal market with department stores like Marshall Field's in Chicago that had begun handling diamonds and fine jewelry around 1890. Other stores, such as Wanamaker's and Gimbel Brothers in Philadelphia, followed in 1904 and 1905, respectively. Jewelry retailers responded, urging one another not to allow themselves to "be driven from the field altogether."[17]

New traditions emerged out of this competitive business context. In 1895, for example, jewelers introduced the "sweet sixteen ring" for girls. Early elaborations of the wedding ring ritual, such as an additional ring called the guard or band keeper ring, appeared in catalogues as well.[18] Retail jewelers also promoted new services. They knew they could not sell their goods at the discounted prices offered by department stores, so they countered with expertise and specialized services, such as the gift registry, in which they informally kept track of a customer's silver pattern. Introduced at the turn of the century as an attempt to centralize the gift-giving process and avoid duplications, it served to keep customers from going to department and chain stores to buy silverware, glassware, clocks, candlesticks, or the ubiquitous vases found on lists of wedding gifts received in the late nineteenth and early twentieth centuries. More than gift sales, however, jewelers focused their energies on the ring purchase, which they claimed forged a long-term relationship between their business and the new household.[19]

As we have seen, the giving of the bride's ring in the ceremony had a complex liturgical history, but with the rise of consumer society wedding ring style became subject to prevailing fashions. Although these ritual goods were not objects of fashion in the manner of other types of jewelry, their design and material reflected broader style shifts, according to etiquette writers and jewelers. By the early twentieth century, the plain gold band that served "by long established custom" as the wedding ring was giving way to different styles.[20] Victorian wedding band styles had been "plain, heavy gold,"[21] but by the early twentieth century, jewelers' catalogues featured bands both in narrow widths and wider, flattened styles, and goods that were art-carved with orange blossom designs, chased with scrollwork, decorated with a fancy edges, or simply plain. Fashions changed rapidly and many different ones existed simultaneously. Jeweled engagement rings appeared in the nineteenth century, sometimes serving as the only ring. According to *Demorest's Monthly* magazine, pearl, solitaire diamond, and diamond, ruby, and sapphire combinations were popular, as well as amethyst rings decorated with a monograph made of small diamonds. Flat gold bands were also seen as acceptable tokens of future marriage.[22]

Jewelers like Tiffany's introduced new elaborations on the wedding ring. In 1886, Tiffany's introduced the diamond solitaire style that became a standard. Unlike earlier solitaire settings that encased the lower part of the stone in a bezel mounting, the "Tiffany setting" raised the diamond on prongs away from the ring's shank, allowing light to enter from below to create a more brilliant stone. (The diamond also appeared larger.) The famed New York jeweler began in 1837 as Tiffany & Young, a New York giftware and fancy goods shop, became Tiffany & Company in 1853, and incorporated in 1868 with Charles Tiffany as president. During the 1870s, when diamonds became more plentiful after the discovery of new sources in Africa, Tiffany's brought popular attention to these gems, displaying unmounted stones and jewelry at the 1876 Philadelphia Centennial and winning awards at the 1878 Paris Exposition. By the 1950s, Tiffany's was one of New York's "big five" jewelers, a list that included Black, Starr & Gorham, Cartier, Van Cleef & Arpels, and Harry Winston.[23]

Other experts also indirectly promoted the diamond engagement ring tradition. Etiquette writers, for example, spoke out on the custom of the bride's engagement ring. In the 1880s, engagement rings were a new enough tradition that couples needed basic guidance. One etiquette book had to point out that the engagement ring was "worn on the right finger of the right hand." As late as the early twentieth century, such books provided instructions on how to handle the bride's two rings during the vows, suggesting that the engagement ring shift to the right hand for the duration of the ceremony and be returned to the left afterward.[24] These etiquette works helped solidify new traditions introduced by the jewelry industry.

In the 1920s and 1930s, while the industry continued to offer a variety of wedding and engagement ring styles to suit a range of pocketbooks and tastes, it searched for new ways to maximize profits. To this end, American jewelers pushed platinum over gold, arguing that it wore better than the yellow metal and was more becoming to diamonds. Happily, they noted, platinum cost "several times as much" as gold.[25] During this period both American and Canadian jewelry retailers began introducing bridal sets consisting of a matching engagement and wedding band, often sold boxed together. These bridal sets marked a greater level of commercialization. Matching rings cost more than an unmatched engagement ring and wedding band sold separately. A matching set with a small solitaire diamond ranging from one-eighth to three-eighths of a carat, even from a mail order catalogue, could be quite expensive in 1927. Depending on the carat weight, these sets, sold as units, ranged from $32.75 to $122.50.[26] A boxed set, moreover, pushed the idea of two rings over one.

Catalogues of the time only reveal the possibilities that were available to consumers. Styles of wedding rings offered separately in catalogues still outnumbered goods presented in more costly matched sets.[27] The American mail-order firm Montgomery Ward, for example, offered only two "combination sets" in their 1927 catalogue, while they featured twelve styles of bands and countless diamond ring styles made of white gold, platinum, and green or yellow gold. Availability, however, did not necessarily mean that consumers accepted the new fashions or were able to afford them. Rings could be worn in ways not intended by the manufacturer or retailer, such as the Depression-era practice of making one ring serve the purpose of two. Consumers also often preferred plain gold bands over the more elaborate carved styles that jewelers advertised.[28] Still, the "endless novelty" in these trade and retail catalogues revealed the broad outlines of an expanding consumer ideal for American weddings.

These new ring traditions were connected to larger shifts in American business. As jewelers invented traditions and promoted their professional services, they participated in the changes taking place in advertising during the 1920s. Trade writers and professional associations for the jewelry industry actively engaged in national advertising as a way to shape consumer behavior and develop a reliable market. In the 1920s, they promoted branded diamond engagement rings using the latest forms of advertising methods, including tie-ins with Hollywood movies and radio programming. For example, movie stills of wedding scenes were used in advertisements, such as the wedding scene from the 1927 Universal picture *Butterflies in the Rain*, which promoted Bristol's Seamless bride and groom rings.[29]

By the 1930s, the jewelry industry elaborated this consumer ideal further with the introduction of brand-name diamond engagement rings. Earlier in the twentieth century, wedding bands were sold under trade names, such as the Orange Blossom line produced by Traub Manufacturers or Bristol's Seamless rings. Diamond rings were often purchased in a different manner. Customers bought a stone, which the jeweler mounted in a selected setting. By the 1930s, however, retailers increasingly began to sell diamond rings in units purchased from manufacturers.[30] This standardized the distribution process, making it easier for chain stores and nonspecialty stores to sell wedding and engagement rings. Couples no longer needed the expert attention of a trained jeweler to make their rings individually.[31]

Brand-name rings marked a higher level of consumerism as customers could now experience the ritual good as a commodity with a particular identity. In previous centuries, rings had marked a binding contract of marriage or a religious sacrament. The rise of brand names helped transform these ritual goods into tokens of romantic love. Brands differentiated diamond engagement rings and wedding bands, allowing the industry to infuse their product with a particular symbolism or cultural reference through advertising campaigns. Couples could choose from brands like Rings o' Romance, Token o' Love, and Love Parade. Such names characterized the diamond ring as a public demonstration or symbol of a man's love for a woman. National advertising campaigns also shaped the meaning of these ritual goods. In the late 1930s, the industry began reaching consumers through a combination of radio and television spots, movie playlets, outdoor posters, and window displays. Keepsake Diamonds, for example, began running national advertisements to create brand-name recognition for their diamonds in teen, women's, bridal, and general-interest magazines. From 1939 through 1944, their ads appeared in forty different magazines, from *Screenland* to *Esquire*, "making a total of 2,073,136,560 reader impressions."[32]

Many of these invented ring traditions appeared during the economic and social context of the Great Depression. During this period, jewelers faced a crisis when economic hardship led many couples to defer marriage. The rate of marriage dropped 5.9 percent between 1930 and 1931, and then dropped by another 7.5 percent between 1931 and 1932. The average age of marriage rose during the Depression. By 1939 it was 26.7 for men and 23.3 for women. In spite of declining marriage rates in the 1930s, jewelers clung to the hope that wedding sales were Depression-proof.[33] Trade writers argued that wedding rings were "staple" articles, something people would not do without: "Whether times are good or bad, whether war or peace, people still get married," ran one trade advertisement. No wonder one Depression-era article on the wedding industry noted that the "bride look[ed] most beautiful of all to the jeweler."[34]

During this period of economic hardship, specialty jewelers continued their efforts to develop the bridal market in the face of increased competition from mass retailers that also sold jewelry. Department stores were hurt during this period, but specialty jewelers suffered more as they could not rely on a broad range of necessity goods to generate profits. Between 1929 and 1933, the number of jewelry stores declined 28 percent. Their sales during this time period plunged 67 percent. The number of department stores, in comparison, declined 16 percent, with sales dropping 41 percent. In 1929, there were 19,998 jewelry stores in the United States. By 1933, that number had declined to 14,313. Sales plunged from approximately $536 million in 1929 to $175 million in 1933.[35]

After the Depression was over, the wedding industry as a whole entered into a new boom time, brought on in part by skyrocketing marriage rates. A striking drop in the average age of marriage was partly responsible for this hike. By 1951, the average age for men was a youthful 22.6, for women, a mere 20.4. Jewelers and others watched the age of marriage drop with dollar signs in their eyes. *Seventeen* magazine promoted its advertising space, saying, "She's spending / She's open-minded / She's older than you think: That Young Women in Her Teens."[36] Early marriage meant that the newly discovered teen market could be turned into a bridal market as well. The jewelry industry sought out this lucrative teen bridal market through advertisements for silverware and engagement and wedding rings in a wide range of magazines and other media. Market researchers in the 1950s instructed manufacturers to reach the bride and bride-to-be through television, newspapers, radio, and school publications. Businesses began targeting the African American bridal market as well through advertisements placed in the black general-interest publication *Ebony*.[37]

THE INVENTION OF THE MALE ENGAGEMENT RING

In their search for new markets, American ring manufacturers and retailers first united in a campaign in 1926 to promote the male engagement ring as a "modern expression of an ancient custom" (figure 5). Men had worn engagement rings in the mid- to late nineteenth century, but examples of the practice were rare.[38] As the enthusiastic campaign got under way, the *Jewelers' Circular* called for the appointment of a committee to organize the merchandizing and advertising program. Manufacturers began using radio advertising and sent out newspaper electrotypes for jewelers across the country to use with their window displays of men's engagement rings. Proposals demonstrated that the campaign created networks of jewelers, working cooperatively to put "this immense idea into the public consciousness."[39]

Implicit in this "immense idea" was a transformation of masculine identity. Advertisements drew on a "common language," one that reflected contemporary ideas about gender.[40] To succeed in the campaign for the male engagement ring, in other words, jewelers and their advertisements had to educate the public and overturn social norms that linked jewelry with femininity. They had to make a man's engagement ring seem like a masculine object. Advertisers who wrote copy and jewelry manufacturers who provided style names for

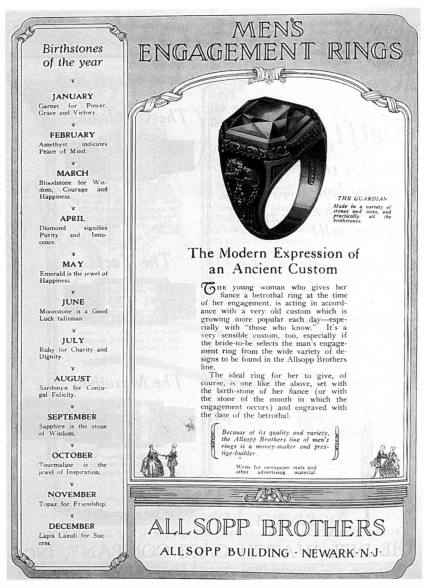

FIGURE 5. In its 1926–1927 campaign, the jewelry industry promoted the invented tradition of the male engagement ring. *Jewelers' Circular* (April 4, 1926), Library of Congress, Washington, D.C.

all types of rings for men in the 1920s tried to appeal to men through gendered language that signaled cultural authority. Men's rings that were not wedding-specific signaled association with power or positions of authority with names like the Pilot, the Advocate, the Master, the Executive, and the Stag (figure 6). A ring like the Major, a carved green gold ring with a blue-white diamond, was advertised as something "for the 'he-man' who appreciates true value."[41] Men who wore these brands had sexual prowess, the ads seemed to say.

To make the prospect of wearing an engagement ring more palatable, the jewelry industry implicitly de-emphasized it as a symbol of changing marital status. While the rings were to be worn on the future groom's left hand like the bride's diamond engagement ring, unlike a woman's they could be any type of ring. A token that did not follow the gender logic of the woman's engagement ring was likely more acceptable to prospective grooms, thus the industry did not adopt one particular style. According to the trade literature advising jewelers how to promote the custom to brides, "none but the engaged couple knows it is an Engagement Ring."[42] Such an object, however, did publicly proclaim a shift in the man's gender identity as he moved into monogamy and gained new responsibilities as husband, provider, and future father. A ring worn as a visible marker of this upcoming transformation, moreover, symbolically placed the groom-to-be on a more equal footing with his future wife, who also wore an engagement ring.

Jewelers masked the radical implications of this campaign by allying themselves with the idea of tradition, one that reproduced established understandings of gender and sexual difference. Ad copy and imagery for the campaign showed that jewelers were trying to legitimize the male engagement ring as a heterosexual tradition. Cooperative advertisements by Newark jewelers promoted the "ancient custom" by using a photograph of a male hand posed with a cigarette, a symbol of sophisticated modernity. To promote the custom, a "bang-up merchandising man" was to design a window-display case of exhibit rings in rugged materials such as iron or bronze, like those worn by men in suitably heroic times, such as "in the ancient Gallic, Roman, Frankish and Pictish ages." Advertisements for the male engagement ring used images of knights going into tournament or battle wearing a token ring. The custom was advertised as a betrothal gift for the man, a practice one ad noted was "still observed by most of the European peoples where the influences of industrial

SUCCESSFUL MEN WEAR DIAMONDS

The PREMIER

636A—Extra heavy 14K green gold ring carved in modern streamline effect is set with AA1 blue-white diamond in white gold top. Examine it Free of Charge and without obligation. Convince yourself of its splendid value. Direct importing reduces price to $87.50
$8.75 down; $7.88 a month

The PHENIX

629A—Man's 18K white gold ring carved with clean cut design and set with brilliant AA1 quality blue-white diamond. The diamond is mounted to display full brilliancy and color. Two triangular, blue French sapphires are set in shank making a pleasing contrast. A good value at............$75
$7.50 down; $6.75 a month

The SAXON

690A—The sturdiness and dash of the fighting Saxon is in this 14K green gold ring with its large AA1 blue-white diamond set in white gold top. Some jewelers would sell it for $175 cash. Our low price on easy terms...........$150
$15 down; $13.50 a month

The EXECUTIVE

692A—A leader of Men chose for himself this artistically carved 14K green gold ring. The sparkling AA1 quality blue-white diamond set in white gold top gives it the appearance of an $85 value. Price only...........$50
$5 down; $4.50 a month

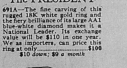

The PRESIDENT

691A—The fine carving of this rugged 18K white gold ring and the fiery brilliance of its large AA1 blue-white diamond makes it a National Leader. Its exchange value will be $110 in one year. We as importers, can price this ring at only...........$100
$10 down; $9 a month

The ACE

643A—A high flying value at the lowest possible price. A good sized AA1 blue-white diamond set in a simply carved, yet handsome 14K green gold mounting with white gold top. A bargain at...........$48.50
$4.85 down; $4.37 a month

The STAG

628A—Proudly - designed 18K white gold ring with AA1 quality blue-white diamond. Two triangular, blue French sapphires are set on either side of diamond. A good investment. Unequalled bargain at...........$100
$10 down; $9 a month

The SAGAMORE

612A—This 14K green gold ring is carved with an effectively simple Old Indian design. A good sized AA1 blue-white diamond mounted on white gold top gives flashing display of brilliance and contrasting colors. Direct importing makes possible the price...........$85
$8.50 down; $7.65 a month

A Sweet diamond one year after purchase is worth 10% more in exchange for a larger diamond

FIGURE 6. Jewelers differentiated their men's rings in the 1920s through design names that signaled status and masculine power. Finlay & Strauss Scrapbook, Archives Center, National Museum of American History, Behring Center, Smithsonian Institution, Washington, D.C.

efficiency have not destroyed time-honored traditions."[43] Perhaps to counter the potentially emasculating image of an engaged man who had lost his sexual freedom, other versions planned for the campaign featured pretty girls giving the rings and, using a popular advertising phrase from the time, "pictur[ed] some 'he-men' wearing 'em."[44]

Jewelers, moreover, knew they had to combat popular notions of gender that assigned consumption to women. Trade writers showed a keen awareness of the conflicts that arose between men and women over the issue of spending. If the groom knew the bride "contemplated purchasing a ring that would cost from $30 to $50" for him, according to one trade writer, "he probably would veto the plan."[45] Trade articles argued that the "psychological time"[46] to sell the bride a male ring was at the time of her engagement and gave suggestions on how to contact the bride without her groom through personal letters with enclosed finger size cards for measuring his ring finger. Jewelers seemed to know that they had to ally with the bride against her groom in order for this tradition to lose its invented status.[47]

It is no wonder the tradition never caught on. A 1927 etiquette book noted the rarity of the custom, suggesting that it was "entirely a matter of individual predilection and is far more the exception than the rule." Unable to overcome "individual predilection" by the 1930s, the male engagement ring custom dropped from view in the jewelry trade literature, only to reappear briefly in 1944, when the Granat Brothers, a leading West Coast ring manufacturer and N. W. Ayer advertising client, promoted a man's gold and diamond engagement ring set to match the bride's as a leap-year idea.[48] In the 1950s, men's engagement ring advertisements appeared, but no concerted effort to change consumer behavior took shape.[49]

These efforts to masculinize engagement rings demonstrate that jewelers must have realized the lack of common knowledge about this supposedly ancient tradition. The industry had to overturn the idea that engagement was something that happened to women. Men were the ones who were supposed to buy the ring for their future spouse, even if such a purchase could be a ticklish matter, as was the case of John O'Rourke of the receiving department at Strawbridge & Clothier in Philadelphia in 1911, who was spotted by fellow employees "examining plain gold rings" and then teased about the incident in the store's company newsletter. Unlike the proposed male engagement ring custom, the purchase of the female engagement ring was an everyday event legitimized by advertisements showing the bride-to-be trying on her ring with her future husband watching. Numerous etiquette books described how women got engaged, who should pay for the ring, and whether the bride should be involved in the selection.[50] While the engagement period itself was historically a time when the woman had more power than she would after marriage, the ring signaled male prerogative. Men proposed, women got engaged. The diamond ring, moreover, showed others a woman was "out of circulation."[51] It was a sign of the man's ability to pay, as well as a symbol of his love. A male engagement ring did not fit this story.

BRIDES OR BOMBERS?

Engagement rings for men did not become tradition in part because they failed to fit contemporary gender mores. On the other hand, rings for the bride were a "natural" part of most marriage ceremonies. Nevertheless, the style of these feminine objects varied widely in the nineteenth and early twentieth centuries. As engagement stones, diamonds were increasingly considered "traditional" in the United States beginning in the late nineteenth century. Still, as we have seen, before the twentieth century those about to marry had many options that did not involve diamonds. In other countries, such as Austria, Germany, Italy, Spain, England, and France, these precious stones did not typically mark an engagement. After 1870, however, discovery of diamond deposits at Kimberley, South Africa, opened up the potential for expanded consumption. Cecil Rhodes, the English founder of De Beers, joined the diamond rush in the 1870s on Johannes De Beer's farm along the Vaal River. Rhodes and others dug for diamonds in an open hole in the ground in what became the famous Kimberley mines. Here, Rhodes began buying up claims and merging his holdings with other mine owners. By 1885, the amalgamated mines Rhodes headed under the De Beers Mining Company name at Kimberley. When Rhodes incorporated in 1888 in South Africa, the De Beers Consolidated Mines, Ltd., controlled 90 percent of the diamond production of the world.[52] In the decades that followed, De Beers invented diamonds as a rarity by restricting their release upon the market and elevating their price. Through mergers, government influence, and merciless control over production and distribution of stones, De Beers managed to construct, as journalist Edward Jay Epstein showed in his exposé of the cartel, "a brilliant illusion."[53]

Advertising played a key role in spreading the diamond engagement ring tradition. This particular wedding custom grew in popularity in direct relation to the economic context of the 1930s and 1940s. During the Depression, diamond prices collapsed as demand decreased, and at the outbreak of war producers found themselves with very large stocks. These excess stocks posed a danger to the industry. To help pull them out of the economic crisis, the De Beers cartel turned to advertising in 1938 under the advice of Harry Oppenheimer, the eldest son of Sir Ernest Oppenheimer, chairman of De Beers since 1929. They hired N. W. Ayer and Son, a prominent full-service advertising agency founded in Philadelphia in 1877. The Ayer agency grew to be an important go-between for the cartel and the American market as De Beers did not retail directly in the United States, but sold uncut stones to the Diamond Trading Company in London. Ayer provided sales help and educational materials to the diamond importers, cutters, wholesalers, and retailers that did business in the United States.[54]

The Ayer agency immediately reported success with its advertising campaigns and various promotions. Advertising focused on the lucrative American marriage market, seeking to expand the numbers who purchased diamond engagement rings but also raise the size and quality of those diamonds.[55] According to market research conducted by the agency for De Beers, American consumption of diamonds had been in decline since the end of World War I. Diamonds had fallen out of favor in part because of the economy, but also, they argued, because of "changes in social attitudes and the promotion of competitive luxuries." Ayer noted jewelers' "alarm" at the "increasing apathy on the part of American youth toward the custom of diamond engagement rings." Diamonds had gained a reputation for being "cheap," "flashy," and "old-fashioned." True or not, Ayer used this idea to promote its services to De Beers. Using the measurement of a cut carat per marriage, an Ayer study found that in 1939, "about a quarter of a cut carat of diamonds were imported" per marriage. In 1940, Ayer claimed success, noting increased cut gem diamond imports to the United States.[56] According to different polls in 1943, anywhere from 75 percent to 98 percent of women received diamond engagement rings, and they became the leading line of jewelry in most department stores. In the 1950s, the Ayer agency noted in internal reports that the "tradition was as strong or stronger than ever."[57] Paralleling campaigns for bigger diamonds, couples were choosing rings with greater carat weight. In 1956 "nearly four-fifths of a cut carat of diamonds were imported per marriage" (up from a quarter of a cut carat per marriage in 1939). Ayer claimed that between 75 percent and 85 percent of brides had diamond engagement rings.[58] According to a 1957 "Hope Chest" study of the youth market, desire for diamond engagement rings became widespread among most teenage girls. (One hundred percent of girls who were thirteen to fourteen years old planned to have a diamond engagement ring.) The power of their advertising campaign extended beyond the wedding day itself, as the industry speculated that the "after-engagement market" absorbed more diamonds as well as couples acquired a diamond engagement ring at some point after the marriage.[59]

Economic prosperity and rising marriage rates certainly must have helped the agency succeed as they did the jewelry industry in general. The Ayer firm, however, was clear to separate its efforts from rising marriage rates, claiming responsibility for increased consumption rather than attributing it to demographics. When marriage rates rose, dipped, or leveled off, they noted, diamond consumption continued to climb.[60] Ayer's assertion that they were responsible for changing the consumer habits of marrying couples, however, was self-serving, in that it encouraged clients to trust that their ad money was well spent. While wartime romance, increased spending power, and rising marriage rates during and after the war were certainly good for business, increased diamond ring consumption did not necessarily follow. Yet, even if Ayer's claims were exaggerated, advertising campaigns and promotions likely shaped the meaning of getting married, making the diamond engagement ring seem a natural step on the way to marriage. Diamonds had been a popular stone for engagement rings before Ayer came on the scene, but the agency helped give new meaning to the tradition and make it more widespread.

In particular, the Ayer campaigns made use of the war to give a new definition to this tradition. De Beers faced a publicity problem during World War II, one that could have threatened its monopoly over the market, as well as the credibility of the diamond engagement ring tradition. Diamonds were a strategic material needed for the industries of both the Allied and Axis powers. Industrial diamonds provided the hard edges and abrasives for cutting precision parts needed in the mass production of weapons of war and conversion of civilian machinery to war production. The stones were also required for jeweled bearings in instruments and guidance systems for submarines and planes. In sum, diamonds were central to war production and a South African cartel controlled the world's supply. The United States had less than a year's stockpile of industrial stones. Keeping a steady supply throughout the war was a concern for President Franklin D. Roosevelt, who held emergency meetings about diamonds in 1940. Roosevelt ordered the War Production Board (WPB), which regulated production of civilian goods and oversaw the conversion of industries, to buy a stockpile of 6.5 million carats from De Beers. The cartel resisted, as its monopoly depended upon controlling the availability of the stones. Sir Ernest Oppenheimer of De Beers opposed any transfer to the United States, arguing that when the war ended, any remaining American stockpile might be released upon the market with devastating effects. Britain pressed De Beers to comply, and eventually it did in a limited way, providing 14 percent of the original request to the United States and creating a Canadian stockpile in addition.[61]

Ayer's advertising campaign sought to dispel public criticism of De Beers by allying the cartel's interest with American war aims. Through a national run of trade and retail advertisements designed by the Ayer agency, De Beers was transformed from a hoarder into a promoter of the war effort.[62] Ayer's campaigns for diamond rings focused on patriotic concerns over wartime conversion and mobilization and the public's belief that gem diamonds would cut into military quotas for the stones. Trade literature sought to educate jewelers and jewelry departments about the distinction between gem stones and the much-needed industrial diamonds so that they would pass on the information to consumers. According to Ayer's ads for the industry, brides did not have to "sacrifice" their diamonds for the war, although advertisements picturing a woman removing her engagement ring showed they were willing to do so to "help give him clearer vision" (figure 7). Ads argued that consuming gem stones in fact furthered the war effort as they were found and mined with industrial diamonds; diamond ring sales helped defray mining costs. Advertisements that asked "For Brides—OR BOMBERS?" answered that diamonds were for both.[63] Diamond engagement rings were thus made central to the war effort. Public relations department promotions also exploited patriotic feelings

MY MOST PRECIOUS

POSSESSION ... BUT Grind it to powder

IF IT WILL HELP GIVE HIM CLEARER VISION!

It will help him most there on your finger, flashing the vision of his constant love for you.

But haven't I heard that only DIAMOND dust can polish the lenses of the navigation instruments he needs to bring him through the perils of the sea — safe back to me?

That is true. A kind of diamond dust made from crushing bort is used to grind and polish lenses for the bomb-sights, range finders, navigation instruments that are so essential to the victory of our armed forces. But you need not sacrifice your diamond for this or for any of the other purposes where diamonds, the hardest substances known, are needed to make wire dies, core drills, saws, precision tools for all our instruments of war.

Why not? No sacrifice is too great if it will help our cause to victory!

Fortunately, the United Nations control almost the world's entire supply of a type of diamonds better suited to that kind of job — rough, tough little industrial diamonds. The diamond he bought for you — and the other gem diamonds being sold today — are helping with the war another way.

How can that be?

They are helping foot the bill for all the industrial diamonds needed in our war industries—about 5,000,000 carats in the United States alone this year. Both kinds come from the same mines, of course . . . but the gem diamond occasionally found is so valued for its eternal beauty that its price defrays a good share of the cost of mining the others.

Then jewel diamonds are still going to be available?

Yes, unlike most luxuries, there are no war priorities on gem diamonds today. Today, more than ever before, they are cherished as the imperishable bearers of life's deepest, tenderest sentiments.

See that your customers understand these points about the dual position and meaning of diamonds in the world at war. Published in the interests of the jewelry trade of America by De Beers Consolidated Mines, Ltd., and Associated Companies.

T—2—1942—1 page—7 x 10—Jewelers Circular-Keystone, Department Store Economist, Jan., 1943—N. W. Ayer & Son, Inc.   9043

FIGURE 7. Patriotism and the diamond engagement ring tradition went hand in hand, as jewelry industry campaigns explained that purchasing gem diamonds helped the war effort by subsidizing the mining of industrial diamonds. N. W. Ayer Advertising Agency Records, Archives Center, National Museum of American History, Behring Center, Smithsonian Institution, Washington, D.C.

to promote diamonds, as in Ayer's New York fashion show titled "Diamond, Bride and Bugle Call," done on behalf of their client, De Beers. The fashion show featured models wearing diamonds and historical bridal costumes from different wartime eras and a color slideshow about industrial diamonds.[64]

The N. W. Ayer campaign for De Beers during the early 1940s also used wartime patriotism as a marketing tool, linking romantic love with the American way of life that soldiers were fighting to protect. In popular culture, World War II was linked to heterosexual romance. Films captured the passion of potential last goodbyes, the strain of separation, and the tearful reunions between husbands and wives when soldiers returned. Like others in the wedding industry, the Ayer agency understood the lucrative potential of romanticizing the emotions surrounding the war. Ads for the jewelry trade focused on getting retailers to exploit the "emotional urgency stimulated by conscription."[65] Diamonds were to be a "token of their pledges" until the couple could marry when the war was over. De Beers ads for the trade encouraged jewelers to depict romance leading to marriage as patriotic, noting that "Defense Is in Cahoots with Cupid!"[66]

Many ads used images of soldiers in uniform—a common occurrence in those days as marriage rates rose—but an image that also made a connection between diamonds and marriage as a religious rite. Promotions for the diamond ring tradition at this time transcended ethnic and religious differences. Ad copy and artwork depicted a country of diverse faiths united under one democratic ideal, something that also suited wartime aims. Ads showed uniformed grooms or couples who had waited to marry because of the war participating in Jewish, Greek Orthodox, and various Protestant ceremonies (figure 8).[67] Advertising copy manipulated the emotions wrought by wartime separations, assuming that all weddings, regardless of religious affiliation, would take place with special intensity: "At last they meet beneath a canopy to part no more. And in the long-awaited vows young hearts find surcease from all loneliness past and hope postponed and waiting. . . . To light the tenderness of such a day, a diamond ring must flame with special purity and joy. Obtain it from a trusted jeweler."[68]

Another Ayer wartime campaign for De Beers linked industrial progress and prosperity with love and romance. Defense spending had brought about the end of the Depression. As factories geared up to produce war goods, and

FIGURE 8. N. W. Ayer's campaign for the diamond engagement ring tradition during World War II appealed to different religious groups. N. W. Ayer Advertising Agency Records, Archives Center, National Museum of American History, Behring Center, Smithsonian Institution, Washington, D.C.

farmers found a market overseas with the Allies, the United States economy improved. Labor shortages led to higher wages, and suddenly men and women found themselves with more money to spend than they had in years. Shortages of goods and rationing put some brakes on consumer spending, but the jewelry industry assured its bridal market that there were no war priorities on gem diamonds that would restrict couples from getting married properly. In fact, the De Beers campaign during the war linked economic recovery to the bridal business as, according to one ad, "Factory Whistles Play the Wedding March."[69] This advertisement noted that defense contractors were spreading $12 billion across the country, removing "the economic barrier to marriage." De Beers encouraged jewelers to take advantage of this engagement market by using the promotional material they provided. De Beers ran other trade advertisements linking prosperity and marriage. "Bugles over America" depicted Cupid flying amidst the factory smoke that signaled American economic recovery. Similarly, "Love in Boom" featured another incongruous pairing of the white wedding with factory imagery (figure 9). De Beers advised jewelers that "as never before the diamond engagement ring becomes a priceless symbol of the deep bonds which men and women cherish most in these times." In these three ads for diamonds, rising numbers of marriages and wartime sentiments were equated with the workings of industry. By using the language of production, here signified by smokestacks, gears, and factory whistles, they connected the power of American capitalism with marriage. The diamond engagement ring was not a consumer good in these ads, it was a tradition that jewelers had to "protect, perpetuate and encourage."[70] Such images mystified production, erasing the exploitative labor in South Africa that provided both gem and industrial diamonds. They also naturalized ties among marriage, the state, and capitalism.

While diamonds in fact were abundant, made precious only through the machinations of the De Beers cartel, as an invented symbol they transcended their commercial origins to become "timeless" or "forever." Trade advertisements and articles urged retailers to promote diamonds as the only suitable "symbol of love and marriage." Their costliness and engineered rareness also made them favorites of the jewelry industry. Not just any stone would do, as De Beers discouraged the consumption of small, inexpensive stones, urging retailers to allow the groom to use credit in order to obtain a finer stone.[71] The indestructibility of diamonds also made these stones potent wedding symbols.

FIGURE 9. N. W. Ayer's diamond advertising campaign linked the white wedding tradition with industrial progress and prosperity. N. W. Ayer Advertising Agency Records, Archives Center, National Museum of American History, Behring Center, Smithsonian Institution, Washington, D.C.

Their ability to survive and become heirlooms that could "keep alive family traditions" was another good reason they were used for engagement rings. (Here the industry skirted the heirloom tradition that ran counter to business's need for new markets.) With copywriter Frances Gerety's 1948 coining of the famous advertising slogan "A diamond is forever," the Ayer agency firmly established the diamond engagement ring tradition in American popular culture.[72] Unlike the much smaller male engagement ring campaign, or the more grassroots movement toward the double-ring ceremony discussed in the next section, these slogans themselves became a part of popular culture.

Advertising campaigns were important for spreading the diamond engagement ring tradition, but N. W. Ayer's public relations department also developed many other ways to shape the market. The Ayer agency became an even more powerful cultural producer in its field in the early 1950s as it began to define its public relations department more broadly, adding product promotion for clients to its traditional publicity work. This expanded merchandising role was reflected in the many promotional materials it developed for De Beers diamonds. Ayer did much more than develop advertisements for magazines and trade journals. The agency had an entire diamond staff that prepared the material on diamonds to educate both consumers and jewelers on the tradition. For example, diamond experts on staff at the agency wrote lectures, such as "Diamonds with a Past" and "Who Sets the Fashions in Diamonds," for distribution among jewelers for talks at social groups and clubs.[73] Ayer's own staff lecturer, Gladys B. Hannaford, known in the industry as the "Diamond Lady," crisscrossed the United States in the late 1940s and 1950s, giving interviews on radio and television, talking at jewelers' association meetings, and lecturing at colleges, high schools, and Rotary Club luncheons on the history of diamonds, mining, and cutting, and most important, on the selection of diamond jewelry. While Ayer noted that some retail experts claimed that retailers threw away most merchandising aids and point-of-purchase material sent to them, they claimed that jewelers found De Beers's aids helpful. To prove this, they circulated in-house the praise from letters written by jewelers from places like West Virginia, Ohio, and Oregon. Their public relations department even provided "direct individual help" in merchandising matters, as for a Cortland, New York, jeweler who wrote them with a question about lighting diamond displays.[74]

In the 1940s and 1950s, the public relations department pushed diamonds on what they called the "school-club-church circuit." Teenage boys and girls, young unmarried men and women, and even mothers of the bride would have had a difficult time missing these innovative promotional efforts for De Beers. From 1945 to 1953, Ayer circulated a film titled *The Eternal Gem* on the "school-club-church circuit." In 1946 *The Magic Stone*, another De Beers diamond film, showed in all Loew's theaters across the country. In 1953, Ayer produced a full-color twenty-seven-minute film titled *A Diamond Is Forever*, which was initially distributed by Columbia Pictures to 3,500 theaters and then shown to nontheatrical audiences in more than 14,000 showings. It featured a jeweler explaining to a bride-to-be how diamonds were mined, cut, and polished. By 1954, the "school-club-church circuit" became the "TV-school-club-church circuit" and viewership soared.[75] The film had a television audience of more than 23 million people in 1954 and 1955 and was shown as well to thousands of clubs, schools, churches, and groups of jewelers. By the late 1950s, the agency claimed in a series of in-house reports on their clients that the "strength of diamond traditions" could be "traced in large part to the advertising, publicity and promotional work done since 1939."[76] Such large-scale education efforts certainly reached broad segments of the population, helping to establish "tradition."

More than any other wedding symbol, perhaps with the exception of the formal white gown, the bride's diamond ring entered popular culture. Photographs or drawings of engaged or married couples consistently used the bride's diamond to denote their transformed status. The image of a feminine gold band, typically with a solitaire diamond, graced the covers of sheet music and bridal paper doll books (figure 10). Covers of bridal magazines and images in etiquette books put the bride and her diamond in the foreground, as if it was her ring that conveyed the desired meaning.[77] After World War II, a diamond engagement ring emerged in popular culture as a symbol of female achievement. While Ayer claimed it "strengthened the desire to buy diamonds," certainly consumers brought their own meanings to their "sparklers" when they gave their rings this name in company newsletter announcements of their engagement.[78] For working women, wearing an engagement ring signified success in the competitive marriage market. Popular culture was full of examples

FIGURE 10. Little girls learned about the diamond engagement ring tradition in places like this bridal-themed paper doll book. Carolyn & Donald Grepke Paper Dolls Collection, Archives Center, National Museum of American History, Behring Center, Smithsonian Institution, Washington, D.C.

of women boasting about their diamonds—the bigger the better—or regretting their lack of this symbol of commitment and marriage.

In the face of such massive campaigns and such far-reaching educational efforts on behalf of De Beers, those about to marry must have felt immense pressure to conform to the tradition. The positive reception to the De Beers campaign, marked by the rapid rise in diamond sales and embracing of the diamond engagement ring tradition, showed that the advertising messages resonated with those about to marry. The fact that diamond engagement rings for the bride were popular before Ayer's extensive promotions suggests that the makings of this tradition were already in place. But by World War II and the early postwar period, when a new cult of marriage worked its way into the national discourse, the custom took on a different meaning that firmly established it as tradition. Diamond engagement rings for women came to be seen as a natural symbol of romantic love and marriage in part because they fit contemporary gender logic in a way the male engagement ring did not. The extensive efforts of N. W. Ayer's advertising and innovative educational campaigns in the 1940s and 1950s tied this consumer good to national prosperity—to ideas of progress, industrial might, and the American democratic consumer ideal.

THE "REAL MAN'S RING"

Unlike the diamond engagement ring, which emerged slowly as a tradition over the late nineteenth and early twentieth centuries, only to be given new meaning and put firmly in place by strong diamond advertising campaigns mid-century, the groom's wedding band became traditional very quickly in the 1940s and 1950s. The popularization of this invented tradition is not merely a story of hapless brides and grooms influenced by advertising, buying new types of consumer goods as soon as they appeared in jewelers' windows displayed in innovative contraptions such as the Rings-O-Bliss tray. American groom's rings had been available since the 1920s, when they appeared in catalogs and in advertisements and came in a variety of styles from the simple band to the art-carved.[79] The first trade article encouraging the "real man's ring," or the groom's wedding band, appeared in 1930. By 1937, the double-ring ceremony appeared in an etiquette book, the first such mention my survey uncovered.[80] In these decades, however, the practice had not yet become tradition for most marrying couples.[81]

By World War II and in the early postwar period, climbing marriage rates and the expansion of middle-class affluence had given both jewelers and department stores increased opportunity to sell all types of wedding rings. It was within this window of consumer readiness that jewelry industry campaigns for the groom's band took place. While no cartel lay behind the promotion of gold or platinum wedding bands for men, the jewelry industry nevertheless played a role in the invention of this tradition. During the war, the Jewelry Industry Publicity Board campaigned widely to promote "the story of the double ring service." Using radio, trade publications, movies, and newsreels, the publicity reached schools, clubs, factories, home economics departments, and country newspapers. The campaign and other efforts were successful. According to one account in 1943, around 80 percent of couples wanted to have a double-ring ceremony. A 1947 *Fortune* magazine article titled "Ring Twice" noted that from the end of the Depression to the late 1940s, the percentage of double-ring as opposed to single-ring marriages increased from 15 percent to approximately 80 percent. The article noted that there was "a time when it was considered odd in the United States for males to wear wedding rings. But those who indulge in the practice now can be assured of being perfectly acceptable."[82]

Consumption of these goods quickly forced religious ritual to change. In the 1940s and 1950s, the double-ring ceremony crossed denominational lines, appearing in Catholic, Unitarian, Baptist, and Methodist churches, among others.[83] The Catholic Church in particular debated the new ritual in the pages of the *American Ecclesiastical Review*. One priest turned to the journal in 1944 for advice on whether the "double ring" marriage ceremony was permitted. If it was allowed, he asked, "is the prayer for the blessing of the ring, as found in the Ritual, said in the plural number, and do groom and bride successively place a blessed ring each on the finger of the other, saying the accustomed words, 'With this ring, etc.?' " Among Catholics and others prior to World War II, most marriage vows took place with one wedding band, which the groom placed on the bride's left hand. Changes in this long-standing practice led the Catholic journal to conclude that as the groom's ring was a matter of custom and not legislation, "it is custom which will govern the manner in which it is to be carried out." The Roman Ritual called only for the blessing of the bride's ring; as custom had it, the ring for the groom was not usually blessed. In 1951, the issue was taken up again, only now the journal concluded that "no objection can be set forth against the blessing of the second ring along with the ring of the bride," even though the Roman Ritual made no provision for the practice. By 1956, the journal's Catholic authorities once again addressed the question, stating finally that the Congregation of Sacred Rites permitted the double-ring ceremony and that the blessing was to be said only once but in the plural.[84] Priests, ministers, and justices of the peace agreed to perform the double-ring ceremony, allowing it to become a new tradition, but first couples had to hear about the practice.

The wedding industry helped transform the wedding ceremony by educating the public about the groom's ring, but consumers also played an important role. Those about to marry learned about the practice informally, by seeing the double-ring ceremonies of friends or family members. Advertisements in window displays and in magazines also educated consumers. Such promotions allowed one Fresno, California, jewelry store to sell "three men's wedding rings for every four engagement-wedding ring combination sold to the brides." The new bridal magazines appearing during this period discussed the double-ring ceremony, making it seem a fashionable thing to do.[85] These publications, however, may have been responding first to consumer demand. One reader of a new California bridal magazine in 1948 wrote in to request an article on the double-ring ceremony, noting that she was "interested in this type of wedding for myself but [knew] very little about it." She wanted to know who bought the groom's band and how the exchange was carried out during the ceremony. Bridal consultants also helped spread the practice. Their manuals discussed the tradition, passing on etiquette tips on things such as who paid for the groom's ring. It is likely that consumer interest spurred these wedding professionals and businesses to provide information on the practice and stock groom's bands. As more people became interested in the practice, the double-ring ceremony entered popular culture and spread from there (figure 11). The Hollywood romance, for example, helped promote the custom in popular culture. Humphrey Bogart chose to wear his first groom's ring when he married for the fifth and final time to Lauren Bacall in 1946, and Shirley Temple had a double-ring ceremony during her wedding as well. By the end of the 1940s the tradition was even used to sell other wedding-related products, such as "1847 Rogers Bros." brand silverware, which was sold in a new "Double Wedding Ring Chest" (figure 12).[86]

Jewelry retailers credited the new interest in the "masculine band" to wartime sentiments, but they also helped shape the contours of this sentiment in ways beneficial for commerce. According to one saleswoman from a jeweler's diamond department, men about to leave for war could be "play[ed] up heav-

With this ring, I thee wed, for richer, for poorer,

FIGURE 11. The double-ring ceremonies of Hollywood stars like Ann Blyth helped popularize the new tradition. "Ann Blyth, Bride of the Year," *Photoplay* (June 1953), 46.

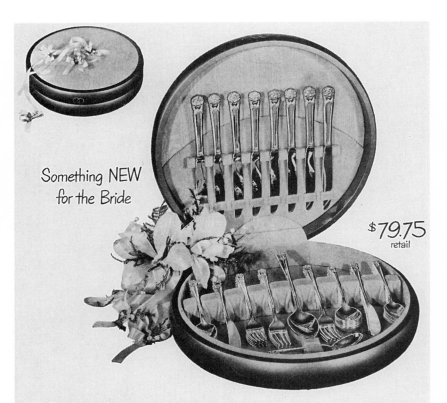

FIGURE 12. The invented tradition of the double-ring ceremony eventually was used to sell other wedding-related goods. *Department Store Economist* (April 1949), 39. Hagley Museum and Library, Pictorial Collections Department, Wilmington, Delaware.

ily."[87] As De Beers had done with diamonds, the industry emphasized the poignancy of separation and potential loss that could be lessened by tokens of love and commitment. The double-ring ceremony highlighted the bonds of marriage and family, bonds that could be extended to include nation and the capitalist "free world." During wartime, men could wear groom's bands as symbols of what they were fighting to preserve.[88] The industry understood that a wedding band could be presented as a manly object in harmony with war aims, as depicted on the cover of *Click* magazine, reprinted in a 1944 issue of the jewelers' trade journal. In the photograph, a handsome soldier holds a letter from home, likely from his wife, as the prominently foregrounded art-carved wedding band suggests. The image captures a personal moment, one that links the soldier with the home front and the wife he left behind. The gun slung over the soldier's arm frames the image on one side, reminding the viewer of the danger faced by men at war. The gun also handily stands as a phallic sign of the soldier's masculinity, something uncompromised by the shiny ring he wears on his left hand.[89] The ad copy accompanying this image heralds the market potential of the soldier when he returns, suggesting that weddings and marriage were seen as suitable symbols of the wartime aim of preserving the American way of life.

While preserving a consumer democracy was the long-term goal, wartime shortages created an immediate problem. The War Production Board, as we have seen, attempted to stockpile diamonds in opposition to De Beers. Potential restrictions on gold also became an issue for the jewelry industry. Men's rings contained three times as much gold as women's, something that had to be justified during World War II. In 1943, the War Production Board limited jewelers to 50 percent of the gold they used in 1941. William Schwab, the president of J. R. Wood & Sons, Inc., the largest manufacturer of wedding rings at the time, campaigned against the WPB restrictions. According to a 1947 *Fortune* article, he had thought about increasing sales by popularizing the double-ring ceremony before Pearl Harbor, but "his chance came during the war when prospective brides and bridegrooms, facing wartime separation— with all its apprehensions—were emotionally susceptible." Schwab argued with the WPB over whether a man's ring was a necessity or a luxury. Likely in response to what were seen as the "religious overtones" of the argument, according to the article, the WPB raised its gold limitation to 75 percent, then eight months later lifted it entirely.[90] The WPB and the government supported the jewelry industry's case for the groom's ring. Jewelers' efforts to popularize the double-ring ceremony succeeded because consumption became a patriotic act. Weddings and marriage had become synonymous with prosperity, capitalism, and national stability.

Although it had the backing of both business and government, the double-ring ceremony would not have become tradition if it did not overcome male consumers' suspicion of jewelry. As in the 1920s, the industry continued to construct gender difference in ways that either reflected its own beliefs or it hoped would appeal to consumers. According to Miss Bierman, a California jewelry saleswoman quoted in a trade article in 1946, "at one time men were inclined to feel a bit 'silly' about the purchase of a wedding ring." After the war, Miss Bierman observed that "sensitivity" to the practice "vanished." Using language reminiscent of the 1926 male engagement ring campaign, even "the most rugged of men now cheerfully exhibit wedding rings." But this time, a new sense of togetherness permeated the ad language: according to Miss Bierman, many men wanted their rings "made up to exactly the same design as those worn by their wives." Women, she noted, were "invariably delighted with the suggestion." Most had forgotten about "this new form of wedding in the excitement of getting ready." In fact, during the war women often purchased the groom's ring, suggesting that things had not changed too much.[91]

As in the 1920s, jewelers used gender-specific merchandising tactics when inventing tradition in the 1940s. One Pennsylvania jeweler established a separate "groom's room" intended to "give cupid a push." The paneled room, decorated with sporting prints on the wall, allowed the groom to avoid the embarrassment of being the focus of attention when shopping for wedding rings.[92] When selling groom's rings to men, Miss Bierman of the Fresno, California, store consciously used a different sales pitch. Her store's policy was never to mention the man's ring until the woman had made up her mind on her own rings. At that point, the salesperson brought out the groom's ring that most closely matched and suggested the double-ring service. Wedding bands for men were also presented to the customer differently. Miss Bierman noted that she "found it excellent sales psychology to keep all men's wedding rings concealed in slide drawers beneath the feminine ring displays in the case."

Women's rings were displayed against blue sateen and were "made as feminine as possible." Men's rings, she observed, "would 'clash' in this atmosphere." In the early 1940s, catalogues featuring such rings distinguished them from the bride's band, noting that they were "wider, heavier and mannish in appearance" or that they were "plain and decidedly masculine."[93]

Psychological approaches to merchandising had the potential to work only if they reflected contemporary social mores. The jewelry industry helped draw the boundaries of what was considered appropriate, but consumers produced their own meanings.[94] Thus, unlike the male engagement ring in the 1920s, the groom's ring must have made sense for those couples embracing a middle-class American identity based upon new conceptions of family and gender roles. According to some, the groom's ring was to make sure a husband "looks married."[95] The popularity of the double-ring ceremony suggests that what historian Margaret Marsh has called "masculine domesticity" returned more broadly as an ideal after World War II. In the early twentieth century, as Marsh has argued, "masculine domesticity" became a desired trait among upper-middle-class suburban men. Suburban husbands assumed an "increased responsibility for the emotional well-being of their children," and began "to spend their leisure with their wives rather than male cronies, and even to take on limited domestic duties." This gender ideal suited a ring custom that symbolically put men and women on a more equal plane. Marsh and others, however, argued that this gender ideal had declined by the 1920s.[96] Perhaps this contributed to the failure of the male engagement ring tradition. In the postwar period, however, "masculine domesticity" returned in a more inclusive sense. With the rise of working-class home ownership and the move to the suburbs, men's role changed as their domestic responsibilities increased and their focus turned toward the family. The symbolism of the double-ring ceremony, with its mutual exchange of rings, was well suited to the era's new emphasis on "togetherness."[97]

As more and more working-class men became suburban husbands tending their gardens and their backyard barbecues, they found that the groom's ring fit. Accounts of marriage among garment workers at the Maidenform Company in New Jersey, for example, showed an interest in the double-ring ceremony during the late 1940s and 1950s. Working-class men, however, did not necessarily always embrace the middle-class domestic role signified by the groom's ring. When employees Doris Ryan and James Farrell had a double-ring ceremony in 1946, the groom's resistance to the ring was the subject for humor in the Maidenform employee newsletter: "As the two gold bands were slipped on, Jimmy began to feel the pressure of his marital chains, the ring Doris put on his finger was just a little too small. Jimmy claims he hasn't yet been able to take it off. He says he tried to convince Doris of the danger of a mechanic wearing a ring while working at machines, but Doris refused to be convinced."[98] The reporters here were drawing on the image of the wife as ball and chain for humorous effect. Farrell's concerns, however, were legitimate. For industrial workers, a wedding band could be dangerous, sparking or catching in machinery. Practical concerns aside, perhaps such golden bands ill fit working-class notions of masculinity rooted in the more homosocial worlds of the trade union, the lodge, and other male-dominated urban spaces. In this context, the Maidenform workers' satire of Jimmy Farrell's opposition to wearing a wedding band can be read as resistance to a middle-class notion of "togetherness." For some grooms, a ring might symbolize marital bonds—a loss of sexual freedom and new financial responsibilities.

Working-class women, however, did not see the double-ring service the same way. Maidenform employee James Farrell's wearing of the ring was of utmost importance to Doris Ryan, perhaps because those bonds were a gain for her in terms of social status and economic standing. The groom's ring stood as a symbol of her success, as well as the man's willingness to participate in his new role. The bride's ring signaled her new role as wife, but did not symbolize companionate marriage, unless the groom also wore a wedding band. In a time when there was a perceived "man shortage," and when being married was extremely important to many women, so much so that those who were not married by twenty-one were considered old maids, a groom's ring signified a bride's claim to her husband.[99]

Moreover, not all men and women about to marry planned to have a double-ring ceremony or carried it out in a fashion that would make the jewelry industry happy. Both black and white men adopted the band, but as Harriette Cole, one late twentieth-century African American wedding consultant, wrote, a bride could not assume her groom would wear a ring.[100] As we have seen, some religious groups refrained from using rings at all. In addition, brides might subvert the double-ring ceremony, taking it out of its commercial context. The jewelry industry certainly intended couples to buy their matching wedding bands. Jewelers even tried to thwart the older heirloom tradition by advertising their ability to replicate family heirloom rings. Generally, *Bride's* magazine aided the industry in this through editorials promoting the custom, but it also related versions of the practice that were counter to the interests of jewelers. One innovative bride, according to a 1943 issue of *Bride's* magazine, had an heirloom gold band enlarged for her groom.[101]

While some ambiguity remained over this invented tradition, the practice was firmly in the mainstream by the early 1950s. The double-ring ceremony, however, did not simply become popular when the requisite object appeared on the market in the late 1920s or because jewelers ran national promotions. Marketing on its own could not change dominant notions of gender, as demonstrated by the failure of the male engagement ring tradition.[102] The practice became the thing to do only when cultural producers and consumers conspired in the act of cultural production, forging new meanings around the ritual of ring exchange.

* * *

The groom's wedding band and the diamond engagement ring were highly visible and symbolic elements of the formal white wedding ideal that emerged as full-fledged traditions by mid-century. Jewelry retailers and manufacturers had a hand in constructing the symbolism of these goods as they sought new ways to capture the lucrative bridal market, linking it to postwar ideas of the American dream. Like the jewelry industry, other commercial enterprises also needed a modern, flexible idea of tradition in order to attract new markets and stay profitable.[103] As jewelers had done with wedding and engagement rings, an increasingly broad range of businesses developed methods to expand all types of wedding consumption and bring consumers to their doors. Through their efforts, marriage came to mean registered wedding gifts, purchased goods for a new home, ready-made wedding clothes for the bride and her pageant of bridesmaids, a flower-bedecked ceremony, a lavish, much-photographed reception with food, drink, and dancing, and a honeymoon to follow. Although separate and diverse businesses with a variety of functions provided these wedding-related goods and services, they came together in the pages of the new bridal advertising magazines that began appearing in the 1930s and 1940s. As we will see in the next chapter, along with etiquette books and women's magazines, bridal magazines helped define and expand the bridal market during this early period, setting the stage for a postwar multibillion-dollar industry.

CHAPTER THREE

Bridal Magazines and the Creation of a Market

Throughout the twentieth century, bridal magazines have done more than just tell young women what to buy—they have made consumerism itself a traditional part of American wedding culture. With the appearance of publications like *Bride's* (1934), *Wedding Belle* (1948), *Modern Bride* (1949), *Bride-To-Be* (1955), and *Bride and Home* (1956), the idea of tradition became a marketing tool. These magazines played a central role in the rise of a national wedding industry. They consolidated and expanded the wedding-related advice, information, and advertising that had long been a staple of women's magazines. Part of a general shift toward market segmentation and advertising-driven publications, bridal magazines gave advertisers a "must-buy" market unlike any before. *Bride's* in particular helped centralize and professionalize the wedding industry, conducting market research, participating in national advertising, and establishing networks with mass and specialty retailers. *Bride's* became the linchpin for a growing industry by hosting bridal clinics for department stores, which in turn helped spread wedding salons and gift registries across the country.[1]

Before specialized bridal magazines appeared in the 1930s and 1940s, however, etiquette writers and women's magazines had already begun shaping wedding tradition. By the last quarter of the nineteenth century, brides were able to turn to a growing number of etiquette books and women's periodicals for information and advice on the social and material aspects of getting married. In the early twentieth century, they began to embrace new ideas about wedding consumption. As an older, more rigid conception of what was correct or "vulgar" fell away, a new code celebrating the bride-consumer took its place. Increasingly, etiquette experts and women's and bridal magazine writers faced a fundamental dilemma: how to persuade consumers to accept new goods and professional services in connection with a ritual that was ostensibly "traditional" and noncommercial. A wedding was not supposed to be a commercial event or a fashion show that displayed the latest in bridal apparel. And yet magazine writers, and in some cases etiquette writers, were in the business of celebrating the "modern" wedding, of persuading brides to spend more money on their marriage celebration and see the need for gift registries, bridal consultants, florists, photographers, and caterers. Through their advertising, editorials, feature articles, and merchandising efforts and promotions, first *Bride's*, and later other bridal publications, naturalized higher levels of consumption and played a key role in the invention of the formal white wedding tradition.

ETIQUETTE BOOKS AND WEDDINGS

Long before bridal magazines came on the scene, etiquette books gave advice to those about to marry. Etiquette books first appeared on the American market in the 1830s. Early etiquette manuals addressed manners and correct conduct for different social situations and either omitted discussion of weddings or treated them in a minimal way. Although religious marriage ceremonies and formal receptions were ritualized occasions that required knowledge of tradition, or the way things were done, they were only one of a number of social events that were a part of elite and upper-middle-class life.[2] For example, Sarah Hale, the editor of *Godey's Lady's Book* from 1837 to 1877, gave only one chapter to engagements and weddings in her 1866 work *Manners; or, Happy Homes and Good Society*. Instead of a discussion of wedding invitations and thank-you letters, silver engraving, floral arrangements, reception menus, or the accumulation of the personal and household trousseau, Hale provided thoughts on what contributed to a happy union, and gave advice on the etiquette of engagement. Weddings, Hale argued, were not governed by "rules." In practice, such things as the number of bridal attendants and the wedding dress always varied according to circumstances.[3] Such advice reflected the informality and simplicity of most ceremonies in the mid-nineteenth century when most weddings did not participate in the formalized ritual and display of bourgeois life.

By the late nineteenth century, however, weddings were a central topic in many different works of etiquette and the manuals had become their own popular literary genre. In a time of great social change, etiquette books had much to offer both middle-class and working-class readers. With rising numbers of immigrants and challenges to racial hierarchies in this period after the Civil War, etiquette books established exclusionary standards that worked to shore up middle-class power. The rules of etiquette acted as a form of social control. Such works, however, also held out the opportunity for emulation and social mobility for those who followed their advice.[4] For guests unsure of what to give an engaged couple, these publications provided gift suggestions that were assured to be tasteful and correct. Etiquette books provided a guide for those unfamiliar with the social intricacies of the middle-class wedding celebration, helping with wording on invitations, the order of the receiving line, the seating arrangement at the wedding breakfast, and the phrasing of thank-you letters.

Wedding advice became increasingly elaborate by the turn of the century, reflecting a growing orientation toward consumerism. Etiquette manuals began to link rites of marrying to rites of acquiring or buying, providing lists of the clothing needed for the trousseau and outlining extensive household linens and goods required to set up house. Margaret Sangster's 1904 *Good Manners for All Occasions* provided a guide for the trousseau, listing two dresses, eight waists, three jackets, four skirts, one wrapper, four vests, and one corset with covers. The same account lists the household linen provided by the bride, a list that included among many other things, six towels and two bath towels for her maid, "if she have one."[5]

Etiquette books now advertised their advice as "modern," suggesting that things had changed, requiring new advice. In fact, over the years, tastes and practices did evolve, and to some degree etiquette manuals record these shifts. As early as 1882, etiquette writers made concessions to new fashions and guided readers through the "latest ceremonials." Just as etiquette writers noted the evolving ring practices discussed in Chapter 2, their manuals also captured other alterations in the ceremony, such as changes in the order of the processional and new ways for the groom to approach the altar. In *American Etiquette and Rules of Politeness* (1882), by no less than professors Walter R. Houghton, James K. Beck, James A. Woodburn, Horace R. Hoffman, and Mrs. W. R.

Houghton, a section titled "The Latest Ceremonials" legitimized the "latest New York form" for presenting the bride at the altar. In this new custom, the bride proceeded down the aisle alone, followed by her parents.[6]

Etiquette experts assesrted their cultural authority and expertise by allying with unchanging tradition—they were the ones who knew how things were done and had always been done. Some etiquette writers criticized changing tastes. Prominent society author Amy Vanderbilt favored luxury gifts long considered traditional and criticized a perceived turn toward useful, more practical gifts. In 1952 she offered a "word of warning" to those brides who rejected offers of sterling silver in favor of household furnishings: *If you don't get your sterling now, you may never get it*" (emphasis hers).[7] These experts, however, also had to deal with changing consumer traditions and with their own need for new markets. In the 1930s and 1940s, women's magazines and bridal magazines came out with their own etiquette manuals that were oriented toward fashion and decorating the home. With the growing consumer orientation of wedding advice came a more flexible attitude toward codes of behavior and notions of taste. As *Vogue's Book of Etiquette* from 1948 noted, etiquette was "full of paradoxes . . . based on tradition, and yet it can change." According to *Vogue*, "certain elements [were] indispensable to every wedding." A ceremony in a judge's or registrar's office or in a church with only the clergyman and witnesses was not "according to Webster or any woman's conception, a wedding." A real wedding required certain essentials, including: "1. a religious ceremony; 2. a father, brother, uncle, cousin, or other male relative, to give the bride away; 3. a best man for the groom; 4. at least one attendant for the bride; 5. a bouquet for the bride; 6. a ring for the bride. And, if possible, 7. a reception, no matter how small, which need only entail a wedding cake and a drink in which to toast the bride." Etiquette books like this presented a wedding ideal that even in its most modest version still followed "tradition," including ritual elements such as the ring, flowers, and cake. More typically, etiquette books produced by these magazines instructed readers to pay attention to the material goods "required" for a wedding, the bride's wardrobe, and the couple's new home.[8]

By acknowledging changes in tradition, these writers demonstrated a continued need for their advice. If wedding etiquette could become as "out of date as grandmother's rocking chair," as the expert Julietta Arthur put it, then brides would need to buy new editions. The number of updated editions and new publications suggests a growing market for etiquette advice in the twentieth century. Particular works achieved phenomenal success in reprint, like Lillian Eichler's *Book of Etiquette*, which was first published in 1921 and had sold over a million copies by 1945.[9]

Emily Post's *Etiquette, The Blue Book of Social Usage*, provided an elite model of the ideal wedding. Published in 1922, her manual sold more than two-thirds of a million copies by 1945. Post's advice worked its way into the larger culture. Her name became synonymous with etiquette (figure 13). Significantly, she stood as one of the more unyielding of advisers.[10] Although she offered a script of the way things were supposed to be done, certainly many did not follow her to the letter. Some consciously rejected her advice. For example, Emily Post made her way into working-class discourse as an object of fun by the 1940s and 1950s. Women appropriated the power of big-name etiquette writers like her and turned it to their humorous ends. Wedding announcements in factory newsletters, for example, used these women to give working-class employee nuptials the mock aura of a society wedding. In 1946 at the Jantzen Yarn mills in Oregon, for example, the Trunks department noted that "from all the recent happenings in our corner of the plant we should be the matrimonial bureau with [employee] Virginia Chamberlain as Emily Post or Dorothy Dix." Post remained a leader in the field in the late 1960s, when wedding professionals, such as the designer and bridal wear manufacturer Priscilla Kidder, claimed that etiquette classics, like Emily Post, were their "bible."[11]

By the early 1960s, for all its elite origins, etiquette advice reflected a more inclusive tone in keeping with the times and displayed even greater flexibility than before. Perhaps in response to changing behavior, etiquette writers began addressing new social circumstances, such as divorce and second marriages.[12] *Modern Bride*'s 1961 volume argued that the rules of etiquette "can be learned by anyone of average intelligence." *Modern Bride* implied that courtesy, and thus good manners, were achievable by all: "Gentlefolk, no matter what their social or racial origins, are those who put consideration for others first in all their dealings." Putting others first meant respecting other cultures' way of doing things, even if it clashed with one's own.[13] Eleanor Roosevelt stated in her 1962 *Book of Common Sense Etiquette* that it was "not just a matter of

What a lovely Wedding!

N̲o one will ever forget the Browning wedding. Everything was just right. And *your* wedding — whether it's for four or four thousand — can be as beautifully memorable an occasion with ETIQUETTE to guide you.

From the simplest ceremony to the most elaborate, Emily Post tells you what to do about invitations, trousseau, rehearsal, reception, and all the myriad details of a wedding. Now as always, the accepted highest authority and best-selling book on all questions of good taste, ETIQUETTE will help you as it has helped thousands of other brides.

EMILY POST'S

Etiquette

THE COMPLETE GUIDE TO GOOD MANNERS
668 pages, illustrated • $5.00 at your bookstore
FUNK & WAGNALLS COMPANY, New York 10

Portrait by

FIGURE 13. The formal white wedding with the bride in a long gown and veil appeared as the ideal, though experts like Emily Post also included the "simplest ceremony" in their advice and appeals to social anxieties. *Bride's* (Spring 1948), 155.

knowing how a lunch or dinner should be served. . . . There are many correct ways of behaving in almost any situation." A large segment of her work was devoted to weddings, outlining the different ritual practices of Roman Catholics, Jews, and Protestants, providing suggestions about wedding preparations, invitation protocol, ring practices, and the various informal and formal ways of celebrating a union. Although always speaking with an authoritative voice, this former First Lady significantly included a section titled "Variations from Custom," which stated, in reference to rules governing who bore the wedding expenses, that "there is nothing sacrosanct about any of these customs." Envisioning a case where a couple might have been on their own financially before their wedding, or a case where the bride was self-supporting, she gave permission for "special arrangements" if such circumstances required a break with past customs.[14] By the 1960s, etiquette experts served commercial ends well, for they allowed for infinite changes in fashions and the addition of new wedding-related goods and rituals. Women's and bridal magazines would take this commercialization to the next level.

THE BIRTH OF THE BRIDAL MAGAZINE

By the late nineteenth century, weddings were a ubiquitous topic in women's magazines and general interest periodicals. Publications like *Harper's Bazaar*, *Scribner's*, and *Atlantic Monthly* explored wedding-related subjects, with articles on weddings and marriage, and poems, short stories, and serialized novels that treated courtship, engagement, wedding gifts, the ceremony, and the honeymoon.[15] Women's periodicals like *Godey's Lady's Book* featured numerous bridal fashion plates and discussions of wedding and trousseau apparel. In addition, women's magazines were sometimes tied to the business of selling paper patterns for home sewing, something that would have found a ready market with the bride-to-be. Aided by improved railroads, the Postal Act of 1879, which allowed magazines second-class mail rates, and the Rural Free Delivery Act of 1896, which provided new access to rural markets, magazine circulation soared by the end of the nineteenth century.[16]

As they grew, magazines became increasingly dependent on selling advertising space. Promotion methods for selling magazines varied widely in the 1890s, including subscription clubs, discounts, and premiums, but these practices declined after the turn of the century as the advertising magazine took shape. With the rise of branded goods, businesses sought to reach a national market by advertising in women's magazines. Magazine advertising dollars grew from $682 million in 1914 to $2,987 million by 1929. The editorial-to-advertising-page ratio also shifted as magazines such as *Ladies' Home Journal* reversed its ratio from 60:40 at the turn of the century to 40:60 by the mid-1920s. By

1930, more than 60 percent of revenue came from advertising. This increased dependence on advertising shaped content as articles and features became product promotions themselves.[17] Such editorial advertising masked the inherent commercial nature of these magazines. Women received instruction on how to be beautiful, keep a clean, efficient house, and have a happy marriage alongside products that would help them achieve these goals.

Magazines increasingly targeted specialized reader groups. Magazine publishers, such as Curtis Publishing, Condé Nast, Hearst, and others, devised editorial formulas to reach particular readers and then sold advertisers access to these readers. Publications that appealed to a homogeneous audience with shared interests, like those about to marry, simplified the editing process and increased advertising value. A host of influential and long-lived fashion magazines appeared, such as *Mademoiselle* in 1935, *Glamour* in 1939, and *Seventeen* in 1944. These magazines refined the female market even further along the lines of age and interests. *Mademoiselle* sold to "smart young women," such as the student or graduate in search of a wardrobe for college or a job-hunting guide after college. *Glamour,* which grew out of *Glamour of Hollywood,* and *Seventeen,* which stemmed from *Stardom,* addressed the concerns of single young women.[18] Along with advertisements for Gorham silverware and Keepsake rings, *Seventeen* magazine featured articles such as "You Didn't Inherit Grandma's Sterling?" and wedding stories with titles like "Maid-of-Honor."[19] By the 1950s, magazines gained their character from the formula, regardless of changes in editorship or personnel. This combination of standardization and market segmentation worked as businesses flocked to advertise in magazines.[20]

Women's magazines also offered a market segment that was likely interested in weddings. Readers were all either potential brides, or the mother, sister, cousin, aunt, grandmother, or friend of a bride or bride-to-be. As advertising publications, moreover, they had the potential to bring businesses together that had an interest in the lucrative bridal market. They provided a centralized source of product and service information for those about to marry. In the early 1930s, the magazine *House Beautiful* attempted to reach these consumers with a bridal package that later became a standard way to target this market segment. In the Philadelphia area, *House Beautiful* sent brides-to-be an elegant white and gold box containing brochures and information on wedding photography, Wanamaker's Trousseau Shop, gift ideas, and honeymoon travel.[21] It is not surprising that women's magazines also fit wedding consumption into their annual seasonal cycle, even after specialized bridal magazines made getting married a year-round business. June regularly found a woman in white on the cover of women's magazines (figure 14). Articles outlining wedding budgets appeared in spring issues, and advertisements for wedding silver were a year-round staple. Some women's magazines like *Good Housekeeping* ran regular wedding etiquette columns.[22]

In the postwar era, general-interest magazines also participated in the naturalization of the wedding industry and its consumer ethic by documenting and celebrating its success. Like *Fortune* magazine in the 1930s, in the postwar period *Life* and *Ebony* published articles on bridal fashion, accounts of the elaborate wedding celebrations of famous people, and features on the success of businesses and entrepreneurs that targeted the bridal market. Such accounts naturalized consumer rites that involved expenditure on wedding gifts, designer wedding gowns, diamond rings, towering wedding cakes, limousines, receptions for hundreds of guests, and honeymoons in exotic locations. First published in 1944, *Ebony*, a general-interest magazine directed at a black audience, participated in the construction of this wedding ideal. Regular features on society weddings or the marriage of famous African American individuals often received full-page spreads with photographs of the bride and groom and their celebration. These articles implied that high levels of wedding expenditure were something to admire and perhaps emulate. Readers' letters, however, also criticized the elaborate consumption documented in the magazine.[23] In *Life*, the white counterpart to *Ebony*, the formal wedding ideal took center stage during this period of soaring marriage rates. The bride who graced the June 1952 cover of *Life*, and the feature article "The Wedding Business: It Profits from the U.S. Sentiment for Brides at the Unsentimental Rate of $3 Billion a Year," celebrated wedding consumption as an expression of the American dream, a natural part of American life.[24]

Although women's magazines delivered advertisers a general female public interested in weddings, specialty bridal magazines provided even finer market segmentation. According to a 1933 *Fortune* magazine article on the wedding business that spurred *House and Garden* advertising manager Wells Drorbaugh to found *Bride's* magazine in 1934, "the rustle of a bride's train [was] music to

June 1933

10 Cents
s

DELINEATOR

BEST STORY NUMBER

T. S. STRIBLING

ELISABETH SANXAY HOLDING

STEPHEN VINCENT BENÉT

RUTH HAWTHORNE

THE SUMMER FASHIONS THAT ARE SMARTEST

FIGURE 14. Before the rise of the bridal magazine, a wide range of women's periodicals regularly featured a formal white wedding gown on the cover of June issues. *Delineator* (June 1933).

thousands of businessmen."[25] *Bride's* magazine, and those publications that followed its lead, played a major role in the development of the bridal market, taking American wedding culture to unprecedented levels of consumerism. Appearing first under the name *So You're Going to Be Married: A Magazine for Brides*, it started as a small operation with a limited northeastern audience. The magazine's offices were in the New York City living room of its first editor, Agnes Foster Wright, a well-known interior designer who was the wife of the editor of *House and Garden*. In order to reach its target audience, the magazine followed a path already established by retailers in search of those about to marry and employed clipping services to track engagement announcements in newspapers. At first it used a free-controlled circulation, meaning it was sent quarterly free of charge to prospective readers in New Jersey, New York, and Connecticut, but it soon achieved national distribution. In response to the 1949 appearance of *Modern Bride* on newsstands, *Bride's* added newsstand sales to its free-controlled circulation of 150,000 and eventually switched over completely.[26] The major publishing house Condé Nast bought the publication from Wells Drorbaugh in 1959.

From the very beginning, the magazine defined the commercial concerns of the wedding industry. Following a format that changed little over the decades, the magazine's advertising and advertising tie-ins focused on etiquette, beauty, bridal fashion, the trousseau, gift giving and receiving, housewares, and entertaining.[27] Providing information about wedding fashions, such as where to find particular styles and designers of gowns, was one of its major functions. The magazine format also outlined what was significant for women about to marry, with regular sections like "The Wedding," "The Bride Gives and Hopes to Receive," "The Bride Creates a Home," "The First Year," and "Special Articles," a section that typically featured a short tribute to the groom's perspective. Each of these sections primarily covered the consumer choices facing those about to marry. Even the "First Year" section, which could have addressed issues relating to marriage, focused largely on future entertaining and the goods to be purchased to that end. Though the magazine appeared during the depths of the Depression, it made few references to a restricted purse other than a regular feature for the "budget bride."[28]

According to Wells Drorbaugh, Jr., the son of the magazine's founder and a publisher of *Bride's* for many years, the magazine worked to "channel" wedding businesses. Advertising pages continually increased, and by 1940, more than forty advertisements preceded the contents page in the magazine. By the early 1960s, advertisers spent more than $2 million in the magazine, which had a circulation of 220,000.[29] Not only did more businesses advertise their goods and services, but an increasing range of companies also sought a bridal market. Significantly, the magazine expanded the types of businesses that were considered "bridal." Advertisements introduced unusual things, such as "showers of steel," clearly expanding what it meant to be "bridal." Barbara Tober, who was editor-in-chief from 1966 to 1994, continually sought to take advertising into new areas. According to her, the magazine had to convince businesses that their product was a "bride thing," as in the case of furniture makers, whom Tober claimed were difficult to persuade. *Bride's* also expanded what was considered "bridal" by regularly publishing lists of different types of businesses across the country that offered services or products for brides. *Modern Bride* duplicated this wedding service in the early 1950s in the feature "To Serve You," which listed businesses from all regions of North America, including 119 U.S. cities and 3 Canadian cities.[30] Such lists put wedding photographers, jewelers, bridal salons, designers of ready-to-wear and wedding gowns, and honeymoon resorts on a par with manufacturers of steel goods, furnaces, carpeting, bedding, and furniture, linking each to the fulfillment of the white wedding ideal. In these ways, bridal magazines helped invent the bridal market itself, defining what consumer goods and services were necessary for the ideal wedding and marriage.

Bride's magazine expanded this bridal market by creating networks with department stores. The magazine developed various campaigns that promoted bridal merchandising, sponsoring store promotions and providing tie-in advertising articles on the events across the country. In 1939, for example, it first ran a contest for its readers that tied into department-store promotions for household goods. "The Home for Two" contest, advertised in *Bride's*, took place at Altman's and at Carson, Pirie Scott. Each department store tagged merchandise for the contest, supplied each contestant with a floor plan and sketches of furniture, and instructed them to choose furnishings for their ideal home. The winners, who were written up in the magazine, had their choices displayed in a special apartment constructed at the store.[31] Such contests fostered store loyalty among new couples at the same time as they linked marriage to a consumer ethic.

Bride's magazine also fostered networks with mass retailers through bridal business clinics. Alexandra Potts, head of merchandising at *Bride's* in the late 1930s and 1940s, developed these innovative clinics for stores interested in opening bridal departments. Potts, who had been a bridal consultant at a New

York department store in the 1930s, had been hired by the magazine to promote specialized services across the United States.[32] At a time when being a career woman often meant also being single, Potts married and had a child as she pursued a highly successful career in the wedding industry and later as a merchandising consultant in the retailing field. At bridal clinics hosted at New York hotels like the Waldorf-Astoria and the Ritz-Carlton, store executives and consultants from all over the United States and even from Canada came to learn about the bride as a "volume customer." New ideas on flower displays and bouquet fashions, bridesmaid dresses, potential bridal costume expenditures, and wartime weddings were some of the subjects addressed at these clinics in the early 1940s.[33] At one clinic held in New York in 1948, the theme was "The Bride is the store's best customer." Attendants were treated well, with a buffet breakfast, a luncheon in the hotel's grand ballroom, and a champagne and caviar party. According to the clinic's program, presentations included talks on the "ideal structure of a store-wide Bridal selling operation," an overview of the bride's shop by a Gimbel's consultant, and discussions of "the gift bureau's important liaison place in the store's bridal operation as well as its unlimited money-making possibilities," led by Carson, Pirie Scott, Chicago; D. H. Homes Company, New Orleans; and Neiman-Marcus, Dallas. Afternoon sessions focused on bridal magazine services, with talks by editors, publishers, and the expert Alexandra Potts. The day was capped with a fashion show tied into the spring 1948 edition of *Bride's*.[34]

Bride's took credit for spreading the "bridal shop idea" that supplied the goods for the traditional white wedding, though several other magazines also played a role. According to *Bride's*, when the magazine first appeared there were only five bridal shops in the United States and only half a dozen manufacturers specializing in wedding apparel. Alexandra Potts claimed that before the war there were seventy-five "real bride shops." By 1948 or 1950, according to another account, there were 500 bride's shops with full-time consultants in stores found in towns of 50,000 or more.[35] Women's magazines also continued to play a role in the expansion and consolidation of the industry through the networks they formed with retailers. In 1948, for example, *Mademoiselle* offered a Bridal Secretaries Clinic where consultants could receive training on new trends and fashions. *Mademoiselle* also provided national statistics on the average bride's expenditure for retailers. More direct competitors with *Bride's* magazine, like *Modern Bride*, also educated retailers about the bridal market. By the early 1950s, the influential Alexandra Potts had moved to *Modern Bride* to become its merchandise counselor and feature writer, and eventually editor-in-chief. Unlike *Bride's*, *Modern Bride* had a board of bridal consultants on staff from department stores in different regions of the country, which it featured on the magazine's masthead. These consultants connected the consumers with whom they had day-to-day interaction with the retailers they represented and the bridal magazine. Like its competition, *Modern Bride* promoted the one-stop wedding through features such as "Real Life Bride," in which the magazine followed a woman as she planned and shopped for her wedding dress, trousseau, and new home, using the bridal salon and gift registries at stores like Abraham & Straus in Brooklyn, or Dayton's in Minneapolis.[36]

The success and the growth of a national bridal market led to new bridal publications that further consolidated the power of the industry. Additional bridal titles did not mean great diversity during this period, however, as new publications followed the format and content of early entrants on the scene. *House Beautiful* came out with *Guide for the Bride*, a semiannual supplement to its publication. By the mid-1950s it had become an independent quarterly publication like *Bride's* with a distribution of 200,000 copies per issue with advertising rates of $1,400, much lower than *Bride's*. Some new publications were short-lived, as was Curtis Publishing's *Bride-To-Be* magazine, which appeared in 1955. This new quarterly, the fourth national magazine in its field, was intended to be a "combination wedding plans book, home planning guide, and counselor of young marriages." Addressing the problem of being able to appeal to brides in different regions of the country and offer them advertisements for goods they could purchase in their area, the magazine adopted a split run, with fifteen selective editions that broke down to one national edition, four regional editions, and ten selective markets.[37] Other magazines continued to appear, though some were simply regional publications that did not have the national scope of *Bride's*. In general, department stores offered free copies of different bridal magazines to customers. One publication, *The American Bride*, was sold to department stores that then distributed it to local women about to marry.[38]

Modern Bride, however, was the main competitor for *Bride's*, though there were more similarities than differences between the two publications. Published by Ziff-Davis, *Modern Bride* was sold on newsstands, driving *Bride's* to adopt that sales format, as mentioned earlier. Both cost more than most fashion and women's magazines of the time. Like other women's magazines, the price of the magazine did not cover publishing costs, requiring advertising revenue, and both competed for advertisers.[39] As the title *Modern Bride* suggests, the new magazine positioned itself as more forward-thinking than its main competitor. In the beginning, it had the potential to offer a less-traditional approach to wedding planning. In the first issue, articles on sex, careers, and working wives appeared alongside more traditional articles on wedding planning, homemaking, and beauty. For the most part, however, the two publications addressed similar traditional concerns, suggesting a conservative approach that perhaps was intended to appeal to the widest possible audience. Along with other lesser bridal magazines that eventually appeared regionally and nationally, these two publications and their consumer message reached a broad audience. According to market studies from the mid-1970s, *Bride's* and *Modern Bride* reached the same readers. Young women, aged eighteen to twenty-four, many of whom worked or went to college, who came from all regions in the United States and were from a range of racial, class, and ethnic backgrounds, were most likely to pick up either one of these magazines as they planned their nuptials.[40] Readers of both were largely rural or suburban, though over 26 percent of readers were urban and came from families that were relatively affluent, though not exclusively. Both publications reached a large proportion of the bridal market by the late 1970s. According to one 1977 report analyzing circulation figures alongside census data, over 86 percent of all first-time brides were bridal magazine readers. *Bride's* and *Modern Bride* were read together in many cases in spite of their relatively high cost, with duplication nearly reaching 60 percent.[41] As these bridal magazines reached more and more readers, and as they helped create networks between businesses, defining and expanding the market and spreading new services such as the department-store wedding salon and gift registry, they were increasingly in a strong position to influence practice and shape "tradition."

BRIDAL MAGAZINES AND MARKET RESEARCH

The new bridal magazines studied the market they helped create, and in the process, helped expand and promote it. Like retailers during the marriage boom after World War II, magazines tracked marriage rates, even in the barren years of the 1930s, and used these figures to convince retailers and advertisers to exploit this "fabulous market" further. Working for *Bride's*, Alexandra Potts conducted some of the earliest market research on the wedding industry. She gathered information about the bridal market by traveling across the United States, taking surveys in both urban and rural areas. She shared this information with department stores, as on one thirty-week tour in 1939 when she traveled to six hundred stores, talking to prospective brides and their mothers.[42] The advice dispensed at these clinics and on these tours appeared in department-store trade journals, thus popularizing the bridal shop idea nationally and furthering ties between the magazine and mass retailers.[43] As a bridal merchandising expert and representative of the first magazine for brides, Alexandra Potts was in the position to shape retailers' conception of the national bridal market. Her research and wedding advice had a wide audience, as she wrote articles for the *Journal of Retailing* and other publications, and was frequently quoted in the trade literature.[44]

Bride's magazine participated in research that ostensibly documented a widespread interest in tradition. During the Depression, the merchandising service of *Bride's* conducted a national survey of bridal departments and specialty shops that found that engaged women spent an average of $250 on their trousseaus alone, which meant $250 million in bridal business. While this was likely an overly optimistic average, it nevertheless represented an ideal that the magazine cultivated for its advertisers and readers. Ostensibly reflecting the consumer preferences of brides across the country during World War II, Alexandra Potts painted a picture of a couple interested in a wedding with all the trimmings, even if they had to postpone their hopes for a home together. Servicemen, noted one trade article reporting on the 7th Annual Bridal Business Clinic in 1944, had a "preference for the traditional wedding." According to Potts, 75 percent of brides married formally in 1948 "due to the end of the war and the settling down period in social affairs."[45] *Bride's* magazine surveys during the 1940s and early 1950s, moreover, confirmed a widespread interest in the formal wedding at a time of soaring marriage rates—good news for the advertisers as well as for the department stores following these market reports.[46]

In the late 1950s and 1960s, for the first time bridal magazines used national market research to understand the business of brides. In 1958, *Bride's* sponsored the first representative study using random sampling methods. The study randomly sampled 3,800 brides from marriage license registrations in fifty sample counties that covered both rural and urban areas. To eliminate bias due to nonrespondents, a certain number of nonresponding brides were interviewed in person or by telephone. For the first time, the wedding industry gathered data about their readers for advertisers to create an accurate picture of the U.S. bridal market as a whole.[47] This early market study helped advertisers and bridal magazines define their target audience more precisely than ever before in order to reach them more effectively. In the process of researching this bridal market, publications like *Bride's* and *Modern Bride* rationalized and standardized the wedding process, turning the men and women who married and set up house into consumers for increasing numbers of markets.

The first bridal study promised a rosy future for the industry. In 1958, it described a young bridal market that attended college in higher percentages than U.S. women at large. The market for household goods appeared promising among this group, with 83 percent starting homes of their own, instead of doubling up with parents or relatives. Those about to marry had purchasing power as well, as 70 percent of brides were employed at the time of their marriage and the combined annual income of the couple was substantially above the median income of all U.S. families. Overall, the study offered advertisers the promise of "*immediate* sales potential" as well as the "opportunity to pre-sell young couples" the goods they would need to acquire in the few years after marriage. According to the study, women about to marry had three "pocketbooks" to spend on advertisers' products and services: one including the combined income of the couple at the time of marriage, one made up of their combined savings and money gifts, and one consisting of the money spent by family and friends on wedding gifts, something "over which the bride exercises considerable direct control."[48]

The consumer message of *Bride's* magazine, moreover, reached a relatively well-off group who as a whole had a higher percentage of participation in the industry and conformity with the white wedding ideal. The market analysis from 1958 found that of the 1,254 marriage licensees interviewed for the study, 349, or 28 percent, identified themselves as buyers of *Bride's* magazine. These readers were mainly middle-class women employed in white-collar, professional, and technical fields and had a higher medium annual income, when combined with their future husbands', than the general population. A dual-income family meant increased purchasing power, but it could also mean that the bride had more control over future consumer decisions that the couple would make, something good for advertisers in *Bride's*. Readers of the magazine also used a gift registry at a higher rate than the rest of the bridal market in the United States. They received a higher percentage of certain wedding gifts, such as silver, fine china, crystal, earthenware, glass stemware, and plastic dinnerware, suggesting that their participation in gift registry or their reading of *Bride's* resulted in a standardization of gifts. Readers also spent more on honeymoons than other American brides. Such statistics would have helped *Bride's* magazine sell advertising space in the late 1950s, as the figures suggest that businesses would reach a relatively well-to-do market, one where there was the potential to gain the consumer loyalty of brides as they furnished their home and began establishing brand preferences. In addition, advertisers were able to reach others as the magazine passed to the bride's family members and friends.[49]

These studies thus served advertisers and the magazines first and foremost, but they also measured the consumer preferences of these young women. To some degree, the creation of the bridal market was a two-way process. Statistics and information that research studies provided gave advertisers increased knowledge about bridal markets, knowledge about consumer preferences that could then be used to influence their choices. In the end, though, it was in the commercial interest of bridal magazines to expand the number of markets, to widen the range of goods and services required when a couple married and established their household. Market research legitimized these ever-expanding markets, helping magazines to attract more and more advertisers, who in turn helped transform wedding practice.

Market research also reflected social norms and values of the time. Following *Bride's*, *Modern Bride* studied the market in a way that defined it as a first-marriage market. *Modern Bride* conducted four in-depth studies of national retail sales to first-marriage brides, two performed by Sindlinger & Company in 1965 and 1968, one by National Family Opinion in 1969, and one by Trendex, Inc., in 1973. According to these reports, the industry understood first-marriage brides to be more desirable consumers since most needed to set up house from scratch and had not yet formed brand or store loyalties. Those who remarried brought everything they needed into their marriage and were already "established shoppers."[50] Through this market research, bridal magazines and the businesses that supported them by purchasing advertising space both defined the ideal wedding as a first-time marriage, naturalizing a particular set of family relations. Market researchers, the bridal magazines that sponsored them, and the advertisers they influenced, however, did not label divorce and remarriage as immoral or even socially undesirable. Yet, when businesses turned to a "first-marriage" market to make more money more efficiently, they in fact reified that social relationship at the expense of alternate arrangements. In this way, the bridal market established and upheld lifelong marriage as a cultural ideal.

TRADITION IN BRIDAL MAGAZINES

To a great extent, the content of bridal magazines mirrored the commercial goals of market research studies of the industry. The formal white wedding ideal that emerged in the pages of bridal magazines embodied the tensions inherent to an industry that was in the business of tradition. Even though they were advertising magazines, they presented themselves as service publications devoted to helping modern women uphold tradition, something that by its nature, however, was not supposed be subject to the changing whims of fashion. From their beginnings into the postwar period, they promoted the wedding as a timeless unchanging ritual, even as they pushed modern goods and new services in pursuit of an increasingly commercial ideal.

Bridal magazines, for example, promoted the idea that weddings were a symbolic link with the past, with the ways things had been done for generations. Advertisers in *Bride's* during this period made repeated use of the theme of tradition (figures 15, 16, and 17). Marriage allowed the couple to become a part of "the traditions and conventions of wedding etiquette [that] belonged to all Brides and Grooms," according to one 1954 article in *Bride's*. Some of these conventions and traditions were supposed to be strictly followed, with the help of the magazine's experts. Regular features underlined the unchanging formal nature of the wedding, with maps that diagrammed the ceremony, positioned the wedding party, and outlined the path of the processional and recessional. Charts rigidly defined which wedding fashions were appropriate for different

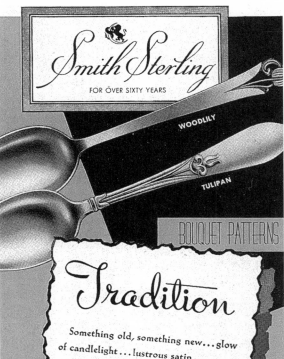

FIGURES 15 and 16. Advertising in bridal magazines often used the idea of tradition to sell goods such as sterling silver. *Bride's* (Spring 1948), 155, 167.

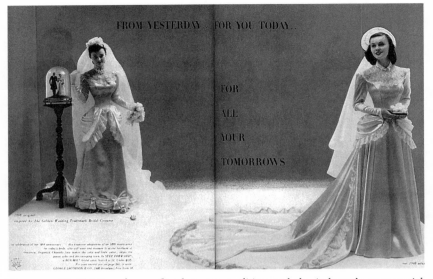

FIGURE 17. Skirting the conflict between tradition and the industry's commercial goals, this advertisement from *Bride's* magazine suggested that the "adaptation of an 1898 masterpiece" would become "the heirloom of tomorrow." *Bride's* (Spring 1948), 26–27.

times of day or types of ceremony. From its inception, moreover, the illustrations and artwork, layout, and the editorial message of *Bride's* all underscored the idea that weddings were serious business, in that they created a permanent union between a man and a woman that had religious and romantic significance. For example, the first contents page in 1934 took the shape of an open book, likely a prayer book, with the couple sketched at the top and the back of a priest or minister figured below. Agnes Foster Wright's first editorial message to the bride emphasized the romance and social impact of marriage, masking her commercial message beneath the mixed rhetoric of love and orange blossoms and information for the bride, in a way typical of bridal magazine writing.[51] In these ways, magazines like *Bride's* balanced their celebration of marriage as a religious rite and the culmination of romantic love with their consumer ethic and business goals. Just as etiquette writers had done in the past, bridal magazines tried to reconcile the belief in marriage as a religious rite with the magazine's advertising focus.[52]

Embracing a consumer ethic predicated upon choice and flexibility, however, bridal magazines also encouraged women to have a hand in the making of their wedding traditions, suggesting that tradition itself could be a product of consumer society. From the Depression through the abundance of the postwar period, bridal magazines set forth the wedding as a woman's chance to express herself fully for the first and most important time through the purchases she made for her wedding and her future home. On one level, these publications envisioned a "modern" bride, not one bound by old-fashioned tradition. Etiquette advice remained open enough to allow for the emergence of the bride's personality through the consumption of goods and services provided by the wedding industry. One of the first issues of *Bride's* advised the bride to remember that through her choices she was "an artist painting a lasting picture." Consumer choices allowed women about to marry to preserve their "subtle individuality."[53] Similarly, in the 1950s the editorial voice wed consumerism to personal fulfillment. Material abundance and variety allowed every woman to "be exactly the Bride she has always wanted to be."[54] Her decisions were supposed to mirror her "own convictions."[55] According to another author, experts were only to offer "guidelines" for achieving the expression of the bride's true self.

There were limits to this self-expression through wedding consumption, however, as women were warned not to change themselves or experiment with things at the ceremony or reception.[56] Bridal magazines simply offered up a range of prefabricated identities, usually delineated by the budget available to the bride. Reflecting class identities, while avoiding the use of the term, these types ranged from the society bride to the solidly middle-class bride to the struggling bride on a budget. Articles like "Trousseau for Audrey" and "Trousseau for Ricki" in *Bride's* and "I Am Joyce" and "I Am Kay" in *Modern Bride* presented alternative consumer identities, with different budgets, tastes, and needs. Pictured with the furniture, home décor, china, and silver they bought or requested as wedding gifts, these white women and their testimonials appeared as ordinary brides—types that were supposed to represent the range of individuals that made up the magazine's readership. Articles like these defined the parameters of women's identity, inasmuch as they offered up ideals against which readers could judge themselves and evaluate their own consumer realities.[57]

Bridal magazines empowered brides as consumers through their covers, format, editorial content, and advertisements. Advertising and editorial messages were always directed at the future Mrs. Consumer, something reflected even by the covers of the magazines. As a "relay text" that sent advertising messages to readers, the cover was too important a place for capturing the business of brides to feature a groom prominently.[58] *Bride's* magazine ran a series of historical-themed illustrations or paintings of a bride and groom on some early covers, but for the most part, the bride in white was ubiquitous. Even when *Modern Bride* put the groom on the cover in an unconventional move in 1949 and then again in 1953 and 1954–55, he appeared obscured by the bride's veil and full white dress, in the background, or even walking off the page with only enough of him showing to signify "groom." For the most part, however, the groom was physically absent or existed as a marginal figure within the pages of bridal magazines. Occasionally, he appeared humorously as the "Forgotten Man."[59] While he usually had his own section in magazines, it is clear that he was not expected to be the reader. Significantly, advertisers sought bridal business, not groomal business. In fact, men were a hindrance to consumption that had to be overcome. Women were to side with the wedding industry against their reluctant grooms: "Let him help you to select your silver pattern. . . . Subtly sell him on the fact that a traditional wedding . . . is the kind he's dreamed about and wanted all his life."[60] Although the groom might resist, one article advised with a condescending tone that "a little gentle persuasion is usually all it takes to convince him that a formal wedding is well worth the effort, the hand-shaking, and all the rest of it."[61] If allowed to have his way, according to one consultant writing for *Bride's*, the groom would "undoubtedly cast his vote for a minimum of 'fuss and feathers.'" Magazines marginalized the groom's role in the wedding preparation in a manner that reflected the gendered division of wedding labor. Information on the groom's financial responsibilities, his gift to the bride, etiquette, appropriate wedding attire, and advice on honeymoons were given to the bride, apparently to be passed on to him.[62] Unlike the jewelry industry, which responded to new conceptions of masculinity that allowed for the adoption of the groom's wedding band and double-ring ceremony, bridal magazines during this period did not pull the groom into the wedding plans in an equal fashion.

In general, bridal magazines were slow to adapt content or attitudes to social change. During World War II, when large numbers of women entered the war industries, bridal magazines only shifted slightly, responding not to new roles for women, but instead to war rationing and the groom's new circumstances. They adapted to the limitations of the "furlough wedding," but they continued to promote the formal white wedding tradition, even linking it to war aims. As we have seen with the jewelry industry during this period, wedding industries benefited ideologically from the war as the bride and patriotism went hand in hand to the altar. Even in a time of rationing, women's war work, and men's commitment overseas, *Bride's* magazine promoted the traditional wedding, something that inevitably used up scarce or potentially scarce resources. The publication justified this stance by stating that most readers wanted a formal wedding.[63]

Bridal magazines fit tradition to wartime circumstances. Bridal magazines romanticized the military wedding, providing information on its special etiquette. Regular features distinguished between the different needs of civilian couples and those in the army or navy. Articles on setting up house after marriage became features on how to deal with military housing.[64] And in the postwar years, they shifted again slightly, placing the bride's individuality in the context of American exceptionalism. The bride could be an individual, at least in her consumer choices, because of the success of American capitalism. According to a 1947 article, brides may be beautiful all over the world, but "there's something pure USA about American Brides." Their distinctiveness was due to the fact that the "pursuit of happiness" was "written into the constitution [*sic*]."[65]

Although marriage rites and the rituals surrounding them grew out of the couple's distinctive religious, ethnic, and class background, bridal magazines made little reference to this diversity during this period. Bridal magazines occasionally covered the etiquette and customs of Jewish and Catholic weddings, and articles at times appropriated or invented customs that were purportedly from other countries. According to the first issue of *Bride's* magazine, women could choose, discriminately of course, from customs originating in other countries: "being gay, young and enthusiastic, and quickly assimilative, [she] often adapts them to her own ceremony." Borrowing "wedding ideas from different countries" was seen as "fun." Whether it was an Austrian crown of myrtle, or planting a small tree after the ceremony in the Bermudian tradition, small variations in dress and custom were allowed in order to impart one's individuality on the wedding day.[66] Ethnic traditions could be an accessory, something decorative to be put on and taken off at will. For the most part, however, bridal magazines elevated the upper-middle or upper-class Protestant church wedding, with a wedding reception in a home, a hotel, or a club. Significantly, society weddings in major northern and southern cities appeared prominently in regular magazine features.

The racial identity of bridal magazines was consistently white through the 1960s. Even though the publications had readers of color, and brides and grooms from a variety of racial backgrounds had weddings with all the trimmings, racial attitudes changed slowly in these publications. With very few exceptions, through the 1960s the couples featured were white, though one 1962 *Modern Bride* issue featured an interracial marriage of a white American lieutenant and a Japanese-American woman. Until the late 1960s, African American brides were completely absent, with blacks only appering as servant figures in advertisements, and then rarely. Black fashion models faced discrimination in general, and bridal magazines were no exception. With the increased urbanization and improved occupational status of African Americans during World War II, marketers began discovering the black consumer.[67] The civil rights movement and growing pressure from black consumers led to changes in mass media. By 1970, however, only two or three African American women commanded top modeling fees. Although after 1968, black women started appearing in magazines like *Bride's*, modeling dresses from Priscilla of Boston and others, it fell to publications like *Ebony* to conceptualize fully the African American white wedding during this period.[68]

In the 1970s, the wedding industry began to find more multicultural ways of marketing its goods and services in bridal magazines. Ethnic content in bridal magazines increased during this period. The "roots" phenomenon that swept the United States led to the passing of the Ethnic Heritage Act in 1974, which supported initiatives to promote distinctive cultures. Businesses responded to this new interest in heritage, coming out with advertising campaigns and products tailored to the interests of particular ethnic and racial groups. According to historian Marilyn Halter, as special events that occurred intermittently, weddings were "highly conducive to part-time ethnicity."[69] By the 1990s, market segmentation, combined with broad social change, resulted in the rise of specialized ethnic bridal magazines. *Latina Bride*, published in

California, appeared in 1997. This new magazine offered bilingual feature articles, and used Latina models. Like other bridal publications, *Latina Bride* also
negotiated the modernity/tradition divide when its creators promoted the
magazine as "more than just ads for pretty dresses," arguing that it offered "a
contemporary perspective with a respect for tradition." Etiquette works like
Jumping the Broom also popularized invented traditions for black men and
women about to marry. These ethnic rituals were eventually incorporated in
dominant white bridal magazines, such as a recent photo essay in *Bride's* on
jumping the broom and ways to decorate the ritual object.[70]

* * *

By the late 1970s, the wedding industry had become an $8 billion bridal
market in which 2.3 percent of total households accounted for up to 13 percent
of all retail expenditures.[71] Over the course of the first half of the twentieth
century, etiquette manuals, women's magazines, and finally bridal magazines
fostered the consumer ethic that supported this massive industry. Through
their market research studies and various merchandising strategies, bridal magazines helped develp and expand the idea of a bridal market segment. Editorial
and advertising content linked tradition and modernity and naturalized the
lavish white wedding. Just as bridal magazines and etiquette books promoted
a new commercial ethic based on flexibility and individuality, others in the
business of brides also had to bridge the tradition/modernity divide. With the
help of advertising and the bridal clinics introduced by *Bride's,* department
stores in particular popularized a host of new consumer rites that helped transform American wedding culture by the postwar era.

CHAPTER FOUR

Department Stores and Consumer Rites

In 1960, when bridal consultant Claire Dreier recalled her role in establishing a Wedding Bureau in 1938 at Eaton's in downtown Toronto, she remembered that the Canadian department store was opposed to her suggestion at first, calling it a "Damnable American idea. Too flamboyant."[1] Dreier had attended at least one of Alexandra Potts's early bridal clinics for department stores where she learned about the market and shared her Canadian experience with American retailers. As she knew, in the United States, department stores were beginning to offer gift registry services and use a range of "flamboyant" merchandising tactics to capture the bridal market. Completely lacking the hesitation of Canadian retailers, U.S. department stores had no compunction about pursuing those about to marry. By mid-century, stores like Strawbridge & Clothier in Philadelphia, Wanamaker's in Philadelphia and New York, Marshall Field's and Carson, Pirie Scott in Chicago, and Neiman-Marcus in Dallas had made the mass retailer a central player in the wedding industry, inventing a host of new "traditions." For the first time, wedding-themed window displays and department-store bridal fashion shows placed the marriage ritual itself in a commercial setting. New gift registry services standardized and rationalized gift-giving customs, eventually offering a blueprint for wedding consumption—elaborate wish lists or lists of preferences that employed the rhetoric of tradition in the service of modernity. And, just as the golden age of department stores was over, a new emphasis on serving the bride took shape in luxurious wedding salons that appeared in urban stores across the country. Before their demise in the 1980s, these department-store bridal salons offered more efficient, modern ways of planning the formal white wedding with all the trimmings.[2] Through salons, window displays, fashion events, and gift registries, department stores shaped the meaning of getting married, turning the commodified, commercialized wedding into a modern tradition by the postwar period.

EARLY RETAILERS AND THE WEDDING TRADE

Before the idea of a bridal market took shape, early mass and specialty retailers supplied everything from the engagement ring, invitations, and wedding gifts to the material for the bride's trousseau and wedding gown. Retailers were only beginning to recognize the possibilities of the wedding trade when L. H. Winans of Rochester, New York, planned her nuptials in 1899 and made a detailed record of her marriage expenses. L. H. Winans was able to turn to a range of suppliers, such as the dry-goods stores that since the 1880s had typically offered high-grade service and sold complete lines of goods in about a dozen or so small departments. Along with other customers, this middle-class Rochester bride may have sorted through goods piled high on wooden counters of a dry-goods emporium or in the dry-goods section of a department store. She might have been assisted by a businesslike clerk who took down items that hung on the wall or from pillars, or helped her with bolts of cloth on shelves or in drawers. There, Winans may have purchased her bridal silk, the name sometimes given to the white silk fabric she recorded in her list of trousseau and marriage expenses. She also budgeted for stationery, either for wedding invitations or thank-you letters, and may have visited a specialty stationer's like Dempsey & Carroll, Society Stationers, in New York, or purchased goods in one of the stationery departments that were fixtures in large stores across the country at the time. Stationery stores catered to the wedding trade in several ways. They carried illuminated marriage certificates printed on parchment and bound with sterling silver mountings, made wedding menus with special designs, and sold keepsake wedding albums to hold souvenirs from the event, such as telegrams of congratulation and pieces of fabric from the gown and trousseau. At a specialty jeweler's or at a jewelry department in a large store Winans may have purchased the $2.50 pin for "Eva" recorded in her list of marriage expenses, following the custom of giving members of the wedding party a token of appreciation.[3] The fact that specialty retailers and department stores sold goods to brides like her, however, did not in and of itself mean that a fully conceptualized bridal market existed at this point.

At the turn of the century, urban brides like L. H. Winans had easy access to a wide variety of retailers, but with the rise of mail-order firms, rural women also were increasingly able to choose from an assortment of goods directed at those about to marry. In the 1870s and 1880s, mail-order firms brought the idea of the wedding trade to the hinterlands. Twenty years after Montgomery Ward began selling things through the mail, its catalogue had more than 1,000 pages and a circulation of 730,000 with two and a half orders per catalogue on average. A rural or small-town bride could admire wedding rings, wedding silver, ready-made bridal lingerie sets, or formal wedding stationery. From the Montgomery Ward catalogue, for a dollar and a half, she might purchase one hundred Wedding, Regret, and Correspondence cards, or five hundred for two dollars, emulating the social niceties of her urban counterparts.[4] Still, while these early mass retailers targeted those about to marry, neither the rural nor the urban bride was part of a clearly defined market segment yet.

The rise of the bridal market was connected to new retailing contexts. Retailing underwent a dramatic change as dry-goods stores divested themselves of their wholesaling function and focused more on the business of selling. By the late nineteenth century, the "palace of consumption" replaced the dry-goods emporium. The department store represented a new organizational form in retailing, characterized by a wide variety of different lines of merchandise and separate departments that were responsible for "buying, selling, promotion, accounting, and control." By 1910, full-service department stores had expanded to include as many as 125 departments, a division that allowed for a new level of rationalization and specialization in labor, space, and finances.[5] Department stores treated female shoppers as guests as well as potential spenders, offering them many services that sometimes had no relation to shopping, cutting into their own short-term profits in order to provide an array of amenities in a luxurious atmosphere. These institutions were worlds unto themselves, with post offices, telegraph offices, hairdressing salons and barber shops, and restaurants. Shoppers could take advantage of free delivery, a children's nursery, and free art exhibitions, and could enlist the personal service staff for difficult shopping tasks. Charge accounts, liberal return policies, and the slogan, coined by retailer John Wanamaker, that "the customer is always right," further elevated female consumers during this golden age of the department store.[6]

The wedding industry in department stores came out of this early attention to the female market segment. Unlike the groom who, once married, ceased to be a groom, a bride kept her bridal status for an undefined period of time, though market researchers would later define a bride as a woman who had been married for no more than a year.[7] A wedding marked only the beginning of a woman's new role as household consumer. Department stores optimistically believed that women formed lifelong brand and store loyalties at the time of their wedding. Through their publicity division, which took on responsibility for "the conversion of one-time purchasers into regular customers," department stores sought the loyalty of the bride.[8] Grooms were sometimes sought after in advertisements for rented formal wear or cut-glass gifts. In the 1920s, Marshall Field's promoted its "Groom's Corner" on the second floor of the Store for Men with humorous ad copy that only served to underline the groom's marginal consumer role: "Oh, that's right . . . there'll be a groom at this wedding too! . . . He'll get the same interested attention that you receive in the Wedding Bureau."[9] For the most part, ads and events were directed at women shoppers. For example, the "Bride's Week" became a staple of department-store merchandising. Events like the "Bride's Jubilee" transformed the interior of Philadelphia's Wanamaker's into a pink and white domestic wonderland for two weeks in 1908. An organist in the grand court played wedding marches and a series of tableaux decorated nearly every floor, featuring such scenes as a bride with her bridesmaids, "the bride at breakfast," and "the bride in the kitchen." Store demonstrators also conducted a cooking school for brides that showed them how to operate new kitchen equipment, preparing them for their future role.[10] Retailers used representations of weddings and scenes from newlywed life throughout the store to display a wide range of consumer goods. At Strawbridge & Clothier, another Philadelphia store, the Women's Suit Department used valuable space on the selling floor to feature a full-size roped-off tableau of "The Famous 'Bridal Party'" in 1915 (figure 18). Bridal promotions even targeted children. In 1914, Strawbridge & Clothier featured a Kewpie doll miniature wedding display in its toy department, replete with Kewpie doll bride, groom, preacher, mother of the bride, ring bearer, flower girls, and guests, "with the chauffeur ready to take the happy couple on their honeymoon."[11] These domestic and sentimental themes must have had broad appeal among married, unmarried, or soon-to-be married women alike, justifying the lavish use of retail space. By the 1930s, department stores

THE FAMOUS "BRIDAL PARTY"

An Interesting Feature of the Notable Spring Opening Display of
Women's Fashionable Costumes, Held in the Women's
Suit Department During the Week of March 8.

FIGURE 18. Department stores like Philadelphia's Strawbridge & Clothier used tradi-
tional wedding scenes to draw interest as early as 1915. Strawbridge & Clothier,
Store Chat (April 15, 1915), 74. Hagley Museum and Library, Pictorial Collections
Department, Wilmington, Delaware.

in cities across the country were targeting the future Mrs. Consumer through
an increasing variety of innovative promotions.[12]

To some degree, these and other department-store merchandising techniques invented new traditions and attempted to transform wedding practice.
Stores tried to shape wedding gift customs, expanding the list of suitable items,
from china, glass, silver, linens and towels to small appliances and other household goods. Stationery departments introduced new versions of the wedding
invitation and later other related items, such as printed matchbooks and napkins for the reception.[13] Certain promotions appeared allegedly in response to
consumer demand. For example, gift wrapping departments appealed to the
lucrative bridal shower market, but also noted a growing "trend to groom
showers" in 1959.[14] Perhaps this trend was an outgrowth from the new emphasis on togetherness, but more likely it was simply wishful thinking on the part
of store management.

Most of these new department-store bridal promotions fell under the category of merchandising, which among the larger retailers was the responsibility of the firm's sales promotion or publicity division. Through this division, department stores invented tradition. Merchandising could mean many things, as department-store executives and professionals associated with New York University's School of Retailing recognized. One expert defined merchandising as "buying and selling, finding customers, providing them with what they want, when they want it, at prices they can afford and are willing to pay."[15] Another argued that it included promotional activities, such as advertising, window display, and arrangement of departments. The director of publicity or the sales promotion division of large department stores, or the advertising manager that performed similar functions for smaller stores, planned and produced a wide variety of store advertising and displays. Promotional activities and delegation of responsibility of course varied among firms, but by the 1930s, this division was generally in charge of such things as radio, newspaper, magazine, and direct-mail advertisements, interior displays using store posters, signs in elevators and fitting rooms, handbills, package inserts, and bill inserts, special announcements on the public address system, special tables, sections, corners, or "shops" for featured items, and telephone solicitation.[16] Advertising and in-store promotions sought to increase storewide sales volume, as well as faster stock turnover, something that "provided some measure of how accurately the firm was projecting and—in the case of specially advertised goods—stimulating consumer demand."[17]

The sales or publicity division also attempted to build goodwill and increase public confidence in their establishment. Bridal merchandising likely helped them in these efforts as wedding tableaux across the store and in window displays had broad appeal and in-store bridal events, such as fashion shows, attracted large crowds. Bridal merchandising also drew different departments together, benefiting the store as a whole. The publicity or sales promotion division typically oversaw "interlocking displays in allied departments" and would have coordinated wedding displays with the heads of different departments.[18] As we will see, bridal salons sold goods from different parts of the store. For the "one-stop" wedding to take shape, the publicity or sales promotion division had to get different departments to work together, rather than compete with each other. And, in cooperation with other departments, this division was typically responsible for the lavish window displays that generated goodwill for the store at the same time as they helped transform weddings into consumer rites.[19]

WEDDINGS ON DISPLAY

Department-store window displays embodied the new consumer ethic. At the end of the nineteenth century, retailers created enticing palaces of consumption through the manipulation of light, color, and glass to evoke a new "land of desire" that catered to the female consumer. Before the 1880s, stores did not pay attention to their displays, and windows collected dust and flies. By the end of the nineteenth century, however, merchandising professionals or window trimmers brought a more sophisticated and theatrical aesthetic to retailing in their attempt to give newly enclosed windows "a new kind of drawing power" that would move goods and increase profits. With the introduction of full-bodied papier-mâché mannequins to stores like Marshall Field's in 1913, professional window trimmers were able to create stylized social settings, such as weddings. Ensembles of different merchandise began to appear against realistic backdrops.[20] Making use of the new display techniques, professional window trimmers helped invent the tradition of the formal white wedding, bringing it first to department stores in major cities like Philadelphia and Chicago, and by the 1920s, even to smaller venues like Bloomington, Illinois, and Charlotte, North Carolina.[21]

Part of the appeal of these windows for consumers was that their contents changed continually, featuring new fashions and displays that marked the changing seasons. In the late 1930s, Wanamaker's fifty street-level display windows changed on a weekly basis. Windows tied in with newspaper advertising and seasonal sales promotions, such as white goods in January and furniture in February and August. Displays celebrating Christmas, Easter, and Thanksgiving became traditions in themselves, something shoppers looked forward to and made special visits to see.[22] Bridal promotions were all-pervasive as stores learned to pursue the wedding trade around the calendar, arguing that brides married in large numbers in every month, not just June. Like the seasonal religious and secular themes discussed by William Leach that were "intricately interwoven into store life," weddings also had the potential to become a part of the store's culture.[23]

Even as window-display techniques grew more artful, and promotional events more elaborate, retailers consistently turned to the traditional figure in white to advertise and promote their wares. Jewelers and florists increasingly relied on pictures of the bride or dolls in bridal finery representing marriage ceremonies in miniature.[24] Department stores used realistic mannequins of the bride in various wedding scenes. These types of window displays had the element of human interest, but they also highlighted events that could be connected with the store's services. They promoted particular goods, such as rings or going-away clothes, and encouraged higher levels or standards of consumption. As with advertising, such scenes provided ritual reenactments of dominant gender roles.

Stores likely turned to wedding scenes again and again in part because they imbued goods with a familiar emotional appeal, an appeal they must have known would draw attention to their store windows and bring customers in the door. Weddings were excellent advertisements and public relations events for a store, something the Louis Pizitz department store in Birmingham, Alabama, was well aware of in 1925 when it held a contest titled "Why Marry?" as a way to celebrate its twenty-sixth anniversary. In a manner reminiscent of today's reality television shows, the winner of the contest had "the honor of being married on the roof garden of the Pizitz store," a publicity stunt that attracted much attention.[25] Most stores, however, did not resort to hosting real-life ceremonies and instead featured a variety of wedding displays that sought to capture the emotions behind this rite of passage. At Wanamaker's in the 1920s, a series called "Steps to the Altar" broadcast such sentiments into the Philadelphia streets. Against dark wood paneling, scenes such as "The Courtship," depicting a couple at a piano, and "The Ceremony," showing the bride, two bridesmaids, and two small flower girls, brought familiar scenes to passersby (figure 19).[26] Details in the window display, such as a raised handkerchief in the bridesmaid's hand and petals on the ground, drew on the sentimental feelings surrounding a rite of passage. These scenes made a connection between tradition and the emotions surrounding a marriage. Through such displays, romantic love became something timeless and universal, forever fixed on the smiling faces of mannequins wearing department-store clothes.

Displays reenacted the different stages of getting married, much like Underwood & Underwood stereograph images of a wedding had done earlier in the

FIGURE 19. By the 1920s, weddings appeared in a variety of department-store window displays, such as this one from Wanamaker's in Philadelphia. Such displays often evoked the sentiment and emotion surrounding a wedding to sell bridal apparel. Historical Society of Pennsylvania, Philadelphia, "Steps to the Altar—The Spring Bride," Wanamaker Collection, 2188.

century with scenes such as "The Proposal," "With This Ring I Thee Wed," "Dressing the Bride," and "Alone at Last."[27] Woodward and Lothrop, a Washington, D.C., department store, for example, featured a series of twelve wedding vignettes in 1926, "commencing with the selection of the wedding ring and concluding with the departure of the bride from her home." Such displays instructed consumers about the goods they needed to perform their duty properly. They also repeated certain elements, strengthening one particular image of the ideal white wedding in popular culture. As the display profession realized, wedding scenes had the potential to be "rather stereotyped in appearance."[28] Displays, such as an in-store tableau at Marshall Field's in 1925, often presented the bride in white, followed by her attendants, surrounded by elaborate candelabra, banked palms, and the requisite cupid in the wings (figure 20).[29] Details like the candelabra added a religious element, while figures like the cupid signaled heterosexual love and romance in the absence of a groom. When these "traditional" details became stereotypes, the formal white wedding ideal had indeed become hegemonic. Department stores' window

FIGURE 20. Bridal window displays like this one from Marshall Field's in 1925 presented a traditional image, with candelabra, decorative palms, and a cupid in the wings. Marshall Field's Archives, Chicago.

trimmers tried "to think up new ideas in connection with them."[30] As a result of their efforts, more modernist wedding displays appeared at Marshall Field's in the 1930s, such as one titled "Of Thee I Sing," which featured a solitary bride, a chair, and two small signs, against a stylized Art Deco background (figure 21).[31] In the context of a store window, however, a bride in white still signified a marriage of romance and commerce, of tradition and modernity. Without the exterior decorative elements that signaled "wedding," however, stylized displays like "Of Thee I Sing" leaned toward the modernity end of the tradition/modernity dichotomy, turning the wedding into a display of pure fashion and design.

In a variation upon the white wedding theme, window displays linked wedding tradition with the past. Displays drew on particular historic events with romantic associations. Jewelers and department stores constructed period scenes from the colonial, Revolutionary, or Civil War era.[32] These tableaux also featured representative brides from countries besides the United States. In

FIGURE 21. By 1932, bridal window displays like Marshall Field's "Of Thee I Sing" became more sophisticated, revealing a new modernist aesthetic. Marshall Field's Archives, Chicago.

a similar vein, department stores hosted pageants of historical wedding costumes. These pageants turned history and tradition toward the very modern end of selling wedding gowns, trousseau clothes, silverware, and other items. They served fashion's imperative to "buy, dispose of, and buy again," but in a way that was masked by the marriage ritual's noncommercial associations.[33] Historical fashion shows and window displays highlighted the store's role in the community and its connection to its traditions.[34]

In the early 1940s, wartime weddings became a popular theme in window displays. A tableau featuring a groom in uniform with his bride likely drew on popular romantic sentiments about soldiers and war, as well as the emotions generated by wartime separation from loved ones.[35] Like jewelers who used wartime patriotism to promote the new tradition of the double-ring ceremony, department stores linked their wedding "traditions" with the American way of life or democracy. With its endless variety of consumer items, the department-store window displays represented the good life the soldiers were fighting to protect. A fashionably dressed bride, a newlywed couple furnishing their home for the first time—these were symbols of prosperity and freedom of consumer choice.

Retailers used weddings to demonstrate their support of the soldiers who, with their future wives, were understood to be important postwar consumers. By the early 1940s mass retailers like Strawbridge & Clothier celebrated what they called the "big business of selling to brides." During the war, this Philadelphia store assembled a display in support for the United War Chest Campaign that employed a bride in white and a groom in uniform. Featured in an article aptly titled "Our Windows Worked for Our Boys" published in the company newsletter, the store window did the triple national service of appealing to the growing number of engaged couples, promoting the patriotic image of the store in the community, and building employee morale in a time of war.[36] Similarly, in a conscious effort to connect bridal promotions to the war, department-store trade literature urged retailers to capitalize on increased interest in silver during these years (something that contradicted etiquette expert Amy Vanderbilt's fears in the early 1950s that Americans were choosing practical gifts over silver). Patriotism and tradition went hand in hand as department stores found that "a chest of silver became the supreme symbol representing the home for which millions of men in the armed forces yearned."[37] Whether representing the "white wedding" of the colonial era or advertising chests of silverware, department-store merchandising embedded the idea of wedding tradition past and present within a national or consumer context.

Like window displays, in-store fashion shows further developed the link between weddings and consumerism. They served a dual commercial function, advertising goods at the same time as they created the atmosphere of luxury and service believed to be so conducive to consumption. Fashion shows first reached a popular American audience in the early twentieth century. By one account, the first American fashion show appeared in 1903 in New York by the Ehrich Brothers. Although fashion shows originated in the elite fashion industry with designers like Coco Chanel, Paul Poiret, and Charles Frederick Worth, they became a popular cultural form and a part of mass culture. Filmed fashion shows, for example, acted as tie-ins for women's fashions as early as 1910.[38] Early department-store fashion shows drew on exotic themes and far-

The Wedding Party from Our Spring Fashion Show

Gateway to Spring, the intriguing title of our Spring Fashion Show, was given on February 21, 22, and 23 to packed audiences. Its climax was the beautiful wedding tableau, shown here. Gowns were from our Bride's Shop, and the little choir boys were members of the Boys' Choir Guild of the *Church of the Holy Apostles and the Mediator*. For "Spring Weddings and Our Bridal Service" please turn to page 2.

FIGURE 22. Department stores like Strawbridge & Clothier hosted popular bridal fashion shows on a regular basis by the mid-twentieth century. Strawbridge & Clothier, *Store Chat* (March 1948), back cover. Hagley Museum and Library, Pictorial Collections Department, Wilmington, Delaware.

away places, such as Gimbel's Parisian focus in "Promenade des Toilettes" in 1910, its "Monte Carlo" casino theme in 1911, and Wanamaker's orientalist "Garden of Allah" fashion show in 1912. By World War I, with the rise of the women's ready-to-wear industry, these popular spectacles spread the concept of ever-changing fashion, bringing wider arrays of styles and colors to a broader spectrum of buyers.[39]

Department-store shows often featured a wedding tableau and by the 1930s and 1940s, special bridal shows appeared in stores across the country, making fashion or the quest for newness a part of wedding tradition (figure 22).[40] Department stores hosted smaller events in-store and took over hotels for their larger fashion shows through the mid-1960s.[41] Bridal fashion shows were publicity events that promoted the store as a whole. Women attended these bridal fashion shows to get ideas for their wedding gown, but in the process, they, and their female relatives and friends, also learned about other goods and services offered by the department store. Fashion shows promoted potential trousseau items, from the going-away suit to lingerie to luggage, as well as the goods a bride might need in her future home. Their focus was consumerism, even though their format and structure reenacted the noncommercial wedding ceremony. The featured goods even sometimes merged with the bride herself, as in one fashion show that staged a pageant of brides and attendants carrying packages of bed sheets in colors that matched their outfits.

Bridal fashion shows and "Bride's Week" became traditions in and of themselves, making stores across the country a natural part of getting married. The Dallas department store Neiman-Marcus claimed to be an early participant in this new trend. After the success of its weekly fashion shows, the store decided to host events featuring wedding and bridesmaid gowns, lingerie, wedding gifts, and different trousseaux for a range of budgets. Stanley Marcus invited the editor of a bridal magazine to serve as commentator and "to lend additional authority to [the] presentation." The shows were hugely successful and helped Neiman-Marcus to dominate the bridal business in its city.[42] Similarly, in Philadelphia in the 1950s, Wanamaker's wedding bureau organized regular June and January fashion shows with titles such as "A Bride to Remember," "Wishes Come True," "Now as Then, Weddings Begin at Wanamaker's." As the titles suggest, these spectacles linked the past with the future, emphasizing their role in creating wedding memories, as well their part in the couple's future life together. In Chicago, at Marshall Field's "Bride's Week" in 1958, the show made wedding traditions the theme for the different events, interior arrangements, and window displays. Throughout Chicago's State Street and Old Orchard stores, table settings for bridal showers and receptions were on display in the linen, china, and silver sections. According to the store's news release for the event, sixteen window displays on State Street pictured "wedding traditions," such as cake cutting, tossing the bridal bouquet, and the "tradition of the wedding gift." One large window also depicted a "complete wedding party."[43] Any visitor to Marshall Field's during "Bride's Week" would not have been able to escape the displays or the crowds attending the different events.

By the 1950s, bridal fashion shows were immensely popular, suggesting the great potential of these merchandising events to influence those about to marry. Free to the public (though by invitation only), the Wanamaker shows did not directly generate revenue, though they must have been considered lucrative ventures from the planning and time the publicity division gave each event. Each show at Wanamaker's drew a huge audience of women to the degree that overcrowding was a concern. Extra elevator operators and "starters to speed the departure of the guests" were on hand. Wanamaker's typically distributed from 1,000 to 4,000 tickets for its January and June shows in its auditorium. Spectators had to pick up their tickets at the third-floor wedding bureau, perhaps in an attempt to ensure that guests visited the bridal salon. With employees handling the PA system, lighting, the podium, runway, steps, ticket taking, fitting, and refreshments, these events were highly coordinated productions. Twelve female models and two male models were typically hired, though at least a couple of times a large group of Marines with sabers took part in the spectacle. In addition, storewide participation and cooperation was required for the success of the event. Gift registry and the china, silver, and gift wrapping departments, men's department, and housewares all arranged for wedding displays in their areas to tie into the fashion show and promote it. These elaborate fashion shows appeared season after season for decades, spreading to suburban branch stores in the early postwar period.[44]

In the late 1960s, a new marketing strategy appeared, one that took the older bridal fashion show and added displays and events from a variety of vendors with goods and services of interest to those about to marry. These new bridal fairs expanded the definition of "bridal," but still along fairly traditional lines. At "New York's First Bridal Fair" in 1969, for example, more than two thousand brides-to-be in their early twenties and their mothers turned out at Madison Square Garden. The event featured a panel of experts giving tips on marriage, as well as two fashion shows. According to a *New York Times* report, the fair also featured twelve commercial exhibits, "ranging from airlines and such wedding staples as photographers and orchestras all the way to Chase Manhattan Bank, which passed out free shopping bags with the word 'LOVE' printed on the sides."[45] While adding a few vendors without explicit wedding trade (banks and airlines were represented), all exhibits conformed to the industry's longtime goal of expanding what was considered "bridal." Each exhibit, moreover, fit into the postwar domestic ideal and upheld the tradition of the formal white wedding with all the trimmings.

Not everyone at these events agreed with these values, however. While it is safe to say that department-store bridal promotions and bridal fairs were well attended and well received, especially in the context of the skyrocketing marriage rates in the postwar period, some opposition to the wedding industry appeared by 1970. The second-wave feminist movement drew renewed attention to inequality in marriage and exploitation of women by businesses and the media. Popular books and unpublished feminist dissertations critiquing the wedding industry appeared during this time.[46] "New York's First Bridal Fair" in 1969 became a target of feminist protest by members of the Women's International Terrorist Conspiracy from Hell (WITCH). Setting mice loose on the exhibit floor and staging a satirical wedding ceremony of their own, WITCH challenged the panel of experts, asserting their belief that marriage was an institution that oppressed women. They also condemned "the commerciality of the Bridal Fair." Not surprisingly, this bridal fair, which is of legendary status among feminist scholars, received scant attention in the *New York Times* account of the event. The article focused on the wedding fashions that debuted at the fair, framing the protest and comments of attendants in a way that belittled the group's critique. The reporter recorded the guests' offhand, almost bored criticism of WITCH and noted that the women at the fair were not scared by the mice, but simply picked them up so they would not get squished. Significantly, no photos of the WITCH protestors were included in the report, only four images of brides-to-be and models wearing wedding fashions.[47] Other critiques of the wedding industry emerged in the 1970s, such as the brief flirtation with anti-materialist, anti-establishment New Weddings, but this opposition did not result in lasting change. At a trade show in 1970, while Priscilla Kidder predicted that "weddings are changing," challenges to tradition appeared simply as shifting consumer tastes or changing fashions. Noting the music played at a bridal trade show, the reporter signaled this change was not radical, as "The girls swung down the aisle to music by Glenn Miller. It wasn't the Rolling Stones, but it wasn't Lohengrin either."[48]

Some real changes did take place, however, as the mainstream wedding industry became more racially inclusive. Department stores attempted to reach a broader consumer base among women about to marry, and bridal fashion shows tried to reach the ethnic market for the first time. Black-owned publications and events, such as *Ebony*'s Fashion Fair, had used African American models, but through the 1960s, Wanamaker's, Strawbridge & Clothier, and Marshall Field's all used white models in their fashion shows. When black models appeared in bridal fashion shows in the 1970s in places as small as the Herbst department store in Fargo, North Dakota, the wedding industry had reached a new level of market outreach—and perhaps a higher degree of acceptance of the formal white wedding ideal by American consumers (figure 23).[49]

DEPARTMENT-STORE WEDDING GIFT REGISTRIES AND OTHER "MODERN TRADITIONS"

Window displays and fashion shows attracted customers and promoted their stores, but department stores also had to compete with other retailers. They therefore came up with a variety of services intended to hold onto their customers' business. Although department-store gift registries were established ostensibly in the older spirit of personal service and amenity—of making the customer happy—they intended to rationalize and centralize gift giving, making the whole enterprise more efficient. New gift registries were marketed as a convenient service for wedding guests and the bride, but the innovation clearly served the purpose of generating sales and keeping it in one place. As we saw in Chapter 2, specialty jewelers recorded a bride's silverware pattern for those who came in search of a wedding gift for her. In the early twentieth century, however, gift givers generally followed their own whims, as the numerous duplications of silverware, silver serving items, crystal, candlesticks, and vases found on elite wedding gift lists from the period suggest. Beyond advertising, offering expert services and advice on etiquette, and cutting prices, retailers could do little to control competition if the choice of gift was left up to the wedding guest.[50] Wedding guests could buy from mail-order catalogues or visit any number of specialty shops or department stores to purchase presents. Registries evolved to solve these problems, emerging as a service that benefited both the retailer and the customer. By the end of the twentieth century, the gift registry experience had become a traditional part of most weddings,

FIGURE 23. By the early 1970s, bridal fashion shows were a seasonal occurrence all across the United States. As this event at the Herbst department store in Fargo, North Dakota, suggests, the wedding industry sought to appeal to an increasingly diverse market by this time. Institute for Regional Studies, NDSU, Fargo (2043.1.9).

spreading beyond department stores and jewelers to all types of retailers, large and small.

Department stores, with their full line of goods, introduced the most comprehensive and potentially commercial type of gift registry. In 1924, Marshall Field's of Chicago was the first North American department store to offer a centralized gift service. Although wedding presents eventually became the only concern of this bureau, at first they were simply lumped in with other special occasions, as the service also furnished "suggestions for parties, table decorations, wedding plans, or gifts."[51] By 1929, more than half of both large and small stores had "gift suggestion departments." The following year, however, the general idea of a gift registry was still novel enough to warrant an article seeking "to educate the public" about its functions and benefits in the *Saturday Evening Post*. Even though during the Depression department stores reduced the number of staff and consolidated services, gift registries spread to stores like Chicago's Carson, Pirie Scott. In the mid-1930s, *Bride's* magazine and Lenox China also began promoting the service.[52]

The appearance of the gift registry service fit into the larger changes taking place in retailing. Gift registries, for example, could be successful only if employees accepted interdepartmental selling. Department-store gift shops had to assert their status as sales departments in opposition to other employees' belief that they were just a display department.[53] Rationalization of the gift selection process was only possible if salespeople worked through the centralized service and did not try to keep the sales within their own department. Department-store management understood there would be opposition to this new way of selling. When Marshall Field's opened its Party, Wedding and Gift Bureau on the second floor of its Chicago store in 1924, it notified all section managers, assistants, division superintendents, and floor men of the service, asking for their cooperation.[54] By consolidating gift purchases in one place, registries marked a shift away from departmental loyalty toward identification with the store as a whole, something that would develop further with the rise of the department-store bridal salon.

For gift givers, registries de-skilled the gift-giving process, taking control of the choice of present from the guest, and saving time as well. Registries permitted the bride more control over her wedding presents, but with the introduction of preprinted forms, this changed. Stores began to outline what sorts of goods the bride "needed." Gift registry forms had the potential to standardize consumption and establish norms for wedding practice, marking a new level of rationalization. *Bride's* magazine first introduced the "long form" for gift registry around 1950, marking a shift away from merely recording "preferences" to actually suggesting to the bride the types of goods and particular items that were appropriate wedding presents.[55] By 1960, Carson, Pirie Scott was issuing a "Bride's Preference List," which provided a full page of preprinted items that recorded what brides "want" and what they "have" already (figure 24). Carson's list provided the dual outlines of suburban easy living and a more formal way of life, with lists of silver items, crystal pieces, bar accessories, china, as well as plastic pieces, carpet sweepers, ironing boards, card tables, lazy susans, casseroles, and TV snack tables.[56] The introduction of these forms marked a shift toward standardized consumption as the retailer now told the bride what she should have in her new home.

Telling the giver what one wanted as a wedding present in this way, however, could be considered vulgar or crass. The mercenary potential of the whole wedding gift enterprise had been the subject of critique in the late nineteenth century, as we saw in Chapter 1. Gift registries opened up another can of worms. The bride not only would have asked for a specific item, she would know its price and thus how much the giver spent. A registry was also clearly impersonal, a fact only emphasized by the use of forms and prefabricated lists. Retailers understood the potentially undesirable commercial aspect of their services and sought ways to elide it. When the gift registry at Marshall Field's opened in 1924, it presented its new service in a subtle way, offering to solve "delicate problems of etiquette . . . rendering first aid to the bride."[57] Some department stores used promotions—or gimmicks—to appeal to prospective customers and mask the commercial nature of this new tradition. In 1944, Bullock's of Los Angeles promoted a "wishing well" where the bride would register her choice in china, glass, linen, and silver patterns in a bride's book, which would be dropped in a wishing well. (It is unclear what actually happened to the bride's book after this.) Symbolically, however, the wishing well turned the act of asking for a particular present into a magical event. At Bullock's, the well helped her "receive," not *get*, the gifts she wanted. And importantly, it allowed her to make a "wish," not a *request*. This novel approach apparently attracted large crowds.[58] Once registered, however, brides

THE BRIDE'S PREFERENCE LIST
Wedding Gift Service St 12000
K 2381

Bride given
"To The Bride"
Cook Book on ____

Cuson Fine Scotias

Bride's Name		Wedding Date
Address		Home Phone
City	Zone	Office Phone
Groom's Name		
Period of Furniture		Color Scheme:

SILVER NAME:	WANT	HAVE	CRYSTAL NAME:	WANT	HAVE	CHINA NAME:	WANT	HAVE
Place Settings			Goblets			Place Settings		
Knife			Sherbets			Fruits		
Fork			Tumblers Ftd.			Soups - Rim - Cream		
Salad Fork			Tumblers 5 oz. Ftd.			Sugar - Creamer		
Butter Spreader			Cocktails			Sauce Boat		
Teaspoon			Wines			Platters - S M L		
Place Spoon			Plates			Vegetable Dishes		
Cocktail Forks			**SILVER HOLLOWARE**			Tea or Coffee Pot		
Iced Tea Spoons			Candle Sticks					
Butter Knife			Well & Tree Platter					
Cold Meat Fork			Salt - Pepper			**BAR ACCESSORIES:**		
Gravy Ladle			Sugar - Creamer			Highballs		
Pickle Fork			Vegetable Dish			Old Fashioneds		
Pie Server			Water Pitcher			Ice Bucket		
Salad Set			Others:			Martini Set		
Serving Spoons								
Sugar Spoon								
Tomato Server								
POTTERY - PLASTIC NAME:			**STAINLESS NAME:**			**MISCELLANEOUS:**		
Starter Sets			Starter Sets			Card Table		
Salads			Serving Pieces			Carpet Sweeper		
Soups			Steak Knives			Carving Board		
Fruits			Carving Set			Casseroles		
Platters			**STAINLESS STEEL HOLLOWARE:**			Chafing Dish		
Sauce Boat						Ironing Board		
Vegetable Dish			Casseroles			Lazy Susan		
Casserole			Platters			Salad Bowl		
Salt - Pepper			Vegetable Dish			TV Snack Tables		
Sugar and Creamer			Water Pitcher					
Others:			Others:					
Casual Glassware								

FIGURE 24. By 1960, the department-store wedding gift registry tradition not only had brides list their preferences, it outlined the goods that they were supposed to "want." Marshall Field's Archives, Chicago.

faced the problem of conveying information about the registry to their guests. B. Altman's in New York advised them to "just drop the hint to your relatives and friends so they can choose your gifts without fear of duplication."[59] Specialty stores had a similar dilemma, one that silverware manufacturers attempted to resolve. One manufacturer warned brides of the dangers of unwanted duplications and simply advocated open communication of one's wishes: "Once there was a bride who read a survey. She learned that most brides receive up to nine times as many cut glass bud vases and monogrammed place mats as they can use—but only half the silverware they ask for. This little bride determined not to suffer a similar fate. So she hurried to her nearest silverware store. There she selected and registered her pattern. And then she told all who were coming to her wedding she had selected her pattern in Gorham sterling . . . and would be delighted if they gave her only two teaspoons or even just a knife and fork."[60] Even behind the scenes, in-store memoranda masked the calculating, commercial aspect of these new services, noting subtly in the passive voice that "often the bride's china pattern or her preferences are known and these serve as a guide to patrons."[61]

In the mid-twentieth century the problem of wedding gifts became the subject of popular satire in Edward Streeter's best-selling 1948 novel *Father of the Bride*. The bride, Kay Banks, is inundated by presents in the weeks before her marriage. As the gifts arrive, they are sorted, recorded, and displayed. In a competitive spirit, Kay sought to beat her friend Booboo Batchelder's record of 234 wedding gifts and reach "235 or bust." Interestingly, although half of her presents came from the Tucker Gift Shop, the story makes no mention of gift registry. Instead, the bride and her mother criticize the "junk" that came from the store, and the father of the bride worries over the duplicates of highball glasses, cocktail shakers, and wineglasses that made his house "look like a setup for *The Lost Weekend*" (a movie about alcoholism).[62] Even though most of these gifts were unwelcome, they were chosen personally by the guests and were important for that reason.

Father of the Bride's satire aside, gift registry services appeared to have some effect on wedding consumption by the postwar period. Gift registries by their very nature were intended to shape custom. The first statistical study of the American bridal market as a whole, performed by *Bride's* magazine in 1958, indicated that registries were successful. According to this random sampling of women, one out of two brides made her preferences for types of wedding gifts known, either through suggestions to friends or through registries at local stores. Women sought basic household items, such as flatware, dinnerware, portable appliances, and housewares, as well as crystal (crystal was considered "basic" by the study). Of those brides who listed "preferences," one-third were more specific, listing desired type, brand, pattern, or color. Readers of *Bride's* magazine were engaged most deeply in these consumer rites, asking for more things, and being more specific in their choices. For example, 47 percent of bridal magazine readers listed sterling, plate, or stainless steel flatware in comparison with the 25.9 percent of the total U.S. bridal market that wanted these goods as wedding presents.[63] And 42.7 percent of readers specified their "brand, pattern, color, or type," while only 22.9 percent of the total U.S. bridal market did so.[64] While it is possible that guests did not listen to the gift advice provided by the bride's registry or that brides did not even use the services available to them, some appreciated the assistance stores provided. One mother of the bride wrote to Carson, Pirie Scott and commended its bridal service for doing a "magnificent and thorough job" of her daughter's gifts, the selection of which made her guests "very happy."[65]

Just as store gift registries became a traditional part of getting married, other departments participated in the invention of new consumer rites. Stationery departments provide an interesting example of the way that retailers were able to shape the meaning of wedding-related customs. Department stores presented their stationery goods as traditional and timeless, but also as modern and subject to changing fashions. At Marshall Field's in the 1920s, for example, engraved wedding cards were advertised as "Modern Traditions / Traditional Modernity: A 'golden mean'—that perfect balance between extremes." The wedding industry had to be both modern and traditional if it was to continue expanding into new markets and be able to adapt to new social circumstances that changed the nature of weddings and their related rituals. Retailers could not afford to stand still, but when their business was tradition, they had to find that "perfect balance."[66]

The tradition/modernity dichotomy allowed for changes to older traditions. For example, it helped stationery departments introduce entirely new practices or types of ritual goods. Eventually, the "tradition" of engraved invitations declined with the introduction of modern techniques that made a close approximation of this old tradition more affordable. Through the 1950s, stationery departments ran profitable engraving workrooms. Retailers offered wedding invitation engraving services and engraved personal stationery with the bride's new name, as well as the traditional writing paper for thank-you notes.[67] A shortage of engravers and a shift to manufacturer's engraving services and the cheaper thermography method, however, changed this. By the late 1950s, department-store trade literature pushed a new and improved form of thermography, or raised printing, as socially acceptable for printed wedding invitations. In traditional engraved invitations, ink was deposited where the surface of the paper was cut, something that could be detected by running one's finger across the print. The new photoplate thermography produced a finished look that was barely distinguishable from engraved work and even maintained the desired feel of the raised printing created by traditional engraving. Stationery departments also introduced entirely new traditions, such as monogramming invitations and imprinting the couple's name on napkins and matchbooks, something that became a standard feature of many wedding packages. In the early 1950s, some stores, like Louis Pizitz Company in Birmingham, Alabama, purchased new stamping machines and trained salespeople in monogramming, using the service to turn their department into a busy gift section.[68] In these ways, department stores helped expand the material outlines of the elite white wedding ideal by altering and creating new, less expensive traditions that allowed for a wider market. Eventually, new department-store bridal salons became a traditional part of getting married as a visit to one became a treasured part of the wedding experience for many brides and their female relatives and friends.

DEPARTMENT-STORE BRIDAL SALONS

In 1924, Marshall Field's was not only the first department store to offer a gift registry, but it also was the first to provide customers with the services of a wedding secretary that same year. Running a sort of bridal salon, this secretary helped women select their trousseau and choose household furnishings, gave advice on presents for attendants and on the correct etiquette for table settings, and kept a list of gifts to avoid duplication.[69] Store employees were supposed to refer customers to her office in the "Gothic Room" on the second floor next to the Elizabethan Linen Room. Wedding secretaries offered a level of service and amenity that was fast disappearing elsewhere as the practice of cost-cutting self-service took hold. Around World War II, the rise of self-service retailing led to a reliance on a part-time sales force and a subsequent decline in skilled selling, and the spread of smaller, less service-oriented suburban stores. The golden age for the department-store customer had ended.[70] But the free services provided by department-store bridal salons were an exception to decades of cutbacks in services.

In the 1920s, when separate bridal salons appeared within department stores, they reflected a movement to offer the atmosphere of smaller specialty shops within the larger framework of the store. Department-store gift shops, for example, adopted this style of retailing. At Neiman-Marcus in Dallas, china, silver, glass, and antiques were "all selected with a specialty store point of view rather than in the traditional manner of the department or jewelry store," according to founder Stanley Marcus. Fine department stores also offered custom dressmaking services in the context of specialty shops within the store that were modeled on exclusive Parisian dressmaking establishments. In the early 1920s, the merchandising concept of the "shop within a shop" took hold, leading to separate exclusive areas within the store, such as corset shops, gown shops, shirtwaist and blouse shops, and "French Rooms."[71] After the rise of women's ready-to-wear clothing by World War I, this form of merchandising helped translate a new material form into terms that would be understood and accepted. Such shops separated out these items, giving mass-produced garments the allure and class associations of custom-made clothing. Whether for gifts or clothing, the shop within a shop promised the expert service and personal attention of specialty retailers, something that could be lost in the acreage of the modern department store. By World War II, bridal salons and consultants appeared in stores all over the United States. In the early 1940s, the New York City area alone boasted wedding bureaus or salons in Altman's, Lord and Taylor, Franklin Simon, Saks Fifth Avenue, Bonwit Teller, J. Thorpe, Macy's, The Tailored Woman, Jane Engle, Wanamaker's, Mary Lewis, and Loeser, as did Bamberger's in Newark, New Jersey.[72]

The success of these new stores within a store likely grew out of the elite image they cultivated. Bridal department advertising and promotions created an upper-class image for the new commercial service, which likely helped them gain acceptance and become a traditional part of the formal white wedding.

Salons offered to take all the shopping details off the hands of the busy bride and pamper her as if she were someone with a lot of money to spend at the store. Advertisements and promotions masked the commercial nature of the bride's visit, turning it into a social occasion. Ads for wedding secretary services or bridal salons promoted this elite image, depicting uniform-wearing attendants serving the bride and her mother tea or lunch, as if this were a personal visit to a friend, not a shopping trip. Store promotions often involved giving the bride a gift, such as a blue garter, helping to support what for one woman entrepreneur was a $175,000 annual business in the early 1950s (figure 25). Such practices promoted invented traditions but also elevated the consumer experience for the bride, turning it into something more than just a shopping trip. A more likely scenario, and one frequently depicted in advertisements, was the presentation of clothing or merchandise for the bride to view with an eye to purchasing. Advertisements and articles on these services typically showed a consultant standing before a seated bride or her mother, holding up going-away outfits and other goods for their inspection. The consultant also sat at a desk, or with the bride and her mother as equals, but still in a manner that suggested that her role was to cater to their every whim (figure 26).[73]

Bridal salons' luxurious settings helped transcend the wedding's link to mass culture. Large, open spaces in the salon drew attention to the gowns when they were brought out or modeled (figure 27).[74] Just as the wedding gown itself was supposed to be unique—for a once-in-a-lifetime event—its purchase was to take place in a special context, away from the hustle and bustle of department-store traffic. According to one consultant in the 1950s, brides viewed their gown as "private and sacred."[75] Salons allowed customers to sit and examine bridal magazines, getting ideas for their own wedding, or pass the time while waiting for the bridal consultant to bring dresses out for private fittings. Furnished with lounges, stuffed chairs, carved tables, desks, chandelier lighting, paintings, and gilt-framed mirrors, the salon was often more like an elegant home than a retail space.[76] Unlike other departments, where goods might be piled indiscriminately on tables, hung crookedly on racks, or shown with dozens of like items, the bridal salon fetishized its merchandise. Open spaces not directly dedicated to the display of merchandise conveyed the idea that wedding consumption was out of the ordinary. When salons attempted to

FIGURE 25. Women entrepreneurs, like Hortense Hewitt, participated in the invention of tradition. *Bride's* (Spring 1948), 199.

FIGURE 26. Advertisements showed department-store bridal consultants in a variety of roles, helping with the wedding gown, invitations, the trousseau, gift registry, and purchases for the bride's new home. *Modern Bride* (Winter 1950–1951). Forsyth Library, Fort Hays State University, Hays, Kansas.

FIGURE 27. The Sosnick & Thalheimer bridal salon in 1950 in Winston-Salem, North Carolina, was typical in that it displayed little merchandise, creating an elite shopping experience through its elegant furnishings and décor. Library of Congress, Prints & Photographs Division, Gottscho-Schleisner Collection [LC-G613-T-56494 DLC].

sell merchandise from other departments in the salon, for example, only a few select items related to the wedding preparations were shown, highlighting the importance of each consumer choice. The gowns themselves were displayed only in a limited fashion, modeled by a single mannequin on a dias, or in a corner. Each item thus took on a ceremonial appearance. The ceremonial presentation of the gowns obscured their ready-made origins, making the bride feel as if she were purchasing an original design made especially "for that most important day of her life."[77]

There were practical reasons, however, for the selective nature of bridal gown displays. Stores simply did not have a lot of goods on hand. In the early 1940s, according to one merchandising expert, few stores carried much stock, but instead took special orders using the *Bridal Book*, a semiannual fashion report that included sketches of bridal and bridesmaid dresses, swatches of material, and price lists.[78] As fragile items that required special storage to protect them and keep them immaculate, bridal gowns could take up expensive retail space. Stores could not afford to stock all the sizes and styles needed. By the early 1950s, stores carried only samples of bridal dresses to allow for adequate display space and customer fittings, but it was acknowledged in the trade that the "best job [was] done by stores that carry some stock."[79]

Although luxurious and spacious, salons also sought an efficient, business-like image, one that was thoroughly modern. Women who worked in other departments flocked to their store's salon when they were about to marry, finding that they saved time and money when they used the service.[80] Salons provided brides with brochures and materials that underlined their role as efficiency experts. In addition to offering free copies of bridal magazines, stores also produced their own publications. In 1939, Marshall Field's offered a *Bride's Book of Plans* that employed the "Kwik-Glance METHOD" in keeping with its emphasis on modern efficiency. It included a section of forms for the bride to fill out that detailed arrangements for flowers, the church ceremony, catering, and a record of gifts given. Much like gift registries, but intended for the bride's own purchases, the forms kept track of the cost of listed items considered to be basic home furnishings and provided pages outlining the personal, household, and kitchen trousseaus. Intended to help the bride "organize [her] time" and "conserve [her] energies," the book attempted to transform getting married into a rational, economic act that could be systematized and standardized through forms and records of expenditure.[81]

These services sometimes extended to the wedding day itself. In 1935, Carson, Pirie Scott of Chicago was the first store in the United States to offer full wedding services.[82] Other major American department stores, such as Strawbridge & Clothier and Marshall Field's, provided services for the bride but did not involve themselves in preparation on the wedding day itself.[83] Eaton's in Toronto was probably the second department store to offer the comprehensive one-stop wedding in North America and contributed to the invention of the commercialized white wedding tradition.[84] Founded in 1938, Eaton's Wedding Bureau followed a sort of vertical integration that covered all aspects of the ceremony and the reception. This well-known Canadian institution advised the bride on her purchase of Eaton's stationery, her trousseau, and wedding gown, and helped her shop for household furnishings for her new home.

Eaton's featured regular promotions, such as fashion shows, and beginning in 1939, a regular bride's week.[85] It also had a men's shop to outfit the groom, as did other department stores. Unlike most of its U.S. counterparts, however, Eaton's also offered to provide the wedding cake, advise on caterers, florists, and eventually photography, and arrange the display of the trousseau and wedding gifts for the Canadian custom of a trousseau tea. The head of the Wedding Bureau, Claire Dreier, and her assistants even supervised the rehearsal and attended the wedding ceremony in order to assist the bride and make sure everything went smoothly.[86]

Although a Canadian institution, Eaton's department store deserves a place in a discussion of the American department-store bridal industry. First, Eaton's presents the most complete set of public archival records on the workings of a bridal salon that my research could generate, one that allows a rare glimpse at the interchange between consumer and retailer. Second, in terms of business relations between the two countries, the border was permeable, with Canadian and American retailers influencing each other. Canadian scholars have suggested that the two countries developed different attitudes toward consumer culture and that Canada developed a national market only in the 1920s, much later than in the United States.[87] Nevertheless, in the case of the bridal business, some analogies and connections between Eaton's and American department stores are warranted. Eaton's early foray into the bridal business provided a model for American stores. In 1942, for example, Marshall Field's sought advice from its northern neighbor when considering implementing a "complete wedding service operation," reversing the situation in earlier days when Eaton's "took [its] cue from them." As the wedding industry matured, it crossed the border with bridal consultants and salon heads going back and forth between Eaton's and Carson, Pirie Scott; Marshall Field's; and others.[88] Consultant Claire Dreier attended *Bride's* magazine's important bridal clinics in New York in the 1940s, where she shared her Eaton's experiences and also picked up new merchandising techniques and crucial information about the bridal market in general. And finally, there is evidence that the American wedding industry influenced Canadian consumers who turned to American bridal magazines as the authorities on customs.[89]

The following case study draws on the rare resources of the Eaton's archive to flesh out the inner workings of an early bridal salon as it dealt with customers, outside businesses, and the department-store community, showing that in real life, such interchanges were filled with conflict and subsequent negotiations. And the invented traditions that this Canadian retailer promoted—many of which were shared by the United States—were the product of these complex negotiations.

EATON'S WEDDING BUREAU

Eaton's Wedding Bureau put on its first wedding on December 3, 1938, in Toronto's Timothy Eaton Memorial United Church, one that must have garnered the new professional service much attention from the society-page-reading public. Margaret Elaine Ellsworth of "Glenalton," Ridley Park, married William Van Allen Holton after a frenzied period of preparation by Eaton's Wedding Bureau and the bride's mother. At the church, against a backdrop of red and white flowers, six ushers assisted the more than five hundred guests entering the church. As the organist played, the wedding party, with all six bridesmaids and the maid of honor clad in white, proceeded down the long aisle of Eaton Memorial. The bridal attendants were dressed alike in Molyneux-inspired gowns, wearing white velvet hats decorated with "tiny white birds posed with outspread wings." They were pictures of the latest fashion, carrying "the new 'Lelong' fan-shaped muffs of white velvet." The bride followed, accompanied by her father who "gave her in marriage." According to the Eaton's write-up for the newspapers that was sent to society editors, Elaine Ellsworth "was a vision of loveliness in her wedding gown of ivory diva Lyons velvet, cut with the classic simplicity of a Molyneux gown," with a deep V-neckline, shirred bodice, and high waistline.[90] The ceremony featured a "unique detail" that was probably the brainchild of the Wedding Bureau. As the procession reached the chancel where the groom and his best man stood, "instead of halting there as is the custom, they mounted the steps and took their positions at either side in front of the choir stalls" with three ushers and three bridesmaids on either side. In all, however, according to Eaton's, "it was really a white wedding, in classic harmony with the ivory and muted colourings of the Church itself."[91]

The Wedding Bureau also orchestrated the reception and the different vendors needed to decorate the house with flowers and cater the traditional affair at the bride's family home. The large house was transformed from an ordinary upper-class home into a ritual space for a wedding celebration of more than five hundred through the red and white flowers and greenery that filled every room, from the drawing room and dining room to the billiards room and library. The red and white theme suited a winter wedding, and was carried out through poinsettias, red roses, and carnations, and white orchids, lilies-of-the-valley, and gardenias, to name just a few. In the tea room the bride's table was set with a white satin tablecloth, crystal candelabra and white candles, mixed white flowers, and a bride's cake, all against a background of red roses and southern smilax, a popular greenery in the U.S. South that must have been imported for the occasion. After the receiving line in the drawing room where the parents and the bride and groom received their guests, everyone assembled in the "great hall." Before taking her place at the table, "the bride paused to perform the traditional ceremony of cutting her three-tiered wedding cake," one likely provided by Eaton's Georgian Room.[92] After the meal, guests wandered through the rooms, visiting the upstairs suite of rooms "devoted to the wedding gifts."[93] The bride then changed into her gray wool going-away costume with its fuschia accessories and the couple left on a honeymoon to Havana, Cuba, one possibly arranged by Eaton's travel service in connection with the Wedding Bureau.

To produce a perfect wedding of this magnitude required an immense amount of detailed planning, coordination, and hard work. Necessarily, this labor was divided among different members of the staff. Miss Kent, acting under Claire Dreier, the head of the Wedding Bureau, made sure a detective had been hired to watch the gifts on the day of the wedding at the Ellsworth house. It was also her responsibility to bring the two white satin kneeling cushions that were placed at the altar rail at the church. There, she was also responsible for the hired girls who directed guests to the ladies' cloakrooms and checked wraps. With more than five hundred guests attending the ceremony at the church and the reception at the house, the logistics merely of entry and exit would have been complex.[94] Another store employee brought in racks for guests' coats at the Ellsworth home where the reception was held. At the church, he brought the sailcloth runway and made arrangements for the laying of this cloth. In the reception room at the entrance to the church he made sure the brown screens, brown carpet, and tall mirrors were in place to set the stage for the bride. J. A. Brockie, Claire Dreier's superior and head of merchandise display at Eaton's, took on the most responsibility, discussing details with the mother of the bride and managing such things as the church plans, the press photographers and newspaper write-up, the gratuities to the minister, organist, Mrs. Gilmour, and the caretaker, and the transportation of the bridesmaids and groomsmen.[95]

Through the Wedding Bureau, the store gained entrance into the family home and into their private lives. Much like the satirical portrait of the wedding caterer in Edward Streeter's novel *Father of the Bride*, Brockie was in a position to evaluate Mrs. Ellsworth and the social status of her family, something the mother of the bride must have been aware of when she self-deprecatingly referred to her "shabby" house and its "really messy background."[96] Brockie would have had little to criticize with this wealthy home, but like the caterer in Streeter's novel, he did order changes to make it suitable for a big wedding. He oversaw the installation of wall treatments, curtains, and rugs, the moving or delivery of furniture by truck, and in a typical *Father of the Bride* moment, the cutting of a new doorway to admit Coles, the hired caterer (though at the last minute Mrs. Ellsworth changed her mind and chose Simpson's, another Toronto caterer, to do the wedding). Having a caterer for the reception meant an even greater transformation of the house, as Simpson's required a kitchen built on the home's terrace that joined with another heated tent.[97]

Held in a stately home during the Depression, the elite Ellsworth-Holton wedding was likely given extra care and attention from the brand new Bureau, but in the following decades Eaton's directed its attention to a wide range of Canadian brides. The Wedding Bureau had dozens of weddings on the books every month but provided full services for a much smaller number. Still, in their busiest week in the period 1939–1941 (the only years for which records could be found), they "serviced" eleven weddings, though one, two, or three productions per week were more common. Able to afford a white wedding, most of these customers were likely at least middle class, especially during the war years in Canada. Suggesting a more diverse customer base, however, Eaton's recognized that the "average home" was not large enough to host a wedding and had to rent a hall, hotel, or small tea room for their reception, choices of venue that also reflected their customers' range of socioeconomic or ethnic backgrounds.[98] By the 1950s, the Wedding Bureau made a number of different appeals to various class and ethnic groups. They encouraged the department store's employees to use its facilities, as did Philadelphia's Strawbridge & Clothier during this period (figure 28).[99] Eaton's directed its Bride's Week promotions at the Garden Club, Canadian Women's Club, the Opera Festival Association, and the University of Toronto College Group, but it also sought the patronage of women in the Ontario Chapter of B'nai B'rith, the Hadassah Bazaar, and the Catholic Women's League.[100] Part of a larger movement to capture the growing immigrant market in Canada after World War II, in 1954 Eaton's Wedding Bureau sought "to interest New Canadians" with an international fashion show as part of its bride's week promotions.[101] Eaton's began to herald the Wedding Bureau as a "Canadian custom," a tradition in and of itself.[102]

Promotions like fashion shows attempted to spread the consumer ideal of the formal white wedding into new markets that may have had different marriage customs and styles of wedding dress. This potentially created conflicts, as consultant Claire Dreier suggested in her talk to an advertising club in 1948. She reenacted various discussions between herself and a prospective bride, including one in which the bride asked her about her mother's wish to wear black at her white wedding. She told the bride that while "many South American and European mothers appear in black gowns at weddings," it is because such dresses were "traditional for older women" in their countries. Dreier advised her that according to "our Canadian custom," mothers should appear "in light or pastel colour or in fall and winter, in warmer jewel tones." In this way, the department store, through its representative from the Wedding Bureau, attempted to change ethnic custom and introduce a more standardized middle-class Canadian taste to consumers.[103]

Bridal salons like those at Eaton's also standardized the physical outlines of nuptial rites, simply through the material and equipment they had at their disposal. Helping with dozens of celebrations each month, the department store had to invest in a wide array of ritual props to be prepared for different situations. Certainly the consultants must have chosen items that they assumed their customers would want, reflecting contemporary fashions and customs. Their inventory included basic items, such as lamps, white rope, gift tables, folding steps, and platforms, indicating that they could build a wedding site from the ground up. Eaton's inventory was dedicated to the church ceremony, suggested by their collection of runners, "church cushions," white kneeling

The Bride's Shop Wishes Much Happiness to these Registered Store Brides

Mr. and Mrs. Robert F. Buzzard who were married on September 17. Mrs. Buzzard was Miss Betty Adams, a member of our Trainee group.

Photograph by Wilbur Boone

Mrs. Robert E. Cross, who was formerly Miss Gladys Parry of our Training Department, was married on September 10, at the First Presbyterian Church, Philadelphia.

Mrs. Peter P. Symanowski and her sister, Anne Thompson, Cashier in our Corinthian Room, who was her maid of honor. The wedding took place on May 26 in St. Francis de Sales Church in Philadelphia.

Photograph by Bill O'Neill

Mr. and Mrs. Kenneth Brownell cutting their wedding cake at the reception following their marriage on September 10. Mr. Brownell is Acting Buyer in our Furniture Department and Mrs. Brownell, the former Peggy Balderston, is secretary to Mr. Severson.

FIGURE 28. Department-store bridal salons like Strawbridge & Clothier's in 1949 served those who worked in the store itself, suggesting that the formal white wedding tradition cut across class lines by mid-century. Strawbridge & Clothier, *Store Chat* (November 1949), 1. Hagley Museum and Library, Pictorial Collections Department, Wilmington, Delaware.

benches, and one church altar.[104] This inventory represented a capital investment, and the items it contained must have been used repeatedly, making such
things as a white church runner a natural, traditional thing to have at one's
nuptials. A guest attending several Eaton's weddings might have noticed some
standardization as well, recognizing a silver urn here and a candlestick there.
Eaton's also owned items of a more fashionable nature, such as twelve shepherd's crooks. Newspaper accounts of shepherd's-crook-carrying bridesmaids
would have spread information about this fashion to a broader Canadian public. Indeed, the practice was present in the United States during the 1920s and
1930s.[105]

Department stores like Eaton's had the power to shape consumers' choices,
but their influence also extended to smaller businesses in the wedding trade. In
the process of arranging for the dozens of weddings it orchestrated each
month, Eaton's came into conflict with small businesses in the Toronto area.
Opposition to the Wedding Bureau fits into the context of long-standing tensions between the two types of merchants. Small merchants, such as specialty
jewelers, had long seen department stores as unfair competitors and "a serious
menace to their existence."[106] In the 1890s, "store wars" erupted when small
merchants organized against their bigger competitors, lobbying for special laws
and taxes directed against department stores. After the 1893 depression in the
United States, hundreds of small merchants went bankrupt, while big retailers
like Marshall Field's survived and were able to drive up real estate values and
force out competitors.[107]

The Wedding Bureau gave Eaton's an even greater power over small retailers in Toronto in that it was in the position to recommend vendors to brides
and direct Bureau business to specific firms, cutting out others and shaping
wedding practice in the process. One such "retail war" took place in 1938 and
1939 between the Wedding Bureau and a local florist. As soon as the wedding
service arrived on the retail scene, Toronto florists such as Adams Flowers,
Tidy's, and Helen Simpson began competing for lucrative orders from Eaton's
brides. Supplying the weddings of prominent brides was a source of revenue,
but it also provided the opportunity for important word-of-mouth advertising
as guests commented on beautiful floral arrangements and mothers of the bride
proudly discussed their origins. In one particular case, Claire Dreier became
involved in a personal and professional struggle with Fred Adams of Yonge

Street, a florist who believed that the Wedding Bureau steered customers away from the business he ran with the help of his daughter. Adams believed that Dreier chose other florists over him because of her own personal "discrimination" against his "religious leaning," though it is unclear what that was. According to Dreier, however, she "switched such orders as [she] could" to Helen Simpson because she "liked her work." The issue became heated enough for Dreier to have to defend herself to J. A Brockie, her supervisor in merchandise display.[108]

As Dreier spelled out the situation, it became clear that the customers' preferences were also involved in this battle between small retailer and department store. The interchanges between Eaton's and Adams Flowers demonstrate the potential for consumers to influence wedding customs and styles. When planning a wedding, Dreier asked her customers which florist they wanted to use, then typically she telephoned them and placed the order or arranged a meeting at the church and reception location. Again, it was the mother of the bride who carried the most power and was able to determine which businesses would profit. In three separate examples, Adams Flowers was cut out of the wedding planning when, according to Dreier, the mothers of the bride decided against it. In one instance, the mother chose a different florist who had done her own wedding and her eldest daughter's. Another mother desired single-branch candelabra, while Adams had only five- and seven-branched ones, causing her to choose a florist who was able to provide what she wanted. In a third case, the mother was completely dissatisfied with the floral decoration presented by Adams Flowers for her daughter's reception. Dreier criticized it as well, telling Brockie that "from a display standpoint it [made] me get 'goose pimples' to even think about it, let alone stand there and look at it." In this case the Wedding Bureau did sway the mother, who had originally asked for this florist for her daughter's wedding. The mother was happy with Eaton's, however, and complimented Miss Dreier by telling "anyone within ear shot" that her daughter's complete wedding arrangements were in her hands and that no final decision was to be made unless she approved of them.[109] In an interview with Brockie, the disgruntled Adams made it clear that he felt that Eaton's had an obligation to give him a "certain amount" of business. Brockie coolly countered that the Bureau "cannot control our customers' wishes," and that "when it comes to a big wedding, they are out to get the best effect as cheaply as possible."[110]

Conflicts between Eaton's Wedding Bureau, Adams Flowers, and other small merchants reveal that what was at stake was an older way of doing business. The Wedding Bureau staff prided themselves on their "modern ideas" and faced criticism from florists and caterers who resisted the changes that were being forced on them by this large and powerful enterprise. The bureau had its own idea of what was tasteful and opposed florists that in its mind overused flowers and created confusing arrangements, even "hanging sprays of flowers over paintings in the room—anything to use up flowers," driving up prices for their customers in the process.[111] Similarly, Eaton's Wedding Bureau also opposed caterers' use of bright colors and sought to impose their own view of food presentation and service on local businesses. Like florists, caterers resisted the Bureau's influence on customers and resented their loss of control over menus and styles of food presentation. The Arcadian Court, one such caterer, fought Eaton's, even going to the point of telling Dreier on the telephone that they did "not want to have anything to do with her or her Wedding Bureau customers." Eaton's acknowledged that they made suggestions on menus, but only at the customer's request.[112] On some level then, consumers played a role in the making of this ideal of the tasteful wedding, suggesting that business's power to shape tradition only went so far.

At the same time, by directing customers to particular firms that complied with the store's standards of taste and their cost requirements, the Bureau asserted its modern vision of the ideal white wedding. As a large distributor of wedding trade to small Toronto businesses, Eaton's was in a strong position to force others to change and adopt its vision. In 1939, the Wedding Bureau sought associations with businesses that, in their very modern-sounding words, "would play ball."[113] Eaton's felt the caterer, the Arcadian Court, would finally realize that their refusal of Wedding Bureau business would not hold up when a client was having "a very large affair, between 350 and 500 guests."[114] Resistance was futile for the small merchant, something another caterer, George Coles, must have realized when he attempted to modernize his food services and follow the Wedding Bureau's suggestions. The Bureau proposed making a formal association with Coles, whom they praised for being able to "play ball," and agreed to recommend him to all their clients.[115] Other caterers who were not so adaptable likely suffered as a consequence.

During this transition period when the Wedding Bureau started up services and made its alliances with Toronto businesses, consumers were still able to exert their taste and choose the caterer or florist that suited their needs. This became clear in the case of another Toronto caterer, Unser's. In 1939, the Wedding Bureau gave Unser's a poor evaluation. They criticized their "older help" and their refusal to stop using "deep colouring in their food," which was allegedly "very objectionable" to their patrons as well as them. And yet, Unser's received more Wedding Bureau business than other caterers, suggesting that many consumers liked their brighter styles over the pastel food colors Eaton's found tasteful. Records of their choices exist only for the first two years of the Bureau, and these suggest that business was spread fairly broadly across the city, with larger proportions of customers in fact choosing, or being assigned to, depending on the perspective, the florist Helen Simpson and the objectionable caterer, Unser's.[116]

Numbers aside, the fact that conflicts made it into the archival records suggests that in the late 1930s and early 1940s, this department store posed a threat to the way wedding trade had previously been conducted in Toronto. Small Toronto businesses seeking the wedding trade had something to worry about as Eaton's Bureau grew more visible and gathered more brides. In the three years that followed its first major production, the number of weddings registered at the Wedding Bureau and the amount of sales of merchandise and services rose rapidly, even though it was wartime. In spring of 1940, Eaton's recorded 255 weddings, meaning that it probably provided the bride with some merchandise, likely wedding gowns. That same spring it provided services for thirty-two weddings, meaning that it likely arranged for the ceremony and reception for that number. The following spring, in 1941, the number of weddings nearly doubled to 446 and the number serviced rose to 53. The less popular fall seasons of these two years followed a similar, but more modest, trajectory. In the fall and spring season together for 1940, Eaton's sold a total of $111,000 in merchandise and $34,865 in services, reporting just over 500 weddings and 74 serviced. Near the end of 1941, it recorded $150,347 in merchandise and $20,226 in services for 848 weddings and 96 serviced. These numbers suggest that while consumers were spending less on the weddings that Eaton's serviced, the Bureau itself was catching on as the number of customers using it continued to grow. Operating costs were a fraction of this revenue, likely making the Bureau profitable for the department store. (By the 1980s, in the United States, bridal departments were no longer seen as profitable in the industry and many began shutting down.)[117]

Some American department stores surely had the potential to influence both consumers and other businesses as well. Independent consultants, for example, were encouraged to keep a directory of local businesses, such as florists, and be familiar with their work so they could give recommendations to the bride. At least through 1960, department stores like Marshall Field's suggested photographers, musicians, caterers, as well as a place for the reception to its customers.[118] By recommending the same vendors over and over again—vendors who likely took pictures in a certain way, played particular songs repeatedly, and served the same menus—Marshall Field's, like Eaton's, was in the position to create a pattern of wedding consumption in Chicago. Although the records are lacking, other U.S. stores may have had the same potential in other cities.

* * *

Department stores strove to make themselves synonymous with weddings and thereby became arbiters of tradition. In Philadelphia, for example, advertising campaigns for Wanamaker's new Wedding Bureau in the early 1950s promoted the "Wanamaker Wedding" and worked to make it a "Philadelphia tradition." Similarly, stores like Hudson's advertised their bridal gowns as a "Detroit tradition" (figure 29).[119] It is likely that retailers succeeded. Many customers appreciated the role department stores played and carried fond memories of their experiences with them. Writing about her visits to downtown Pittsburgh department stores in the 1950s, historian Susan Porter Benson remembered that she and her friends saw their future stretched out before them as "a series of department-store shopping trips: for camping outfits, prom dresses, college clothes, wedding accoutrements, home furnishings, baby layettes—the cycle of life underlined as a stately progression from department to department." From a perspective that attributed less agency to consumers, William Leach described department stores as "merchandising virtually every moment in the human life cycle."[120] Wedding-themed window displays, bridal

A DETROIT TRADITION—YOUR BRIDAL GOWN FROM HUDSON'S

Lohengrin-lovely, this bridal gown of French lace and tier upon tier of net... our bridal consultant, Carolyn Chase, adds a Breton bride's veil of accordion pleated tulle and dainty lace flowers. Made especially for us by Lilly Daché.

HUDSON'S
DETROIT

FIGURE 29. Department stores like Hudson's in Detroit highlighted their role in shaping their city's wedding tradition. Store bridal consultants also figured prominently in ads for gowns. *Bride's* (Spring 1948), 83.

fashion shows, bride's cooking classes, and "Bride's Week" events certainly did become a part of life in the postwar period. New services like the gift registry became traditions in and of themselves. And the department-store bridal salon orchestrated the entire event in a way that emphasized modern efficiency. All these new retailing practices were very popular, and through them department stores were able to invent new traditions, naturalize more extravagant levels of consumption, and construct the lucrative formal white wedding ideal that came to dominate American wedding culture in the postwar era.

While the stores themselves played a major role in the rise of consumer rites, individuals—women in particular—also contributed to the formulation of different elements of wedding culture. The next chapter looks at the women who labored in the industry as department-store bridal consultants, independent bridal secretaries, wedding gown manufacturers, and designers, all of whom contributed to the rise of perhaps the most significant invented tradition—the once-worn, ready-made white wedding gown.

CHAPTER FIVE

Bridal Consultants, the Fashion Industry, and the Business of Tradition

Women who worked in the wedding industry made the invention of tradition their business. By the 1970s, wedding entrepreneurs like Priscilla Kidder, the famous founder of Priscilla of Boston who dressed White House brides in the Johnson and Nixon years, were extremely vested in the success of tradition, just as changes in American society appeared to bring it into question. Propped up on Kidder's desk at her non-union wedding gown factory in Boston during this period was a sign that appropriately read: "Don't Elope."[1] In the decades before, however, women involved in the designing, manufacturing, and selling of bridal apparel and their professional organizations had already come to advocate a particularly lucrative version of tradition—the once-worn, formal white wedding dress. Bridal consultants and the wedding apparel industry lobbied against the practice of using heirloom dresses, thus playing a significant role in the invention of the tradition of the once-worn long gown. Not only did a formal wedding gown potentially cost more than informal bridal styles, it also encouraged greater expenditure on related apparel for the wedding party and guests. According to bridal magazines and etiquette books, the bride's dress set the tone for the wedding, determining whether it was informal, semi-formal, or formal. Expenditures on the invitations, gifts, flowers, attendants' dress, photography, and reception were generally higher for a formal wedding. Even at simple traditional affairs, the bridal gown was an important part of the wedding and took up a substantial portion of the planning budget.[2] Wedding entrepreneurs actively sought to promote this potentially lucrative tradition across a broad consumer spectrum and thus played a major role in the commercialization of American wedding culture.

The success of department- and specialty-store consultants, bridal fashion designers, and other experts in spreading this invented tradition was partly the result of the gendered nature of wedding work and its elite class associations. Women who worked in the field claimed an expertise that grew out of their domestic role, as well as out of their membership in commercial beauty culture. In this way, the wedding industry reinforced proscribed roles for women in society and upheld unequal gender relations. At the same time, however, the industry provided social mobility and economic independence for the women who worked in it. Professional organizations shored up women's cultural authority, helping to standardize and naturalize the new consumer rites they promoted. By the postwar period, some were able to build successful modern careers inventing the tradition of the white wedding.

BRIDAL CONSULTING AS A PROFESSION

Before women became wedding experts for department stores or specialty bridal shops, men associated with religious institutions or hotels acted as advisers to the bride. In 1855, for example, a church deacon at Grace Church in New York City acted as a coordinator or "undertaker of weddings." In the 1870s, "masters of ceremonies" appeared. According to one 1882 etiquette writer, the master of ceremonies made "all the necessary arrangements at the church for the reception of the bridal party," and saw to such details as the white ribbon that was stretched across the aisle for special guests.[3] A "Woman of Fashion" in 1909 made a stronger case for the use of this professional, warning that weddings risked being "ridiculous if they were not done in order," and as a result, were usually "put into the hands of some experienced manager" who did all the arranging.[4] By 1925, elite weddings in New York City, especially those held in hotels, might employ the services of a man who was a "new species of specialist, the master of marriages," according to a *Saturday Evening Post* account of the growing number of "purveyors to the bride." Although rigid in matters of etiquette, such as the correct number of attendants and the need for a wedding rehearsal, the 1920s master of marriages or wedding director was able to adjust to new circumstances, and in this way was a thoroughly modern invention. His role was to deliver a tasteful wedding that conformed to the wishes of the family and upheld their class position, but he also had to be flexible and deal with increasingly complex social arrangements, such as interfaith ceremonies. According to the *Saturday Evening Post*, the master of marriages was "an old hand at handling such problems." Hotel ceremonies were understood to be a solution to interfaith weddings that might have been barred from a religious institution. These new experts also dealt with the problems raised by crowded city living. As specialists in hotel ceremonies, they were seen as a "savior of that army of apartment dwellers" whose accommodations were too small to host a reception.[5] In spite of such celebratory accounts in etiquette books and popular periodicals, the male master of ceremonies was not a widespread phenomenon, limited principally to an elite urban clientele.

As weddings became accepted as a consumer rite, men no longer had a "natural" role in the industry. Significantly, criticism of male wedding professionals typically had a gendered component. A male wedding planner challenged traditional associations between femininity and consumption. According to one midwestern clergyman writing on wedding and funeral practices in the mid-1940s, this "new profession" was not "a man's job."[6] Although he gave no reason for his views, the clergyman perhaps assumed his readers would conjure up stereotyped images of the effete homosexual in a feminized occupation, such as the wedding director stereotype that later appeared in *Father of the Bride*. In this 1948 novel, the wedding director was given a foreign-sounding name and a fringe moustache (in an era of clean-shaven faces). Described as "obviously a young man who knew his way about," Mr. Massoula of Buckingham Caterers lorded it over the Banks family, revealing their insecurities and lack of knowledge of the way things were supposed to be done. The appearance of a satirical portrait of a wedding professional at this time is evidence that knowledge of this new occupation had spread through the culture.[7]

While male wedding professionals introduced the idea of the managed wedding, by the early 1930s bridal consulting was attached to retailing and became a job for women. Bridal consulting grew out of department-store and specialty-store salons, as well as small bridal shops, all of which employed female sales-clerks to sell goods to women.[8] Unlike the more elite master of ceremonies that served at society weddings, department-store bridal consultants were in the position to assist a broader public. The occupation began to attract comment in professional advice literature, appearing for the first time in a revised and enlarged 1934 edition of *Careers for Women*, the same year that *Bride's* magazine appeared, and one year after a *Fortune* magazine article heralded the business of brides. Writing for *Careers for Women*, Marion Porter of the Marion Porter Bridal Service in Boston described the occupation first and foremost as a sales position, or a "liaison officer between the bride and merchant or group of merchants."[9] Career advice emphasized the commercial possibilities of the "bridal business," suggesting that the consultant use the bride "as a radiating point for merchandising."[10] Department-store consultants harbored no illusions about their sales role. For example, although Wilma Allen, a famous New York consultant who was the subject of a *Life* magazine feature article in 1952, wept when one wedding was postponed because the groom suddenly took ill (and the dress was returned), she was well aware of the commercial aspect of her job. According to *Life*, her long years in the business gave her "an unusual attitude toward weddings which is evident in her comments: 'She was a lovely bride—$295'; or 'It was a beautiful wedding—$750.' "[11]

Department-store bridal consultants were salesclerks, but they were also experts on tradition and as such helped shape American wedding culture. Bridal salons like Wanamaker's wedding bureau, founded in 1952, fell under the management of the merchandise division, along with other lines, such as girls' wear, teens apparel, costume jewelry, rings, and leather goods.[12] Consultants thus had to sell their line of goods, just as salesclerks did in these other areas of the store. But due to the special nature of wedding consumption, bridal shop employees had a much larger role than other sales employees in the purchasing choices of their clientele. Customers turned to them for information on etiquette and custom, as well as for information on the latest bridal fashions (figure 30). In the business of tradition, they had to reconcile their position as etiquette experts with their commercial need for innovation. According to a 1960 promotional booklet from Chicago's Carson, Pirie Scott, the Joan Adair bridal consultant could "easily adapt any information to any given need as each wedding brings about new and different situations." At the same time, however, "she does not hesitate to refer again and again to Emily Post and Amy Vanderbilt to reconfirm her answers." In case there was any doubt of this, the promotional booklet included a photograph of two well-groomed, middle-aged women looking through Emily Post's book.[13] Their expertise was appreciated by mothers of the bride who wrote to the Joan Adair Bridal Ser-

FIGURE 30. Bridal consultants, like those at Marshall Field's, projected an image of both efficiency and service. Marshall Field's Archives, Chicago.

vice in 1960 commending their ability to put on a "perfect wedding." According to one thankful customer, the bridal consultant "came into a house full of fluttering, excited bridesmaids and found the maid of honor just arrived from the Loop in street dress, one hour before the wedding. The way she quietly and efficiently took over everything amazed me. She dressed my daughter, arranged her for the photographer while still in the house, accompanied her down the front steps (caring for the gown as if it were a small boy) and held the gown for further photographs outside the house, folded her into the limousine and rode with her to the chapel."[14]

Given the sensitive nature of wedding consumption, wedding professionals were perhaps able to exert more influence than ordinary salespeople. According to Eaton's Claire Dreier in the 1940s, some brides came to her Toronto store "full of expectation," open to all they could do for her, while others came in "with their minds made up because of what they have read in an ad, a picture they have seen." In both cases, she argued, advertisers "wield[ed] such power" making it questionable as to which rang the louder, "the church bell or the cash register."[15] Brides were not just victims of advertising, however, as they too wielded power to shape tradition. Potentially, bridal consultants were what historian Regina Blaszczyk called "fashion intermediaries"—those individuals who were in the position to influence production by taking consumer tastes back to the manufacturer or supplier. In letters to bridal gown manufacturers like Priscilla of Boston, bridal salon consultants noted customer approval of particular styles and the services provided.[16]

In addition, customers used wedding professionals to execute their aesthetic vision of things and persuade others to accept it. Such was the case with the 1938 Ellsworth-Holton wedding in Toronto when Mrs. Ellsworth asked J. A. Brockie, the store's merchandise director, to speak to her daughter Elaine at the church and "present the picture," something she had said nothing about to that point "fearing her reaction to what sounds may be a bit striking." Mrs. Ellsworth asked his help as she had trouble "visualizing this wedding," and complained to him that "beyond the dresses and hats, [she] had *no* idea of what the picture is to be." The Wedding Bureau was supposed to be the expert on tradition, yet Mrs. Ellsworth had many ideas about the big picture and also wanted to oversee many of the details as well. Her communications with Brockie reveal the pressure the mother felt as a hostess as the day approached and she found the Bureau's progress lacking. Turning control over the wedding to a professional like this could often cause anxiety as weddings were once-in-a-lifetime events that required substantial financial investment. Mrs. Ellsworth revealed her anxiety when she complained in a letter to Brockie that "Everyone seems to be expecting a knock-out wedding, and everyone seems to be coming—well over 500—I am sure, and I can see only a long line and you . . . I am sending this to your house to-day for on week days I have visions of you only—with your coat tails flying between Eaton's—winter fair and all the little places in between. Poor *you*, but poor me also." The mother's communications reveal that though the Wedding Bureau provided the expertise on tradition, consumers still had the last say on things. Mrs. Ellsworth queried Brockie about the flower arrangements, the candles, the time the church opened, the placing of the furniture in the home, the parking, and the photography, feeling that her "little party [was] still very vague."[17] The Bureau had things well in hand, though, with internal agendas of everyone's duties. Each of Mrs. Ellsworth's requests and questions was answered and assigned to the proper staff member for completion.

The emotional nature of a wedding coupled with the expectation of perfection created great potential for conflict, something that those who worked in the field well understood. According to one 1925 account allegedly quoting a male wedding director, "If you think, as you watch a bridal party marching down the aisle in well-ordered fashion, that they took their places with little ado, you are much mistaken. All may be as calm as a moonlit sea, but there have been storms, and many of them. Really weddings bring out more temperament than grand opera."[18] Career advice literature for women in the 1930s advocated that those interested in the field gain department-store sales experience as it taught one "how to endure graciously many small annoyances," possibly foreshadowing the future conflicts a consultant might have with the bride and her mother.[19] Consultants in the 1950s appeared to expect fainting or hysterical brides and came equipped with wedding kits that included "smelling salts, spirits of ammonia, sedative pills and a complete set of cosmetics."[20] The wedding industry's prescriptions were also sometimes met with resistance, something those in the profession in the 1990s recognized. Brides and their families created problems for wedding coordinators, according to Angela Thompson, by "rejecting expert advice" or simply postponing tasks they were assigned to do.[21]

In spite of potential difficulties with mothers of the bride, among other things, consulting could still be a relatively glamorous career for women. In some cases, women achieved fame and fortune, reaching a wide audience with their consumer message. Independent consultants like Marie Coudert Brennig in the 1930s, and department-store women like Claire Dreier and Wilma Allen in the 1940s and 1950s, had national reputations in the wedding industry, appearing in newspaper articles, general-interest and bridal magazines, as well as in career literature for women. Other lesser-known figures in the field were written up in bridal magazines, giving readers fashion and household advice, tips on etiquette, and suggestions for old and new customs. Many other consultants appeared just as a "name," in that they were listed in bridal-shop and department-store advertisements in bridal magazines. Brides-to-be paging through these articles, advertisements, and listings would have been able to attach a name to the particular salon or shop, and in some cases even know something about the consultant herself.

More than any other store department, in bridal salons, the glamour of the goods—the diamond engagement ring, the white satin dress, the crystal and silver wedding gifts—rubbed off on the consultant, who held the bride's dreams in her well-manicured hands. Historically, department-store work in general was more desirable than domestic work and more prestigious than higher-paying factory work for women. By the 1920s and 1930s, department stores attracted young college women and entered popular culture in film as a potentially glamorous place to work.[22] This was particularly true for the bridal salon, the place where women came to shop for what was seen as the most important dress of their lives. The glamour associated with selling wedding gowns was partly the result of the field's close connections with commercial beauty culture, which had long been a source of opportunity for women. A key task of the consultant was to make her customer look her best on her special day, and someone who understood beauty was best suited to the job. According to career advice, "good looks [were] always useful" in bridal work.[23] "Name brand" wedding experts appeared in regular bridal magazine features along with their glamorous photographs.[24] Youth was also important, as stores preferred to hire consultants who were close in age to the bride. There were exceptions, however, as married or older women were seen as appropriate managers for bridal salons. In the late 1930s, for example, Mary Ellen Fogarty, a twenty-five-year veteran at Macy's Mirror Room, was a "grandmother and yet [had] the smartness and chic and motherliness which endear[ed] her to the often bedazzled bride-to-be."[25]

Glamour aside, bridal work provided economic independence for women who needed to support themselves and sometimes a family. Throughout American history, when women needed to support children after a spouse died or divorced them, they frequently faced economic uncertainty. The wedding industry provided an opportunity for these individuals. After World War II, Marie Enck of Minneapolis found herself divorced and the sole supporter of three children. In her forties, she went to work. One of the growing number of women who entered the labor force in the early postwar period, she worked in the bridal departments at Dayton's and Young-Quinlan's. Bridal consultants like her were saleswomen who helped in the selection and fitting of wedding gowns and the trousseau, but they sometimes provided assistance with the wedding itself. Like Claire Dreier's at Eaton's, Marie Enck's duties included attending wedding rehearsals and going to the bride's home and church to help the wedding party dress. She often stayed until the bride was safely down the aisle. In later years she also did freelance work at weddings held at several Minneapolis-area synagogues. Over the years, bridal work provided her with a successful career and financial stability for her family.[26]

When the profession first developed for women, some consultants used their department-store experience to become businesswomen and launch their own small bridal specialty shops or become independent consultants. According to women's career advice literature, the "best possible training" for bridal consulting was general sales experience in an exclusive department store, where one could "learn the discipline and rhythm of a business day, meet people, learn how to sell."[27] Between 1944 and 1950, female-owned businesses expanded from 650,000 to nearly a million.[28] Bridal shops would have been a part of this business growth.[29] Others moved from department-store salons into independent consulting businesses. Marie Coudert Brennig, who was called the "dean of the bridal shop ladies," developed the bridal business at Altman's department store in 1927, then headed the bridal department at Saks Fifth Avenue before starting her firm, the Wedding Embassy, in 1930. Her Embassy provided "advisory services" only and published a *Wedding Embassy Year Book* filled with discussions of etiquette, different religious customs, the role of attendants, the personal and household trousseaus, gifts, receptions, flowers, music, and the honeymoon. Independent consultants like Brennig operated closely with magazines and vendors who either advertised or sold goods and services to the bride. Each *Year Book* channeled bridal advertisers, such as *Vogue*; *House & Garden*; Elizabeth Arden; Great Western Champagne; the Meyer Davis Orchestras of New York, Philadelphia, and Washington; and the Chateau Frontenac, a hotel in Quebec. Many department and specialty stores advertised in its pages, but the *Year Book* was nationally circulated through one large department store in major cities throughout the country that also received Brennig's "consultation service."[30] In Philadelphia, for example, Strawbridge & Clothier provided a free copy of her "beautifully bound and finely printed book" to every bride-to-be who visited them. The Wedding Embassy provided its advice free as well, earning revenue from the advertisers in its *Year Book*.[31] In these ways, consultants like Brennig contributed to the rise of a national wedding industry and an elaboration of the formal white wedding tradition.

Women such as Marie Coudert Brennig drew on their elite status to gain legitimacy as wedding experts, a tactic common in the field even at the level of department store consulting. Career advice suggested that it was a "business for the woman of culture, refinement, education, and social background whom necessity has forced into the business world." In addition to other qualifications and training, a successful consultant needed to have more than one generation of "education and good-breeding" behind her.[32] The founder of the Wedding Embassy exemplified this ideal. Marie Coudert Brennig had been a New York debutante and was the niece of publisher Condé Nast (who would later acquire *Bride's* magazine and eventually *Modern Bride*) and daughter of Baron Frederic von Brennig, a position that gave her the "social connections" she needed when the Depression pushed her into business. Consultants did not have to be society women like Brennig, but the field did require one to be at least middle class, and, it would have been understood, white. College women fit the bill, and flocked to find out more about this "fascinating business," as at one 1939 talk on bridal consulting at Radcliffe College by Kathleen Blackburn, the prominent head consultant at New York's Lord & Taylor.[33]

These women's elite backgrounds allegedly allowed them to know when they could play with tradition and bend the rules of etiquette. By 1939, Brennig had assisted with more than five thousand weddings, allegedly ranging from "the $50 trousseau of a Texas cow-girl to the famous DuPont-Roosevelt wedding." This vast experience enabled her to note "changes in traditional custom" and be a "judge of their advisability." According to career advice literature, the profession called for "a gentle-woman who knows that good taste often supersedes convention, and can guide instinctively the bewildered girls who seek her help and advice."[34] Using their class position, women like Brennig made a commercialized wedding—replete with advertisements for champagne, hotels, and magazines—a socially acceptable phenomenon.

Class standing empowered these women, legitimizing their role as cultural authorities on taste and matters of etiquette, but conventional gender mores also made them authorities on wedding tradition. Gender empowered women to enter fields tied to "feminine" pursuits. Since the nineteenth century, when

Ellen Demorest argued that women were better suited than men to sell sewing patterns to female consumers, links between gender and consumption have shaped women's wage-earning potential. By the late teens, advertising trade literature and adwomen like Helen Resor of the famed J. Walter Thompson agency heralded this connection. Women "naturally . . . understand women's clothes better than men," noted one 1941 career advice book. And "naturally, a woman customer wants a woman to wait on her—perhaps advise her a little."[35] Purchasing the trousseau and wedding gown, shopping for household goods, opening and acknowledging wedding gifts, and planning the ceremony and reception were recognized as women's work. Though such thinking reinforced gender inequality, it also enabled women to establish a niche in the industry. The gendered nature of this work protected it from competition from men during the Depression, when married women who worked were criticized for allegedly taking jobs away from men.[36] According to *Independent Woman* in 1939, the wedding industry provided "at least one line of work which the genus masculinus [had] not yet taken over." The dual nature of wedding work was especially evident during World War II, when large numbers of white and black women moved into high-paying manufacturing jobs, potentially threatening the social order.[37] Women who worked in the wedding industry were part of this influx, yet their work served to promote the white wedding ideal and played an integral part in the reestablishment of women's traditional domestic role as wife and homemaker.

Bridal work had close connections to this domestic sphere, even though it took place in the world of business. Career advice manuals suggested that it required a woman to "be something of a home decorator," and to have knowledge of "different menus for the wedding reception and be ready with recipes and attractive, original ways of serving in case finances preclude a caterer." Department stores also made the connection between domesticity in marriage and bridal work, suggesting that being married and "home-minded" *was* job experience.[38] Entrepreneurial women who were part of a family business that catered to the bridal market might move into wedding consulting informally. In the 1950s, Peg Davies, who worked in a florist shop in which her husband had invested, served briefly as a wedding consultant. She drew on her association with the florist, as well as her church connections, and used etiquette books she had consulted when planning her own wedding. Her interest in weddings and flowers came out of her love of entertaining. A self-proclaimed "stickler for doing things right," she had always appreciated good silver and china, interests that must have helped her with her bridal work.[39]

Although these entrepreneurs who built businesses out of their domestic skills, their "natural" affinity for beauty culture, or their consumer role did not challenge traditional divisions of labor, the wedding industry did broaden the avenues for women's social and economic mobility. By the early 1950s, bridal consulting was available to a wider range of women, including black women. Into the 1960s, in the South and elsewhere, department stores prevented black women from trying on wedding dresses.[40] Some department-store bridal salons in the 1940s and 1950s had served African American brides, but their bridal consultants were white. In response to these racist practices, and in recognition of the economic potential of the African American bridal business, some black women became independent consultants. By the late 1950s and 1960s, black middle-class women began to be hired as bridal experts by large enterprises like the Curtis Arboretum in Cheltenham Township near Philadelphia.[41] Smaller firms that sold wedding-related goods also hired black women. In 1965, Sylvia Little, an African American woman who in her mid-thirties with six children may have needed to work, found success with Bridal Services, Inc., in Golden Valley, Minnesota. A field trainer for the company, she taught new personnel "the often special techniques in servicing brides, their families and friends." She ranked first among forty "salesmen" after eight months with Bridal Services.[42] Just as department stores began hiring black models for bridal fashion shows, companies likely saw the benefit of hiring successful black women like Sylvia Little as bridal experts if they wanted to capture what came to be known by the 1970s as the "ethnic market."

With urbanization and the expansion of the black middle class, businesses began to take notice of African American consumers out of self-interest. As historian Robert Weems has argued, economic pressure on white-owned businesses by black consumers transformed advertising and corporate practices. Department stores, which were at the heart of consumer rites, typically only hired African Americans to work behind the scenes in stockrooms or in menial positions. Boycotts pressured white-owned stores to hire black salespeople to work in establishments where African Americans shopped. Organized movements also pressured retailers to desegregate their facilities. If stores did not comply, some black entrepreneurs offered alternative services. For example, in 1951 Estanda Thomas Cogdell, who ran a bridal salon in Washington, D.C., consciously sought to counter the continued racist practices of a Washington department store that "served Negroes in its bridal shop and Jim Crowed them in the cafeteria."[43]

Black women's success in the industry attests to the broad cultural acceptance of the commercial white wedding ideal. By the early postwar period, the white wedding was not just for whites. Women of color, for example, read *Bride's* magazine. According to a 1975 study of the bridal market, out of a national sample of 21,000 respondents, 10.7 percent of the magazine's readership was black and 15.3 percent had Hispanic surnames.[44] Popular black-owned magazines like *Ebony* featured African American models in bridal fashion shows and wedding fashion articles. *Ebony* frequently featured articles on society and entertainment industry weddings with all the trimmings. Accounts of black couples marrying on radio shows and winning exotic honeymoon trips furthered the sense that African Americans embraced the cultural ideal of the white wedding promoted by the industry. Though its origins in elite white culture continued to be reflected throughout popular culture, the meaning of the white wedding shifted as, at least in the black media, it provided a celebration of black feminine beauty.[45] And, as we have seen, it also provided an avenue of social mobility and economic independence for some black women entrepreneurs.

PROFESSIONALIZATION OF BRIDAL SERVICES

As soon as the wedding industry began to conceptualize the bridal market and understand that those about to marry constituted a specific market segment, the field began to professionalize. The first signs of professionalization appeared in the 1930s when *Bride's* magazine attempted to organize department-store bridal salons through clinics, as we have seen. In the 1940s, women's magazines also sought to assert their role as wedding experts and influence the shape weddings would take. *Mademoiselle* first published a *Handbook for Bridal Consultants* in 1946, written by the editor of its "Bridal Information, Please" section. The handbook was a reference guide intended to provide a "memory aid" for the immense amount of bridal information that was supposed to be familiar to consultants, but that "no one Consultant can know letter perfect."[46] By the early 1950s, the first professional organizations in the wedding industry appeared, likely in response to growing numbers of department-store and bridal-shop consultants, the jewelry industry's interest in competing with department stores for the bridal market, and the efforts of bridal magazines.

The National Bridal Service (NBS), founded in 1951 by jeweler Jerry Connor, was the first organization that trained bridal consultants. Connor gained his expertise in the bridal market through his work as a jeweler and retailer. In 1926 he designed a system for registering sterling flatware at his jewelry store in Champaign, Illinois. Connor followed this innovation by developing education programs for jewelers, traveling across the United States to promote the jewelry industry's wedding market. He offered manuals and training courses, such as the "Bridegroom's Guide," a "man-to-man letter" designed to involve the groom, for bridal consultants who were on the staff of jewelry stores. At first, the NBS provided training for women who worked at jewelry stores in the areas of gift registry, sterling, china, crystal, invitations, announcements, thank-you notes, and reception napkins. Stores that offered "NBS Coordination" sometimes also loaned items for the reception, such as candelabra, punch bowls and cups, and serving trays, likely in an effort to promote the use of these luxury goods and encourage the purchase of similar items. The organization grew rapidly and by 1954 had members in forty-one states, as well as an international membership in Australia. Eventually, NBS expanded to organize independent wedding planners not associated with a retailer, adding a division called Weddings Beautiful in 1954 to serve their needs. Other organizations followed, such as the American Association of Professional Bridal Consultants (1955), which was the predecessor of the Association of Bridal Consultants (ABC), formed in 1981. In the early 1980s, the Association of Wedding Professionals appeared. Regional associations and additional national organizations were formed in the 1990s.[47] At the end of the twentieth century, following a wedding industry trend at large and employing the resources of the Internet, a host of new specialized organizations appeared. Associations began to cater to professionals serving specific market segments, such as the National Black Bridal Association in 2001.[48]

In the early 1980s, after the decline of the department-store bridal salon, independent bridal consultants became the main source of professional advice to brides. The Association of Bridal Consultants was established for these independent bridal and wedding consultants as well as those employed by companies with wedding-related businesses. As of 1997, ABC had had 1,300 members in 46 states and 12 foreign countries. Its goal was to increase the professionalism and recognition of the field through its certification programs. After joining the organization, members could take a series of five home-study courses on etiquette, sales and marketing, planning and consulting, wedding day receptions, and related services. Completion entitled a member to the Professional Bridal Consultant designation, which was valid for three years, after which a proficiency exam was required. After passing this exam, attending an additional seminar or workshop, and providing references, the member earned an Accredited Bridal Consultant certificate. Three years later, she or he was eligible to become a Master Bridal Consultant.[49] The association also provided a support network for established consultants by offering assistance with advertising, publicity, and referrals.[50] As had *Bride's* and *Modern Bride* in earlier years, it provided industry statistics on the market. According to ABC, in 1991 American couples spent $2.2 billion on bridal consultants.[51]

With the rise of the bridal consulting profession and the wedding industry itself, women found a professional home for traditional pursuits. Historically, when women organized their occupations, forming associations and educational institutions that trained or licensed new members, they were able to move into a previously male-dominated field. Early businesswomen, for example, formed the National Federation of Business and Professional Women's Clubs (BPW) in 1919. Women also organized in ways that gave traditional pursuits legitimacy. The new field of home economics, for example, rationalized women's domestic labor, giving it the cultural authority of a science.[52] The rise of professional organizations in the wedding industry worked in a similar way, establishing professionally trained women as experts in a field that had once been seen as simply the natural province of women. Preparing for a wedding and readying the bride had long been women's work, though the rise of the master of ceremonies and the professional caterer shifted some of this responsibility to men in the late nineteenth and early twentieth centuries. Professional bridal consulting organizations upheld the authority of women like salon-owner Mary Klemmer in Lancaster, Pennsylvania. According to Klemmer, during the 1960s and 1970s she belonged to what she called the "Bridal Institute out of Virginia." This organization was a source of information and would "back her up" if she had any problems. There were limits to the power these professional organizations provided women, however. As in many fields where women dominated the lower ranks and men held leadership positions, such as the food and fashion industries, by the 1980s, men held the top leadership positions in the wedding industry's professional organizations.[53]

The rise of professional bridal consulting organizations had the potential to shut women out of this lucrative field. A side effect of this professionalization was that female family members became unqualified for planning a wedding. Professional organizations of course advocated the services of trained consultants to ensure the desired perfect wedding. As Dion Magee, founder of the National Black Bridal Association, wrote on his company's Web site, your "Aunt Melba, Sister Rita, or Cousin Lucie aren't professional wedding planners. . . . Weddings are more complex these days and require the attention of a professional."[54] Nevertheless, women continued to operate outside of these organizations, consulting from their homes, finding clients among friends and family or their church membership.[55] As organizations like the National Bridal Service began offering certificates that consultants could frame, announcing their expertise and legitimacy with a hierarchy of titles, irregular or informal participants in the field certainly faced increased competition.

The appearance of these organizations was an important benchmark in the rise of a national wedding industry, signaling that a fully conceptualized bridal market was now in place. Shared information on etiquette and customs helped consultants naturalize particular customs and practices on a potentially national scale. Professional organizations centralized and rationalized a consultants' business, providing each with important resources and information on advertising, local vendors, and the composition of the bridal market itself. These organizations allowed new businesses to work more efficiently and rationally, aiding their efforts to capture new customers and establish a need for their expert services. As the number of professional groups grew and membership expanded across the country in the following decades, a national culture of weddings took shape.

THE WEDDING DRESS TRADITION

Much of the bridal consulting profession focused on promoting the tradition of the white wedding dress—the most visible material element of the formal white wedding ideal. Department-store bridal consultants sold the bride her gown, but this process involved much more than just taking her money. Consultants might measure the bride for a proper fit or supervise an employee who performed this task. If the gown was ready-made, the consultant would order the gown in the correct size, then adjust and press it, a task that required some skill, and finally, she might help the bride get into the taxi or car and then out again with her long, and sometimes massive, white gown and veil intact. The dress had become more than just an everyday item of clothing—it was the focal point for the marriage ritual, a key material element that signified "wedding" and "bride." It could take on a life of its own, becoming something that the bridal consultant cared for, in the words of one satisfied mother of the bride, like a "small boy."[56]

The traditional white wedding gown was set off from the everyday by its color, its style, and its once-worn status, but this was not always the case. The color of the twentieth-century wedding gown itself was an invented tradition, meaning that it evolved into something seen as unchanging and timeless, though it was not always so. As historians, costume experts, and even popular writers have acknowledged, dresses for marrying have not always been white. Before 1800, American brides dressed in the prevailing fashion of their day in gowns that differed only in the richness of their fabric.[57] In the early republic, many brides wore brown, gray, or other colors, though white was sometimes worn.[58] Scholars and experts in the wedding industry have pointed to the wedding of Queen Victoria as the beginning of the color white's popularity for bridal dress. Unlike royal brides before her, Queen Victoria chose a pure white satin gown, trimmed with orange blossoms. The plethora of accounts describing her dress and the wedding popularized the color white, and soon etiquette books were helping turn it into tradition. The color white, reflected in the dress, the veil, the bride's shoes, and the wedding cake's icing, became the traditional bridal color during this period.[59] White wedding gowns were first the province of elites, and then they spread to the middle class. As late as the 1930s and 1940s, however, a white gown could not necessarily be assumed, as various working-class and middle-class women then consciously called the white wedding gown "traditional," suggesting that it was not necessarily a natural event, especially during hard times when many chose less costly civil ceremonies or informal church weddings.[60]

In popular culture, the color white became a symbol of the bride's status, carrying a connotation of innocence and sexual purity. Etiquette books, popular writing, and eventually the wedding industry continued to evoke this symbolism throughout the twentieth century. Fashion designers like Jean Charles Worth made similar associations, envisioning their wedding dresses as "the last gown of virginity . . . a sacred gown . . . a gown of ritual." Even though whiteness was linked with this gender ideal in popular culture, however, consumers wearing white did not necessarily understand this association or accept it. In his scholarly study of British wedding cakes, for example, Simon Charsley suggests that until the mid-nineteenth century, there was no connection between "whiteness" and the occasion for which the cake was used: the "symbolic meaning attached to white, white dresses and veils for brides, and white-iced cakes had all been possible long before they were welded into a pattern of compelling coherence in the later nineteenth century." Using bakers' trade literature, cookbooks, and other sources, Charsley demonstrated that cakes became whiter and whiter over time. By the 1880s, new meanings were attached to whiteness, associating it with purity. Charsley's study, moreover, found the majority of first-time brides adopting the white gown "without question or qualification."[61] Wearing white simply could have been the thing to do because it was what others were wearing, and had worn in the past.

In the past, the wedding gown's style and cut simply followed women's fashions. No one style signified "bridal," thus any dress could become a wedding gown. Women's fashions changed enormously each decade from the mid-nineteenth to the early twentieth century, something mirrored in white by fashionable bridal apparel. Dressmakers and consumers looked to Paris and to fashion plates from *La Mode Illustrée* for the latest styles. They also turned to women's magazines like *Godey's* that translated these fashions for American tastes. In the 1860s, wedding gowns followed women's fashionable dress with an immense skirt held out by a crinoline. At the hem, these skirts could measure five yards around and used a tremendous amount of material. Over the decade, they gradually flattened in front, and by the 1870s the material of the skirt was drawn up in the back into a bustle, shifting attention to the rear of the dress. By 1880 the silhouette had changed again and, according to costume curator JoAnne Olian, the bride was "encased in an unyielding hourglass-shaped bodice and pencil-slim skirt that gave way to a revival of the bustle in the mid eighties." In 1890, the bustle deflated in the rear, the hemline flared out, and the puffy leg-of-mutton sleeve, which had been popular in the 1830s, returned. By the end of the decade, the S-shaped corset transformed the silhouette again, creating a monobosom effect in front and a prominent lower half behind. Around 1900, the neck of the wedding gown was covered in a wide band of tulle or lace. Veils covered the hair and framed the face.[62] The length of the wedding dress followed fashion, as did the train and veil. In the 1920s, bridal dress became shorter in front, revealing the ankles and some of the lower leg (figure 31).

The twentieth-century tradition of wearing the wedding gown only on the wedding day was also invented. If a bride wore white in the nineteenth century, it was acceptable and likely that she wore her gown again, minus the orange blossoms and veil if she had one. At the turn of the twentieth century, brides continued to wear their gowns again in the first year of marriage. As late as 1914, a woman might wear her bridal gown at wedding-related events in the months following her marriage.[63] Millinery trade literature advised that wedding gowns be reused, and noted that some were even designed with removable collars so the dress could shift from modesty to décolleté. As late as 1926, *Good Housekeeping* advised the "practical bride" to select fabric and styles that could be adapted for afternoon or evening wear. According to one costume historian, the tradition of the once-worn gown was in place by the late 1930s and early 1940s. Millinery trade writers, however, noted much earlier in the century that the "preservation till time immemorial" of the bridal gown was understood to be one of the "old-time customs," suggesting that the meaning of the wedding gown was in flux. The once-worn gown was on its way to achieving iconic status in 1900 when trade writers called it "the most important dress she will ever have occasion to wear."[64] The decline of the practice of wearing the wedding dress again signaled a new level of conspicuous consumption and a marked shift toward the wedding as a consumer rite.

The commercially produced tradition of the once-worn, formal white bridal gown also replaced the traditional ethnic wedding costume of immigrants to the United States. As historian Elizabeth Pleck has shown, by the third generation, ethnic intermarriage and the rise of multiethnic neighborhoods, changing religious affiliation, and of course the persuasive power of the wedding industry gave rise to the formal wedding.[65] When bridal gowns varied from the

THE SPRING BRIDE, IF SHE'S SMART, WILL EXPLOIT THE RUSSIAN INFLUENCE
IN HER COSTUME AND THOSE OF HER ATTENDANTS

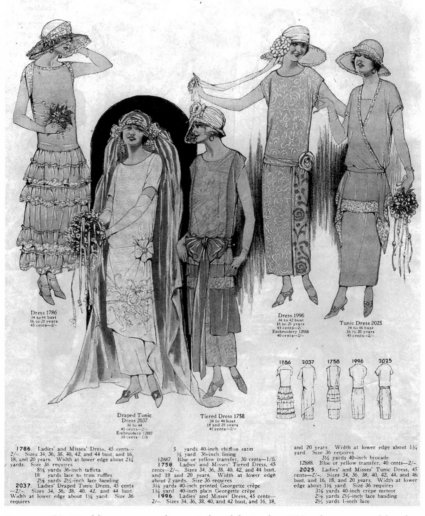

Dress 1786
34 to 44 bust
16 to 20 years
45 cents—2/-

Dress 1996
34 to 42 bust
16 to 20 years
45 cents—2/-
Embroidery 12888
40 cents—2/-

Tunic Dress 2025
34 to 44 bust
16 to 20 years
45 cents—2/-

Draped Tunic
Dress 2037
34 to 44
45 cents—2/-
Embroidery 12887
30 cents—1/6

Tiered Dress 1758
34 to 44 bust
18 and 20 years
45 cents—2/-

1786   2037   1758   1996   2025

1786. Ladies' and Misses' Dress, 45 cents—2/-. Sizes 34, 36, 38, 40, 42, and 44 bust, and 16, 18, and 20 years. Width at lower edge about 2¼ yards. Size 36 requires
8½ yards 36-inch taffeta
18   yards lace to trim ruffles
2½ yards 2½-inch lace banding
2037. Ladies' Draped Tunic Dress, 45 cents —2/-. Sizes 34, 36, 38, 40, 42, and 44 bust. Width at lower edge about 1¾ yard. Size 36 requires

5   yards 40-inch chiffon satin
⅜ yard 36-inch lining
12887. Blue or yellow transfer, 30 cents—1/6.
1758. Ladies' and Misses' Tiered Dress, 45 cents—2/-. Sizes 34, 36, 38, 40, 42, and 44 bust, and 18 and 20 years. Width at lower edge about 2 yards. Size 36 requires
3¼ yards 40-inch printed Georgette crêpe
1½ yard 40-inch plain Georgette crêpe
1996. Ladies' and Misses' Dress, 45 cents—2/-. Sizes 34, 36, 38, 40, and 42 bust, and 16, 18,

and 20 years. Width at lower edge about 1¾ yard. Size 36 requires
3½ yards 40-inch brocade
12888. Blue or yellow transfer, 40 cents—2/-.
2025. Ladies' and Misses' Tunic Dress, 45 cents—2/-. Sizes 34, 36, 38, 40, 42, 44, and 46 bust, and 16, 18, and 20 years. Width at lower edge about 1¾ yard. Size 36 requires
2½ yards 2½-inch lace banding
2½ yards 1-inch lace

FIGURE 31. Wedding gown styles varied widely in the 1920s, demonstrated by this pattern for an embroidered draped tunic wedding dress. *Pictorial Review, The Fashion Book* (Spring 1924), 10. Costume Library, National Museum of American History, Behring Center, Smithsonian Institution, Washington, D.C.

traditional white they were an attempt to differentiate oneself from the dominant American practice in a self-conscious way. The wearing of national dress did not mean a wholesale rejection of American "traditional" practices, however, and couples mixed customs. In 1952, for example, when Olgar Solsvik from the Oregon Jantzen Mills mending department married Gerald Magar, their company newsletter noted that the bride wore her "Norwegian National dress," a dark costume decorated with embroidery. The newsletter included a photograph of the couple at their reception in the bride's home in what was by then a standardized pose of the cutting of the cake. In this context, traditional ethnic wedding dress reflected pride in one's cultural heritage, something that could coexist with an American consumer ethic. Eventually, by the early 1970s, ethnicity became a fashion choice as designers began offering bridal styles incorporating Mexican peasant blouses, Aztec prints, and embroidered, laced "gypsy" bodices.[66]

The white wedding gown tradition also played with the boundary between fashion and "costume." According to Priscilla of Boston designer John Burbidge, wedding gowns were more allied with costume than with fashion. In his view, wedding styles trailed shifts in fashions, staying much the same over the years with their white satin, beads, laces, train, and long sleeves. In a similar vein, fashion historian Anne Hollander argued that the use of a single fabric gave wedding dresses a "ceremonial look," much like that of parade uniforms or religious habits.[67] However, as a product of the fashion industry, wedding apparel underwent seasonal style changes, some that were occasionally quite dramatic.

THE FASHION INDUSTRY AND THE WEDDING DRESS

By the end of the twentieth century, wedding dresses, like those by Priscilla of Boston, were the product of a billion-dollar fashion industry. The context of the production and consumption of these traditional goods had changed dramatically over the course of the twentieth century. Into the early part of the century, middle-class and elite brides typically employed dressmakers for important clothing, such as the wedding dress. Clothes were "made-to-order," "custom-made," or "couture," indicating those "personal, individual, one of a kind garments made to measure, fitted with care, in colors of our own choosing," as defined by costume expert Priscilla Wood.[68] Custom production allowed the consumer more control than was possible with ready-to-wear clothing. Women might visit dry-goods stores to select the fabric, laces, ribbons, and notions themselves, then bring the material to their dressmaker, as did Rochester bride L. H. Winans at the turn of the century.[69] Shopping for fabrics and having the wedding clothes made could be a time-consuming, elaborate process that many middle-class and elite women enjoyed with female friends and family, as reflected in diaries and letters and commemorated in scrapbooks or the bridal books that were in use at least as early as 1889.[70]

The rise of ready-to-wear women's clothing transformed the wedding gown tradition. In general, the shift from custom-made to ready-made clothing took place slowly for women. What were called "slop dressmakers" provided ready-made clothing for women as early as the 1840s, but their fashions offended middle-class notions of good taste. Trade press articles, newspapers, and advertisements pressured women to buy factory-made clothes and heralded ready-to-wear as progress.[71] By the 1880s, inexpensive ready-made dresses or partially ready-made dresses that required fitting were produced and widely offered through mail-order catalogues, along with some wedding fashions. Women's fashions, which closely fitted the upper body, however, resisted mass production techniques for most of the nineteenth century. The poor fit and shoddy quality of early ready-made women's wear meant that it was not widely adopted by the middle class.[72] By the turn of the century, as women's fashions became looser and it was easier to produce sizes that had the potential to fit more women, brides began to purchase ready-made trousseau items from department and specialty stores.

Although ready-to-wear wedding apparel was available, women's trousseaux continued to be a mixture of custom production and ready-made purchases into the 1910s. For example, Mamie McFaddin, a white elite southern bride, detailed her wedding preparations in 1919, noting that she "got a Miss Shea to make my wedding dress. Got 4 dresses at Neiman-Marcus . . . got an evening dress at Sanger's . . . fitted and shopped all day."[73] Less-elite brides and those in urban centers were able to follow the white wedding gown tradition more easily when the gowns appeared in department stores like Strawbridge & Clothier as early as 1911. Wedding dresses were available through mail order by this period as well (figure 32).[74]

The rise of department stores and the women's ready-to-wear industry by

FIGURE 32. Ready-made wedding gowns were widely available by mail order by the teens. These gowns were not necessarily white, and the same styles sometimes doubled as party gowns, suggesting that the once-worn, formal white wedding gown tradition was not yet fully in place. *Standard Mail Order* (Summer 1916), 7. Costume Library, National Museum of American History, Behring Center, Smithsonian Institution, Washington, D.C.

World War I hurt the small female-run shops that provided custom clothing and millinery to brides like L. H. Winans and Mamie McFaddin. Wedding apparel and the clothing associated with the bride's trousseau had long provided business opportunities for dressmakers and milliners.[75] In New York City alone at the end of the nineteenth century there were approximately four hundred dressmakers who employed between two and ten assistants and worked in their own "flats."[76] When a middle-class bride wanted to assemble her trousseau clothing, wedding gown, and veil, unless she had a lot of time and a high level of dressmaking and millinery skill herself, she would have had to hire a dressmaker to visit her home, or visit a dressmaking and millinery establishment to be fitted, and have her clothes and headwear custom made. In the 1880s, Sophie Carlisle, a Pittsburgh milliner, worked in her home making bridal hats, veils, headpieces, and Easter hats. An independent woman by nature, she began her business, Carlisle's of Pittsburgh, after she divorced, though she married once or twice again, allegedly once to the mayor. Expanding to include ready-made bridal fashions by the 1930s, Carlisle's of Pittsburgh prospered and recently claimed to be the oldest bridal business in the United States.[77]

As historian Wendy Gamber has shown, the rise of mass production and mass retailing in the fashion industry transformed a female economy of dressmakers and milliners into a male-dominated field. Dressmakers tried to adapt but could not withstand the power of factories and department stores. Between 1910 and 1920, their numbers declined by half. While the "high-class custom establishment" and the dressmaker who "served the needs of a local, often ethnic or working-class, clientele" remained, custom production and small-scale retailing were clearly on their way out.[78] In the wedding industry, this shift also took place as department-store bridal salons selling ready-to-wear spread across the country beginning in the 1930s and manufacturers of ready-to-wear bridal apparel expanded, all of which allowed the once-worn, white wedding dress tradition to find a broader market.

New wedding gown manufacturers appeared in the late 1910s, and by the 1930s, ready-made gowns appeared more widely. For example, Pandora Frocks, a Seventh Avenue garment district manufacturer, began operation in the late 1910s and was still making wedding gowns in New York in the late 1960s. Manufacturers like the Alfred Angelo Company, founded in 1940 in

Philadelphia by Alfred Angelo Piccione and his wife, Edyth Piccione, established strong reputations in the design of wedding gowns, bridesmaid, mother-of-the-bride, and prom dresses. As marriages boomed, wedding gown companies prospered, and by the mid-1940s more than a dozen big manufacturers produced ready-to-wear bridal apparel.[79]

The rise of this industry was certainly connected to the dispersal of the white wedding gown tradition across a broader socioeconomic spectrum. Less expensive than custom-made clothing, ready-to-wear gowns allowed the ordinary woman to emulate glamorous custom-made fashion. Hollywood movies featuring specially designed custom wedding gowns often found their creations copied and widely disseminated, as was the case with the dress in the 1932 Joan Crawford picture *Letty Lynton*.[80] In *Gone with the Wind*, MGM studio publicists used Scarlett O'Hara's wedding gown to promote the film before its release. Interestingly, while most of the film, as in the novel, focused on the Reconstruction period, designers drew on the brief antebellum scenes, likely finding the moonlight-and-magnolia southern ideal a more suitable tradition for selling "white" wedding gowns and trousseau fashions. Drawing on a minor scene in which Scarlett married Charles Hamilton and Ashley Wilkes married Melanie Hamilton, bridal apparel businesses created merchandising tie-ins. In the film, Scarlett appeared in a white satin wedding gown made of "Flirtation" brand rayon satin, decorated with appliquéd fabric leaves. Capitalizing on the trend, *Bride's* magazine featured a ready-made copy of the gown, which could be purchased for $85 from Best & Company in New York. Interestingly, in Mitchell's novel, Scarlett had worn her mother's wedding dress and veil for her first wedding. The MGM wedding costume was made to look as if it were an heirloom gown and had been passed down from Ellen O'Hara to her daughter Scarlett.[81]

Growth in the industry was rapid in the postwar period. By the end of the 1960s, the United States had about one hundred manufacturers of wedding gowns. In the 1970s, Alfred Angelo, Inc., became one of the largest producers of wedding gowns in the United States.[82] One 1968 industry study, however, reported that about 270,000 brides-to-be avoided the ready-to-wear industry by employing a dressmaker, making their gown themselves, or borrowing their wedding dresses. A little more than half of all first-time brides acquired their gowns ready-made by 1975, while the rest made their gowns, had them custom-made, or wore an heirloom dress.[83]

With the rise of the ready-made wedding gown, a few women achieved fame and fortune in the bridal apparel industry. Beginning in the 1940s, Priscilla Kidder and Phyllis Bianchi became major leaders in the wedding apparel wholesale business. By the late 1970s, Priscilla of Boston and the House of Bianchi were among the top four bridal couturiers in the United States. Priscilla Kidder moved into the wedding business through her training at the New England School of Design and her experience as a buyer for Boston's R. H. White.[84] Kidder, who started her retail operation in the mid-1940s and moved into wholesale in 1949, sold more wedding apparel than other manufacturers in the above-average price range by 1969. Her bridal gowns, known for their lacework, were not in the lowest range, but most sold for about $265 in the late 1960s. Priscilla of Boston was thus responsible for bringing the exclusive white wedding gown to the masses (figure 33).[85]

What Priscilla did with laces, her competitor the House of Bianchi did with beaded work. Phyllis Bianchi started out working at her Italian immigrant mother's dressmaking shop in North Cambridge, Massachusetts. Bianchi also attended a fashion design school in the early 1940s, and after her marriage in 1944, continued working in her mother's retail business. She founded a wholesale business, the House of Bianchi, in 1949, which continued as a successful family business until 1997, when her family was bought out (the business moved and then abruptly closed its doors in 2001).[86]

These manufacturers of wedding gowns cultivated differently gendered images that aided their success. Priscilla of Boston gowns were repeatedly associated with the "designer" herself, though in fact Priscilla Kidder hired designers like John Burbidge and Jim Hjelm to come up with new lines and styles.[87] Kidder worked more as the businesswoman behind the scenes and the symbol of the company in front of the camera. As was often the case with women in the fashion or beauty industries, her stylish and attractive physical appearance was repeatedly commented on as if to correlate it with her competence in the field. She likely owed some of her financial success in bridal design to the image she cultivated as Priscilla of Boston. Although from a working-class background, she became known as "Queen of the Aisle," gaining fame from her association with royal and White House weddings.[88] Kidder had a promi-

1955

FIGURE 33. With their conservative lines and heavy use of lace, Priscilla of Boston gowns typified the once-worn, formal white wedding dress tradition at mid-century. Priscilla of Boston Collection, Archives Center, National Museum of American History, Behring Center, Smithsonian Institution, Washington, D.C.

nent Newbury Street retail store in Boston, which further linked her name
with luxury, while the House of Bianchi did not sell gowns retail. Unlike
Priscilla Kidder, Phyllis Bianchi took a backstage role in her company's publicity, citing her desire to have more time to spend with her children. Bianchi's
image was more domestic and family oriented than Kidder's, though both had
children. At the House of Bianchi factory, as one publicity article mentioned,
the founder's elderly Italian mother even sewed at her side.[89] As glamour
girl or family-oriented mother, both entrepreneurs drew on different gender
"traditions" to promote their businesses.

Wedding gown manufacturers and other businesses were vested in the formal white wedding and fought to establish industry standards that would keep
consumption levels high. Formal weddings required long white gowns. In
times of war, obtaining such luxury items could be difficult. Local associations
of bridal shops faced shortages of white wedding gowns during World War
II. Lobbying clergymen to gather support for a campaign against wartime
restrictions, one local association wrote that "the disappearance of the white
ceremonial Wedding Gown would detract from the dignity of religious wedding services and do injury to those who set great importance on its enduring
associations in their memories."[90] The bridal apparel industry fought the ex-
emptions placed on manufacturers during the war, arguing that long white
gowns were vital for morale. They were successful and received an exemption
from the War Production Board restrictions. Bridal gowns, like wedding rings,
were seen as part of the war effort—what the country was fighting for.[91] In
war bond ads, the fashion industry called for consumers to make sacrifices in
other areas: to "do without an evening gown today" so that they might have
"a wedding dress tomorrow" (figure 34). Any dress would not do, however.
After the war, the Bridal and Bridesmaids Apparel Association (BBAA), a
professional organization founded in the 1950s, tried to counter the short-dress
trend. Popular ballerina-length dresses, they argued, were appropriate only for
the "second or third wedding," not a formal first wedding—the type of celebration that entailed the greatest level of consumption.[92]

Those about to marry were apparently very receptive to the industry's
emphasis on this invented tradition. Bridal salons reported a great demand for
long white dresses and weddings with all the trimmings. According to an
Eaton's study of American wedding bureaus in the New York area and Chi-

Will you do without an evening gown today—

FOR A WEDDING DRESS TOMORROW?

THAT'S a gorgeous evening gown you're thinking of buying. It's so gay and glamorous — and what a flattering neckline! It's YOU.

But who's going to see you wear it—if America loses the war?

Not that soldier you kissed good-bye in a mist of tears! He won't see it until it's years out of style if America should lose the war.

Remember! Germany knocked out France in June, 1940. And today millions of Frenchmen are *still* Nazi prisoners.

That's the pattern—of defeat.

So, if you want that soldier of yours home before too many springtimes have passed—if you want that big church wedding *soon*—you won't buy that evening gown!

You'll buy U. S. War Bonds instead and make sure we win the war!

Just what are U.S. War Bonds? They're the incendiaries that will rain on Tokyo and Berlin— the landing barges that will win back the Philippines!

They're your anchor to windward—your nest-egg for the future.

They're your white satin wedding dress, your coronet of lace, that little house you dream of.

And they're the safest, soundest investment in all the history of mankind!

Here's what War Bonds do for you!

1 They are the safest place in all the world for your savings.

2 They are a written promise from the United States of America to pay you back every penny you put in.

3 They pay you back $4 for every $3 you put in, at the end of ten years ... this is interest at the rate of 2.9 per cent.

4 You may turn them in and get your cash back at any time

FIGURE 34. The "big church wedding" and the "white satin wedding dress" were the reward for wartime sacrifices and patriotism. War bond ads depicted them as part of the American dream. Ad*Access On-Line Project—Ad # W0162, John W. Hartman Center for Sales, Advertising & Marketing History, Duke University Rare Book, Manuscript, and Special Collections Library.

cago, business had increased 100 percent during 1941, "with the formal business topping the list" as 82 percent of brides wanted a traditional wedding. Similarly, in 1942, a survey by *Bride's* magazine indicated that 80 percent of women about to marry wanted a formal wedding.[93] Bridal consultants and salons advertised bridal services for the furlough wedding, and claimed to be able to do a "complete job on 6-hour notice." By following a "prearranged routine," for example, Davison-Paxon, an Atlanta store, was able to deliver a complete wedding package, including flowers, music, and ushers. Wedding gowns themselves became patriotic symbols. With its connection to romance, marriage, and the family, the white wedding gown, like the diamond engagement ring, was a part of the American dream, something the soldiers overseas were fighting for.[94]

As we have seen, fashion designers and manufacturers had a vested interest in one particular version of the white wedding gown tradition—the long formal dress purchased new for one occasion only. By the time wedding dresses were being widely ready-made, they were not being reused. In an interesting shift in symbolic meaning, when the well-crafted original gown became the machine-made, standardized dress, it turned into something to immortalize and preserve for posterity as a unique, once-worn object. The once-worn gown fit the consumer ethos of the wedding industry. Businesses were able to promote this consumerist tradition without seeming crass or commercially minded because they clothed the practice in sentiment and introduced a new discourse on the practice of heirloom gowns. By the 1930s, interest in wearing a dress that belonged to one's mother or grandmother may have declined. According to one saleswoman at a New Haven bridal shop during this period—someone who would have been vested in selling new wedding finery—very few brides wore heirloom gowns.[95]

Criticism of heirlooms came from many different camps—from women's magazines, from etiquette writers, and from the fashion industry itself. The practice of using heirloom gowns had to be eliminated, even as it was promoted in the future in a vague sort of way. Right after the war, a professional bridal consultant handbook published by *Mademoiselle* tactfully handled the implicit conflict raised when commercial interests were allied with tradition. It argued that "wearing an heirloom wedding gown simply because it is old or simply because it has sentimental value does not guarantee a beautiful wedding." Implicitly linking new gowns with democracy and the "American Way of Life," the handbook argued that it was the bride's "inalienable right" to look her best on her wedding day. Amy Vanderbilt's 1952 *Complete Book of Etiquette* equivocated on the matter, arguing that even though it was "traditional" in some families for the bride to wear a "family gown," no family pressure was to be exerted. She should be free to choose a "modern gown" if she wanted.[96] Similarly, the fashion industry was against heirlooms because they understood that the styles had to change and people had to continue to buy new gowns if they were to survive. Fashion designers like Priscilla Kidder spoke on the issue repeatedly, advocating instead their own designs that incorporated the past, but in a new way. In the 1960s, for example, brides allegedly did not want their mother's dress, but they did admire their grandmother's, so designers responded with romantic Gibson Girl styles.[97]

While the modern bride was not supposed to wear an inherited or borrowed gown, according to *Bride's* magazine editor Agnes Foster Wright in 1936, she could "start her own heirloom." Businesses eventually realized that there was money in preserving these dresses for the future. By the 1950s, companies like Heirloom Laboratories in New Haven advertised their "scientific" services in *Modern Bride* (figure 35).[98] Heirlooming became an additional cost in the wedding budget. This new commercial service itself became a tradition, one that successfully transcended the inherent contradiction between modernity and tradition. Creating a kind of future nostalgia, the heirlooming process allowed a bride to look fondly to some day ahead when her daughter would wear her well-preserved gown. The bride upheld tradition by paying to preserve her new dress to be worn by a future bride, a future that the industry hoped would never materialize as the cycle of consumption repeated itself.

Brides sometimes interfered with this cycle of consumption, however, much to the chagrin of the fashion industry. Wedding gown manufacturers were particularly perplexed by new trends toward informality during the late 1960s and 1970s. During this period, the wedding industry fought against what journalist Marcia Seligson called the "New Wedding." A self-consciously anti-materialist celebration, the New Wedding took place outdoors or in a noncommercial space, with handmade or hand-me-down wedding clothes. In response to the less-expensive informal wedding, the industry lobbied for formal weddings, citing them as a solution for rising divorce rates in the postwar period.

FIGURE 35. Businesses like Heirloom Laboratories emerged at mid-century to preserve the once-worn wedding dress for the future, even though the wedding industry discouraged the use of heirloom gowns. *Modern Bride* (Spring 1955), 37. Forsyth Library, Fort Hays State University, Hays, Kansas.

Priscilla Kidder, for example, argued that big weddings gave marriage greater "stature and meaning." She stated for the record that "If the bride gets married in a short dress in a justice of the peace's office, it seems too quick and easy and not too important. But if the bride and her family go to a lot of trouble arranging a big wedding—and her father has paid a lot of money for it—she'll think twice about running home to Mother after the first tiff." In a 1970 interview, Kidder argued in favor of tradition, noting that "there isn't anything you can think of that doesn't benefit from weddings. . . . Marriage is the most important part of our culture."[99]

Popular culture in the early 1970s captured the elements of the countercultural New Wedding that gave the wedding industry reason to be concerned. In apartment weddings, television brides like Gloria Stivic (Sally Struthers), in a 1972 episode of *All in the Family*, wore her grandmother's wedding gown. In a 1974 episode of *Rhoda*, Rhoda Morgenstern (Valerie Harper) ended up taking the New York subway to her ceremony, wearing her wedding dress. Business concerns over ratings and advertisers limited television's potential for social experimentation, as when the network resisted actress Valerie Harper's wish to have Rhoda and her boyfriend, Joe Gerard (David Groh), just live together, rather than ending her cutting-edge status as an independent, single television character with a marriage. Wedding entrepreneurs may have lamented the turn away from tradition, but in fact they also capitalized on countercultural trends, seeking to give their products a youthful, hip image. Designers like Priscilla of Boston made forays into cutting-edge contemporary fashions with their gowns, as with the perhaps unfortunate introduction of the trapeze dress in the late 1960s (figure 36). She also introduced space-age wedding dresses and mini-dresses, fashions that were not meant to be worn by a mass audience, but nevertheless gave the business a modern image.[100]

The New Wedding never really spread beyond the middle-class counterculture movement and the intellectual classes in the 1970s. Perhaps in part because of the growing success of middle-class suburban conservatism, as well as the concerted efforts of the wedding industry, white wedding gowns continued to find a ready market among most people throughout the 1960s and 1970s.[101] In the late 1960s, a time when the counterculture supposedly made inroads into wedding consumption, those having formal white weddings had an average of four attendants, each of which averaged $40 for dresses and $6 for headgear.

FIGURE 36. Wedding gowns followed broader shifts in women's fashions, as represented by Priscilla of Boston's adoption of the radical lines of the trapeze dress in 1967. Priscilla of Boston Collection, Archives Center, National Museum of American History, Behring Center, Smithsonian Institution, Washington, D.C.

According to the industry, in 1968, the majority of one and a half million first marriages were celebrated with "the traditional long white or ivory dress with train and veil, the costume they, or their mothers, had for years dreamed of wearing." In spite of the rhetoric about the end of tradition, manufacturers of bridal apparel saw 15 percent to 20 percent increases in 1969 over the level of 1968, which itself was a peak year for them. In one 1979 study, 98 percent of readers of *Bride's* magazine had a formal wedding, something to be expected among this self-selected group. According to Barbara Tober in 1980, editor of *Bride's*, "practically everyone in the United States married formally."[102]

White weddings even spread to second marriages by the 1980s. Women marrying for the second time, however, were less likely to wear a formal wedding gown. In 1983, "only 21.2 percent of all second-time brides wore formal gowns," according to the National Bridal Service. This statistic can be read as an indicator of significant compliance with the industry's consumer ethic. Such formal gowns might not have been white, but they suggest an elaborate second marriage celebration, a wedding with all the trimmings instead of the "quiet affair" prescribed by etiquette. Etiquette prescriptions warned against wearing white for second marriages. But the wedding industry, in spite of its emphasis on tradition and the value of marriage, sought repeat business. Betsy Kidder, Priscilla's daughter, stated that "the more often a woman gets married, the better it is for business." Priscilla of Boston's "Contemporary-Romantic" line in the 1980s was even promoted to brides who, according to designer John Burbidge, were "marrying for the first to third time in a semi-formal atmosphere."[103] In the context of consumer capitalism, tradition and social mores had to bend to the profit motive.

While sewing one's gown, having it custom made, or buying it ready-made were consumer scenarios discussed frequently in trade literature and bridal magazines, bridal apparel rental services were never a part of the discourse. With the rise of the wedding industry, the once-worn gown came to have a special, ritual significance. Worn only for a single day by one person, it preserved the individuality of the bride. Renting a gown that had likely been worn many times before undercut this ritual meaning. In addition, a once-worn gown was a form of conspicuous consumption. Renting challenged this consumer idea even as it allowed for a wider swath of brides to embody it. Rented wedding gowns existed outside the middle- and upper-middle-class world of *Bride's* magazine and Emily Post, and would have been anathema to businesswomen like Priscilla Kidder who had climbed through the ranks as well.

Even though the established wedding industry did not recognize such inexpensive (environmental, even) alternatives, some women turned to rental businesses in order to keep with their idea of tradition. In the 1930s, Jewish brides in New Haven often rented wedding gowns and borrowed veils from friends who had been married. Similarly, during the 1950s in New York's Lower East

Side, wedding dresses were available for rent for $25 in an atmosphere very unlike department-store bridal salons or luxurious specialty shops. Such shops on the Lower East Side bought their gowns wholesale on Orchard Street and Grant Street, an area known as the wedding dress district. Every season, they would usually buy about five dresses in only a couple of sizes. The dress would be fitted to each bride when needed. The bride would pick up the dress on Friday, get married, and return the dress on Monday. According to Priscilla Wood, whose father was a photographer in the Puerto Rican community in New York during this period, women would have their photograph taken in their rented gowns. She would help her father by assisting in the fitting of the dresses.[104]

Men also rented wedding clothes, but in a different ideological context. Like many other things, there existed a double standard—it was acceptable for a groom to rent, but not the bride. It was common, expected really, that working-class men would hire their "morning suit" for the day, as textile worker Henry Boucher did in Rhode Island in 1922. Working-class wedding guests also met such occasions with hired "tails." By the 1930s, according to the Waldorf's Men's Shop, almost all New Haven grooms marrying formally attired brides rented their suits. Most did it "just to please and satisfy the bride." Grooms rented in order to avoid spending money on something they might "never use again."[105] Men likely did not romanticize their wedding clothing and adopted a practical, thrifty attitude instead. Interestingly, the rental business hindered drastic yearly fashion changes as they required stores to purchase new stock to replace outdated men's styles. Unlike rental businesses for women, which never became widespread, formal wear rental became the norm for men. Wedding rentals accounted for about 40 percent of the yearly total of formal wear for men. Rental businesses standardized men's wedding apparel for the most part. Not only would groom after groom literally appear in the same suit, the range of fashions was highly limited compared to bridal apparel. According to one 1976 study, most rental establishments handled one or two brand names and a small number of colors and styles. Unlike the growing number of women's wedding apparel manufacturers during the period, three major distributors dominated the men's industry—After Six, Lord West, and Palm Beach. In 1979, the groom's apparel rental business grossed $400 million.[106]

By the postwar era, women entrepreneurs in the bridal consulting and fashion industries transformed the ready-made, once-worn, formal, white, "heirloomed" wedding gown into a cultural icon. Their efforts were so successful because networks of manufacturers, buying associations, mass and specialty retailers, designers, and advertising magazines were fully in place by this period. Consumers had little choice in the face of such organization. Yet some variations remained. Some women rented their gowns or made their own. And manufacturers and retailers continued to be concerned with the heirloom threat. Some brides in the 1970s did marry outside of the white box, but by the 1980s, the big wedding was back, according to the industry, if it had ever left at all. Women's acceptance of the white wedding ideal, even as their own lives changed dramatically, suggests the power of the wedding industry to flex with changing social mores. By couching their search for new and ever-expanding markets in the rhetoric of traditional modernity, wedding professionals were able to convince the modern woman of the suitability of a formal white wedding gown.

Dressed in white and off to become Mrs. Consumer, the postwar wedding industry's ideal bride continued to express her individuality and modernity. The ceremony and reception venues she chose, however, were historically connected to ethnic or class traditions and came into conflict with the commercial goal of the wedding industry, as the following chapter explores.

CHAPTER SIX

Catering to the Bride: The Rise of Commercial Wedding Venues

Beginning in the late nineteenth century, a host of businesses turned their attention to the reception—the celebration after the marriage ceremony that eventually became synonymous with the lavish white wedding. Professional caterers, commercial hotels, restaurants, and halls began to provide goods and services that were once the product of family labor. More and more brides began to choose the large over small, the public over private, the professionally done over homemade. Weddings became more commercial in the sense that a catered affair at home, in a hotel or club, or even in a hired hall was more costly and connected to the market in ways that a family affair was not. By the mid-twentieth century, diverse businesses participated in the wedding industry, catering to a wide range of celebrations. Professional caterers and hotels introduced new traditions and elaborated upon older customs. Wedding palaces and halls offered package-deal receptions. And new commercial wedding chapels promised a romantic, out-of-the ordinary alternative to the bureaucratic civil ceremony conducted in a county clerk's office. Increasingly supported by professional organizations and etiquette experts, caterers and commercial venues for both the ceremony and reception invented new standards of consumption and contributed to the rise of a multibillion-dollar wedding industry by the end of the century. This new standard of consumption itself became tradition, something that was difficult to do without and still have a "proper" wedding.

Unlike much of the rest of wedding industry that was soon dominated by chains and large corporations, however, these businesses remained remarkably adaptive to a wide range of markets and corresponding needs and tastes. The diverse demand for wedding ceremony and reception venues, moreover,

opened the door for a host of entrepreneurs, including African Americans
and women. Like the entrepreneurs and firms themselves, wedding practice
varied widely throughout the nascent period of the industry. Many ceremony-
reception configurations existed across the country among different groups.

By the mid-twentieth century, however, most engaged couples encountered
the formal white wedding tradition. With the increasing prosperity of the
postwar period, the majority of Americans were able to incorporate at least
some of its elements. Most married in a double-ring ceremony, most brides
wore white, and most had some sort of wedding reception. This is not to say
that brides and grooms consumed passively; instead, one can imagine couples
and their families employing different "tactics," picking and choosing their
ceremony and reception location according to intersecting desires and less-
desirable practical realities.[1] Even as couples encountered a wedding ideal constructed by the industry to justify its expanding role in the celebration of
marriage, their wedding ceremonies and receptions continued to reflect ethnic
and class preferences, as well as regional differences. From elopements, civil
ceremonies, and private affairs, which minimized wedding consumption, to
church weddings and home receptions that built on middle-class notions of
restraint and decorum, to the communal ritual of the public hall wedding, to
the more lavish celebrations in wedding palaces and luxury hotels, "tradition"
appeared in many forms.

CHANGING PRACTICES

As we have seen, before the rise of the catered affair in the late nineteenth
century, American wedding practice defied generalization. Even as the wedding industry took shape from the 1920s through the 1950s, venues for the
marriage celebration varied widely across the United States. Consumer rites
took hold more slowly in particular regions of the country. In the rural Mid-
west, for example, weddings were simple family affairs through the 1920s. In
the urban Midwest, couples living in cities began taking advantage of the wide
range of commercial venues available to them, increasingly choosing halls,
clubs, and restaurants after the 1920s. Small-town couples went from having
intimate parties in private homes to hosting larger affairs in church buildings
by the 1950s. Although a reception in a church hall was still a modest event, it

marked a shift toward urban consumer rites. Marrying in a public space, even a church venue, often signaled a more elaborate wedding involving printed invitations; numerous gifts; a double-ring ceremony; formal dress; flower decorations; a runner for the church; a prayer book; arm bouquets, corsages, and boutonnieres; and pre-printed wedding souvenirs for guests.[2]

Northeastern immigrant and working-class couples also changed, but in ways difficult to quantify. Several studies based on regional newspaper announcements have been written, but these favored white, native-born Protestant weddings. In fact, as Ruby Jo Reeves discovered in her 1938 study of northeastern marriages, society editors openly admitted that they used race, ethnicity, and class in their selection of wedding and engagement announcements. One society editor eliminated all African American weddings, and selectively screened Italian weddings along class lines, omitting ones that were, in her words, too "woppish."[3] Condescending evaluations of the tastefulness of these weddings were part of a long American tradition of nativism. Wedding announcements typically published in company newsletters, however, provide a window into working-class wedding culture. My study of these sources documents the marriage practices of working-class and lower-middle-class African American, Jewish, Irish, and southern and eastern European employees who worked in factories, department stores, and offices. Though it is clear that many of these men and women had small, inexpensive affairs or civil ceremonies, study of company newsletters reveals that many of these workers had big celebrations. Announcements discussed the bride's dress, detailed the ceremony and reception location, listed the wedding attendants, and described the floral decorations and wedding cake. Often, the newsletter included photographs of the bride and groom at their wedding. According to these rich sources, white working-class and lower-middle-class couples flocked to the many public halls in their cities to celebrate their unions. In the 1940s, at the Maidenform company in New York and New Jersey, for example, the majority of those who reported their weddings to the *Maiden Forum* had a church wedding, and 66 percent followed with a reception in a hired hall. Among these workers, who were largely of Italian and eastern European Jewish descent, the hall remained the preferred location into the 1950s, but it fell a little in popularity as these workers perhaps took advantage of increased prosperity to celebrate in clubs, hotels, and church-related buildings.[4]

During the first half of the twentieth century, taste, religious background, and perhaps restricted finances led to the continued popularity of the home reception, and in some cases, even the home ceremony. At the Jantzen mills in cities in Oregon and Washington, most textile workers in the 1930s had church ceremonies, but 37 percent still married at home. Only a small number reported receptions in their newsletter, though, but the majority of these noted a reception at home. These working-class home weddings were not necessarily simple private affairs. When Jantzen worker Ella Sturm and Walter Israel married in 1932, for example, they had a "beautiful home wedding" attended by sixty-nine relatives. Similarly, when elevator operator Isaac Lewis from Provident Insurance in Philadelphia was married at the bride's home in 1936, one hundred guests attended the ceremony. At their wedding they received so many beautiful gifts that the groom was "sure the depression [was] over."[5] As late as the 1950s, even in the face of cultural pressure from the wedding industry and its formal white wedding ideal, such variations in wedding location persisted. Couples like Jantzen employees Elvie Paivanen and Everett Savo continued to marry in private homes with only relatives and close friends attending. Contrary to etiquette, their wedding was held in the groom's parents' home, not the bride's. Labeled a "family affair" in the company newsletter announcement, the Paivanen-Savo wedding did not lack in significance in the minds of those who attended. All agreed that "the wedding was beautiful and the bride lovely" against a "setting of soft music, flowers, and candle light."[6]

In general, however, by the late 1940s' marriage boom most couples chose to "middle-aisle" it, something that made the wedding industry happy.[7] As opposed to the civil ceremony or simple home wedding, the etiquette-bound formal wedding performed in a religious setting was the bread and butter of the wedding industry. Religious ceremonies, when public, were generally elaborate and formal, involving a greater number of guests, attendants, and gifts, all of which created business for those in the wedding trade. Not surprisingly, with the rise of the wedding industry, prescriptive literature began actively discouraging the home ceremony. According to *Vogue*'s etiquette expert, a home wedding "lacked the spiritual significance and beauty of a church ceremony." Other etiquette writers advocated church weddings, arguing that they were "less trouble" than a home ceremony. Less trouble, however, did not mean less expensive.[8] A long-held custom of paying a fee or making a gift of money to the minister and organist made the church service a more expensive wedding than one performed in the bride's home. By 1947, according to one industry expert, a church wedding cost $75 to $100 more than an identical home wedding because of church fees. Even when cost was not an issue, some brides continued to follow the tradition of the home wedding. Elite Protestant brides sometimes chose to marry in their family's spacious home. These society events appeared in women's magazines and bridal publications—their lavishness and glamour acting as a model for consumption, however, and not a recommendation for a simple home wedding. Like royal, presidential, or Hollywood weddings, these accounts of society affairs provided a dream ideal that could be emulated but never fully lived by ordinary brides.[9]

Elite weddings may have provided a model of consumption, but in fact, etiquette writers, bridal consultants, women's magazines, and even general-interest publications typically outlined a wide range of reception budgets. In the 1930s, *Fortune's* article on the Depression-proof wedding industry presented a costly minimum budget of $5,000 that few could afford (a society wedding "with all the trimmings" was estimated to cost $15,000 in 1929). Etiquette books also outlined an elaborate ideal for the formal white wedding reception that included "music, decorations, food, champagne, other beverages, wedding cakes, [and] boxes of wedding cake," among other things.[10] Other suggestions exacted a lesser penalty on the father of the bride. Jeanne Wright's 1938 *Wedding Book* noted that reception refreshments should be 5 percent of the total budget, which as a whole varied according to one's means. According to Wright's budgets for different types of weddings, the bride's family could expect to spend more on the bridal gown, personal trousseau, and household trousseau than on the reception. This standard became more elaborate after World War II. According to a 1947 article in *Ebony*, the cost of the average African American wedding reception was $300, a high estimation for just the reception alone. Refreshment expenses were still low in relation to other costs during this period. When Susan Strange's upper-middle-class parents married in the 1950s, for example, they had a large formal white wedding, yet food and drink costs took up a small portion of their wedding budget by today's standards.[11] For those on a more limited budget, experts advocated cutting back on professional services and substituting family labor in order to have the required cake, refreshments, flowers, and white wedding gown. Informal civil ceremonies were another way to cut costs, though wedding experts viewed a justice-of-the-peace wedding as a last resort and something to be avoided if possible. The wedding industry ideal that took shape by the postwar period, however, promoted one particular tradition—the lavish reception catered by a professional in a commercial venue. Wedding professionals increasingly came up with ways for working-class and middle-class couples to splurge on their big day and uphold the new "tradition" of the dream wedding.

CATERERS

Before the rise of the catering industry, wedding receptions were typically family affairs produced by women's labor. Early American advice books and literature on entertaining were not focused on weddings and merely placed these simple events in the context of a wide range of social occasions. Many mothers of the bride and their cooks must have turned to Lydia Maria Child's famous handbook, *The American Frugal Housewife*, for its recipe for "good common wedding cake," a rich concoction that included four pounds of currants, two pounds of raisins, twenty-four eggs, and half a pint of brandy.[12] Menu books also suggested possible courses for different types of wedding receptions or wedding-related events like the bridal luncheon. Early twentieth-century women's magazines contained recipes and menus for wedding breakfasts or receptions, suggesting that the family-produced wedding still enjoyed favor.

By the early 1920s, however, a bride's mother turning to etiquette books for advice on how to put on a reception learned that the cake was supposed to be provided by a professional caterer, and not by her own kitchen. The catered reception began appearing regularly in etiquette books during this period, a sign that broader segments of the population now employed caterers (and hence were in need of instruction about what they did). Such prescriptions legitimized the replacement of family labor with commercial services. The widely read Emily Post, for example, included caterers in her outline of professional services for a formal wedding. Other etiquette experts began promoting "the art of a skilled caterer" as a necessary part of a proper wedding. Such professionals were needed to fill the labor gap created by the decline of household servants in middle-class households. Etiquette experts, for example, argued that caterers "should be hired if possible" in order "to do away with unnecessary labor and responsibility."[13] Moreover, as the ideal wedding reception became more elaborate and formal, these events began to require extensive preparation and work, something that female relatives or households without servants could no longer adequately provide.

Caterers had begun advertising their services specifically to those about to marry as early as the 1860s, making them one of the first businesses to target the bridal market. They benefited from the busy social calendar of elites, but the weddings of a broad segment of the population likely provided a steady stream of income. Some offered to host parties in their own commercial venue, as did the New York City confectioner W. H. Barmore. Also a "Ladies & Gents' Restaurant," Barmore furnished weddings, dinner parties, and evening entertainments (figure 37). Such venues allowed families who did not have a large home or who preferred a public space to host elaborate affairs. Early caterers also provided off-site entertainments in private homes. In the 1880s, S & J Davis in Newark, New Jersey, offered multi-course meals, a range of wedding cakes made to order, china, glass, silverware, awnings, and "floor crash," as well as "waiters and cooks sent out at short notice." Even in small southern cities in the 1880s, caterers advertised their commercial services for wedding parties.[14] These offers to rent goods suggest that these businesses served those who did not own the requisite silver and china or have the staff needed to put on large celebrations. The wealthy, however, also hired professionals to ensure a perfect affair. Even they were not always able to host a large party or ball on their own, as Edith Wharton's *Age of Innocence* depicted. In this novel, the fabulously nouveau riche Beauforts "had been among the first people in New York to own their own red velvet carpet and have it rolled down the steps by their footmen, under their own awning, instead of hiring it with the supper and the ball-room chairs." Nevertheless, professional services like caterers did not appear in etiquette manuals until the 1910s, when weddings were on their way to becoming consumer rites for a broader range of marrying couples.[15]

Catering businesses had always served a variety of ethnic groups, tailoring their goods and services to fit different cultural needs. For example, S & J Davis served the German-speaking community in Newark, New Jersey, by

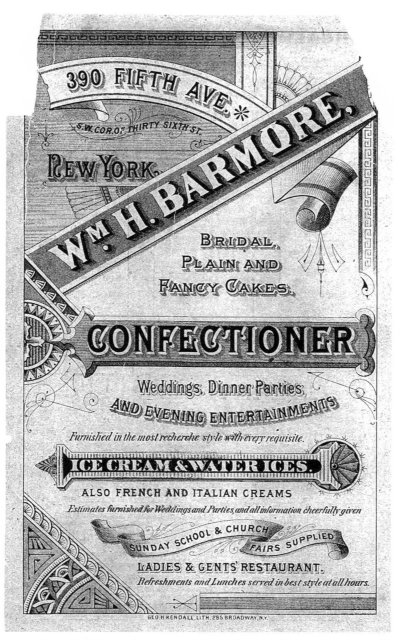

FIGURE 37. In the nineteenth century, caterers and confectioners sought the wedding trade, advertising their reception services and wedding cakes. Warshaw Collection of Business Americana—Confectionery, Archives Center, National Museum of American History, Behring Center, Smithsonian Institution, Washington, D.C.

touting a "fine line of German Mottoes and Favors."[16] Businesses or organizations serving particular ethnic communities sometimes followed the dominant white wedding ideal to the letter. The Harmony Club, a Jewish social organization in Galveston, Texas, catered Jewish weddings in the "prevailing fashion," according to one contemporary account. In 1903, for the wedding of Henry Oppenheimer and Hattie Kempner, the club served a "tower-like bridal cake" at the bride's residence. The wedding cakes caterers provided, however, did not always follow all-white prescriptions and showed the influence of different cultural tastes. In Upton Sinclair's opening chapter of *The Jungle*, the Lithuanian immigrant wedding featured a bridal cake in the shape of "an Eiffel tower of constructed decoration, with sugar roses and two angels upon it, and a generous sprinkling of pink and green and yellow candies." In one strange case at the turn of the century, a Jersey City commercial baker mixed ethnic stereotypes with prevailing wedding traditions and a little bit of showbiz flair in order to promote his wedding cake business. As a publicity stunt, he invented a cake that could talk (using a phonograph recording) and play the standard wedding music from *Lohengrin*. The cake, which was a three-foot-high four-decker, was sent as a gift to an American bride marrying in Germany. According to an account in the trade journal *Supply World*, it was decorated with cupids and "queer little fat Germans holding steins aloft, and looking as if they were exclaiming 'Prost!'"[17] Not surprisingly, such commercially produced wedding cakes stood outside the emerging middle-class white wedding ideal. For the most part, however, the catering profession shunned such stunts and sought to make itself an indispensable part of the ideal wedding by cultivating an image of taste and expertise in etiquette and correct social form.

While the catered affair became a part of the ideal wedding by the 1920s, less costly family affairs continued to take place. During hard times in the 1930s, for example, menus and recipes for the reception appeared in magazines, along with hints for economizing. In the 1930s, manuals such as one produced by *Ladies' Home Journal* outlined what a caterer or partial catering service could provide, but also included menus for the reception and recipes for cakes.[18] During the Depression, *Ladies' Home Journal* likely recognized that a home-baked cake was a necessary economy for many readers, as well as an expression of the domesticity the *Journal* promoted in its publications. In a 1931 radio talk on weddings, even Emily Post, who had earlier promoted the use of caterers, acknowledged that although you "must of course have wedding cake," it could "be baked at home and iced at the confectioners." By the postwar period, etiquette books like *Amy Vanderbilt's Complete Book of Etiquette* noted that "the tiered wedding cake may be a caterer's dream," but then still grudgingly acknowledged that it might be suitably made "in the kitchen of the bride and be as simple or as elaborate as the cook can manage."[19] Etiquette books published at the time by women's magazines, however, consistently advocated professional services, such as caterers, florists, and bridal consultants.[20] And famous caterers, like Sherry's in New York City, advertised their wedding receptions as the "one traditional gesture [that] stands out above all the rest" (figure 38).[21]

With the rise of the catering profession and the catered affair, men played a larger role in upholding and ultimately shaping wedding tradition. At first, catering was a male profession. Men ran the trade journals, formed the professional organizations, and held the top positions in the field, such as hotel banquet manager and chef. Hotel trade literature, such as the *Mid-west Hotel Reporter* and *Tavern Talk*, included articles on caterers and the profession written by men in the field. Caterers and related businesses established *Supply World* in 1888. At the turn of the twentieth century, their professional organization, the Steward's Club, appeared. In the 1920s, the Caterers Association organized and then merged with the Steward's Club in 1932. By the 1950s, after the term *steward* lost status and new titles, such as Food and Beverage Manager or Catering Director, appeared, the organization changed its name, eventually becoming the International Food Service Executives Association in 1976. By the mid-twentieth century, catering textbooks and handbooks for the food service industry came out, outlining proper practices and suggesting different marketing methods. This professional literature advocated the benefits of the bridal market in ways that paralleled developments in other areas of the wedding industry. Just as jewelers and department stores were advised to follow marriage rates and peruse the society column for engagement announcements, and write letters to brides and women in the wedding party, so too were caterers.[22]

Diverse groups of male caterers shaped the tradition of the wedding reception. African Americans were some of the earliest entrants, establishing a niche in this and other service industries. In the eighteenth century, black-owned

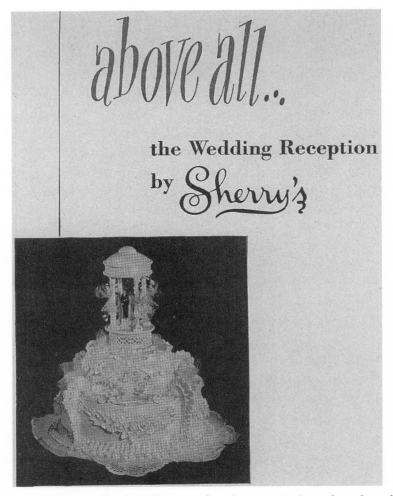

FIGURE 38. Caterers like the well-known Sherry's in New York sought to downplay their commercial status and highlight their long-standing reputation among brides. *Bride's* (Spring 1948), 83.

bakeries and catering establishments opened in Providence, Newport, Philadelphia, and New York. Prominent black caterers were largely men, though their businesses were often family run. By the 1840s, these caterers had an elite clientele. For example, Edward V. Clark, an African American jeweler and a caterer, supplied silver and glassware to New York's "upper ten" in the 1840s before his business folded after the Panic of 1857.[23] Gaining positions of relative wealth and prominence during this period, African American caterers worked to professionalize the field. Such efforts continued after the Civil War in the face of increased competition from white male caterers. When professionalization of white businesses worked to exclude black business owners, they responded by forming their own organizations.[24] In the food service industry, a variety of African American–run groups emerged to protect the interests of black entrepreneurs and workers. For example, the Corporation of Caterers, the Public Waiters Association, which later became the Waiters' Beneficial Association, and the Philadelphia Caterers Association organized in an effort to compete with white capital. Similarly, the Caterers Manufacturing and Supply Company purchased wholesale goods, such as tables and chairs, glassware, silver, china, and linens, which it then sold at cost or rented to its black members.[25]

In the face of increased competition from whites, some black caterers developed a broad-based wedding trade. Caterers like Charles H. Smiley, a prominent Chicago businessman, offered an innovative range of wedding services in the early twentieth century. Smiley provided the usual refreshments and wedding cake, but he also arranged for the flowers, church decorations, and even security guards to watch the gifts. One of the leading black businessmen in Chicago, he was the largest employer of African Americans in that city during that era. Although it was increasingly unusual after the Civil War, some African American businesses continued to attract a white clientele.[26] In Philadelphia, Albert E. Dutrieuille Catering, a family-owned business from 1873 to 1975, served both a black and a white clientele. Ledger accounts for the 1920s and 1930s show that its catered events ranged widely in price. One lavish 1920 reception for 150 guests cost $343, with china, glass, and linen provided. A big wedding celebration did not always break the bank, however, as one 1933 Dutrieuille reception for 200 cost only $75. At this modest event, guests were served ice cream and cakes, and the caterer provided linens, china, and a waiter. Another black-owned Philadelphia business, the John W. Holland Company, catered thousands of weddings, including those of Main Line elites. Founded in 1877 by John Holland, a former butler, the company was bought by William Newman in 1914. Newman gained his catering expertise moving up the rungs of the food service industry, overcoming racial discrimination at Horn & Hardart's in the 1890s to become the first African American busboy at this famous lunchroom across from Wanamaker's department store. Later, Newman worked as a cook and chef at several different restaurants, on steamships, in Army camps, and on railroad diners, and eventually became a partner in Holland's catering business. After becoming sole owner of the firm, he brought it from a five-person "horse-and-buggy catering business" to a company that around 1950 had 100 regular employees, 300 temporary workers, and grossed $200,000 annually.[27]

Ironically, caterers like Holland's used their authority as tradition experts to introduce new customs as socially correct or desirable. Holland served the consumer who needed his expert knowledge of tradition, or how things were supposed to be done. As *Ebony* magazine pointed out in its story of the successful Philadelphia caterer in 1950, "social climbers will come to Holland's because they know that better than anyone else, William Newman knows what tradition demands in social entertaining." At the same time, Newman introduced new customs and elaborated old ones, all the while allying himself with tradition. This invention of tradition sometimes came in response to consumer demand. Individual brides sometimes made seemingly impossible demands. Newman met the request of one client who "wanted a 75-pound wedding cake put inaccessibly in the center of a large table" by devising a way of "mounting the cake on wheels and pivots so that it could be moved in any direction by a slight tug on a satin ribbon." Caterers sought ways to serve large numbers of customers, inventing things like electrically rotating hors d'oeuvres tables the size of a small merry-go-round and electrically operated champagne fountains.[28] In a way seen time and again throughout the wedding industry, caterers combined innovation and tradition by adding new elements to wedding celebrations, while at the same time invoking custom to assert the correctness of their menus, table settings, and service. Eventually, fancy innovations like the champagne fountain became traditions in their own right, repeated at wedding after wedding.

Black and white men were prominent in the field through the first half of the twentieth century, but as women increasingly entered the wage force in the postwar period they began to play an important role. Catering was well suited to women trying to create a bridge between their domestic role and economic needs. They could enter the industry without professional training. Moreover, wedding cake baking drew on domestic skills, required minimal capital, and could take place at home, while knowledge of etiquette and the ability to decorate a room and table were widely seen as female specialties.

Married women in particular fit the bill. Farmwives in the Midwest, for example, ran small catering businesses on the side, contributing to the postwar commercialization of weddings in rural areas. Mrs. Clifford Anderson, a Minnesota farmwife who had no children, started baking birthday cakes for people in her area in the early 1940s. This expanded into her own busy catering business in the 1950s and 1960s. According to Barbara Howard, whose 1962 wedding reception was catered by Anderson in Elbow Lake, local brides visited her home and sat in her well-tended house while discussing their wedding plans and looking at photographs of cakes she had made.[29] Businesses like Anderson's operated on very small budgets and catered only to a local clientele. Such cake-baking and catering businesses continue to be run out of women's homes today. (Martha Stewart is the most prominent example of this type of caterer. By using her home, Turkey Hill, as the center of her catering business, she allowed her homemaker image to continue even as she created a business empire.)

While cake baking and catering could be viewed as extensions of "women's work," domestic skills sometimes translated into financial success and a prominent career. Mrs. Anderson's simple tiered wedding cakes and the service she provided in her farmhouse dining room were different only in degree from those produced by prominent wedding cake designers like Cile Bellefleur-Burbidge. In the 1950s, Cile Burbidge had worked helping her husband, John Burbidge, a wedding gown designer for Priscilla of Boston. After having several children and leaving work, she became depressed. Her doctor, who must have been on the same wavelength as Betty Friedan, told her to "get out of the house." She began taking an evening class at the YWCA on cake decorating, which led to a career in designing elaborately decorated, architecturally inspired wedding cakes that were featured in books, in window displays at Tiffany's and Priscilla of Boston's, and at bridal fairs. Another female entrepreneur, caterer and confectioner Edith McConnell, ran a successful business in Wilmington, Delaware, from the 1920s to the 1950s, serving elite clientele like the DuPont family. Wedding cakes were her specialty and she actively sought out the business of brides, advertising at the Wilmington Flower Market and in the *Brides Book*, a national advertising publication that featured local businesses. In 1941, she directed 44 percent of her total advertising budget specifically at the bridal market. As other caterers did, she served a range of budgets, suggesting that a variety of socioeconomic backgrounds engaged the wedding industry at this point. Her cakes in the 1950s were priced from $6.50 to $75 for wedding receptions with guests numbering from twelve to three hundred. The average cost of her wedding catering, from available records, was a little more than $200 in the mid-1950s.[30]

Even though the catering industry itself was diverse, wedding reception tradition became increasingly standardized by the first half of the twentieth century. Whether a family affair or a catered extravaganza, the wedding reception by definition was an event that revolved around hospitality and the provision of food and drink for guests. Menus created by household labor likely reflected personal tastes, family recipes, and perhaps dishes considered customary or traditional for a wedding. Commercial caterers, on the other hand, had to please their customers, but they also had to pay attention to the bottom line and to their business reputation. Those attending their events were potential judges of the quality and quantity of food and drink. Caterers had to provide refreshments that would please and be profitable to produce as well. Dishes that were proven successes helped them achieve their goals, and certain ones thus became "traditional" fare. No sit-down wedding breakfast or standing reception, for example, appeared to have been complete without either chicken à la king or lobster Newburg, the ubiquitous dish allegedly first introduced in the 1860s by Charles Ranhoffer, the chef at Delmonico's in New York.[31] As they did with food, catering businesses were also in a position to shape "traditions" for both the ceremony and the reception. Like the Eaton's department-store bridal salon in the late 1930s, caterers supplied all the necessary items for transforming a private home into a ritual space for the ceremony. According to Emily Post, for example, caterers had "the necessary standards to which ribbons are tied, like the wires to telegraph poles." They also rented out the goods needed for off-premise catering, a list of items that expanded greatly over the decades. Customers of course had some choice, but they made their choices within a range established by the business.[32]

The potential for endless styles and nonstandard cakes, however, certainly existed. The companies that supplied catering firms were also in the position to influence tradition and perpetuate certain wedding symbols. Bakery supply companies like H. A. Johnson & Company of Boston and Jaburg Brothers of New York sold their cake-making goods to commercial bakers and hotels by the gross. These goods were remarkably diverse in the nineteenth century. Cake decorating catalogues listed a wide variety of wedding cake boxes made of moiré paper or embossed paper with silver edges and a panoply of ornaments, such as gumpaste brides and grooms, roses, flower baskets, doves, bells, horns of plenty, and cupids playing violin. Certain items supported other cake rituals. According to custom, the white bride's cake was supposed to conceal a "ring, thimble and dime indicating marriage, single blessedness, or wealth" for guests who found the object in their slice.[33] Confectionary supply companies provided these symbolic items that were supposed to be baked into the cake. Even though they did not cater directly to those about to marry, businesses like these shaped wedding tradition by establishing the (albeit broad) boundaries of what was possible in commercially produced cakes. At the same time these early businesses and experts shaped wedding consumption through the goods and services they provided, they also had to please their customers. Bakery supply companies needed to provide gumpaste cake toppers and decorative symbols that caterers thought would sell, such as the kewpie doll figures popular in the early twentieth century.

Caterers also helped make more elaborate wedding cake customs traditional. With a few exceptions, like the *Lohengrin*-playing cake, this tradition followed a particular mold. Caterers and the etiquette writers that outlined their services promoted the custom of having two cakes. Etiquette writers typically discussed the differences between these two cakes, described the cutting ritual, and outlined the practice of individually boxed slices (figure 39). The cake cutting ritual involved the white bride's cake, made of a pound, sponge, or white cake (though this was confusingly sometimes called the wedding cake). The wedding cake was traditionally a rich black fruitcake covered in white icing. Caterers cut this concoction up and wrapped the pieces in fancy boxes for guests to take home—a tradition that was possible without the accoutrements provided by caterers, but one that was certainly aided by these decorative boxes.[34] Significantly, the fact that etiquette experts had to explain these customs suggests that they were spreading to those unfamiliar with the "tradition" and that perhaps caterers had a hand in their construction.

As the field professionalized, the potential for standardization increased. Professional institutions eventually opened the door for women's greater participation in the cake-making trade and in the process contributed to an in-

Two Suggestions FOR THE BRIDE-TO-BE

First Suggestion: Serve dark, rich, handsome fruit cake (the groom's cake) at your wedding feast! And, please be sure that you serve genuine Hoenshel Brandied Fruit Cake, the aristocrat of all cakes. You have excellent social authority for serving fruit cake, for in the 1947 edition of ETIQUETTE, Emily Post writes—"When this is the only cake to be offered . . . the cake is usually black fruit cake."

Hoenshel Brandied Fruit Cake is crammed with fine glacéd fruit and choice nuts. It is mellowed with imported brandy and distinguished sherry, and has the delicious, tangy old-world flavor that makes it supremely suitable for this great event. Can be appropriately served with a light wine or champagne.

Second Suggestion: Present every guest with one of those dainty silver and white boxes containing a generous portion of

the groom's cake. Emily Post, in the 1947 edition of ETIQUETTE also remarks— "There are, at all weddings of importance . . . little individual boxes of wedding cake —'black' fruit cake. Each box is made of white moire or grosgrain paper with the last initial of the groom combined with that of the bride . . . and tied with white satin ribbon . . ."

The great stores listed in this announcement can supply you with these smart individual packages, also with the Hoenshel Brandied Fruit Cake for your wedding. See the Bridal Consultant. She will gladly take care of the details. Or, if none of these stores happen to be convenient for you, write direct to us and we will see that you are supplied.

HOENSHEL FINE FOODS, INC.
1024 Hancock Street   Sandusky, Ohio
Largest Individual Makers of Fruit Cake in the World

PLUM, FIG AND FIG-DATE PUDDING • BRANDIED HARD SAUCE

These Dainty white and silver boxes of the groom's cake, given to guests and sent to friends to "dream" upon, fulfill an interesting old tradition. Bless your friends this way!

HOENSHEL
Brandied Fruit Cake
"KNOWS NO SEASON"

FIGURE 39. Businesses evoked "tradition" when elaborating upon customs, such as the serving of cake at a wedding. Here, Emily Post's "social authority" legitimized the use of fruitcake as a second, groom's cake or as the cake that is sent home with guests in individual boxes. *Bride's* (Spring 1948), 32.

creasingly elaborate yet standard wedding ideal. For example, Chicago's Wilton School of Cake Decorating offered courses and published series of books on cake decorating that held out the promise of entrepreneurial independence for women willing to follow formulas. Founded in 1929 by a family of cake decorators, the Wilton School in Chicago offered a ten-day course that taught students how to make the elaborately tiered wedding cakes, using Wilton's line of cake-making products (figure 40). The course granted a diploma and title of "Master Cake Decorator," suggesting the masculine nature of the occupation, though women were the prime audience for their magazines. By the 1970s, the Wilton School became the largest in its field training thousands of bakers, hotel chefs, home economists, and homemakers. The company still publishes how-to books on cake decorating and sells a line of related products, such as "fountains of love," bride and groom figurines, and glass tumblers to store cake toppers for eternity (figure 41).[35] Although wedding cake styles have changed over time and Wilton's magazines offered a wide range of designs, this publication by its nature provided a standardized model for home bakers and consumers to follow.

By the late twentieth century, caterers developed new marketing techniques that pushed consumers to spend more on their wedding reception. The "package," which presented the consumer with set groupings of goods and services, was a key innovation. Catering literature, now written by women, advocated restricting the price range of packages as a way to increase how much customers spent on their reception or other affair. If packages had a wide price range, customers were forced to make a "value judgment." Professionals in the field believed that consumers did not want to have to be forced to feel cheap when presented with a wide range of prices. The ideal was to have a difference of $12 to $15 between the lowest and highest package, making all choices acceptable. In the same vein, businesses refined their catering packages for the wedding receptions. As outlined in catering textbooks, package prices included "a number of catering services for a total per-person price." These package prices outlined the goods and services deemed necessary for a proper wedding, including such things as a cocktail reception, dinner, flowers, entertainment, after-dinner bar, and gratuities and taxes. This pricing method encouraged expenditure, creating the illusion of a good deal while actually adding items and services that the couple might not have originally intended to purchase.

Candlelight ceremony...

FIGURE 40. Wilton School of Cake Decorating taught homemakers how to make elaborate wedding cakes using their decorating products and standardized methods. A cake such as "Candlelight ceremony," which served 400 and could be made to match the bride's color scheme, gown, and flowers, was a tribute to the formal white wedding ideal. *Magic for Your Table . . . Cake and Food Decorating by Wilton* (Chicago: Wilton Enterprises, 1970), 100. Used with permission from Wilton Industries, Inc. ©1970 Wilton Industries, Inc.

*S*hining dome

to shelter your

loveliest memory!

A charming idea from the Victorian era—now revived and thriving.
A sparkling, crystal-clear dome on a wood-look base displays
and protects your precious wedding ornament forever and ever after!
It's clear plastic, holds nearly all Wilton ornaments.

FIGURE 41. The wedding industry introduced new goods that elaborated upon existing customs, often suggesting that such items were a revival of past traditions. *Magic for Your Table . . . Cake and Food Decorating by Wilton* (Chicago: Wilton Enterprises, 1970), 87. Used with permission from Wilton Industries, Inc. ©1970 Wilton Industries, Inc.

Any number of services could be included in the per-person price, such as flowers and entertainment, and then added into the total package price. According to one catering textbook, this created "the impression for the customer that the overall price for the function is less expensive than if flowers and entertainment were charged separately at a flat fee." Caterers also understood that putting different services together in a package provided additional sources of revenue by capturing a portion of the income that might otherwise be spent on outside vendors, such as musicians, florists, and photographers. Catering menus often followed a fixed-price format for a set range of items. By the early

1990s, however, à la carte pricing was introduced as it allowed caterers to respond to consumer demand for a wider menu choice. This pricing structure also allowed caterers to respond to increasing food costs.[36]

Such packages created a standard framework that was repeated in wedding after wedding, with the exception of à la carte pricing. The package strategy also forced consumers to use the same network of businesses to provide all out-of-house goods and services. As some department stores had done earlier, caterers turned to their own network of local contractors for flowers, photography, and music. According to one catering textbook, these outside participating services typically lowered their costs in order to guarantee this business. The catering service itself also charged a percentage for its role in obtaining the optional outside services. The extra cost borne by the consumer was justified by the time-saving convenience of having a professional handle the details, such as contracts and payments. From the caterers' point of view, package pricing allowed them to "control the quality of optional services, assuring the customer that the entire function will run smoothly."[37] Through such attention to marketing, professionals in the food service industry contributed to the rise of a national wedding ideal.

HOTELS

While caterers sometimes had their own venues or restaurants, the rise of the hotel industry created new commercial spaces for both the ceremony and reception. The early luxury hotel first appeared in urban centers between 1825 and 1860, growing out of taverns and inns that served an elite clientele. Concentrated on the eastern seaboard, they included Boston's Tremont House, New York's Astor House, Philadelphia's Continental, and the St. Charles in New Orleans. Luxury hotels like the Tremont House acted as an extension of their wealthy guests' homes, "serving as the venue for public dinners, celebrations, and casual association."[38] The weddings and honeymoons of the rich, however, were only a small part of this early hotel trade. Some early hotels like Boston's Parker House, for example, were visited primarily by men who used them as a club.[39] Moreover, the geographic limitations of these establishments and the fact that most people did not have a formal wedding meant that the business of brides played a minor role in the early luxury hotel business. Beginning in the late nineteenth century, however, another type of establishment—the commercial hotel—began to transform the industry. With the rise of the railroads, travel became easier, creating a demand for places for tourists, traveling salesmen, and others to stay. A new business culture fueled a building boom as the lucrative convention trade spurred construction of numerous large commercial hotels in the early twentieth century. In New York City alone, one hundred new hotels were built between 1902 and 1905 at an estimated cost of more than $39 million.[40]

As the commercial hotel spread across the country, from the Waldorf-Astoria in New York City to the Blackstone in Chicago to the Hotel Cornhusker in Lincoln, Nebraska, to the Hotel President in Waterloo, Iowa, increasingly broader segments of the marrying public had unprecedented access to luxury and convenience.[41] The Waldorf-Astoria on Fifth Avenue in New York, for example, was known for its lavish catered affairs. When completed in 1897, it was the first hotel in the world to have 1,000 guest rooms. With more than forty public rooms, each decorated in a different historical theme, it had a prominent banquet and food service business.[42] Unlike earlier exclusive luxury hotels, these massive commercial hotels were well suited to host weddings. Typically, modern hotels like the Waldorf tried to serve both their guests and the local community with a variety of ballrooms or banquet halls for private social occasions, costume balls, club meetings, conventions, and sales events. Their maze of public rooms allowed many events to take place simultaneously. For example, the Edgewater Beach Hotel in Chicago hosted 168 wedding parties in June 1928 alone (figure 42). In spite of their size, every event held in a hotel ballroom was assured a sparkling, correctly set table and an elaborate multi-course menu. (Not all was sterling, however, as commercial hotels were huge consumers of silverware and spurred silver manufacturers like Reed & Barton to come out with new lower-priced hollow wares that could be sold in volume.)[43] And not all hotel wedding events were big splashes, as hotel restaurants or public dining rooms also hosted bridal dinners or small wedding receptions consisting of only the immediate family (figure 43).[44] For the most part, however, wedding experts in the first half of the twentieth century associated these modern hotels with the costly big white wedding.[45]

Commercial hotels gave birth to a new type of professional that helped shape American wedding culture. In keeping with their need for efficiency and goal of customer service, these establishments hired a variety of protocol ex-

FIGURE 42. The hotel wedding was a very popular tradition by 1930, as indicated by this announcement board from the Edgewater Beach Hotel in Chicago. On one day, June 16, 1930, the hotel hosted six wedding breakfasts, three wedding ceremonies and dinners, three wedding dinners, two separate wedding ceremonies, and one wedding reception, all in private rooms, though many more took place in the hotel's public dining rooms. *Hotel Monthly* (May 1930), 60. General Research Division, New York Public Library, Astor, Lenox and Tilden Foundations.

FIGURE 43. Around the turn of the twentieth century, the Hotel Cadillac in Detroit provided traditional decorations for a wedding ceremony, including palms, an arch and bell, and flowers. Library of Congress, Prints & Photographs Division, Detroit Publishing Collection [LC-D4-62022 DLC].

perts and managers who served the bride. In 1919, for example, the McAlpin Hotel hired Mrs. Leonora Crook as an entertainment hostess, a title and position the hotel noted was "unique" and "unusual," likely because she was a woman in what was then a male-dominated field. Her role was to play hostess at luncheons, meetings, and weddings held at the hotel. More typically, male hotel professionals filled the new role of banquet manager or catering manager.[46] One famous maitre d'hotel, Oscar Tschirky (1866–1943), became one of the first banquet managers in the hotel industry in 1893. Known internationally as Oscar of the Waldorf, his name carried the prestige of the great New York hotel in which he worked. Authoring books on weddings and entertaining and quoted in numerous trade articles, he represented a new level of professionalism in the field.[47]

As the hotel industry professionalized, it began offering new goods and services for the bride and groom and their wedding guests. Many of the extras that hotels provided were intended to capture future trade. Like other businesses with wedding trade, hotels recognized that a marriage not only brought increased opportunity for point-of-sale purchases but also the possibility of creating new lifelong customers. Trade literature advised the maitre d'hotel to act as a "salesman" for newlyweds, showing them extra courtesies that would encourage them to come back to the hotel for their anniversary. As early as the 1920s, establishments like the Edgewater Beach Hotel cultivated future customers, offering couples who married there and returned to celebrate their anniversaries a special anniversary wedding cake.[48] Hotels continued to develop new ways to capture the wedding trade through the mid-twentieth century. As jewelers and others were doing, hotels produced their own booklets to distribute to prospective brides in their cities. For example, in the 1940s the Deshler-Wallick Hotel in Columbus, Ohio, designed a wedding book for recording information about the engagement, showers, trousseau, gifts, wedding gown, the marriage record, the honeymoon, new home furnishings, "and finally, plans for the future." Distributed through the city's Welcome Wagon service, it reached a hundred newly engaged women every month. Like those booklets and magazines circulated by jewelers, furniture companies, department stores, and others, this "goodwill promotion idea" linked their commercial services with, in their words, the "usual sentiment attached to the wedding ceremony."[49]

At the same time as the hotel industry began targeting the business of brides, prescriptive literature also began promoting commercial venues for the wedding reception. By the 1920s, etiquette writers explained the format and necessary expenditures for a hotel ceremony or reception. Interestingly, some resistance to the hotel wedding remained. Emily Post, for example, continued to favor receptions in private homes. In her words, the most simple wedding breakfast in a private house had "greater distinction than the most elaborate collation in a public establishment." Public spaces lacked "sentiment" and a "'home' atmosphere." She conceded to changing contexts, however, noting that if the bride's house was very small the wedding breakfast might be hosted in a hotel or assembly room. Commercial caterers with their own salons also criticized the "commercial atmosphere of a hotel."[50] The wedding industry at large, however, promoted hotel receptions. *Bride's* magazine, for example, noted that they allowed one to put "all the cares and contingent problems into the hands of an expert," and a special wedding issue of *House Beautiful* warned that a "home reception will mean additional work for your family and you may find it will be easier all around if the reception is held elsewhere."[51]

While hotel and club weddings were more expensive and elite than most other options, by the mid-twentieth century couples who celebrated their marriage there were not necessarily elite themselves.[52] While most families could not afford a lavish white wedding reception in an expensive hotel, these catered affairs were nevertheless no longer the province of the elites. For example, when Jean West, who worked in the New York office of Binney & Smith, the makers of Crayola, and Anthony Falzone, a printer for the Typographical Service Company, married in 1959, they had a big reception in the Louis XVI Suite at the Waldorf-Astoria. After the ceremony at St. John the Evangelist Roman Catholic Church, the bride in a formal gown and the groom in white tie and jacket celebrated their marriage with coworkers and others at this famous hotel. Following tradition, the couple had studio portraits taken and honeymooned in the Poconos, a popular working-class resort area. With its old-world service and opulent architecture and decoration, the Waldorf-Astoria provided working- and middle-class families with a one-time access to wealth and luxury and created a glamorous backdrop for a wedding that was very different from everyday life.[53]

Early on, the commercial hotel industry also sought the Jewish bridal market. Jewish weddings took place in a variety of venues. Excluded from private country clubs, Jews formed their own. Well-to-do brides in the 1930s, for example, married at the Brook Country Club in New Haven.[54] Certain hotels, like the luxurious Hotel Astor, had long catered to Orthodox Jewish weddings. Early in the twentieth century, some establishments provided commemorative wedding favors for guests at Jewish weddings, such as a "pocket-sized bencher, or grace-after-meals booklet, bearing the couple's name and date of the wedding." Around the turn of the century, according to an 1899 report on immigrant life, ceremonies in the Lower East Side took place in the synagogue "when the extra expense [could] be borne."[55] Increasing numbers of synagogues built their own accommodations with catering departments for weddings and other occasions. Jewish caterers provided the wedding banquet and ceremonial items, such as the chupah and yarmulkes, and dealt with the rabbi and cantor, arranging for the "music, flowers, menu cards, cigars, cigarettes, coat check and the kashruth supervisor." By the interwar years, synagogues themselves faced "stiff competition from hotels and halls" for the business of brides. Hotel trade literature in the 1930s revealed an industry still working to capture the Jewish market. For example, articles encouraged the maitre d'hotel to sell himself as a master of ceremonies for Jewish weddings because of the "certain formality which is followed" at "orthodox, semi-modern, or modern" nuptials. This attention to the Jewish bridal market continued into the early postwar era. Professional catering literature directed at hotel managers and independent caterers, for example, described dishes, such as stuffed cabbage, that would appeal to Jewish tastes and advised the hiring of Jewish women to prepare specialty food.[56]

By the 1940s and 1950s, black-owned hotels also began offering luxurious settings for African American weddings. The black-owned hotel industry took shape in the early twentieth century, catering exclusively to African Americans barred from white-owned hotels by Jim Crow practices.[57] Between *Plessy v. Ferguson* in 1896 and the *Brown* decision in 1954, black-owned businesses rose to fill the consumer needs of African Americans in both the North and the South. In Atlanta, Georgia, alone, the black community saw the opening of the European Hotel in 1895, the Mackie Bee Hotel in 1901, the Hawk Hotel in 1913, the McKay Hotel in 1921, and the Savoy Hotel in 1937.[58] Professional literature for the hotel industry noted when African American businessmen purchased or built new hotels for black consumers, thus legitimizing Jim Crow accommodations, even setting them in a "progressive" New South context. For example, when the Arlington Hotel in Pine Bluff, Arkansas, was sold in 1929 to "a group of Chicago and Little Rock negroes" who were represented by a former president of the black Arkansas Mechanical and Normal School, a trade article in *Tavern Talk* praised the new ownership. The sixty-room building was "to become one of the finest negro hostelries in the South" as the new owners expected to invest significant funds remodeling and repairing it.[59] Most hotels open to African American trade were modest, however, and would not have provided wedding venues comparable with those furnished in whites-only establishments. Black middle-class travelers often had few options. The black-owned Adams Hotel in St. Louis, where baseball player Jackie Robinson chose to stay, for example, lacked air conditioning. According to an *Ebony* article in 1950, "travel-conscious Negro America is weary of fourth-rate hotel accommodations with their usual accompaniment of frowzy bellboys, dingy bathrooms and flippant desk clerks." In southern cities, visiting African Americans sometimes had to turn to places like the YMCA and YWCA, which were also segregated.[60]

Newly modernized black-owned hotels like Detroit's Carlton Plaza thus created a splash when they opened. The Carlton Plaza, built in 1933 in the Brush Park neighborhood of Detroit, was newly renovated and opened to African Americans in 1949 under the management of Edward Swan, a former head of the local NAACP branch. *Ebony* magazine heralded this 200-room establishment in 1950 as "the most beautifully decorated and most elaborately furnished hotel for Negroes anywhere in the U.S." Available services matched many white-owned and white-patronized hotels. Honeymooners and other visitors at the Carlton Plaza were met by uniformed doormen and bellboys who offered to carry their luggage. The hotel offered first-rate wedding services for African Americans. Receptions and bridal parties there took place in the glamorously titled New Orleans Suite and the Hollywood Room, a five-room suite. Guests and others could visit the hotel barbershop, beauty shop, tailor's shop, cocktail lounge, gift shop, and portrait photography studio. Located near downtown shopping and a theater district, the Carlton was a vibrant social center until the fortunes of the Brush Park neighborhood declined. Today this hotel stands vacant and boarded up, owned by the state.[61]

The Gotham Hotel in Detroit's Paradise Valley district provided another prominent wedding venue for African Americans. Built in 1924 by Albert Hartz and bought by John J. White and Irving Roane in 1943, the Gotham flourished as a luxury hotel and was visited by many prominent personalities, including Langston Hughes, Billie Holliday, and Thurgood Marshall. Wedding parties celebrated in its banquet space, the Holiday Room, or in the popular Ebony Room, a dining room known for its African carvings, fresh flowers, and multi-course meals. Society brides housed out-of-town wedding guests in well-appointed rooms at the Gotham furnished in solid mahogany.[62] By 1962, its fortunes turned and the Gotham closed, finally falling victim to the wrecking ball of urban renewal in 1964.[63]

HALLS

Although an increasingly broad range of marrying couples celebrated their union in commercial hotels, the cost associated with these catered affairs excluded most. A host of other public venues, however, stepped in to serve the bride. Urban white working-class and immigrant couples turned to less-expensive public venues hired out by their ethnic or fraternal organizations, social clubs, community centers, dance halls, or local saloons. Halls connected with a particular religious community had long been associated with working-class and immigrant life. Catholic church halls and Jewish community centers, for example, were frequently used for wedding receptions and other functions. As depicted in Upton Sinclair's novel *The Jungle*, a hall in the back of a saloon, rented for $15, furnished another common wedding reception venue.[64]

Large public halls could be rented for reasonable rates. The Lower East Side alone had more than fifteen halls that provided a venue for weddings, nightly dances, dancing schools, and large balls. Two of these, the New Irving Hall and Liberty Hall, could accommodate from 500 to 1,200 people. As with hotels, weddings were fairly closely scheduled. At the turn of the century, Liberty Hall saw three weddings a week. Jewish couples had their reception there after a synagogue wedding ceremony, but if they could not afford to do that, they married at the hall. New Irving Hall rented for only $30 a night for a wedding at the turn of the century. Unlike hotels, which had an on-site catering manager or banquet manager who took care of all details, early hired halls generally just provided a space for the wedding reception. The parents of the contracting parties rented the hall, hired an orchestra, provided refreshments, and divided the expense. The space was rented for a "nominal sum," making it a more affordable option than a hotel.[65] Public halls or community centers also served African American brides and grooms across the country. Barred from many public spaces, African Americans had formed their own clubs and fraternal lodges since the nineteenth century. Some of these groups acquired meeting sites that were used to host wedding receptions, among other events.[66]

Beginning in the late nineteenth century, public spaces played a central role in the social life of immigrant New York City. Hall venues were one response to city life, a means of bringing communities together in a public space to celebrate a marriage when homes were not large enough to have more than a family party.[67] According to the New York Settlement Society, a Progressive group that would have had an interest in praising what they deemed to be authentic ethnic customs, weddings celebrated in halls "displayed the collective social spirit which plays so large a part in holding people together within a fixed geographical limit." While those with the money and the desire might hire banquet halls in hotels for this function, the hired public hall provided an affordable option and allowed those with limited means to extend hospitality and reaffirm ties to their ethnic group. In the 1930s, according to one Italian immigrant living in New England, Italian-Americans hosted their wedding celebrations in community centers because they held many people and had a bar, which in turn let everyone have a good time dancing and drinking to the health of the bride.[68] In general, these hall weddings were very large. Working- and lower-middle-class couples often had hundreds of guests at their wedding. One 1916 wedding of a Strawbridge & Clothier salesman had 500 guests at his Jewish ceremony at the New Auditorium Hall in Philadelphia, including over fifty men and women from the department store. Although big weddings like these certainly mounted debts, costs could be cut with the addition of family labor or a simple repast in a way not possible at a hotel. At one Italian wedding reception held in a rented hall in New Haven in the 1930s, "sandwiches, soda pop, cookies, crackers, and fruit were spread on long, uncovered boards sup- ported by sawhorses."[69] Receptions in hired halls where hundreds of guests were served sandwiches and pitchers of beer came to be called "football wed- dings," allegedly because different types of sandwiches were passed back and forth.[70]

Ethnically identified public halls abounded through the 1960s. Some hired halls were not linked overtly to any specific ethnic group, such as the Tatamy Fire House and the Bloomsbury Hose Company Hall in Pennsylvania. Ac- cording to one 1967 popular study of weddings, around World War II people married in the hall of the organization they belonged to, such as the American Legion, the VFW, or the Elks.[71] Many also chose wedding venues that signaled their identification with a particular ethnicity or religion. Jantzen employees in Portland, Oregon, in the 1930s and 1940s frequently celebrated at the Italian Federation Hall and the Norse Hall. In the 1940s and 1950s, Maidenform employees in Bayonne, New Jersey, favored the Polish-American Hall and the Ukranian Hall and National Home. Strawbridge & Clothier employees in the 1950s kicked up their heels at the Kosciuszko Polish Club, in the Italian- American Citizens League Building, and at the Devon Bocci Club. Among different communities of workers, public halls generally fit the ethnic groups of the employees, though not always. A couple like Stella Rogers and Louis La Grand might choose to have a big reception and dance at Portland's Norse Hall in 1940 without expressing any identification with Scandinavian customs. In a similar vein, Italian-American Maidenform employees used the Polish-American Hall and at least one Episcopal employee of Binney & Smith held a wedding reception at the Catholic Knights of Columbus Home in Danvers, Massachusetts.[72]

Where one celebrated a wedding made a public statement about one's social status and taste, as well as one's ethnic identity. As we have seen, in the nineteenth century, the Protestant ideal became a church wedding and home reception. Public halls were generally associated with the non-Protestant working class and historically reflected one's ethnicity. Omitted in etiquette books, the lower-status but very popular public hall wedding remained on the margins in the early twentieth century.[73] Associated with the working class and different generations of eastern and southern European immigrants, the wedding in a hired ethnic hall stood outside the native-born white Protestant ideal defined early on by the wedding industry. Through the mid-twentieth century, wedding receptions in hired halls had a lower class status than home weddings or celebrations in private clubs or hotels (figure 44).[74]

For second-generation immigrants, a church wedding and a reception in a commercial or public space expressed one's identification with American culture and middle-class identity.[75] Including elements of the formal wedding ideal, however, did not necessarily mean that a family had turned their back on their ethnic community. Wedding receptions often effortlessly merged old traditions with new. Chinese-Americans in San Francisco in the 1920s, for example, often mixed Western and Chinese traditions when they married. According to one study, large Chinese weddings took place in a church, hotel, or public hall. The couples wore Western dress, married to strains of Wagner or Mendelssohn, had cake and refreshments, and then were driven home in a limousine festooned in red paper and silk. A fifteen- to twenty-course wedding feast followed the next day in Chinatown.[76]

In the postwar era, a different type of hall emerged out of the food service industry—the wedding hall or wedding palace. Unlike public halls, these new wedding halls were wholly profit-driven ventures. They were not ethnically based or connected to any particular community or organization, and con-

FIGURE 44. The wedding reception of Cecilia Wrazen and Bronislaus Nowak was held at a public hall in Buffalo, New York, in 1943. According to the FSA/OWI photographer, the couple "apologized for the smallness of the wedding, blamed it on rationing of food, [and] talked of how their parents' weddings had lasted for four days of feasting." Library of Congress, Prints and Photographs Division, FSA/OWI Collection [LC-USW3-024716-DDLC].

sumption under their roof took on a different meaning. Their goal was to sell more goods and services to the bride, not just provide her with a space for a celebration that may or may not have been professionally catered. These wedding palaces became the "East Coast phenomenon" that writer Kitty Hanson observed in the 1960s, but they also appeared elsewhere in the United States right after World War II. To Hanson's critical eye, catering halls in the early postwar era resembled a "high school gymnasium, tricked out with some tired draperies, battered tables, and folding chairs." This was not always the case, however, as one West Coast "Wedding Manor" in 1948 offered such luxuries as having a wedding on board the yacht *Amici*. By the 1960s, catering halls had certainly moved to a new level of consumerism, creating thematic venues that turned the bride into a queen for a day, or at least for a few hours.

Catering halls became wedding palaces, complete with mirrors, paneling, fountains, chandeliers, and a variety of thematic décor. Some went beyond being restaurants or simple venues for a catered wedding and became "wedding castles," places where the focus was on the bride's presentation. In these venues, the bride appeared as part of a spectacle—behind netting, amid dry-ice smoke, or on a revolving platform.[77]

Like other businesses with wedding trade, these commercial venues developed new ways to increase consumption and expand the bridal market. As part of the catering profession, wedding halls also used the "package deal" marketing idea. Venues like the Lord Fox Restaurant in Foxboro, Massachusetts, or the Thatched Cottage and Leonard's of Great Neck on Long Island offered package deals that included all the "traditional" elements of the formal white wedding, plus many more of their own invention. Broader in reach than catering packages that simply addressed the refreshments at the reception, the wedding hall package deal focused on the entire wedding as a marketable commodity. In 1960, for example, the "straight Lord Fox package deal" included a three-piece orchestra, flowers for the head table, the wedding cake, and wine. Packages at the Thatched Cottage, a 500-seat restaurant by 1961, were even more extensive, adding pre-wedding publicity, travel services for the honeymoon, and a hostess for the reception who called times for the toast and cake-cutting (figure 45).[78]

Wedding palaces carried standardization to a new level. In general, these venues created a standardized final product—the reception buffet or dinner. In order to serve many brides efficiently and cost-effectively, menus and services were customized only in small, superficial ways. Menus were limited and wedding parties typically selected items from a range of choices. Consumers were able to exert their tastes within the constraints of these packages and price ranges. At Lord Fox, chicken à la king was the favorite wedding breakfast item. Sauterne and vin rosé (for its color) were the two most popular wine choices. Similar tastes prevailed at the Thatched Cottage in 1960, but there is some evidence that consumers influenced the "producer" in this case. The owner, Warren Bittner, noted that his clientele preferred a less dry champagne, contrary to accepted opinion, and thus made that a standard in wedding packages.[79] Moreover, unlike caterers and department-store bridal salons at Eaton's and Carson, Pirie Scott, wedding halls generally did not work with outside

FIGURE 45. Commercial venues for the wedding reception introduced new traditions, such as making a wish at an allegedly 316-year-old wishing well at the Thatched Cottage. *Modern Bride* (August–September 1970), 344.

vendors, something that potentially would have varied the final product. Instead of searching for different florists, photographers, musicians, caterers, and wedding cake providers, and then worrying about business contracts, payment, and the logistics of the wedding location itself, the customer purchased a standardized package that drew on the wedding hall's on-site services. Creating the true one-stop wedding, these halls provided all the material elements of the formal white wedding except the bridal gown. Although consumers shaped the package deal to some degree, for the most part what emerged from these commercial venues was the same white package.

Even as wedding palaces standardized the formal wedding, they also elaborated it and expanded what could be considered traditional. Like others in the service industry for the bride, wedding halls invented traditions as they sought to distinguish their business from others and attract more customers. For example, Lord Fox kitchen staff carved ice sculptures to decorate tables. The Thatched Cottage, which worked harder to come up with new ways of doing things, featured an "authentic Indian wishing well with its romantic legend" and illuminated three-tier champagne fountains. They also presented the bride and groom with champagne glasses inscribed with their first names. Couples who chose the "champagne and dinner plan" had their champagne toast served from a 102-ounce bottle of champagne, which they later received as a memento. Each couple had an 8 x 10 color photograph permanently mounted in the restaurant's "bridal gallery." The Thatched Cottage also promoted something that would later become a standard—the buy-now, pay-later wedding. In the earliest example I have found, in 1961 it offered financing so that you could "have your wedding now, pay on easy monthly payments."[80]

Although such innovations created a sense of uniqueness and variety, on another level the logistical requirements of their operation turned each wedding into something of an assembly-line production. Like hotels, wedding halls hosted numerous weddings at a time. To deal with this, their spaces were carved into a variety of ballrooms and salons. Each separate room received its own name in a way that gendered the space and distinguished it from other locations. The names added feminine glamour, as in the Thatched Cottage's Cinderella Room with its bandstand-pumpkin and murals of Cinderella, or the rustic masculine ambience created at Lord Fox Restaurant's Pine Room, Tack Room, Bull Lounge, and Stag Room, with their soft pine and stone background.[81] Weddings in these rooms were scheduled and organized in such a way as to prevent brides from different parties seeing each other. According to the hostess at Lord Fox in 1960, brides found it very upsetting to come in sight of each other. To prevent this disaster from happening, and to push as many parties through as possible, weddings were broken down into different stages. The hostess kept the event to a strict, minute-by-minute schedule as the couple and hundreds of guests were ushered through the different rooms and sometimes called in from the lawn by loudspeaker. While one bridal party arrived at eleven o'clock and was ushered into the Colonial Room, their 200 guests arrived and were assembled in the Tack Room for coffee and sweet rolls. The couple had their pictures taken in the Victorian parlor, then moved to the receiving line in the Hilary Room and the buffet. At noon the same day, 115 guests arrived for a second wedding, only one hour later than the previous wedding. This wedding party went through the same motions, only in a different set of rooms. Each bride threw the bouquet and disappeared to the brides' dressing room, one at three o'clock, the other at four. The Lord Fox hostess, when interviewed for an article in a restaurant trade journal, joked that she "never [gave] the bride to the wrong groom."[82]

WEDDING CHAPELS

At the same time as these palaces and package deals elaborated the formal wedding, spreading it to a wider bridal market, an alternate wedding industry emerged in places as diverse as the bordertown of Yuma, Arizona, the neon strip in Las Vegas, and the Smoky Mountains of Tennessee. Between the 1920s and the 1950s, commercial wedding chapels appeared on the scene, providing civil or religious ceremonies for eloping couples. Often cheap, always quick, commercial chapels either shunned most of the commercial trappings of the mainstream wedding industry or embraced them in a funhouse mirror fashion that included Elvis serenades or hillbilly ministers. Rooted in the Gretna Green wedding tradition, these "marriage mills" grew in response to tightening state controls over marriage and a demand for civil ceremonies that went around these restrictions (figure 46).

The "Gretna Green" marriage, as it came to be known, was one that took place with few legal obstacles or formalities. The phrase stemmed from the village of Gretna Green in Scotland just across the English border. English couples in the mid-eighteenth century circumvented laws prohibiting marriage without parental consent by traveling to the Scottish village, where they merely had to declare themselves husband and wife before any two witnesses to become legally married.[83] The Gretna Green marriage spawned its own American industry in bordertowns in states where marriage laws were more lenient. For example, a Jantzen employee living in Portland in the 1950s might have crossed the Columbia River into Washington to marry in Vancouver, thereby avoiding the blood test required by Oregon. On the other side of the country, when couples preferred or needed to marry without delay they traveled to places like Elkton, Maryland, the elopement capital of the East. Beginning in 1913 when neighboring Delaware passed waiting laws and public notification laws, Maryland became a destination for couples seeking to avoid a waiting period or residency requirement. The state required a church service for these quickie weddings, spawning the industry. By the 1920s and 1930s, Elkton had fifteen private wedding chapels, such as the Little Wedding Chapel, offering special package deals that included all the trimmings.[84]

FIGURE 46. Wedding chapels offered a low-cost, no-frills alternative to the catered affair. According to the FSA/OWI photographer of this wedding chapel in Yuma, Arizona, many Californians eloped across the border in order to avoid a three-day law, which required three days between application for the license and the ceremony. Library of Congress, Prints and Photographs Division, FSA/OWI Collection [LC-USF34-072104-D DLC].

For many arbiters of good taste, these secret unions were beyond the pale of tradition. In the nineteenth century, etiquette writers strongly condemned elopements. To elope was to break with society's conventions, something that itself came to have its own appeal. One justice of the peace from Pocomo City in North Carolina in the 1930s believed that "there's a touch a romance in running over the line to another state and getting the knot tied unbeknownst to the neighbors."[85] With the rise of the commercial wedding chapel in places like Elkton, Maryland, the secret wedding became its own romantic tradition. Couples who married in secret at Elkton were not shunned, but they still received a lot of attention when they returned to work. For example, when Ralph Greco, a presser in the ladies' alterations at Strawbridge & Clothier, eloped "to famed Elkton, Maryland" with Patricia Walsh in 1955, he was honored with a bridal shower when he returned to work.[86] While not the shivaree that cowboy William Wall had received earlier as punishment for not giving a wedding dance, this humorous bridal shower served as a reminder that breaking with tradition still had consequences.

Unlike the elopement, the civil ceremony was always socially correct. Civil ceremonies had their own etiquette prescriptions. Bridal apparel, for example, was supposed to avoid any feeling of pageantry or drama. A civil ceremony was typically very small, involving the couple and their witnesses. According to one etiquette expert in the 1930s, a city hall wedding meant that the bride and groom had "decided to forego orange blossoms and Loehengrin" in favor of getting married in the simplest possible way.[87] On rare occasions, a civil ceremony provided more spectacle than a formal church wedding, as in the case of early fad weddings performed as "publicity stunts" in the 1920s, including weddings on horseback, on airplanes, and over a lion's cage.[88] (Such spectacle weddings prefigured reality television weddings.) For the most part, however, couples were expected to shun the "shoes and rice" when they chose to marry at city hall or to elope.

By their nature, the civil ceremony and the elopement had few or none of the material trappings of the formal religious wedding. Couples often chose them for this very reason. Of all the marriage options, they were the least costly and time consuming. As a result, they suited the demands of working-class life. According to the justice of the peace from Pocomo City in the 1930s, couples chose them mainly for economic reasons. Not surprisingly, during the Depression, church weddings declined overall and city hall weddings rose.[89] According to one New Haven justice of the peace in the 1930s, who beginning in 1916 kept track of all the civil weddings he performed, some wanted to avoid the fuss of a church wedding, but most chose this type of ceremony for social reasons—because of premarital pregnancy or because it was a second marriage or a racially or religiously mixed union. Justices of the peace were sometimes even able to help pregnant brides back-date their marriage by giving them blank marriage certificates. Those remarrying also had higher rates of civil ceremonies. The resident status of the bride and groom—whether they were from the area in which they married—was another factor. In more recently settled regions of the country, such as the West, civil ceremonies were thus more popular.[90]

FIGURE 47. Couples wishing to marry quickly thronged to places like the Little Wedding Chapel in Elkton, Maryland, where restrictions on marriage were fewer. After these restrictions in other states were removed, Elkton remained a traditional place to marry. Collection of the author.

In spite of the association of the civil ceremony and the elopement with cost cutting and potential scandal, between the 1920s and the 1950s, a variety of entrepreneurs and businesses saw their commercial potential. Wedding chapels took the economic and social need for a quick marriage and couched it in the language of romance. The romantic image these marriage mills developed sometimes remained when they no longer provided quickie marriages. For example, Elkton remained a "traditional" place to marry even after a forty-eight-hour waiting period was put in place in 1938. Little Wedding Chapel continued to draw couples, offering "lovely weddings at a small fee." With its decorated chapel, organ music, candlelight service, and nonsectarian service, it advertised itself as a place "where your reverent vows of today become tender memories tomorrow" (figure 47).[91] These commercial wedding chapels offered a ceremony that cost much less than a formal church wedding. Such businesses allowed poorer couples, or those who simply did not want to spend much money on the ceremony, to partake in American wedding culture as it emerged in the postwar years.

The commercial chapels that emerged during this period became a new fixture on the wedding scene, albeit one outside the mainstream of *Bride's* magazine and Emily Post. In what came to be known as a "destination wedding," couples married in places like Gatlinburg, Tennessee, the "wedding capital of the South." This southern state had no waiting period, no residency requirement, and no blood test requirement. A popular tourist destination in the Smoky Mountains, the town drew those seeking a holiday or a romantic destination for their wedding. Dozens of religious and nonreligious commercial venues, such as the Cupid Chapel of Love, the Sweet Magnolia Wedding Chapel, the Band of Gold Wedding Chapel, and Sugarland Weddings, offered package deals. In recent years, for example, one could have a "Hillbilly Wedding" performed by a bib-overall-wearing minister. Ironically, these chapels sought to keep the standards of their profession high and promote an image of respectability by joining the Wedding Association of Gatlinburg and advertising their membership.[92]

As with the catering profession and hotel industry, this marriage market attracted black entrepreneurs to serve a clientele facing de facto and de jure segregation. After World War II, for example, Charles P. Coleman, an ex-G.I. and African American Baptist minister, converted his gas station on the outskirts of Yuma, Arizona, into a drive-in wedding chapel. Coleman drew on the Californians who eloped to Yuma to avoid a three-day law that required a waiting period between the application for a license and the ceremony. In 1948, more than 20,000 traveled across the state line at the Colorado River to marry in one of the many wedding chapels that sprang up on Highway 80 and in the town of Yuma. Coleman's wedding chapel was the first business that many saw as they entered the state. He served both black and white couples who drove into his chapel, though in an interview in *Ebony* magazine the minister noted that most whites preferred to be married by a white officiant and many left his establishment once they discovered his race. Suggesting a recognition of the socially marginal nature of such business, with tongue in cheek *Ebony* titled the report on Coleman "Quickie Drive-In Wedding Chapel." The chapel building itself fully embraced the business side of matrimony, demonstrating a modern, flexible idea of tradition with a sign that featured Coleman's name prominently, and another sign that directed drivers to pull under the carport into the "drive-in chapel" where there was "free parking." The article also noted that the owner was "not happy with his matrimonial business" and wanted a church of his own and more education to fulfill his ambition.[93]

The Southwest became the heart of this diverse market for Gretna Green marriages. Wedding chapels reached their most modern early postwar expression in Las Vegas. The Las Vegas wedding industry grew side by side with the gambling industry. After 1931, when legalized gambling came to this desert town, the hotel and casino industry blossomed, bringing tourists and potential brides and grooms. The first casino, the Flamingo, appeared in 1946, followed by resort hotels and big-name entertainers. As Las Vegas developed a glamorous image, it attracted marrying couples to places like the Candlestick Wedding Chapel, which opened in 1954. Another well-known older business was the Little Chapel of the East, one of the few free-standing chapels that looked like it was designed as a church, though it was not. Such chapels played with the iconography of the wedding, picking and choosing elements to distinguish themselves from competing businesses. The interior décor varied from a "traditional church interior" to medieval design. Unlike churches, however, wedding chapels had gift stores that sold decorative marriage certificates and T-shirts and coffee mugs with the date and name of the chapel on them. Like a church, hotel, or wedding hall, Las Vegas chapels facilitated big weddings as well. They varied in seating capacity, catering to the traditional small elopement or the lavish white wedding. Most significantly, however, they were available twenty-four hours a day year round, allowing spur-of-the-moment weddings. The Clark County Marriage License Bureau also co-operated with extended hours seven days a week. During the 1970s, hotels in Las Vegas began adding on-site chapels, providing competition for the historic wedding chapels on the strip. In recent decades, the Las Vegas wedding has gained popularity as a relatively inexpensive alternative to a formal church wedding, with the basic ceremony and license costing $100 and rising to $300 with the addition of flowers and videos.[94]

By 1996, when the first scholarly study of this Las Vegas tradition appeared, there were thirty-five wedding chapels in the city. These enterprises used package deals in much the same way as wedding halls had done in the Northeast in the 1950s and 1960s. Instead of selling each good or service individually or à la carte, which added time to the planning process, chapels grouped popular items together, such as flowers and music, and gave a small discount. The Las

Vegas chapel industry, like so many others in the wedding trade by the mid-twentieth century, tied marriage and commerce together. "Your happiness is our business" was a frequent motto. In order to make their customers happy (perhaps for repeat business), they introduced new traditions and transformed old ones, offering Elvis wedding packages, Middle Ages–style ceremonies, and "rich and famous"–style celebrations in which couples rode in a hot-tub-equipped thirty-five foot limousine.[95]

The Las Vegas wedding at the end of the twentieth century certainly took the wedding industry to a new level of commercialization. At the same time, this pinnacle of modern consumer culture brought greater inclusivity to the formal white wedding ideal. Ironically, it allowed those who wanted to take part in American wedding culture to bypass the myriad businesses that emerged to serve the bride by the postwar period and that created this consumer ideal in the first place.

* * *

As more and more couples hired professionals and turned to commercial venues, the meaning of the white wedding tradition changed. The catered affair—whether it was in a private home, hotel, public hall, or "wedding castle"—differed dramatically from the wedding of past centuries. An emblem of modernity, the catered affair served urban, industrial life and its bourgeois culture of manners and civility. With the rise of commercial wedding chapels, the etiquette-bound formal wedding was turned on its head by couples searching for a way to marry that fit their modern needs. In these new commercial venues, the marriage ceremony itself became a consumer rite, the subject of advertising and merchandising. As weddings became more strongly connected to the market, businesses were able to give new meaning to the idea of tradition. Increasingly standard, rational, and efficient, yet also playfully flexible in response to the need for new markets, the elaborate formal white wedding tradition became a central modern consumer ritual of the postwar period as what was once an elite practice became the "rite" of everyone.

Wedding Tradition at the Turn of the Twenty-First Century

Many invented traditions remained traditional at the end of the twentieth century. Brand-name diamond engagement ring sets, bridal magazines, wedding consultants, bridal salons, once-worn and ready-made heirloomed formal white gowns, gift registries, and catered affairs continued to be a ubiquitous part of American wedding culture. After an alleged break in the 1970s with the rise of the anti-establishment New Wedding, in the luxury-obsessed 1980s tradition returned, perhaps best symbolized by the lavish 1981 fairy-tale wedding of Lady Diana Spencer and Prince Charles, watched by more than 750 million people worldwide. According to many accounts, after this weddings became "really big," with the average cost quadrupling from $4,000 to $16,000 between 1984 and 1994.[1]

By the late 1990s, however, while wedding consumption remained at an all-time high, the idea of the traditional wedding itself underwent a sea change. Experts who helped establish the American wedding as a consumer rite around the middle of the century—women such as Marie Coudert Brennig, Emily Post, Alexandra Potts, and Priscilla Kidder—would have raised an eyebrow at the seeming implosion of tradition in the past decade, most vividly symbolized by the popular reality wedding shows that play every night on cable television and money-making or corporate-sponsored million-dollar celebrity weddings.[2] Weddings had long been turned into publicity stunts for individuals and institutions, but never to such a degree and certainly not in the same way. By the late 1990s, American wedding culture took an ironic turn, becoming a postmodern pastiche of invented rituals, adopted customs, and ironic play on identity. In many cases, weddings became a spectacle that broke free of the boundaries of the traditional wedding, collapsing hierarchies of sexuality, gender, and class.[3]

Just as businesses, entrepreneurs, and wedding experts invented the "modern wedding" in the mid-twentieth century, they too had a hand in the creation of this new, more playfully inventive celebration by the century's end. In particular, a host of retailing innovations during this period changed the way businesses reached different bridal markets and challenged the idea of tradition that had been the mainstay of the nascent industry. Most significantly, these new ways of doing business, which included e-commerce, discount bridal apparel retailers, wedding expositions, and monopolistic partnerships between the different sectors of the wedding trade, increased the power of the wedding industry and strengthened its hold on the buying public. By the turn of the twenty-first century, through the efforts and innovations of this industry, a "language of commerce and the commodity" openly permeated American wedding culture, decentering the very idea of the traditional wedding, yet still upholding its place as a central consumer "rite."[4]

In the 1990s, businesses began adopting Internet technology to target different segments of the bridal market. Companies developed Web sites that advertised their goods and services and allowed consumers to make arrangements or shop directly through their online site. The nature of wedding Web sites allowed for an even greater market segmentation. Brides and grooms searched the Web to find just the right photographer, florist, and consultant to reflect their taste or budget or to choose the perfect ring, wedding gown, or assortment of household items for the gift registry. By 2000, according to one Internet research company, about 30 percent of couples used the Internet to plan their weddings. New wedding media and service companies brought together vendors and professionals in the field with those about to marry. For example, companies like the Wedding Channel allowed shoppers to find local resources in their area, such as bridal salons and florists.[5] Another dominant company in the field, The Knot, Inc., Weddings for the Real World, attracted advertising dollars to its online wedding-planning site launched in 1996. Much like *Bride's* magazine had done beginning in the mid-1930s, The Knot became a linchpin for the industry, channeling wedding businesses in a way that further consolidated the bridal market. The Knot also engaged in e-commerce, becoming the largest Internet retailer of wedding supplies, favors, and gifts for wedding attendants. In addition to its online services, it offered print publications, such as *The Knot*, a national wedding fashion publication, and *Weddingpages*, which appeared as a regional magazine in more than thirty different markets in the United States. The Knot also produced a book series with Random House and Chronicle Books. In conjunction with its online site, these publications helped The Knot develop a highly recognizable brand name for its service.

The Internet and e-commerce helped shape late twentieth-century wedding consumption, giving it a new immediacy and flexibility. Founders of the wedding industry, such as *Bride's* magazine, invested in new members of the industry, such as weddingchannel.com, a major online wedding planning and content resource. By forming an "exclusive strategic alliance," *Bride's* and weddingchannel.com were able to pool their marketing activities and extend the reach of their brands. Other Internet companies, however, positioned themselves in opposition to traditional members of the wedding industry. Press releases for The Knot promised that the company's shopping guides "[broke] the mold of old school bridal mags." Unlike print magazines published monthly or seasonally, Internet publications were continually updated and could claim to be in the moment in a way not possible with older media that yellowed and tattered with age. The Knot, for example, claimed to offer "to-be-weds exactly what they want: up-to-the-minute wedding style straight from the runways and real weddings, plus carefully organized directories to nuptial essentials . . . to help them make informed buying decisions while shopping for the big day."[6] Its Web site, moreover, noted that the company "pioneered the online wedding space" by "curing the clutter of the highly fragmented bridal industry" through its wedding planning Web site that provided the tools and resources for organizing a wedding.[7] With their endless ability to layer information link by link, Web sites like The Knot centralized the wedding industry in a way not possible in traditional publications. Yet this very layering and endless linking created its own type of fragmented virtual world where time and space collapsed—an anti-space in which information from vastly different sources only appeared to be connected, but in fact was severed from any single context or unifying authorship by the nature of the medium. In a matter of seconds, one might click from advertisements for gay wedding reception sites to department-store gift registries to articles condemning the commercialization of marital rites.

Less tradition-bound than older retailers, more flexible in their search for markets, online wedding entrepreneurs saw the wide-open potential of the Internet to reach previously ignored consumers, such as the gay and lesbian wedding market. This market began taking shape openly by the mid-1990s, with the publication of commercial gay wedding guides. Although the debate over legalizing gay marriage continues, businesses are poised to tap into what they see as a potentially lucrative market. In 2004, the projected purchasing power of the national lesbian and gay market was $485 billion a year.[8] According to *Forbes* magazine, if same-sex marriages were legalized and 92 percent of gay couples currently living together married (the percentage of co-habitating heterosexual couples that married in 2000), the result would be an expenditure of $16.8 billion. Numerous Web sites emerged to cater specifically to this market segment. After Vermont enacted a civil union law in April 2000, for example, Web sites began connecting gay couples with the local wedding industry. Right after the law passed, gayweddings.com sent approximately 3,000 couples to Vermont for civil unions. Businesses with a primarily heterosexual market also broadened their definition of the traditional wedding. According to Carley Roney, co-founder of The Knot, magazines like *Bride's* had to catch up to the Internet, which was a pioneer in this market.[9] The Knot featured a gay couple in 2000 and increasing editorial content and features on same-sex marriages (though according to another source, The Knot has been covering gay weddings since 1997). Attention to this market grew after the November 2004 Massachusetts ruling that gay couples had a right to marry under the state constitution.[10]

On a level not seen in the wedding industry before, wedding planning Web sites built synergies through partnerships with media and retailing giants to deliver this newly expanded bridal market to its advertisers and create profits for its investors. In 2003, and again in 2004, The Knot joined the women's cable network Oxygen to produce a television miniseries called "Real Weddings from The Knot." These television specials were filmed in "reality" style, following six couples through their wedding planning and preparations in the weeks leading up to their marriage. The Knot also built on past innovations in the business of brides. In a form of tie-in seen decades earlier between *Bride's* magazine and department stores, The Knot's Web site provided information about the gowns, flowers, favors, and reception sites featured in these televised "real weddings."[11] As on other reality shows, here wedding consumption merged with entertainment as the planning and preparation became the main point.

During this period, other areas of the wedding industry increasingly concentrated their hold on the bridal market. The jewelry industry's path, for example, mirrored that of mass retailers. Family-run businesses founded in the 1920s became chains in the early postwar period, and then merged with other chains in recent years to create organizations with immense brand reach and market share. By the twenty-first century, mass discounters like Wal-Mart began claiming a piece of this lucrative market, in spite of an image that ran counter to traditional ideas of wedding luxury and exclusivity.[12] Bridal magazines also consolidated their hold on the market. *Bride's* magazine and *Modern Bride*, which had been major competitors since their founding in 1934 and 1949, ended their rivalry in 2002 when *Bride's* publisher, Condé Nast, purchased its rival for $52 million. A new competitor for print magazines—Internet wedding planning sites—did the same, forming alliances with different major department store chains that gave them unprecedented access to millions of consumers.[13]

Partnerships with traditional retailers furthered the influence of these industry newcomers. For example, weddingchannel.com sold a stake in its company to Federated Department Stores, another major chain of mass retailers. Weddingchannel.com created ties with wedding gift registries at Federated stores in an attempt to overcome one of the weaknesses of e-commerce—brides and guests were reluctant to register for gifts or purchase gift items online without having seen the goods personally. According to the co-founder of weddingchannel.com, consumers wanted face-to-face contact with sales clerks and a place to return merchandise. The new alliance between wedding channel.com and department stores operated by Federated solved this problem as consumers could register their gift list at Federated stores, which in turn would promote weddingchannel.com and encourage brides to sign up with the Web site. Guests could then buy the items online from weddingchannel.com. Similarly, in 2002, The Knot acquired the backing of the May Department Stores Company, the second largest department store chain in the United States as of 2004.[14] A $14.2 billion company, May operated 439 department stores, including Lord & Taylor, Hecht's, Strawbridge's, Filene's, and Foley's, among others. This alliance launched a multi-platform marketing campaign, with online advertising, in-store promotions, direct mail and e-mail campaigns, as well as advertisements in The Knot publications. The Knot also promoted the wedding gift registry sites of May Department Stores companies.[15] The retailing world changed again in 2005 with the merger of these two goliaths, May and Federated.

Such synergy created unprecedented growth. According to its company Web site, The Knot had 3 million members by 2002 and 5.1 million by June 2004, "the largest audience—bar none—of wedding-obsessed, cash-wielding brides."[16] The May Department Stores Company created its own synergy with other retailers, expanding into the wedding apparel industry. In 2000, it spent $436 million to purchase the country's biggest wedding gown retailer, David's Bridal; in 2002, it acquired the industry pioneer Priscilla of Boston.[17] The creation of May's Bridal Group provided "a platform for sales growth" as David's Bridal customers then shopped and registered at May Department Stores (20 percent of registrations in the company's full-line department stores were from David's Bridal customers). The fate of this bridal group is unknown in 2005 after Federated purchased May Department Stores and is discussing whether to sell David's Bridal.

Wedding gown manufacturers and retailers changed dramatically during this period. Priscilla of Boston and David's Bridal represented two different phases of the wedding apparel industry—the era of the independent retailer and U.S. manufacturer that was replaced by the present-day phenomenon of discount and chain retailers and out-sourced production. As we have seen, Priscilla Kidder's bridal salons and Boston manufacturing concern emphasized expert service and fitting, as well as custom production. Though Priscilla popularized her name with ready-made designs, her brand suggested an American-produced couture, especially in its heyday of White House weddings in the late 1960s and early 1970s. Its success was tied to these elite associations, as well as to her own glamorous image. By the end of the twentieth century, Priscilla of Boston represented an older, more traditional style that faced many challenges from new market conditions. At the time of Priscilla of Boston's purchase by May, it was a "high-end company with a chain of ten stores and a good, if languishing, reputation."[18]

David's Bridal, on the other hand, was partly responsible for what writer

Rebecca Mead has called the "Wal-Martization" of the wedding industry. While David's originated as a small chain of bridal stores in Florida in the 1970s, it became well known as the first wedding gown discounter after 1990, when it opened a warehouse-like outlet store. Bridal retailers had offered discounts in the past, as in the case of Filene's Basement's traditional daylong sale on bridal gowns, held since 1947. But, for the most part, the specialty bridal shop built its allure on an image of exclusivity and luxury, as had department-store salons before their decline in the 1980s. Unlike Priscilla of Boston and others in the field who did not carry full lines of stock for customers and required appointments, ordering, and fittings, David's Bridal pared its services and costs down. In a break with tradition, when David's first entered the scene they performed no alternations, took no appointments, and sold their gowns in a wide range of sizes off-the-rack. Eventually, after their purchase by May Department Stores and reflecting this chain's desire to move David's away from its discount roots, David's introduced special-order designer dresses and began to follow traditional bridal salon culture in that they now took appointments from customers, though these were not required as they were in other more exclusive stores. Gowns were of cheaper quality as well, purchased directly from manufacturers in Taiwan, and later, from factories in China, Vietnam, the Philippines, Thailand, and Sri Lanka, where the firm established its own factory. These practices generated tremendous profits, while allowing their dresses to retail on average $500 (the average bride in the United States spent $800 on her gown). David's Bridal ads, offering "your dream gown at a great value," regularly command large portions of advertising space in bridal magazines.[19]

Not surprisingly, as was the case with other discounters and mass retailers, the rise of David's Bridal and these mergers hurt traditional independent bridal salons and wedding apparel and men's formalwear manufacturers. In the case of Priscilla of Boston, giving in to the goliath seemed to have been the solution. As of 2003, there were still 3,000 independent bridal retailers fighting for survival. These businesses competed with the seemingly unstoppable David's by emphasizing their expert service and elevating the whole consumer experience, marketing techniques long in use in the wedding industry. Some, like designer Vera Wang, found a niche in the luxury wedding gown market, selling gowns that averaged between $2,000 and $7,000. Other independents also entered the discount market.[20]

Those in the tuxedo business had to contend with these new trends. Wedding rentals were the mainstay of this estimated $1 billion industry in 2003 (tuxedos were rented in 90 percent of weddings). As it did with bridal apparel, May Department Stores consolidated the tuxedo business, creating an unprecedented united front. In 2001, May acquired After Hours, an Atlanta-based men's formalwear franchise that itself was a consolidation of competitors in that region and elsewhere. Soon after, May purchased Modern Tuxedo, a 26-store Chicago chain, Desmonds Formalwear, a 66-outlet firm in the Midwest, and 125 Gingiss stores, one of the oldest names in men's formalwear. Independent tuxedo stores tried to compete in this business by affiliating themselves with a bridal shop in order to get "bridal leads" and access to the consumers who made the decisions. This strategy helped May Department Stores. Because of its association with David's Bridal, May's newly merged tuxedo concerns had "one big advantage," according to Robert Huth, president and chief executive of May's bridal group—"first shot on [sic] the bride."[21]

Unlike earlier bridal salons, David's Bridal offered an experience and a product that further exploded the idea of wedding tradition, even as it drew on it for power and legitimacy. David's made visible what had been hidden before—the mass-produced, ready-made gowns masquerading as one-of-a-kind creations that turned a woman into a queen for a day. Independent and department-store bridal salons, as we have seen, displayed show models but generally maintained little stock and kept what sizes they did carry in protected spaces. Racks and racks of gowns in all sizes did not convey the sense of uniqueness or luxury created by the minimalist modernist display often used in department-store salons or specialty bridal shops. David's accepted the disconnect between the production and the experience of the good. Rather than hiding this incongruent relation, David's and presumably their customers simply did not pay attention to it. A woman who chose her less-expensive gown at these pared-down outlets could still be a beautiful bride and experience her wedding the same way as in the past.

Other innovations during this period broke with the founders of the industry, marking a shift toward a less hierarchical and more inclusive American wedding culture. Wedding planning Web sites and online shopping, for example, potentially challenged the expertise of wedding professionals built up in the postwar period. These new ways of selling gowns and reaching the bridal market de-centered the traditional wedding expert. Though brides continued to draw on her knowledge and use her authority, she was no longer the central mastermind behind the wedding who worked in conjunction with the bride's mother. While wedding consultants and their professional organizations used Web sites to attract clientele and promote their services, the nature of online shopping shifted much of the planning to the consumers—the bride and groom themselves. David's Bridal, for example, encouraged brides to visit their stores on weekdays, when salespeople were less busy, and to prepare for their appointments by perusing the online catalogue and coming in with printouts of dress styles they wanted.[22] Internet wedding planning sites where couples could register for gifts and plan every detail of their wedding and honeymoon allowed consumers to research their options from home and at all hours, rather than visiting department stores, bridal salons, florists, photographers, jewelers, and the commercial venues for the reception. The bride could come to her wedding planner with a clear vision of her dream wedding, armed with information about vendors and different types of weddings gleaned from the Internet. This new commercial context empowered brides, giving birth to the "Bridezilla," a term very postmodern in its incongruous self-mocking union of "bride" and "Godzilla." (The Bridezilla is an acquisitive, controlling woman who focuses on the material elements of her celebration and runs roughshod over guests, the wedding party, and vendors, especially her bridal consultant.)[23] New types of wedding planning books that empowered the bride to make her own traditions replaced older etiquette authorities. As Dennis Hall has pointed out, *Weddings for Dummies* (1997), part of the immensely popular "For Dummies" series that attacks a variety of topics and problems in life, broke with earlier conduct books. According to Hall, where Emily Post was authoritative and hierarchical and in her time was among a small group of experts in the field, *Weddings for Dummies* competed within a huge universe of conduct books by focusing narrowly on its topic, presenting its wedding advice informally and nonlinearly, and in a way that indulged in the "bracketing and winking, self-reflexivity, and cheap irony" associated with postmodern texts.[24] Traditional experts like the Emily Post enterprise, however, also adapted to new circumstances, producing multimedia wedding planning software.[25]

At the same time, this plethora of options seems to have increased the labor involved in planning marital celebrations. Although heralded as a way to save time, it is likely that the endless choices provided by online vendors and the round-the-clock availability of Internet shopping escalated the effort that couples put into their wedding plans, effort that bridal consultants had long made it their business to save. Instead of turning to an expert or professional, whether it was a travel agent or a wedding planner, the consumer took on the often daunting task of trying to find the "best deal," aided by bargain bridal handbooks and Internet research. In the 1990s, for example, planning a wedding involved visiting on average thirty different retail locations. The work of consumption also spread as the groom-to-be took more of a role in the wedding planning and made more consumer decisions with the rise of this type of shopping.[26]

Early entrants in the industry also changed as bridal magazines, which had begun as authorities on etiquette and wedding fashion, displayed a more playful and ironic sensibility at the turn of the twenty-first century. In the early postwar period, these consumer publications emphasized flexibility and individual taste. Bridal magazines today continue to do this, repeating the idea that a wedding should reflect the personality of the bride (or "the couple" in recent years).[27] But in the past, this emphasis on individuality and personality did not mean that "tradition" itself could be dispensed with or even questioned. In decades past, weddings, romance, and the beautiful bride were serious business. In recent years, though, mainstream books and popular Web sites on wedding planning celebrated the perspective of the "anti-bride" and critiqued American wedding culture. In bridal magazines, beauty products for the big day appeared in a humorous vein, with articles titled "Lash Track—How to apply mascara so magnificent, it's mesmerizing." Occasionally, ads poked fun at the patriarchy of the ceremony itself or playfully bent the gender roles of the bride and groom. An online bridal registry, fortunoff.com, for example, ran a series of ads depicting a bride-and-groom wedding cake topper in which the bride was strangling the groom.[28] Ads for the big-box store Target, and its gift registry service "ClubWedd," featured men singing into their mops while the bride smirked self-consciously into her feather-duster bridal bouquet, suggesting an awareness of the past and a retro playfulness with long-standing divisions of labor. In contemporary bridal magazines, even the consumerism of the industry and the irrationality of over-the-top wedding consumption itself was a subject of occasional humorous comment, as in the case of a one-page feature poking fun at the cost of being a Hollywood bride—"$415,811— Before the Flowers," a total that included $1,200 for a "poof-ect pooch" or dog, and $8,000 for breast implants.[29]

Though contemporary bridal magazines expanded "tradition" in new directions and even challenged it, they never completely abandoned it. Much remained the same, as bridal magazines continued to advise couples on wedding etiquette and on the correct format for such things as the procession and recession in different religious ceremonies.[30] In other places, however, these publications also broke down long-standing rules of social conduct. Some advice went in radical new directions, collapsing hierarchies of sexuality. In 2003, for the first time, *Bride's* broke with tradition and addressed the issue of gay marriage in a short, one-page, though much heralded piece. The magazine's editor, Millie Martini Bratten, explained the decision to include the article, noting the gay wedding market's gift registry business and readers' questions about gay wedding etiquette. According to Bratten, the current generation getting married was more inclusive than ever before, something the magazine was trying to address. The article placed the movement as "a natural progression and assertion of civil rights." More in keeping with the light tone of the magazine, however, it also offered advice for guests invited to a gay wedding. Interestingly, the article also undermined its radical potential, noting that "same-sex affairs can be nearly as traditional as heterosexual ones."[31]

Contemporary bridal magazines and other wedding experts also depicted wedding styles and consumer choices that broke with earlier social strictures. New wedding fashions drew self-reflexively on past traditions for meaning. This shift was visible in advice on the traditional white. In the past, etiquette writers advised brides who did not fit the standard of the young virginal bride not to wear white. For example, pregnant or repeat brides were admonished not to choose white and older women were advised to select a color that was flattering to their appearance. In 1977, *Modern Bride* began addressing the "mature" bride and also began formally recognizing second weddings with a "married again" section. This early recognition of an older or repeat bridal market focused on appropriate dress styles and etiquette. By the late 1990s, however, experts urged nontraditional brides, such as the visibly pregnant bride or the older bride, to have the more lucrative traditional "white" wedding.[32] By 2003, *Bride's* magazine featured women who married in formal white gowns at age thirty and forty.[33] In both cases, the formal white wedding was the accepted standard, only now it could be appropriated by new groups and interpreted in a variety of ways. In general, what was considered to be appropriate wedding apparel also expanded during this period, as bridal fashions ran the gamut from gowns with full crinoline skirts to spare slip dresses, from the high-necked, long-sleeved dress to backless outfits or gowns with plunging necklines. Colors and patterns other than solid white also appeared regularly. Wedding planning Web sites, such as The Knot, helped to change "tradition" by announcing to millions of consumers such things as "pink is the new white in weddings."[34]

Advertisements for contemporary bridal fashions in these publications began to adopt a more self-reflexive, playful aesthetic. This is not to say that bridal fashion photography changed wholesale. Many ads continued to follow a representational style much in keeping with that found in bridal magazines from the early years of the wedding industry. Then and now, many ads feature a model standing in a designer gown against a solid color background or traditional wedding location. While some ads began to depict brides in suggestive poses, lying supine on a bench for example, the photographs still foregrounded the fashion details of the dress, rather than the metaphorical meaning generated by the context or background.[35] Some contemporary ads, however, broke with this older representational style through a distinctively postmodern embrace of the "irreverent pastiche" and "the language of commerce and the commodity."[36] Many ads depicted wedding gowns (and the women who wore them) as works of art by placing the model in museum-like settings, in front of a painting or draped over a piece of classical sculpture. Others more explicitly turned the bride and her gown into something to be admired and perhaps purchased by placing her within a gilded frame. One 2003 ad for Reem Acra wedding dresses, for example, used explicit "language of commerce" and turned the bride into a commodity. In a two-page advertising spread at the front of *Bride's*, two models wearing long white Reem Acra gowns appeared with skin and hair painted gold (à la Ian Fleming's *Goldfinger*) in front of a gilt backdrop of painted trees, wall, and a classical bust. Both were draped with layers of heavy gold jewelry, while one, as if to make the obvious connection between sex and money clear, wore big gold earrings that read "sexy" in capital letters. The elegant white embroidered wedding dresses stood out in stark relief, while the two women wearing the gowns melded into the golden background as props.[37]

In a similar vein, bridal magazine articles about wedding fashions sometimes adopted a postmodern historical referentiality. Modernist ideas of time collapsed in these articles. For example, one piece, subtitled "Past Forward," paired new bridal fashions with photos of the eclectic "vintage styles" that inspired them. Such styles were not intended to be nostalgic—instead, they were represented as "anchored in the past but reinterpreted for modern times." In this article, wedding fashion did not develop in a linear way; instead, it embraced discontinuity. Styles appeared in a pastiche of different time periods and gender norms, from "traditional geisha glamour" inspired by a 1904 image of Puccini's Madama Butterfly to the Hollywood fashions from the 1930s and 1950s to Jacqueline Kennedy's style as First Lady.[38]

Just as bridal magazines sometimes reflected a new wedding aesthetic, the tradition of the bridal fashion show and bridal fair also changed, expanding into the more inclusive "wedding expo." As we have seen, bridal fashion shows were typically associated with one retailer, while bridal fairs featured a broader range of goods and services from different retailers and manufacturers all under one roof. Over the past twenty years, massive wedding expositions mirrored the expansion of the wedding industry.[39] The wedding expo featured many more exhibitors and attendants than earlier bridal fairs. These big sales events were held repeatedly during the year in all cities across the country. One early entrant on the scene, the "Original Wedding Expo," advertised its advantages to potential vendors, noting that it featured 150 exhibitors on average at convention center events and attracted an average of 1,500 brides and 3,000 guests. Hotel venues for the expo were smaller, but still on a much grander scale than before. Also held in convention centers, these events were billed as extravaganzas, offering "one-stop shopping for the wedding of your dreams." Expos continued to expand the definition of bridal, including vendors for such things as insurance and housewares, as well as the many goods and services now traditional, such as candles and limousines or florists, photographers, and videographers.[40] Unlike earlier bridal fairs, the more recent wedding expo also included exhibits from vendors selling gym memberships and diet plans, adding a new dimension to the traditional beauty industry that had targeted brides.[41] Rather than simply selling beauty products for grooming and "making up," these vendors catered to a new idea of the "buff bride"—a bride who remade her body for her wedding day—an ideal celebrated on reality television shows of that name.

With the arrival of the first gay wedding exposition at the turn of the twenty-first century, tradition took a new turn. Bridal fairs, such as the New York event protested by WITCH in 1969, celebrated consumerism and upheld traditional gender roles. Wedding expositions, with their expanded list of vendors and broader market reach, simply elaborated these values and took them to a wider audience. The gay exposition, however, played with the idea of "tradition." These events challenged heteronormative gender roles and definitions of marriage or couplehood, all the while fitting radical new social relations into a familiar consumerist context. As they borrowed invented traditions, such as the white bridal gown, wedding cake toppers, the double-ring ceremony, and the catered affair, they unhinged them from their original gendered meaning.[42]

In keeping with the larger purpose of the wedding industry, gay wedding expos were largely commercial, but they were also understood as a means for achieving equality—an equality based on consumer citizenship as well as social belonging. On one level, this market segment of the industry challenged dominant heterogender ideals and social roles. Businesses adapted quickly to this potential new market, bringing the promise of broader social change. Gender-neutral terms have appeared in department-store and specialty-store gift registries, and department stores have even begun hosting same-sex wedding expos.[43] Commercial venues for wedding receptions have also seen the potential. The first same-sex wedding expo in New York was held in 2001 at the Thatched Cottage, the Long Island catering hall known for decades for its thematic package-deal weddings. Unlike traditional commercial fairs or expos, this event was sponsored by Marriage Equality New York, a group advocating the legalization of gay marriage. According to a *New York Times* article on the event, some came to the Thatched Cottage in support of this civil rights issue, noting that "gowns and triple-decker cakes, for all of their frivolity, were

FIGURE 48. The gay wedding market created a need for new goods and services. Same-sex items, such as wedding cake toppers, allowed gays and lesbians to uphold "tradition" when they married. Collection of the author.

significant symbols on the path toward legal recognition." One exhibitor asserted that gay couples, like others who marry, also desire "roses and orchids and ice sculptures."[44]

Some firms catering to this market tried to avoid being "controversial" and expressed a desire to be "mainstream" and appeal to both the gay and heterosexual wedding market.[45] The more ironic aspects of gay culture expressed in cross-dressing and mock weddings did not play a part at these events. Some businesses do cater to the more transgressive aspects of the gay wedding with humorous products that playfully challenge heterosexual norms (figure 48). But wedding expos are big business and thus are typically conservative events. For example, the 2004 Gay and Lesbian Wedding Expo held in Garden Grove, California, featured exhibits from American Express and Wells Fargo Mortgage, as well as photography, catering, and tuxedo firms. The Garden Grove Expo, according to the minister who organized it, was simply for "run-of-the-mill couples just looking to arrange weddings." Like mainstream wedding expos, these events promoted consumption through the "package deal." In 2004, for example, a same-sex wedding expo held in Manhattan promoted the usual exhibits, such as vacation packages for gay couples, but hotel packages sometimes adopted names with a political cachet, such as the "Freedom to Marry" honeymoon package, or the "Proud to Be in Love" package. Even these commercial events, however, addressed serious issues and featured exhibits with a political edge. Expos offered legal advice on adoptions and domestic partnership agreements.[46]

* * *

The postmodern American wedding culture of recent years may not in fact be a break with tradition, but merely the continuation (or completion—it remains to be seen) of a process long under way. Recent retailing innovations of course differ from what came before in that they give the wedding industry unprecedented access to consumers and power to shape wedding practice. Coupled with the recent boom in weddings in popular culture, as seen in magazines, movies, and television, new social institutions like The Knot and David's Bridal are able to spread the formal white wedding to every corner of American society in a way that would have been unimaginable thirty-five years ago. As always, individuals continue to find ways to oppose this industry and host celebrations in keeping with their values and tastes.[47] In recent years, however, even opposition to over-the-top wedding consumption found its own niche in the wedding industry, with Web sites and planning guides dedicated to green weddings, the anti-bride, and the indie bride.[48]

The economic and cultural power of the wedding industry today should come as no surprise now, given its history. The gay wedding industry and other seemingly tradition-breaking trends in the mainstream wedding industry, for example, built on the modernity/tradition dichotomy employed by past innovators in the field. Wedding expositions, wedding e-commerce, discount bridal retailers, and the consolidation of bridal retailing through mergers and the new synergies they created are all a logical extension of the consumer rites established during the middle decades of the century. As we have seen, between roughly the 1920s and the 1950s, diverse businesses and entrepreneurs established and legitimized a nascent wedding industry by simultaneously drawing on and deconstructing the power of "tradition." By creating new rituals, bridal magazines, etiquette writers, jewelers, department stores, wedding consultants, caterers, and others turned it into a flexible marketing tool in pursuit of the lucrative bridal market. It was not until the rise of a national wedding industry and this new use of tradition that certain consumer rites became codified and the costly celebration with all the trimmings became a cultural expectation. Inventing traditions and promoting new professional services as essential for the traditional wedding, the wedding industry expanded the material outlines of the marriage ritual and linked it, seemingly inextricably, to a modern consumer ethic.

$\mathscr{Notes}$

INTRODUCTION

1. The wedding industry provides its own figures, which are used by bridal magazines to attract advertisers. See http://www.forbes.com/2002/05/09/0509feat.html and http://www.condenet.com/press/condenet/wedding.html for the $70 billion figure. Also, see "The May Department Stores Company and The Knot Announce Marketing Alliance," http://www.theknot.com/02.25.02.shtml. For the $30,000 figure, see http://www.entrepreneur.com/article/0,4621,290139,00.html and http://money.cnn.com/2005/05/20/pf/weddings/. This is up from 2002, when the average wedding cost $22,360.

2. "A Little Light Reading Anyone?" *New York Times* (April 11, 2000), 6.

3. For example, most undergraduates in my spring 2003 women's studies course at Hartwick College, "Weddings, Marriage, and the Family: Feminist Perspectives," embraced the formal white wedding ideal and accepted the wedding industry in our class discussions and in the questionnaires I circulated at the end of the course.

4. "Trade on Tradition," *Jewelers' Circular-Keystone* (October 1944), 168.

5. Eric Hobsbawm, "Introduction: Inventing Tradition," in *The Invention of Tradition*, ed. Eric Hobsbawm and Terence Ranger (Cambridge: Cambridge University Press, 1983), 1.

6. Ibid., 1–3.

7. Elaine Tyler May places the rising marriage rates, baby boom, and domestic focus of this period in the context of Cold War fears of communism and nuclear annihilation, but does not discuss weddings. See her *Homeward Bound: American Families in the Cold War Era* (New York: Basic Books, 1988). Also, see Beth Bailey, *From Front Porch to Back Seat: Courtship in Twentieth-Century America* (Baltimore: Johns Hopkins University Press, 1988).

8. "Marriages; The Blushing Bride is a Mighty Economic Force," *Better Living: DuPont Employee Magazine* 7 (November–December 1954), 17; "Tin Anniversary: 10th Postwar Year Sets Record for Wedding Celebrations in the U.S.," *Better Living: Du Pont Employee Magazine* 10 (May–June 1956), 26–27; "Ten Years Later . . . *Better Living* Records Decade of Unequaled Progress for Employees," *Better Living: DuPont Employee Magazine* 10 (November–December 1956). Hagley Museum and Library, Wilmington, Delaware (hereafter Hagley). For a discussion of the attitudes toward affluence during this period, see Daniel Horowitz, *The Anxieties of Affluence: Critiques*

of American Consumer Culture, 1939–1979 (Amherst: University of Massachusetts Press, 2004).

9. Lizabeth Cohen, *A Consumers' Republic: The Politics of Mass Consumption in Postwar America* (New York: Alfred A. Knopf, 2003), 11; Betty Friedan, *The Feminine Mystique* (New York: W. W. Norton, 1963); Nancy A. Walker, ed., *Women's Magazines, 1940–1960: Gender Roles and the Popular Press* (Boston: St. Martin's Press, 1998); Joanne Meyerowitz, ed., *Not June Cleaver: Women and Gender in Postwar America, 1945–1969* (Philadelphia: Temple University Press, 1994).

10. For an excellent sociological and cultural studies approach to weddings in contemporary popular culture, see Chrys Ingraham's *White Weddings: Romancing Heterosexuality in Popular Culture* (New York: Routledge, 1999). For a scholarly treatment of the meaning of the white wedding in the United States and the world, see Cele Otnes and Elizabeth Pleck, *Cinderella Dreams: The Allure of the Lavish Wedding* (Berkeley: University of California Press, 2003). Also, see Barbara Penner, "A Vision of Love and Luxury: The Commercialization of Nineteenth-Century American Weddings," in *Winterthur Portfolio* 39 (Spring 2004). A recent journalistic work on weddings, Carol McD. Wallace's *All Dressed in White: The Irresistible Rise of the American Wedding* (New York: Penguin, 2004), drew extensively on my 2000 dissertation, "American Weddings: Gender, Consumption, and the Business of Brides" (Ph.D. diss., University of Texas at Austin), largely without attributing the source of its information. Wallace's book, moreover, is poorly written and without footnotes, an index, or full bibliography. Readers interested in serious contemplations of the topic are better served by the work of Cele Otnes and Elizabeth Pleck or Chrys Ingraham, or the forthcoming work by Katherine Jellison. In addition, a popularly written, though intellectually serious, feminist work by Jaclyn Geller is also relevant: *Here Comes the Bride: Women, Weddings, and the Marriage Mystique* (New York: Four Walls Eight Windows, 2001).

11. Lloyd Wendt and Herman Kogan, *Give the Lady What She Wants!* (Chicago: Rand McNally, 1952). The consumer sovereignty thesis favored by some business and cultural historians problematically naturalizes the producer perspective, in that it implicitly accepts at face value and validates the producer's own desire to meet demand.

12. In this way, *Brides, Inc.* is part of a recent movement to bring the consumer into business history, reflected by Kathy Peiss's book on the cosmetic industry and American beauty culture, and Regina Blaszczyk's study of ceramics and glass industries in the United States. Kathy Peiss, *Hope in a Jar: The Making of America's Beauty Culture* (New York: Metropolitan Books, 1998); Regina Lee Blaszczyk, *Imagining Consumers: Design and Innovation from Wedgwood to Corning* (Baltimore: Johns Hopkins University Press, 2000). *Brides, Inc.* also connects with a feminist historiography of women's labor history that integrates discussions of production, labor, and consumption, best represented by Wendy Gamber's book on the dressmaking trade and Alison J. Clarke's work on Tupperware. Wendy Gamber, *The Female Economy: The Millinery and Dressmaking Trades, 1860–1930* (Urbana: University of Illinois Press, 1997);

Alison J. Clarke, *Tupperware: The Promise of Plastic in the 1950s* (Washington, D.C.: Smithsonian Institution Press, 1999).

13. *Brides, Inc.* challenges the liberatory potential of consumerism, especially in the context of recent developments, such as the rise of global corporations and the deindustrialization of the United States. For an overview of different views of consumption, see Gary Cross's synthesis, *An All-Consuming Century: Why Commercialism Won in Modern America* (New York: Columbia University Press, 2000), which discusses the history of the "jeremiad" tradition, as well as more celebratory perspectives on consumerism.

14. While women in the early twentieth century may have appropriated mass culture for political ends, at the end of that century it was more difficult to find such appropriation and resistance in the face of all-encompassing corporate power. For discussions of early twentieth-century consumer agency and working-class women, see Nan Enstad, *Ladies of Labor, Girls of Adventure: Working Women, Popular Culture, and Labor Politics at the Turn of the Twentieth Century* (New York: Columbia University Press, 1999). Also, see Kathy Peiss, *Cheap Amusements: Working Women and Leisure in Turn-of-the-Century New York* (Philadelphia: Temple University Press, 1986).

15. See Nancy F. Cott, *Public Vows: A History of Marriage and the Nation* (Cambridge, Mass.: Harvard University Press, 2000), for a discussion of marriage and ideas of citizenship.

16. John Gillis, *A World of Their Own Making: Myth, Ritual, and the Quest for Family Values* (Cambridge, Mass.: Harvard University Press, 1997), 150–151.

17. "Wedding Profits for Jewelers," *Jewelers' Circular* (May 1932), 30; "Cupid Really Mows 'Em Down in First Quarter of 1946," *Jewelers' Circular-Keystone* (June 1946), 348.

18. See Karen Dubinsky, *The Second Greatest Disappointment: Honeymooning and Tourism at Niagara Falls* (New Brunswick, N.J.: Rutgers University Press, 1999). For a discussion of wedding photography, a major area of the wedding industry, see Charles Wesley Lewis, "Working the Ritual: Wedding Photographs as Social Process" (Ph.D. diss., University of Minnesota, 1994); Charles Wesley Lewis, "Hegemony in the Ideal: Wedding Photography, Consumerism, and Patriarchy," *Women's Studies in Communication* 20 (Fall 1997), 167–187; Charles Wesley Lewis, "Working the Ritual: Professional Wedding Photography and the American Middle Class," *Journal of Communication Inquiry* 22 (January 1998), 72–92.

CHAPTER 1. THE EVIL OF ELABORATE AND SHOWY WEDDINGS

1. Daniel Horowitz, *The Morality of Spending: Attitudes Toward the Consumer Society in America, 1875–1940* (Baltimore: Johns Hopkins University Press, 1985), 68–69; Elaine Tyler May, *Great Expectations: Marriage and Divorce in Post-Victorian America* (Chicago: University of Chicago Press, 1980), 20–21. The "dawn of history" cited in Edith Wharton, *The Age of Innocence: Complete Text with Introduction, Historical Contexts, Critical Essays*, ed. Carol J. Singley (Boston: Houghton Mifflin, 2000), 154.

2. Cott, *Public Vows*, 30–32.

3. For an example of an eighteenth-century slave wedding in New Jersey, see Susan E. Klepp and Billy G. Smith, eds., *The Infortunate: The Voyage and Adventures of William Moraley, an Indentured Servant* (University Park: Pennsylvania State University Press, 1992), 96. For examples of nineteenth-century slave weddings, see Dorothy Sterling, ed., *We Are Your Sisters: Black Women in the Nineteenth Century* (New York: W. W. Norton, 1984), 35–37; John Larkin, *The Reshaping of Everyday Life: 1790–1840* (New York: Harper & Row, 1988), 64–65.

4. Larkin, *The Reshaping of Everyday Life*, 65–66, 240; Laurel Thatcher Ulrich, *A Midwife's Tale: The Life of Martha Ballard Based on Her Diary, 1785–1812* (New York: Vintage Books, 1990), 146–147, 140–141; Ellen K. Rothman, *Hands and Hearts: A History of Courtship in America* (New York: Basic Books, 1984), 76–77.

5. Quotation in Mrs. H. C. Gates, American Life Histories, Library of Congress, Manuscript Division, WPA Federal Writers' Project Collection (hereafter American Life Histories). John Mack Faragher, *Sugar Creek: Life on the Illinois Prairie* (New Haven: Yale University Press, 1986), 80–82; David Hackett Fischer, *Albion's Seed: Four British Folkways in America* (New York: Oxford University Press, 1989), 282; Brenda E. Stevenson, *Life in Black and White: Family and Community in the Slave South* (New York: Oxford University Press, 1996), 64–65, 228–229; Bertram Wyatt-Brown, *Southern Honor: Ethics and Behavior in the Old South* (New York: Oxford University Press, 1982), 445–446, 448.

6. William Simon Wall Interview, American Life Histories.

7. Ibid.

8. Peter Ward, *Courtship, Love and Marriage in Nineteenth-Century English Canada* (Montreal: McGill-Queens University Press, 1990), 111; Blanche M. Ellis, Diary, 1890–1891, December 3–4, Joseph Downs Collection of Manuscripts and Printed Ephemera, Winterthur Library, Wilmington, Delaware.

9. Rothman, *Hands and Hearts*, 76, 77–78, 80, 167; Larkin, *The Reshaping of Everyday Life*, 63–64.

10. Larkin, *The Reshaping of Everyday Life*, 71; Katherine Grier, *Culture and Comfort: Parlor Making and Middle-Class Identity, 1850–1930* (Washington, D.C.: Smithsonian Institution Press, 1988), 79. Etiquette books also referred to the parlor wedding. See M. S. Rayne, *Gems of Deportment* (Detroit: Tyler & Company, 1882), 193.

11. For a discussion of True Womanhood, see Vicki Howard, "Courtship Letters of an African American Couple: Race, Gender, Class, and the Cult of True Womanhood," *Southwestern Historical Quarterly* (July 1996); George Elliott Howard, *A History of Matrimonial Institutions*, vol. 2 (Chicago: University of Chicago Press, Callaghan & Company, 1904), 140; "A Woman of Fashion," *Etiquette for Americans* (New York: Duffield & Company, 1909), 108.

12. Frank Norris, *McTeague: A Story of San Francisco* (New York: Doubleday & McClure, 1899; reprint, New York: Penguin Books, 1964), 30; Robert S. Lynd and Helen Merrell Lynd, *Middletown: A Study in Modern American Culture* (New York: Harcourt Brace Jovanovich, 1929), 112.

13. "Record of Trousseau and Marriage Expenses," in Warshaw Collection of Busi-

ness Americana—Matrimony, Archives Center, National Museum of American History (hereafter NMAH); Behring Center, Smithsonian Institution, Washington, D.C. "The Decoration of a Church for a June Wedding" and "Church Wedding in June," *Florist Exchange* 29 (June 4, 1910), 996; "Seventeen Distinguished Authors," *Correct Social Usage* (New York: New York Society of Self-Culture, 1903), 133–135.

14. Belle Spauling, "A Home Wedding in June," *Boston Cooking-School Magazine* (June–July 1900), 12–13; "Menus for Wedding Feasts and Class Spreads," *Boston Cooking-School Magazine* (June–July 1908), 35; Alice Kessler-Harris, *Out to Work: A History of Wage-Earning Women in the United States* (New York: Oxford University Press, 1982), 113.

15. Mrs. H. C. Gates, Lexington, Missouri, American Life Histories; Upton Sinclair, *The Jungle* (New York: Doubleday, 1905. Reprint New York: Signet Books, 1980), 10; Blanche M. Ellis, Diary, 1890–1891, December 3–4; the 1906 quote on wedding cake is from Til to Miss H. E. Purvis, October 19, 1906, George C. Purvis & Family Papers, Hill Memorial Library, Baton Rouge, Louisiana (hereafter HML).

16. Wanamaker's sought the June wedding trade and promoted sterling silver as "the accepted and conventional wedding present." "Silverware: Push Stocks This Month," *Dry Goods Economist* (June 8, 1901), 42; *Store Chat* (October 15, 1909), 273, Strawbridge & Clothier Collection, Hagley; "Our 1905 Rose Festival an Event Without Precedent," *The Evening Bulletin—Phil*, June 3, 1905, newspaper advertisements, series 8, box 75, Strawbridge & Clothier Collection.

17. "Wedding and Gift List from an Unknown Bride," box 1, Tennessee State Library and Archives, Nashville; Titcomb-Shepard Wedding Album, Massachusetts Historical Society, Boston.

18. Cathy Luchetti, *"I Do!" Courtship, Love and Marriage on the American Frontier* (New York: Crown Trade Paperbacks, 1996), 173; Rothman, *Hands and Hearts*, 167–168.

19. Mary Paul to Howard Bland, September 13, 1905, Mary Paul to Howard Bland, 1905, box 3, Bland Family Papers, University of Maryland, College Park; Pauline Wright to Irby Nichols, June 19, 1918, Irby C. Nichols and Family Papers, HML. For a more extended discussion of wedding gifts, see Howard, "American Weddings," 241–242. My discussion of wedding gifts focuses on cultural meanings that are historically determined; scholars from different disciplines have explored other complex meanings of the gift. For example, see Amanda Vickery, "Women and the World of Goods: A Lancashire Consumer and Her Possessions, 1751–1781," in *Consumption and the World of Goods*, ed. John Brewer and Roy Porter (London: Routledge, 1993), 280–286, 294. Other, more structural ways of studying gift behavior come from sociology and anthropology. For a landmark text, see Marcel Mauss, *The Gift: Forms and Functions of Exchange in Archaic Societies* (New York: W. W. Norton, 1967), 9–10. For a contemporary sociological study of North American gift behavior, see David Cheal, "The Social Dimensions of Gift Behavior," *Journal of Social and Personal Relationships* 3 (1986), 423–439.

20. Card from August Schneider to Mary Moody Northern, n.d., Moody Mansion,

Galveston, Texas; For other examples of southern and handmade gifts, see Pauline Wright to Irby Nichols, June 10, 1918, Irby C. Nichols and Family Papers; Mabelle Martin Bryant interview by Judith Linsley, March 14, 1989, McFaddin-Ward House Museum, Beaumont, Texas.

21. Henry Ward Beecher, "Wedding Bazaars," *Godey's Lady's Book and Magazine* (March 1870), 295. An earlier critique of the consumer goods acquired through marriage appears in Lydia Maria Child, *The Frugal Housewife etc.*, 3rd ed. (Boston: Carter & Hendee, 1830), 102.

22. Beecher, "Wedding Bazaars," 295. This type of critique also appeared in the early twentieth century: Margaret Woodward, "The Evil of Elaborate and Showy Weddings," *Suburban Life* 14 (June 1912), 418. For a discussion of Victorian concern over hypocrisy, see Karen Halttunen, *Confidence Men and Painted Women: A Study of Middle-Class Culture in America, 1830–1870* (New Haven, Conn.: Yale University Press, 1982).

23. "Seventeen Distinguished Authors," 116. Also, see Margaret E. Sangster, *Good Manners for All Occasions* (New York: Christian Herald, 1904), 131;

24. Charles Hanson Towne, *Gentlemen Behave* (New York: J. Messner, 1939), 62–63; N. C., *Practical Etiquette* (Chicago: A. Flanagan, 1899), 53. Emily S. Bouton, *Social Etiquette: The Usages of Good Society*, 7th ed. (Chicago: F. Tennyson Neely, 1882; 1894), 182; quote taken from "Wedding Cards," *Godey's* (January 1873), 96.

25. Rayne, *Gems of Deportment*, 202.

26. Edith Wharton, *House of Mirth* (1905; New York: Bantam Books, 1984), 85–86; Wedding scrapbook, newsclipping, Caldwell-Chrisman wedding, n.d. McFaddin-Ward House Museum; Rothman, *Hands and Hearts*, 168; quotes from Wedding scrapbook, newsclipping, 1914, McFaddin-Ward House Museum.

27. Beecher quoted in T. De Witt Talmage, *The Marriage Ring: A Series of Discourses in Brooklyn Tabernacle* (New York: Funk & Wagnalls, 1886), 79–80.

28. Rayne, *Gems of Deportment*, 176.

29. Anne Randall White, *Twentieth-Century Etiquette* (Chicago: Wabash Publishing House, 1904), 278.

30. In Wharton's *Age of Innocence,* there is a "stormy discussion as to whether the wedding presents should be 'shown.'" The character Mrs. Welland refused to have her daughter's gifts displayed: nearly in tears, she stated that she "should as soon turn the reporters loose in [her] house" (156); 1847 Rogers Bros., 1915–1916, box 80, folder 2, N. W. Ayer Advertising Agency Records, NMAH.

31. Beecher, "Wedding Bazaars," 295; "A Woman of Fashion," *Etiquette for Americans*, 109.

32. Wharton, *House of Mirth*, 85; Mary Roberts Coolidge, *Why Women Are So* (New York: Henry Holt, 1912; reprint, New York: Arno, 1972), quotations from 25–28, 29, 21–22.

33. Sangster, *Good Manners for All Occasions*, 131.

34. Abraham Cahan, "A Ghetto Wedding," in *Yekl and the Imported Bridegroom and Other Stories of Yiddish New York* (New York: Houghton Mifflin, 1898; reprint, New York: Dover, 1970), 226.

35. In the 1850s, Beecher went into debt shopping. See Horowitz, *Morality of Spending*, 11.

36. Robert E. Weems, *Desegregating the Dollar: African American Consumerism in the Twentieth Century* (New York: New York University Press, 1998); Ted Ownby, *American Dreams in Mississippi: Consumers, Poverty, and Culture, 1830–1998* (Chapel Hill: University of North Carolina Press, 1999), chapters 2–4; Cindy S. Aron, *Working at Play: A History of Vacations in the United States* (New York: Oxford University Press, 1999), 214–216; Peiss, *Cheap Amusements*, chapter 3; John Kasson, *Amusing the Million: Coney Island at the Turn of the Century* (New York: Hill & Wang, 1978).

37. May, *Great Expectations*, 51, 2, 7.

38. Quote from "A Rambling Batchelor," *Matrimonial Ceremonies Displayed* (London: H. Serjeant, n.d.), v; Peter Lacey, *The Wedding* (New York: Madison Square Press, Grosset & Dunlap, 1969), 243.

39. Also, see De Witt Talmage, *The Marriage Ring*, 36.

40. Royal Jackman, May 6, 1936, Anthony, New Mexico, American Life Histories; Johnny Haselton Interview, 1939, American Life Histories.

41. Enstad, *Ladies of Labor*, 27, 29–30.

42. According to sociologist Pierre Bourdieu, taste derived from "cultural capital," something closely linked to education and social origin. In Bourdieu's words, taste classified the classifier. Bourdieu, *Distinction: A Social Critique of the Judgement of Taste*, trans. Richard Nice (Cambridge, Mass.: Harvard University Press, 1984), 13, 6–7; Wharton, *Age of Innocence*, 35.

43. Rayne, *Gems of Deportment*, 193; Thorstein Veblen, *Theory of the Leisure Class: An Economic Study of Institutions* (New York: Macmillan, 1899; reprint, New York: New American Library, 1953), 64–65. See also Horowitz, *Morality of Spending*, 28.

44. Woodward, "The Evil of Elaborate and Showy Weddings," 418.

45. David E. Shi, *The Simple Life: Plain Living and High Thinking in American Culture* (New York: Oxford University Press, 1985), 181, passim; Jennifer Scanlon, *Inarticulate Longings: The Ladies' Home Journal, Gender, and the Promises of Consumer Culture* (New York: Routledge, 1995), 51–52; Enstad, *Ladies of Leisure*, 31.

46. Susan Glenn, *Daughters of the Shtetl: Life and Labor in the Immigrant Generation* (Ithaca, N.Y.: Cornell University Press, 1990), 208; For a general discussion of the New Woman, see Carroll Smith-Rosenberg, "The New Woman as Androgyne: Social Disorder and Gender Crisis, 1870–1936," in *Disorderly Conduct: Visions of Gender in Victorian America* (New York: Oxford University Press, 1985), 245–296.

47. Quotes from Joyce Antler, *Lucy Sprague Mitchell: The Making of a Modern Woman* (New Haven, Conn.: Yale University Press, 1987), 191–192; Desley Deacon, *Elsie Clews Parsons: Inventing Modern Life* (Chicago: University of Chicago Press, 1997), 55–56.

48. Edith Ordway, *The Etiquette of To-Day* (New York: George Sully and Company, 1913), 198, 200; Woodward, "The Evil of Elaborate and Showy Weddings," 418. For another example of this critique, see Edward Bok, "His Daughter's Wedding," *Ladies' Home Journal* (June 1904), 20. Cited in Ellen M. Litwicki, "Showering

the Bride: A Ritual of Gender and Consumption," paper presented May 30, 1998, at the Conference on Holidays, Ritual, Festival, Celebrations, and Public Display, Bowling Green University, Ohio. Also, see Margaret Wade, *Social Usage in America* (New York: Thomas Y. Crowell, 1924), 146–147.

49. Antler, *Lucy Sprague Mitchell,* 69; Robert H. Wiebe, *The Search for Order, 1877–1920* (New York: Hill & Wang, 1967), chapter 7.

50. Horowitz, *Morality of Spending*, 50, 61.

51. Margaret F. Byington, "Homestead: The Households of a Mill Town," in *The Pittsburgh Survey: Findings in Six Volumes* (New York: Charities Publication Committee, 1910), 150, 149.

52. WPA accounts of Polish, German, and Italian weddings describe the different ways that guests gave money at the reception, including collections in the apron of the mother of the bride, plate-breaking contests, dances with the bride, and money envelope collections. See American Life Histories: Mrs. Mary Mathews Toman, March 7, 1939, Lincoln, Nebraska; Vito Cacciola, January 17, 1939, Living Lore in New England; Elmer Dellett, September 21, 1938, Lincoln, Nebraska.

53. "Living in New England," Vermont Quarry, American Life Histories.

54. Cahan, "A Ghetto Wedding," 226; Jenna Weissman Joselit, *Wonders of America: Reinventing Jewish Culture, 1780–1950* (New York: Hill & Wang, 1994), 24.

55. Sinclair, *The Jungle*, 18, 20.

56. "June Brides a Fair Mark," *Dry Goods Economist* (June 8, 1901), 43. See also "Cheap Tableware Fairly Active," *Dry Goods Economist* (May 18, 1901), 15.

57. "Silverware," *Dry Goods Economist* (June 8, 1901), 42.

58. Woodward, "Evil of Elaborate and Showy Weddings."

59. Horowitz, *Morality of Spending*, 135–137.

60. See Susan Strasser, *Satisfaction Guaranteed: The Making of an American Mass Market* (Washington, D.C.: Smithsonian Institution Press, 1989).

61. Roland Marchand, *Advertising the American Dream: Making Way for Modernity* (Berkeley: University of California Press, 1985), 6–8, 12; Nancy Walker, *Shaping Our Mothers' World* (Jackson: University Press of Mississippi, 2000), 59–62.

62. Recent studies have shown how consumer culture also widened the distance between those who had access and those who did not. For example, for a discussion of rural consumers and their adaptation of the telephone, automobile, and electricity, see Ronald R. Kline, *Consumers in the Country: Technology and Social Change in Rural America* (Baltimore: Johns Hopkins University Press, 2000). For a discussion of the way African Americans and poor whites experienced consumer culture in the South, see Ownby, *American Dreams in Mississippi*. For a discussion of the way different ethnic groups experienced mass culture and made it their own, see Lizabeth Cohen, *Making a New Deal: Industrial Workers in Chicago, 1919–1939* (Cambridge: Cambridge University Press, 1990), chapter 3.

63. "Advertising and Selling Suggestions for June," *Jewelers' Circular* (May 16, 1929), 46. Also, see fig. 44a in Carl A. Naether, *Advertising to Women* (New York: Prentice Hall, 1928), 271; Marisa Keller and Mike Mashon, *TV Weddings: An Illustrated Guide to Prime-Time Nuptials* (New York: TV Books, 1999), 13–14.

64. John W. Rogers, Jr., *Wedding Presents: Play in One Act* (New York: Samuel French, 1926), 1, 3, 5–6.

65. Jane Grant, "Purveyors to the Bride," *Saturday Evening Post* (September 5, 1925), 23, 89. For a discussion of the gendered language of advertising copy and literature about consumer culture during the 1920s, see Simone Weil Davis, *Living Up to the Ads: Gender Fictions of the 1920s* (Durham, N.C.: Duke University Press, 2000).

66. Grant, "Purveyors to the Bride," 23.

67. Horowitz, *Morality of Spending*, 169. For a discussion of later intellectual debates, see Horowitz, *The Anxieties of Influence*. Ruby Jo Reeves, "Marriages in New Haven Since 1870" (Ph.D. diss., Yale University, 1938).

68. *Jeweler's Advertiser* (Chicago: Jeweler's Advertising Company, 1908), 213. "Selling More Gifts for the June Bride," *Jewelers' Circular* (May 11, 1927), 117.

CHAPTER 2. RINGS AND THE BIRTH OF A TRADITION

Portions of this chapter are based on material that appeared previously in Vicki Howard, "'A Real Man's Ring': Gender and the Invention of Tradition," *Journal of Social History* 36, no. 4 (Summer 2003).

1. In addition to rings, retail jewelers sold jewelry and novelty items deemed suitable gifts for the wedding attendants and advertised a wide range of goods for wedding presents, helping spread the increasingly elaborate formal white wedding ideal. This chapter focuses, however, on their role in the invention of ring traditions. "Trade on Tradition," *Jewelers' Circular-Keystone* (October 1944), 168; "First, the Engagement Ring," *Department Store Economist* (July 1944), 62. This idea continued into the 1950s. According to the Ayer agency in 1955, "Sentiment still is the biggest word in Selling." "De Beers," Ayer News File (January 3, 1955), 11, box 252, N. W. Ayer Advertising Agency Records, October 2001 Addendum, NMAH.

2. The jewelry industry recognized its historical role in introducing new traditions. See "Introducing the Diamond Anniversary Ring: The Biggest Idea Since the Diamond Engagement Ring," De Beers, 1981, box 72, N. W. Ayer Advertising Agency Records, October 2001 Addendum.

3. George Frederick Kunz, *Rings for the Finger* (Philadelphia: J. B. Lippincott Company, 1917; reprint, New York: Dover Publications, 1973), 1; Lillian Eichler, *The Customs of Mankind: With Notes on Modern Etiquette and the Newest Trend in Entertainment* (New York: Nelson Doubleday, 1924), 228; Jeanne Wright, *The Wedding Book* (New York: Rhinehart, 1947), 3. See also George Elliott Howard, *A History of Matrimonial Institutions*, vol. 2 (Chicago: University of Chicago Press, 1904); Ethel Lucy Hargreave, *A Short History of Marriage: Marriage Rites, Customs, Folklore in Many Countries and All Ages* (Philadelphia: D. McKay, 1913).

4. Scholars have explored the intersection of American imperialism with gender and racial ideologies. See Janet Davis, *The Circus Age: Culture and Society Under the American Big Top* (Chapel Hill: University of North Carolina Press, 2002), 10, 199.

5. Accounts of the ancient origins of ring customs appeared in many different places. See "That Most Important Occasion," *Brides Book* (Spokane, Wash.: Paxton & Barney Photographers, n.d.), in Matrimony, box 1, Warshaw Collection; *The Art of*

the Wedding (New York, N.Y.: The Hallmark Gallery, 1964), 5–6, in Matrimony, box 1, Warshaw Collection. Simon Charsley argued that J. C. Jeaffreson (*Brides and Bridals*, London: Hurst and Blackwell, 1872) wrote a history of the white wedding cake that was "myth-making," influencing later histories, which would link contemporary nineteenth-century practice to ancient Rome. See Charsley, *Wedding Cakes and Cultural History* (London and New York: Routledge, 1992), 29–30.

6. Gail F. Stern and Ruth Leppel, "Wedding Traditions: A Cultural History," in *Something Old, Something New: Ethnic Weddings in America*, ed. Gail F. Stern (Philadelphia: The Balch Institute for Ethnic Studies, 1987), 5; Barbara Tober, *The Bride: A Celebration* (Stamford, Conn.: Longmeadow Press, 1984), 50.

7. " 'Wedding Americana' for Bride's Shop," *Department Store Economist* (April 1944), 18; "Here Comes the Bride," *Bride's* magazine (Spring 1942), 70; Martha Stewart, *Weddings* (New York: Clarkson N. Potter, 1987), xii; Kunz, *Rings for the Finger*, 194.

8. Liturgy is defined as the "patterns, forms and words through which public worship is conducted" (http://www.england.anglican.org/services/). Kenneth Stevenson, *Nuptial Blessing: A Study of Christian Marriage Rites* (New York: Oxford University Press, 1983), 92, 173; Kenneth R. Stow, "Marriages Are Made in Heaven: Marriage and the Individual in the Roman Jewish Ghetto," *Renaissance Quarterly* 48 (Autumn 1995), 452–453.

9. Stow, "Marriages Are Made in Heaven," 450.

10. Stevenson, *Nuptial Blessing*, 132–133, 134, 136 (quotations), 81–82.

11. Stow, "Marriages Are Made in Heaven," 445; Stevenson, *Nuptial Blessing*, 139.

12. David Cressy, *Birth, Marriage, and Death: Ritual, Religion, and the Life-Cycle in Tudor and Stuart England* (New York: Oxford University Press, 1997), 347 (quotation), 342, 345. David Hackett Fischer, *Albion's Seed: Four British Folkways in America* (New York: Oxford University Press, 1989), 81; Howard, *A History of Matrimonial Institutions*, 127.

13. Fischer, *Albion's Seed*, 81; David C. Brown, "The Forfeitures at Salem, 1692," *William and Mary Quarterly* 50 (January 1993), 85–111; quotation from 101.

14. Stevenson, *Nuptial Blessing*, 147, 158.

15. Stevenson, *Nuptial Blessing*, 162, 163. Stephen Scott, *The Amish Wedding and Other Special Occasions of the Old Order Communities* (Intercourse, Pa.: Good Books, 1988), 30.

16. Philip Scranton, *Endless Novelty: Specialty Production and American Industrialization, 1865–1925* (Princeton, N.J.: Princeton University Press, 1997), 353.

17. "Hints for Retailers," *Jewelers' Weekly* 20 (May 15, 1895), 10. Also see "Hints for Retailers," *Jewelers' Weekly* 20 (June 19, 1895), 19; "Dry Goods Cheapness Exposed," *Jewelers' Weekly* 20 (July 3, 1895); "Diamonds Sell Slowly but Surely," *Department Store Economist* (Sept. 1940), 98.

18. "Sweet Sixteen Rings," *Jewelers' Weekly* 20 (September 18, 1895), 19; The Robert Simpson Company, Limited, Fall and Winter catalogue, 1917–1918, 322; The Robert Simpson Company, Limited, Spring and Summer catalogue, 1922, 220.

19. Barbara Tober, *The Bride: A Celebration* (Stamford, Conn.: Longmeadow Press,

1984), 78; "Can a Ring Make a Woman Remember?" *Jewelers' Circular* (May 1926), 11.

20. Adelaide Shaw, *Etiquette for Everybody* (New York: Homemaker's Encyclopedia, 1952), 174; Millicent Fenwick, *Vogue's Book of Etiquette* (New York: Simon and Schuster, 1948), 166, 174–175; Kunz, *Rings for the Finger*, 227; Edith B. Ordway, *The Etiquette of To-Day* (New York: George Sully and Company, 1913), 197–198 (quotation).

21. Harvey Green, with Mary-Ellen Perry, *The Light of the Home: An Intimate View of the Lives of Women in Victorian America* (New York: Pantheon Books, 1983), 18–19.

22. Walter R. Houghton et al., *American Etiquette and Rules of Politeness* (Chicago: Rand, McNally & Company, 1882), 201; *Demorest's Monthly* discussed in Green, *Light of the Home*, 18.

23. "Diamonds Next Door," *Journal of Retailing* (April 1944), 47; A. Kenneth Snowman, *The Master Jewelers* (New York: Harry N. Abrams, 1990), 174–188. "De Beers," Ayer News File (August 1, 1955), 10, box 252, N. W. Ayer Advertising Agency Records, October 2001 Addendum.

24. Houghton et al. *American Etiquette and Rules of Politeness*, 195. Ordway, *The Etiquette of To-Day*, 206.

25. "Budget for a Bride," *Fortune* (June 1933), 41.

26. Bridal sets appeared in the mail-order catalogue of the Simpson Company, a Canadian retailer, between 1932 and 1936. Eaton's, a Canadian department store, did not feature bridal sets in its catalogues in the 1920s and early 1930s, but it did offer many different styles of diamond engagement rings and wedding bands sold separately. Montgomery Ward, Baltimore, Spring and Summer, 1927, 308–309, trade catalogue, Hagley.

27. "Wedding Rings: Gain in Marriages Encourages Jewelers and Manufacturers," *Jewelers' Circular-Keystone* (February 1937), 5. Catalogues from the late nineteenth century through the 1920s sold engagement rings separately from wedding bands. Catalogues featured both single engagement rings and separate wedding bands, as well as the new bridal sets, in the 1930s. For example, see Bennett Brothers, Inc., trade catalogue, 1937, Hagley.

28. Decades after the 1930s, jewelers sought to sell an expensive ring to the bride's mother who had married in the Depression. See "Prosperous Jewelers," *Financial World* (March 30, 1966), 7; N. W. Ayer, *125 Years of Building Brands*, in-house publication, N.W. Ayer Advertising Agency Records; "Wedding-Rings: Gain in Marriages Encourages Jewelers and Manufacturers," *Jewelers' Circular-Keystone* (February 1937), 5; "Merchandise Surveys Published," *Department Store Economist* (November 1944), 117.

29. "Bride and Groom Rings, Bristol Seamless Ring Co., New York," *Jewelers' Circular* (June 1, 1927), 11; "Keepsake Diamond Rings, Magazine Advertising Schedule for Fall 1944," *Jewelers' Circular-Keystone* (October 1944), 167; "Joseph H. Jacobson & Sons, Inc.," *Department Store Economist* (March 1947), 43; "New Wedding Rings Tie-Up with Movie Stars," *Jewelers' Journal* (June 1929), 47.

30. "The Diamond Ring Becomes a Unit," *Printer's Ink* (May 15, 1930), 126;

"Keepsake Print Campaign Offers Teens Advice on Dating—Diamond Rings Sell, Too," *Advertising Age* (August 25, 1958), 2.

31. For a discussion of the manufacture of rings, see "All America Knows, Wood Rings," *Jewelers' Circular-Keystone* (February 1937), 5.

32. "The Diamond Ring Becomes a Unit," *Printer's Ink* (May 15, 1930), 126; Eugene Gilbert, *Advertising and Marketing to Young People* (Pleasantville, N.Y.: Printer's Ink Books, 1957), 307; quote from "Magazine Advertising Schedule for Fall 1944," *Jewelers' Circular-Keystone* (October 1944), 167. Also see "Keepsake Print Campaign," *Advertising Age* (August 25, 1958).

33. Bailey, *From Front Porch to Back Seat*, 42; "Wedding Profits for Jewelers," *Jewelers' Circular* (May 1932), 30.

34. "Get This Angle in Buying Wedding Rings," *Jewelers' Circular* (October 1931), 10; "Budget for a Bride," *Fortune* (Spring 1933), 41.

35. In spite of this, jewelers appear to have held their own against department stores' jewelry sales. In 1929, the value of jewelry sold in specialty stores was almost thirteen times that sold in department stores. Eventually, however, jewelers lost ground to department stores and chains. In 1948, consumers spent almost twelve dollars in jewelry stores to every one they spent on jewelry in department stores. By 1963 jewelers outsold department stores by slightly more than four dollars to one. U.S. Department of Commerce, *Fifteenth Census of the United States: 1930 Distribution, Vol. 1, Retail Distribution, Part 1* (Washington, D.C.: United States Government Printing Office, 1933), 47, 49; U.S. Department of Commerce, *Census of American Business: 1933, Retail Distribution Vol. 1, United States Summary: 1933 and Comparisons with 1929* (Washington, D.C.: United States Government Printing Office, May 1935), A-1, A-12, A-13. U.S. Department of Commerce, *United States Census of Business: 1948, Vol. I, Retail Trade-General Statistics, Part 1* (Washington, D.C.: United States Government Printing Office, 1952), 1.02, 1.04, 1.05; U.S. Department of Commerce, *United States Census of Business: 1948, Vol. 2, Retail Trade-General Statistics, Part 2 and Merchandise Line Sale Statistics* (Washington, D.C.: United States Government Printing Office, 1952), 18.03, 19.02, 24.03; U.S. Department of Commerce, *1963 Census of Business, Vol. 1, Retail Trade Summary Statistics, Part 2: Merchandise Line Sales* (Washington, D.C.: United States Government Printing Office, 1963), 7A-7, 7A-14–16, 7A-24–25. Chain jewelry stores also provided competition for individual family-run stores. By 1965 it was "farewell to Mom and Pop" as family jewelry businesses lost out to chains. "Not Just the Carriage Trade: Jewelry Is Shifting from a Class to a Mass Business," *Barron's* (April 19, 1965), 3.

36. Bailey, *From Front Porch to Back Seat*, 42; quotation from *Department Store Economist* (September 1951), 130.

37. Gilbert, *Advertising and Marketing to Young People*, 307; "Magazine Advertising Schedule for Fall 1944," *Jewelers' Circular-Keystone* (October 1944), 167; "Keepsake Print Campaign," *Advertising Age* (August 25, 1958). See Cohen, *A Consumers' Republic*, for a discussion of market segmentation. For a discussion of African American magazines, see Tom Pendergast, *Creating the Modern Man: American Magazines and*

Consumer Culture, 1900–1950 (Columbia: University of Missouri Press, 2000), chapters 2 and 4.

38. "Men's Engagement Rings: The Modern Expression of an Ancient Custom," Allsop Brothers, *Jewelers' Circular* (April 14, 1926), 32. Green, *The Light of the Home*, 19; Rothman, *Hands and Hearts*, 161–162.

39. "Popularizing Engagement Rings for Men," *Jewelers' Circular* (May 29, 1926), 53; "Stimulating a Stagnant . . . ," *Printer's Ink* (October 21, 1926); "Making 'Men's Engagement Rings' All the Vogue," *Jewelers' Circular* (June 16, 1926), 105.

40. Marchand, *Advertising the American Dream*, xix, xx.

41. Jane Wells, "Your Money's Worth in Jewelry: Etiquette of Gift Giving" (New York: L. W. Sweet, Inc., n.d., ca. 1920s), pamphlet, Finlay & Strauss Scrapbook, NMAH.

42. "Popularizing Engagement Rings for Men," 53; "Stimulating a Stagnant . . ."; quote from "Making 'Men's Engagement Rings' All the Vogue," 107; "In League with Love," Goldsmith, Stern & Co. *Jewelers' Circular* (April 28, 1926), 47.

43. "A Betrothal Gift for a Man Which Reflects His Personality," Larter & Sons, *Jewelers' Circular* (April 13, 1927), 43.

44. For a discussion of masculinity in advertising in the 1920s, see Simone Weil Davis, *Living up to the Ads*; "Popularizing Engagement Rings for Men," 53; "Stimulating a Stagnant . . ."; quote from "Making 'Men's Engagement Rings' All the Vogue," 106.

45. "Making 'Men's Engagement Rings' All the Vogue," 106.

46. "Popularizing Engagement Rings for Men," 53.

47. "Making 'Men's Engagement Rings' All the Vogue," 105–107.

48. Mrs. Massey Lyon, *Etiquette: A Guide to Public and Social Life* (London: Cassell and Company, 1927), 87; "Granat Brothers," Ayer News File (October 9, 1944), 5, box 249, N. W. Ayer Advertising Agency Records, October 2001 Addendum.

49. Otnes and Pleck, *Cinderella Dreams*, 67, 69.

50. *Store Chat* (April 15, 1911), 1. Strawbridge & Clothier Collection, Hagley. "Popularizing Engagement Rings for Men," 53; "Making 'Men's Engagement Rings' All the Vogue," 106–107; "The Most Important Sale You Make," Traub Manufacturing Company, *Jewelers' Circular* (May 4, 1927), 25; *Store Chat* (April 15, 1911), Strawbridge & Clothier Collection, Hagley; Lyon, *Etiquette*, 87. Lyon's book was published in England, as well as Canada, yet American brides likely still turned to it for advice. It included references to the rare practice of a male engagement ring.

51. Rothman, *Hands and Hearts*, 164; Green, *Light of the Home*, 17; *Rainbow Reporter* (October 1948), 7, Binney and Smith Collection, NMAH.

52. "Meet Our Clients: De Beers," Ayer News File (August 31, 1953), n.p., box 251, N. W. Ayer Advertising Agency Records, October 2001 Addendum.

53. Edward Jay Epstein, *The Rise and Fall of Diamonds: The Shattering of a Brilliant Illusion* (New York: Simon and Schuster, 1982).

54. Theodore Gregory, *Ernest Oppenheimer and the Economic Development of Southern Africa* (New York: Oxford University Press, 1962), 322, 298; "De Beers," Ayer

News File (April 18, 1957), 10, box 253, N. W. Ayer Advertising Agency Records, October 2001 Addendum.

55. For a discussion of the Ayer agency, see Jackson Lears, *Fables of Abundance: A Cultural History of Advertising in America* (New York: Basic Books, 1994), 90–94. Diamonds for rings up to this point averaged under $80. Epstein, *The Rise and Fall of Diamonds*, 121–122. Epstein's journalistic work was used to reconstruct the Ayer campaign in Pleck and Otnes's discussion of De Beers. I have drawn on Epstein's excellent journalistic account, but I have also had the opportunity to go into more detail using a new collection at the Smithsonian Archives Center that appears to have been the Ayer corporate material that Epstein used when researching his book.

56. "Diamonds," Ayer News File (May 10, 1940), 1, box 248. "De Beers," Ayer News File (August 25, 1958), 1, box 253; "Diamonds," Ayer News File (April 7, 1941), 1, box 248; Epstein, *The Rise and Fall of Diamonds*, 123; "Diamonds," Ayer News File (April 7, 1941), 1, box 248. "Three-in-One," Ayer News File (September 18, 1941), 3, box 248; N. W. Ayer Advertising Agency Records, October 2001 Addendum.

57. Quotation from "De Beers," Ayer News File (August 26, 1957), 2, box 253. "Selling Diamonds Today," *Department Store Economist* (March 1943), 49; Marc Koven, "Diamonds Next Door," *Journal of Retailing* 20 (April 1, 1944), 49; "Fields Knows How to Sell Fine Jewelry," *Department Store Economist* (March 1948), 143; "De Beers," Ayer News File (August 26, 1957), 2, box 253; the agency reported increased retail sales during the war. "De Beers Consolidated Mines Ltd.," Ayer News File (February 3, 1942), 5, box 248, and (June 2, 1941), 1, box 248, N. W. Ayer Advertising Agency Records, October 2001 Addendum.

58. Quotation from "De Beers," Ayer News File (August 26, 1957), 1, box 253. "De Beers," Ayer News File (May 11, 1953), 1–2. According to this internal report, Ayer pushed larger diamonds than it had previously in a series of ads run in *Vogue*, *Harper's Bazaar*, and *Town and Country* in 1953–1954; "De Beers," Ayer News File, (August 26, 1957), 1, box 253; "De Beers," Ayer News File (April 25, 1955), 3, box 252; "De Beers," Ayer News File (August 1, 1955), 10, box 252. According to the Ayer agency, their surveys indicated that in 1954, 70 percent of marriages were preceded by a diamond engagement ring gift. "De Beers," Ayer News File (April 25, 1955), 3, box 252, N. W. Ayer Advertising Agency Records, October 2001 Addendum.

59. Gilbert, *Advertising and Marketing to Young People*, 272, 303; "De Beers," Ayer News File (August 26, 1957), 2, box 253. For the new emphasis on "deferred engagement rings," see "De Beers," Ayer News File (April 26, 1954), 1, box 252; (April 23, 1951), 1, N. W. Ayer Advertising Agency Records, October 2001 Addendum.

60. "De Beers," Ayer News File (April 25, 1955), 3, box 252; "De Beers," Ayer News File (April 26, 1954), 1, box 252. Ayer was concerned over dropping marriage rates in 1952 as well. "Public Relations," Ayer News File (December 8, 1952), 11, box 251, N. W. Ayer Advertising Agency Records, October 2001 Addendum.

61. Epstein, *The Rise and Fall of Diamonds*, 89–90; Stefan Kanfer, *The Last Empire: De Beers, Diamonds, and the World* (New York: Farrar, Straus & Giroux, 1993), 270–272; "Meet Our Clients: De Beers," Ayer News File (August 31, 1953), n.p., box 251,

N. W. Ayer Advertising Agency Records, October 2001 Addendum. For a definition of wartime stockpiling, see Walton Hamilton, "The Control of Strategic Materials," *American Economic Review* 34 (June 1944), 263–264.

62. Drawing on the Ayer archives and other sources, my 2000 dissertation discusses the way the wedding industry used World War II to legitimize different elements of the formal white wedding, such as the diamond engagement ring, silver gifts, bridal salon services, and the white wedding gown. See Howard, "American Weddings," 79, 82–83, 95–98.

63. "Grind It to Powder," advertising tear sheet, box OS 148, De Beers, 1942–1943; also, see "Could these wings of my heart help tool the wings of his victory," advertising tear sheet, box OS 148, De Beers, 1943; "Fighting Diamonds," advertising tear sheet, box OS 148, De Beers, 1942–1943, N. W. Ayer Advertising Agency Records, October 2001 Addendum; "For Brides—Or Bombers?" *Department Store Economist* (June 1943), n.p.

64. "De Beers," Ayer News File (May 12, 1943), 3, box 248; "Public Relations Dept. Notes," Ayer News File (October 8, 1943), 4, box 248; (August 21, 1944), 4, box 249, N. W. Ayer Advertising Agency Records, October 2001 Addendum.

65. "The Marriage Bureau Hums," advertising tear sheet, De Beers, 1940–1941, box OS 148, N. W. Ayer Advertising Agency Records, October 2001 Addendum. This ad also pointed to the return to prosperity as something working in the industry's favor.

66. "Defense Is in Cahoots with Cupid!" advertising tear sheet, box OS 148, De Beers, 1940–1941, N. W. Ayer Advertising Agency Records, October 2001 Addendum.

67. "Smiling Bride," advertising tear sheet, De Beers, 1945–1946, box OS 148, N. W. Ayer Advertising Agency Records; "Sunny Wedding," advertising tear sheet, De Beers, 1945–1946, box OS 148, N. W. Ayer Advertising Agency Records. The Greek Orthodox wedding depicted demonstrates this theme in the ad copy, although it is not clear whether the groom is in uniform. "Our wedding day," advertising tear sheet, De Beers, 1945–1946, box OS 148, N. W. Ayer Advertising Agency Records, October 2001 Addendum.

68. "Bridal Ritual," advertising tear sheet, De Beers, 1941–1945, box OS 148, N. W. Ayer Advertising Agency Records, October 2001 Addendum.

69. "Factory Whistles Play the Wedding March," advertising tear sheet, box OS 148, De Beers, 1940–1941, N. W. Ayer Advertising Agency Records, October 2001 Addendum.

70. "Love in Boom," advertising tear sheet, 1941–1942, box OS 148, N. W. Ayer Advertising Agency Records, October 2001 Addendum.

71. "112,032,208 times," *Department Store Economist* (March 1947), 41; "Diamond Advertising Spotlights," *Department Store Economist* (March 1948), 142; "New Diamond Advertising for You," *Department Store Economist* (September 1951), 93. Advertising tear sheet (February 3, 1942), De Beers, box OS 148, N. W. Ayer Advertising Agency Records.

72. *125 Years of Building Brands*, 41. Otnes and Pleck, *Cinderella Dreams*, 65–68.

73. "Public Relations," Ayer News File (April 28, 1952), 4, box 251; (December 8,

1952), 11, box 251; "De Beers," Ayer News File (July 6, 1954), 4, box 252. The agency even influenced the name change of movies featuring diamonds. "Adventure in Diamonds," Ayer News File, box 148, OS folder 1, N. W. Ayer Advertising Agency Records, October 2001 Addendum.

74. "De Beers," Ayer News File (April 13, 1953), 8, box 251; "De Beers," Ayer News File (September 10, 1951), 3, box 251; (October 28, 1946), 6; "De Beers," Ayer News File (July 6, 1954), 3–4, box 252; quote from "De Beers," Ayer News File (June 4, 1951), 5, box 251, N. W. Ayer Advertising Agency Records, October 2001 Addendum.

75. "Ayer Filmmakers Report," Ayer News File (April 15, 1946), 3, box 250; "De Beers," Ayer News File (August 3, 1953), 1, box 251; "De Beers," Ayer News File (March 15, 1954), 11–12, box 252. Other television programs on diamonds for De Beers ran as early as 1951. "De Beers," Ayer News File (October 22, 1951), 4, box 251, N. W. Ayer Advertising Agency Records, October 2001 Addendum.

76. "De Beers," Ayer News File (January 31, 1955), 4, box 252; "De Beers," Ayer News File (August 25, 1958), 1, box 253, N. W. Ayer Advertising Agency Records, October 2001 Addendum.

77. Adele Bahn's content analysis of bridal magazines in the 1960s and 1970s quantified the symbols found most frequently. She listed rice, flowers, veils, the color white, rings, and the wedding cake as the most frequently discussed symbols and images. Bahn, "Changes and Continuities in the Transitional Status of Bride into Wife: Content Analysis of Bridal Magazines, 1967–1977" (Ph.D. diss., City University of New York, 1979), 131. Her findings ring true with my survey of bridal magazines from 1934 through the 1950s as well. The diamond solitaire engagement ring increased in popularity in 1950. "De Beers," Ayer News File (April 23, 1951), box 251, 1. Examples of the solitaire in popular culture abound. For example, see Roy Lichtenstein's 1962 painting *The Ring*.

78. Quotation from "De Beers," Ayer News File (April 25, 1955), 3, box 252, N. W. Ayer Advertising Agency Records, October 2001 Addendum. "Sparklers" quotation from *Leading Edge* (March 11, 1944), 8, Pratt & Read Collection, NMAH.

79. Traub Manufacturing Company's Orange Blossom line offered groom's rings in 1928. "A Million Weddings, Traub Manufacturing Co., Detroit," *Jewelers' Circular* (June 7, 1928), 22; Montgomery Ward & Company, Catalogue 106, Baltimore, Spring and Summer, 1927, 308. Groom's rings that matched the bride's wedding band could be quite elaborate. For example, see the wide range of patterns depicted in *The Allen Monthly, June Wedding and Graduates Special*, Chicago, 1947, 6, Hagley.

80. Otto S. Liberman, "Wedding Links Set the Fashion," *Jewelers' Journal* (October 1930), 28. The earliest bride and groom sets I have found were from the late 1920s. See "A Million Weddings, Traub Manufacturing Company," 22–23; See *58th Annual Illustrated Price List of Jewelers' Merchandise*, Otto Young & Company, 1929, trade catalogue, Hagley. The 1931 wholesale jeweler catalogue for Benj. Allen & Company, Inc., in Chicago featured a bride-and-groom ring set. *1931 B. A. & Co. Annual Catalogue*, Chicago, 146, Hagley. Many different styles of matched sets of bands for men and women or rings sold separately to brides and grooms appeared in the wholesale

catalogues by the late 1930s. See *Illustrated Fort Dearborn Gift Book & General Catalog*, 1936, Fort Dearborn, Illinois, 19, 21, 24, trade catalogue, Hagley. Also, see *The Oskamp Molting Co. Wholesale Jewelry, Giftware*, Cincinnati, Ohio, 1938, 14–15, trade catalogue, Hagley. Not every trade catalogue in the 1930s featured groom's rings, however. For example, see Bennett Brothers, Inc., trade catalogue, 1937, Hagley. For an early citation in etiquette books, see Harriet Brooks, *Etiquette for All Occasions* (New York: Reader Mail, 1937), 31. I have found no earlier examples.

81. Ruby Jo Reeves, "Marriages in New Haven," VII–52.

82. "Why the Jewelry Publicity Board," *Jewelers' Circular-Keystone* (June 1944), 158; "The Big Business of Selling to Brides," *Store Chat* (December 1943), 12, Strawbridge & Clothier Collection, Hagley; "Ring Twice," *Fortune* (November 1947), 148.

83. Department-store employees at Strawbridge & Clothier and factory workers at Maidenform reported double-ring ceremonies in their company newsletters.

84. The Roman Ritual "contains the texts and ceremonies for all sacraments administered by a priest. It served as a standard for all Rituals, but local Rituals were still allowed and used in some cases." Adrian Fortescue, *The Ceremonies of the Roman Rite Described* (Westminster, Md.: Newman Press, 1953), 377; "The Double Ring Ceremony," *American Ecclesiastical Review* (October 1944), 311; "The Double Ring Ceremony Again," *American Ecclesiastical Review* (February 1947), 146; "Double Ring Ceremony," *American Ecclesiastical Review* (September 1951), 225–226; "Double Ring Ceremony," *American Ecclesiastical Review* (May 1956), 351–352.

85. "Wedding Rings for the Men Build Volume for This Store," *Jewelers' Circular-Keystone* (April 1946), 220. The store attributed its success to this campaign and to its buying efforts to coordinate styles for men's and women's rings. "Confetti," *Bride's* (Summer 1943), 49; "The Fable of the Enchanted Diamond," *Wedding Belle* (June 1948), 33.

86. "In the Editor's Mail Box," *Wedding Belle* (July 1948), 5; Robey Lyle, *Mademoiselle's Handbook for Bridal Consultants* (New York: Street & Smith, 1946), 37; "'1847' Double Wedding Ring Chest," *Department Store Economist* (April 1949), 39.

87. "Wedding Rings for the Men," 220; Other attempts to use wartime sentiment to sell rings appeared. For example, jewelers promoted the friendship ring, which consisted of a clasped hand symbol. See *Criterion, Rohde-Spencer*, 1942, 21, trade catalogue, Hagley.

88. Robert Westbrook makes a similar argument about working-class womanhood and pin-ups as "objects of obligation." See Robert B. Westbrook, "'I Want a Girl, Just Like the Girl that Married Harry James': American Women and the Problem of Political Obligation," *American Quarterly* 42 (December 1990): 596–604, 605–606. For a discussion of the links among consumption, democracy, and citizenship in a pre–World War II context, see Charles McGovern, "Consumption and Citizenship in the United States, 1900–1940," in *Getting and Spending: European and American Consumer Societies in the Twentieth Century*, ed. Susan Strasser, Charles McGovern, Matthias Judt (Cambridge: Cambridge University Press, 1998), 37–58.

89. "Men in the Armed Services: Most Important Post-War Influence," *Jewelers' Circular-Keystone* (January 1944), 14–15.

90. "Wedding Rings for the Men," 220; quote from "Ring Twice," 148.

91. "Wedding Rings for the Men," 281.

92. R. W. Corrigan, "'Groom's Room' Idea Bids for the 'Forgotten Man,'" *Jewelers' Circular-Keystone* (September 1946), 250; Bob Corrigan, "'Groom's Room Store Gives Cupid a Push,'" *Jewelers' Circular-Keystone* (November 1946), 242. For a discussion of male consumerism, see Mark A. Swiencicki, "Consuming Brotherhood: Men's Culture, Style and Recreation as Consumer Culture, 1880–1930," in *Consumer Society in American History: A Reader*, ed. Lawrence B. Glickman (Ithaca, N.Y.: Cornell University Press, 1999), 207–240. Lizabeth Cohen has noted the new attention given to male consumers in the postwar period. See her *Consumers' Republic*, 148.

93. "Wedding Rings for the Men," 279; *Criterion, Rohde-Spencer*, 1942, 24–25, trade catalogue, Hagley.

94. See Michel de Certeau, *The Practice of Everyday Life*, trans. Steven Randall (Berkeley: University of California Press, 1984).

95. "Talk to Advertising Club" (October 7, 1948), p. 4, box 6, Wedding Bureau, 1948, Eaton's Collection, Archives of Ontario, Toronto, Canada.

96. Marsh, *Suburban Lives*, xiv, 184–185.

97. Jessica Weiss, *To Have and To Hold: Marriage, the Baby Boom, and Social Change* (Chicago: University of Chicago Press, 2000), chapter 4.

98. *Maiden Forum* (February 1947), 4. Maidenform Collection, Archives Center, NMAH.

99. Weiss, *To Have and To Hold*, 23; Bailey, *From Front Porch to Back Seat*, 34–35.

100. "Ebony Contest Winner Takes a Bride," *Ebony* (June 1960); Harriette Cole, *Jumping the Broom: The African-American Wedding Planner* (New York: Henry Holt, 1993), 40.

101. Black Starr and Frost-Gorham, "For the Ceremony," in *An Invitation to the Bride*, 38, pamphlet, 1933, Joseph Downs Collection of Manuscript and Printed Ephemera, Winterthur Library; "Brides on Parade," *Bride's* (Spring 1943), 34.

102. But as one trade advertisement noted, "A Bride Decides and the Jeweler Provides." The Diamond Heart Company, New York, *Jewelers' Circular* (October 1931).

103. New ring traditions continue to appear. For example, in 2000 the "Ah Ring" was introduced for single women. "New Diamond Ring Marketed to Single Women Creates Coast to Coast Demand," *Business Wire* (May 16, 2002), cited at http://www.marriage-planner.com.

CHAPTER 3. BRIDAL MAGAZINES AND THE CREATION OF A MARKET

1. *Bride's* magazine started a "long form-sheet" gift registry that standardized the process. "The Retailer—Happy as the Bride," *Sales Management* (May 1, 1950), 8.

2. John Kasson, *Rudeness and Civility: Manners in Nineteenth-Century Urban America* (New York: Hill & Wang, 1990), 5, 44, 46. Kasson provides a bibliography of etiquette books in which the earliest manual to address weddings by title is *A Guide to Good Manners, Courting, Hints on Etiquette, Morals . . . Weddings, Balls* (Fitchburg, Mass.: Shapley, 1848). Also, see Arthur Schlesinger's *Learning How to Behave: A Historical Study of American Etiquette Books* (New York: Cooper Square Publishers, 1968), 33–34.

3. Sarah J. Hale, *Manners: Happy Homes and Good Society All the Year Round* (Boston: J. E. Tilton and Company, 1868; reprint, New York: Arno Press, 1972), 128; Walker, *Women's Magazines*, 6.

4. Kasson, *Rudeness and Civility*, 5, 44, 60; Richard Bushman, *The Refinement of America: Persons, Houses, Cities* (New York: Vintage Books, 1992), 290–292.

5. Sangster, *Good Manners for All Occasions*, 115. See also *Vogue's Book of Brides* (New York: Doubleday, Doran & Company, 1929), 23–28.

6. Walter R. Houghton et al., *American Etiquette and Rules of Politeness* (Chicago: Rand, McNally & Company, 1882), 200; Rayne, *Gems of Deportment*, 187–188; White, *Twentieth-Century Etiquette*, 271, 277.

7. *Amy Vanderbilt's Complete Book of Etiquette: A Guide to Gracious Living* (Garden City, N.Y.: Doubleday, 1952), 99.

8. Millicent Fenwick, *Vogue's Book of Etiquette* (New York: Simon and Schuster, 1948), 3, 166. See also Joan McClure, *McCall's Engagement and Wedding Guide* (New York: Saturday Review Press, 1972), 93–102.

9. Julietta K. Arthur, "Here Comes the Bride's Business," *Independent Woman* (June 1939), 183; Schlesinger, *Learning How to Behave*, 51.

10. Schlesinger, *Learning How to Behave*, 51. Much like her Gilded Age predecessors, Post's work elevated Protestant, middle-class simplicity and an exclusionary vision of refinement. In a narrative chapter, titled "The Day of the Wedding," Emily Post provided a script for the tasteful, socially correct wedding, describing the various parts of the players, such as the best man's multiple roles as "expressman," "valet," and "companion-in-ordinary," and the various scenes, such as "at the house of the bride," "the procession to church," and "after the ceremony." Emily Post, *Etiquette: In Society, in Business, in Politics, and at Home* (New York: Funk & Wagnalls Company, 1922; 1923), chapter 22.

11. *Jantzen Yarns* (October 1946), 11, Jantzen Collection, NMAH. For a similar use of Emily Post's name on the east coast, see *Maiden Forum* (June–July 1955), 9. Maidenform Collection. Priscilla Kidder quoted in Elizabeth Hawes, "The Lady Who Marries the Best People," *McCall's*, June 1969, 123, clipping, box 10, folder 3, Priscilla of Boston Collection, NMAH.

12. In a similar fashion, later etiquette books, such as *McCall's Engagement and Wedding Guide* from 1972, advised on "traditional wedding customs and rituals," but also explained "the striking modifications that our rapidly changing times are making in the certain once-rigid social rules." McClure, *McCall's Engagement and Wedding Guide*, xvii.

13. Emma Aubert Cole, *The Modern Bride Book of Etiquette and Entertaining* (New York: Ziff-Davis, 1961), vii.

14. Eleanor Roosevelt, *Book of Common Sense Etiquette* (New York: Macmillan, 1962), ix, 296. Etiquette books prescribed rigid adherence to codes of conduct as late as 1939, holding out the prospect of social "embarrassment" and the possibility of being "regarded as ill-bred, crude, discourteous." M'Ledge Moffet, *When We Meet Socially: A Guidebook to Good Form in Social Conventions* (New York: Prentice-Hall, 1939), iii.

15. Walker, *Women's Magazines*, 2–3. A keyword search in the Library of Congress American Memory online collection "The Nineteenth-Century in Print: Periodicals," performed March 23, 2001, found thirteen items containing the word "bridal," thirty-one items containing the word "brides," and fifty-two items containing the word "wedding."

16. Butterick, McCall, Curtis, and the Pictorial Review Companies, for example, all published magazines that they sold at department stores offering paper patterns. Walker, *Shaping Our Mothers' World*, 36; Mary Ellen Zuckerman, *A History of Popular Women's Magazines in the U.S., 1792–1995* (Westport, Conn.: Greenwood Press, 1998), 31.

17. Walker, *Shaping Our Mothers' World*, 56–62, 129–135; Zuckerman, *A History of Popular Women's Magazines*, 159, 161; Theodore Peterson, *Magazines in the Twentieth Century* (Urbana: University of Illinois Press, 1964), 23–25, 184–185; Ellen Gruber Garvey argues that this occurred earlier in elite magazines in the 1890s and then was more widespread by the 1910s as magazines began running fiction on nonconsecutive pages, embedding stories within advertisements. Garvey, *The Adman in the Parlor: Magazines and the Gendering of Consumer Culture, 1880s–1910s* (New York: Oxford University Press, 1996), 15.

18. Zuckerman, *A History of Popular Women's Magazines in the United States*, 117–119; Peterson, *Magazines in the Twentieth Century*, 71; Walker, *Women's Magazines*, 3–4; Kelly Schrum, " 'Teens Means Business': Teenage Girls' Culture and *Seventeen Magazine*, 1944–1950," in *Delinquents and Debutantes: Twentieth-Century American Girls' Cultures*, ed. Sherrie A. Inness (New York: New York University Press, 1998), 152–153.

19. "Introducing Gorham Melrose," *Seventeen* (November 1948), n.p.; "You Didn't Inherit Grandma's Sterling?" *Seventeen* (September 1948), 132, 179; Vernon Smith, "Maid-of-Honor," *Seventeen* (November 1946), 162–278.

20. Peterson, *Magazines in the Twentieth Century*, 118–119; Zuckerman, *A History of Popular Women's Magazines*, 203.

21. "For the Bride Elect," pamphlet, Joseph Downs Collection of Manuscripts and Printed Ephemera, Winterthur Library.

22. "Vogue Prepares Five Budgets," *Vogue* (May 10, 1930), 168; Walker, *Shaping Our Mothers' World*, 46–47; Caroline Gray, "The Wedding Council," *Good Housekeeping* (August 1938), 84.

23. "Front Page Wedding," *Ebony* (January 1947), 12; "Lady Florists," *Ebony* (November 1948), 49; "Speaking of People: Bridal Consultant," *Ebony* (December 1951), 5–6; "Bridal Gowns," *Ebony* (June 1953), 85; "Speaking of People: Bridal Sales Expert," *Ebony* (September 1965), 6.

24. "The Wedding Business: It Profits from the U.S. Sentiment for Brides at the Unsentimental Rate of $3 Billion a Year," *Life* (June 1952): 119–135.

25. "Budget for a Bride," *Fortune* (June 1933), 39.

26. Peterson, *Magazines in the Twentieth Century*, 262–263; Wells Drorbaugh, Jr., interview by author, telephone transcript, November 19, 1997; Wells Drorbaugh, Jr.,

Princeton, New Jersey, to Vicki Howard, Austin, Texas, October 27, 1997, transcript in the possession of the author; "Curtis Publishing Brings Out Bride-to-Be Magazine," *Printer's Ink* (July 29, 1955), 33.

27. Wells Drorbaugh, Jr., interview, November 19, 1997; Wells Drorbaugh, Jr., to Vicki Howard, October 27, 1997.

28. Table of contents, *Bride's* (Autumn 1934); "The Budget Bride," *Bride's* (Summer 1938), 70; "Four Budget Brides," *Bride's* (Summer 1939), 64.

29. Drorbaugh interview, November 19, 1997; Drorbaugh to Howard, October 27, 1997; Peterson, *Magazines in the Twentieth Century*, 262–263.

30. Barbara Tober, interview by author, telephone transcript, January 25, 2000; "At Your Service," *Bride's* (Autumn 1954), 189; "To Serve You," *Modern Bride* (Winter 1953), 131.

31. "Domestic Trousseau Is Upper-Bracket Promotion," *Department Store Economist* (May 10, 1939), 16. Also, see *Bride's* Spring 1939 and Autumn 1939 issues.

32. Drorbaugh interview, November 19, 1997; Drorbaugh to Howard, October 27, 1997.

33. Agnes Ash, "Bridal Consultant Aids in Nursery Decoration," *New York Times* (June 17, 1957), 31; "One Thousand Brides," *Department Store Economist* (July 1944), 36; "Max Schling's Talk," Bridal Business Clinic, July 8, 1941; "Flower Talk by Irene Hayes," Bridal Business Clinic, July 8, 1941, F229–151, box 6, #166, Wedding Bureau Promo, 1943. Eaton's Collection.

34. "*Bride's Magazine*—Programme of the Day," ca. 1948, F229-151, box 6, #167, Wedding Bureau, 1948, Eaton's Collection.

35. Alexandra Potts, "How to Capitalize on Bridal Business," *Journal of Retailing* (April 1948), 69; "The Retailer—Happy as the Bride," 8.

36. Potts, "How to Capitalize on Bridal Business," 71. For lists of bridal consultant board members see the contents pages in *Modern Bride*. "Real Life Bride," *Modern Bride* (Spring 1955), 48–58; "Real Life Bride," *Modern Bride* (Fall 1955), 174–179. Also, see editorial feature on three brides in *Modern Bride* (Winter 1955), 56, 65, 86–87, 108–109, 66–67.

37. "Curtis Publishing Brings Out *Bride-to-Be Magazine*," 33.

38. "Housewares Bridal Registry," *Department Store Economist* (April 1955), 119; "Curtis Publishing Brings Out *Bride-to-Be Magazine*," 33.

39. "The Human Side," *Sales Management* (May 1, 1950), 8. *Modern Bride* was acquired by Condé Nast in 2002. "Primedia to Sell Modern Bride Group to Condé Nast Publications for $52 Million," January 14, 2002. http://www.primedia.com/htm12/news/pressRelease_114.html. In 1962, both magazines cost 35 cents; in 1967, both cost 75 cents, and in 1977, two dollars. Bahn, "Changes and Continuities," 35–37.

40. African Americans and Spanish-surnamed readers, according to one study, were overrepresented in proportion to the general population. Bahn, "Changes and Continuities," 61. Bahn is using a 1977 Trendex Buyership Index study and a Target Group Index study from 1975. I was unable to locate these materials to confirm her analysis.

41. Bahn, "Changes and Continuities," 56–60. She is citing a 1978 Trendex publication.

42. Potts, "How to Capitalize on Bridal Business," 69; Julietta K. Arthur, "Public Spender Number 1: The Bride," *Nation's Business* (June 1939), 17, 115, 18.

43. "Retail Calendar," *Department Store Economist* (January 1949), 100; "One Thousand Brides," *Department Store Economist* (July 1944), 36; "Bridesmaids Dresses [*sic*]," *Department Store Economist* (February 1947), 142; "Wedding Americana for Bride's Shop," *Department Store Economist* (April 1944), 18.

44. "Bride's Magazine—Programme of the Day," ca. 1948, F229-151, box 6, #167, Wedding Bureau, 1948, Eaton's Collection; "News of the Advertising and Marketing Fields," *New York Times* (May 22, 1956), 51.

45. Arthur, "Public Spender Number 1," 17; "One Thousand Brides," 36; Potts, "How to Capitalize on Bridal Business," 69.

46. "100% Increase in Brides Points Up Bridal Shop," *Department Store Economist* (February 25, 1942), 29; studies of course only measured a self-selected audience—those who submitted to the survey or completed the questionnaire *Bride's* provided. Of 2,000 questionnaires in 1950, 500 were returned and of these respondants, 436 were wed in bridal gowns, mainly in "church with all the trimmings." "The Retailer—Happy as the Bride," 8.

47. *Bride's* first study was *The Bridal Market: An Authoritative New Study* (Philadelphia: National Analysts, Inc., 1958). For references to studies by *Modern Bride*, see "Traditional or Modern: Stainless Steel Bridal Promotions Go Year-Round," *Merchandising Week* (October 24, 1966), 26. Also, see *Modern Bride's A Study of Bridal Market Retail Spending* (New York: Ziff-Davis, 1975).

48. *The Bridal Market*, 1–3, 12.

49. *The Bridal Market*, 8–13, 16–17, 24, 31.

50. *Modern Bride, A Study of Bridal Market Retail Spending* (New York: Ziff-Davis, 1975), 5.

51. "The Right Kind of Manners for Your Kind of Wedding," *Bride's* (Winter 1954), 104; Agnes Foster Wright, "To the Bride," *So You're Going to Be Married: A Magazine for Brides* (Autumn 1934), 16.

52. Admonitions from 1927 against the ceremony becoming merely a "fashion show" that overshadowed the "deep spiritual appreciation of the significance and beauty of the wedding sacrament" coexisted with a celebration of the formal wedding over the unfortunate informal ceremony: "Sad it is, but necessary, the bride must, in this exigency, readjust her plans to the dress of a 'real bride.'" Mrs. John Alexander King, *Weddings: Modes, Manners and Customs of Weddings* (New York: Delineator, Butterick Building, 1927), 69–70.

53. Virginia Pope, "Here Comes the Bride," *Bride's* (Autumn 1934), 5, 24.

54. "Fortune's Favored Child—the Bride," *Bride's* (Winter 1953), 89. See also *Bride's* (Spring 1949), 89; Agnes Foster Wright, *Bride's* (Summer 1939), 55; Marian E. Murtfeldt, *Bride's* (Winter 1946), 97; Martha Ellyn Slayback, "Home Wedding Reception," *Modern Bride* (Winter 1949–1950), 68.

55. "To Thine Own Self Be True," *Bride's* (Winter 1954), 75.

56. "Portrait of You—The Bride," *Bride's* (Summer 1947), 103–104.

57. "Trousseau for Audrey," *Bride's* (Winter 1954), 94. Also, see "Wedding-Day Fashions They Prefer," *Bride's* (Autumn 1959), 146–148; "I Am Joyce," *Modern Bride* (Fall 1949), 68; "I Am Kay," *Modern Bride* (Fall 1949), 69.

58. *Modern Bride* (Fall 1949); *Modern Bride* (Fall 1953); *Modern Bride* (Winter 1954–1955); Front covers, tables of contents, and editor's columns operate as "relay texts" according to Ellen McCracken, *Decoding Women's Magazines: From Mademoiselle to Ms.* (London: Macmillan, 1993), 46.

59. *Bride's* (Summer 1940), 108.

60. *Modern Bride* featured a section from 1949 to 1954 titled "His Highness the Bridegroom," and *Bride's* started a section, "John Groom, Esq.," in 1938 that ran through 1945. A new section called "Modern Groom" appeared in 1955 in *Modern Bride*. Quote from *Bride's* (Summer 1949), 77.

61. "The Right Manners for Your Kind of Wedding," 138.

62. Barbara Morrow, "It's His Wedding Too," *Bride's* (Summer 1949), 96. "Beautiful Wedding," *Bride's* (Winter 1947–1948), 142; *Modern Bride* (Summer 1956), 4.

63. "100% Increase in Brides Points Up Bridal Shop," *Department Store Economist* (February 25, 1942), 29.

64. "In Permanent Headquarters," *Bride's* (Autumn 1942), 60; "In Temporary Headquarters," *Bride's* (Autumn 1942), 64; "Mr. and Mrs. A—a Civilian Couple," *Bride's* (Autumn 1942), 58; "Mr. and Mrs. B—of the Army—of the Navy," *Bride's* (Autumn 1942), 62.

65. "America Loves Brides," *Bride's* (Spring 1947), 82; 128.

66. "Coup de Marriage," *Bride's* (Autumn 1934), 46. "Inspired by the Bride in 'Brigadoon,' " *Bride's* (Winter 1954), 81.

67. Bahn, "Changes and Continuities," 150, 141; Weems, *Desegregating the Dollar*, 70–71.

68. "Have Black Models Really Made It?" *Ebony* (May 1970), 152. For examples of black women modeling Priscilla of Boston gowns, see the following citations: Untitled tear sheet from *Bride's* (May 1969), box 8, series 6, tear sheets, 1950–1994, Priscilla of Boston Collection; "Majestic silhouettes in taffeta and silk faille," tear sheet from *Bride's Magazine* (September 1970), box 8, series 6, tear sheets, 1950–1994, Priscilla of Boston Collection; "Reflections of Romance," tear sheet, *Modern Bride* (August–September 1971), box 8, series 6, tear sheets, 1950–1994; Priscilla of Boston Collection.

69. Marilyn Halter, *Shopping for Identity: The Marketing of Ethnicity* (New York: Schocken Books, 2000), 5, quote on 116.

70. Ibid., 118–119. Macy's participated in locally sponsored events, such as the African Brides of Distinction Fair or the Greek Bridal Show (pp. 116–117).

71. Bahn, "Changes and Continuities," 59–60. She is citing a 1978 Trendex publication.

CHAPTER 4. DEPARTMENT STORES AND CONSUMER RITES

1. Tom Alderman, "How to Run 40,000 Weddings, Yet Not Get Married," *Liberty* (December 1960), 58, box 38, Merchandise—Wedding Bureau, Eaton's Collection.

For a history of this Canadian institution, see Joy L. Santink, *Timothy Eaton and the Rise of His Department Store* (Toronto: University of Toronto Press, 1991).

2. Department stores began closing their bridal salons in the early 1980s. For example, Hudson's and Lord and Taylor ended theirs by 1982. J. C. Penney shut theirs down in 1978, but reopened in 1982. See Marj Jackson Levin, "Romantic Look Returns," *Detroit Free Press*, 1982, newsclipping, box 10, Priscilla of Boston Collection. According to Kidder, department stores began to close their bridal sections across the country due to the labor intensiveness of the bridal business. See Randi Henderson, "Despite Ailments, Priscilla Still Designs Bridal Gowns," *Baltimore Sun*, 1983, newsclipping, box 10, Priscilla of Boston Collection.

3. "Record of Trousseau and Marriage Expenses," 1899, Warshaw Collection of Business Americana—Matrimony; Karle & Rhines, Rochester City Directory, 1900; Edward Filene, *Next Steps Forward in Retailing* (Boston: Edward A. Filene, 1937), 29, 53, 57; Leach, *Land of Desire*, 72–73; *Marriage: Correct Forms for Wedding Invitations, Announcements and Receptions* (New York: Dempsey & Carroll, Society Stationers, n.d. [ca. 1900]), 7, 18–19, box 1, Warshaw Collection of Business Americana—Matrimony; "Pamphlet, Reed & Barton Company, New York: 1905," box 3, Warshaw Collection of Business Americana—Silver; A. T. Stewart's, 1908, Drawer 4. Gibbons Card files, Wanamaker Collection, The Historical Society of Pennsylvania, Philadelphia (hereafter HSP). A stationery department appears on the ground floor of Wanamaker's in 1911. "Ground Plan of John Wanamaker's Store," box 29, folder 22, Dedication, 1911, Ephemera, Wanamaker Collection, HSP; Marshall Field's had a stationery engraving room as well. "Engraved Wedding Cards," *Fashions of the Hour* (Spring 1923), 33, Marshall Field's Archives, Chicago, Illinois.

4. For a general discussion of mail order, see Strasser, *Satisfaction Guaranteed*, 212–215; Nancy F. Koehn, *Brand New: How Entrepreneurs Earned Consumers' Trust from Wedgwood to Dell* (Boston: Harvard Business School Press, 2001), 99; Montgomery Ward & Company, Spring and Summer 1895, trade catalogue, no. 57, 38; Montgomery Ward & Company, Baltimore, Spring and Summer 1927, trade catalogue, no. 106, Hagley.

5. Quotation in Norris A. Brisco, *Retailing*, 2nd ed. (New York: Prentice-Hall, 1947), 5. See also Filene, *Next Steps Forward in Retailing*, 29, 53, 57; Leach, *Land of Desire*, 72–73; Strasser, *Satisfaction Guaranteed*, 207.

6. Benson, *Counter Cultures*, 82–91. Benson lists weddings as one of the personal services offered by department stores; Marshall Field's publication *Give the Lady What She Wants!* rolls weddings into this service. As we have seen, Field's did start a wedding secretary service in 1924, but this service was limited to shopping assistance, advice on caterers and honeymoon travel, and the like. It did not typically include the planning and execution of the wedding and reception. Lloyd Wendt and Herman Kogan, *Give the Lady What She Wants!* (Chicago: Rand McNally, 1952), 358.

7. *A Report on Acquisition of Home Furnishings by the New Household Formation Market*, conducted by Trendex for *Modern Bride* magazine (New York: Ziff-Davis, 1973), n.p.

8. Edwina B. Hogadone and Donald K. Beckley, *Merchandising Techniques* (New York: McGraw-Hill, 1942), 13.

9. "Here Comes the Bride's Book," insert in *Fashion of the Hour Presents*, 2, ca. 1939, Marshall Field's Archives. Wanamaker's also had a Groom Shop where formal or informal attire for weddings could be rented. "In Case You Didn't Know . . . ," *The Eagle Speaks* (December 1953), 8, Wanamaker Collection, HSP; "Formal Wear Rental Service in the Modern Manner," Wanamaker's, *Bride's* (Summer 1956), 24D, Store Records, box 91B, Wanamaker Collection, HSP. For a discussion of men as nineteenth-century consumers of crystal, see Blaszczyk, *Imagining Consumers*, 16–18, 31–32.

10. Leach, *Land of Desire*, 84.

11. Window displays (photographs), box 121, Women's Fashions—Weddings, Wanamaker Collection, HSP. Quotation in "The Kewpie Wedding," *Store Chat* (February 15, 1914), 61, Strawbridge & Clothier Collection, Hagley; "The Famous 'Bridal Party,'" *Store Chat*, April 15, 1915, 74, Strawbridge & Clothier Collection, Hagley.

12. "Domestics Trousseau Is Upper-Bracket Promotion," *Department Store Economist* (May 10, 1939), 16; E. B. Weiss, *How to Sell to and Through Department Stores* (New York: McGraw-Hill, 1936), 73; "Brides' Week," *Dry Goods Economist* (May 24, 1930), 43.

13. "Merchandising Calendar," *Dry Goods Economist* (May 1935), 21; "Copy and Layout Material Planned for June Use," *Dry Goods Economist* (May 24, 1930), 43; "Paper Products Personalized," *Department Store Economist* (August 1952), n.p.

14. "Who Is Getting Your Gift Wrap Business?" *Department Store Economist* (May 1959), 32.

15. Paul H. Nystrom, *Fashion Merchandising* (New York: Ronald Press, 1932), 3. Merchandising also included promotional activities, such as advertising, window display, and arrangement of departments. Nathan M. Ohrbach, with foreword by Kenneth Collins, *Getting Ahead in Retailing* (New York: McGraw-Hill, 1935), 154–156.

16. Ohrbach, *Getting Ahead in Retailing*, 154–156; Weiss, *How to Sell to and Through Department Stores*, 72. Some stores "placed the publicity division subordinate to the merchandise division." Brisco, *Retailing*, 63.

17. Quote from Koehn, *Brand New*, 126. Stock turnover was the number of times during a certain period that the average stock of merchandise was bought and sold. The rate of turnover was determined by dividing the average inventory at retail for the period in question into the sales for the same period. Stock turnover was commonly used as an index of merchandising efficiency. Brisco, *Retailing*, 203–204.

18. Brisco, *Retailing*, 451; quotation in Weiss, *How to Sell to and Through Department Stores*, 72–73.

19. Some stores also might try to hire outside design firms to handle their windows. Howard Kratz to J. P. Lachaud, June 6, 1938; Howard Kratz to J. P. Lachaud, May 28, 1938, Store Records, Sales Division, Display Department, box 50, Wanamaker Collection, HSP.

20. Leach, *Land of Desire*, 55, 59 (quotation), 64, 69; Benson, *Counter Cultures*, 102.

21. Bridal windows, October 1925, box 242, folder 16, Marshall Field's Archives; "June Bride Display" at C. W. Klemm, Inc., *Dry Goods Economist* (May 8, 1926), 15.

22. JCN, Display Director, to Seymour S. Sussman (May 6, 1939), Store Records, Display Department, letters, box 52, folder 4, Wanamaker Collection, HSP; Wendt and Kogan, *Give the Lady What She Wants*, 310.

23. "Electric Housewares Gift Campaign," *Department Store Economist* (January 1952), 136; "It's Shower Time for the October Bride," *Department Store Economist* (August 1962), 94; "Overlooked Profits in Stationery," *Department Store Economist* (February 1955), 109; quote from Leach, *Land of Desire*, 84.

24. "June Brides," *Jewelers' Circular* (May 4, 1927), 131; "This Window Made 25 Silver Sales," *Jewelers' Circular* (October 1931), 107; "Advertising and Selling Suggestions for June," *Jewelers' Circular* (May 16, 1929), 44; "Window Display of Houghton-Gorney, Boston," *Florists' Exchange* (June 19, 1920), 1403.

25. "Five Thousand Attend Wedding at Pizitz Roof Garden—Good Ad Stuff," *Dry Goods Economist* (July 4, 1925), 14.

26. Window displays (photographs), box 121, folder 1, Women's Fashions—Photographs, Wanamaker Collection, HSP.

27. For example, see "Dressing the Bride," 04332, n.d.; "Decorating for the Wedding," 08349, n.d., Underwood & Underwood Collection, NMAH.

28. Quotation in this paragraph taken from William Nelson Taft, *Handbook of Window Display* (New York: McGraw-Hill 1926), 115.

29. Bridal windows, October 1925, box 242, folder 16, Marshall Field's Archives.

30. Taft, *Handbook of Window Display*, 111, 115 (quotation).

31. "Of Thee I Sing," Hedrich Blessing Studio, September 1932, box 243, folder 3, Marshall Field's Archives.

32. These displays drew on popular historical pasts, in keeping with an early twentieth-century fad for historical pageants. David Glassberg, *American Historical Pageantry: The Uses of Tradition in the Early Twentieth Century* (Chapel Hill: University of North Carolina Press, 1990), 137.

33. Leach, *Land of Desire*, 92. Sociologist Eva Illouz explores the relation between romance and capitalism in *Consuming the Romantic Utopia: Love and the Cultural Contradictions of Capitalism* (Berkeley: University of California Press, 1997).

34. In 1921, Wanamaker's proposed one to mark its diamond jubilee, perhaps to underline the store's place in American history. "Motife: The Expression of 60 Years in Merchandise, Fashion, Art, Music, Methods," box 37, memo, "Diamond Jubilee—1861–1921, 25 Years in NY Begins April 8, 1921," Wanamaker Collection, HSP. Also, see photographs "As Mother Looked," "Dixie Darling," "War of 1812," and "Colonial Bride," *Store Chat* (December 1943), 10–11, Strawbridge & Clothier Collection, Hagley.

35. "Our Windows Worked for Our Boys," *Store Chat* (May 1944), 13, Strawbridge & Clothier Collection, Hagley.

36. "The Big Business of Selling to Brides," *Store Chat* (December 1943), 9, Strawbridge & Clothier Collection, Hagley; "A Bride Is Worth $3300 to a Department Store," *Store Chat* (February 1956), 6, Strawbridge & Clothier Collection, Hagley; "Our Windows Worked for Our Boys," 13.

37. "New Flatware Patterns Stimulate Silver Purchases," *Department Store Economist* (September 1949), 96. See also "Your Store in June," *Department Store Economist* (May 10, 1942), 8.

38. Leach, *Land of Desire*, 101–102. Elite designers Coco Chanel, Paul Poiret, and Charles Frederick Worth each claimed the first fashion show in the late teens. Charlotte Herzog, "'Powder Puff' Promotion: The Fashion Show-in-the-Film," in *Fabrications: Costume and the Female Body*, ed. Jane Gaines and Charlotte Herzog (New York: Routledge, 1990), 134. Otnes and Pleck date the department-store fashion show to New York City in 1857. *Cinderella Dreams*, 34.

39. Leach, *Land of Desire*, 101–103, 110.

40. "Our Fall Fashion Show Was Brilliant and Beautiful," *Store Chat* (October 1950), 7. These fashion shows were a regular feature, according to this article, thus it must have been held during the 1940s; "Five Star Fashions," *Store Chat* (February 1951), 2.

41. "Girls Are Rapt but Practical When Watching Bridal Show," *New York Times* (January 15, 1965), 24. Manufacturer's bridal trade shows also exhibited at hotels. "$49 Bridal Gowns Lead Show Buying," *New York Times* (January 4, 1951), 50.

42. Stanley Marcus, *Minding the Store* (Boston: Little, Brown, 1974), 72.

43. News release, February 8, 1958, Bridal Promotion File, Marshall Field's Archives.

44. Bridal Fashion Show memos, box 67, Planbook 1956–62, Wanamaker Collection, HSP. On overcrowding, see Memo to Mr. Funk from Mr. Wetherill, 1957, box 67, Store Plans, January–August 1957, Wanamaker Collection, HSP. On bridal fashion shows in suburban branch stores, see "Special Events Calendar," *Store Chat* (February 1975), 5; News release, 1975, Bridal Promotion File, Marshall Field's Archives; Koehn, *Brand New*, 133.

45. Judy Klemesrud, "It Was a Special Show—And The Audience Was Special, Too," *New York Times* (February 17, 1969), 39. See also Leslie Maitland, "A Fair for Seekers of Perfect Wedding," *New York Times* (February 18, 1975), 34; "The Original Wedding Expo," http://www.originalwedding expo.com/.

46. Bahn, "Changes and Continuities," 18, 182–183; Marcia Seligson, *The Eternal Bliss Machine: America's Way of Wedding* (New York: William Morrow, 1973); Kitty Hanson, *For Richer, For Poorer* (New York: Abelard-Schuman, 1967).

47. Klemesrud, "It Was a Special Show," 39.

48. Morris, "Bringing the Bride up to Date," *New York Times* (April 14, 1970), 56.

49. Herbst Department Store Collection, North Dakota Institute for Regional Studies, Fargo.

50. Elsie Bell Grosvenor's Honeymoon Scrapbook and Journal 1900, box 36, Grosvenor Family Papers, Manuscripts Division, Library of Congress, Washington, D.C.;

Louise Conway Schoenberger, Wedding present list, June 1, 1908, Joseph Downs Collection of Manuscripts and Printed Ephemera, Winterthur Library; Titcomb-Shepard Wedding Album, 1899, Massachusetts Historical Society, Boston; "The Brides Are Always With Us: June Weddings Represent Only a Small Per Cent of the Year's Total," *Dry Goods Economist* (March 8, 1930), 55.

51. Memo from General Manager, D. M. Yates, November 8, 1924, Marshall Field's Archives; quotations from *Fashions of the Hour*, Christmas Number 1924, 1, Marshall Field's Archives.

52. Benson, *Counter Cultures*, 85, 93–97; Marion Edwards, "Wedding Presents Made Easy," *Saturday Evening Post* (March 15, 1930), 52; Brisco, *Retailing*, 287–288; "Services for Customers," *Store Chat* (August–September 1950), 4, Strawbridge & Clothier Collection, Hagley. On Lenox and gift registries, see Blaszczyk, *Imagining Consumers*, 257–258.

53. Benson, *Counter Cultures*, 50; "The Gift Shop Is a Sales Department," *Store Chat* (March–April 1930), 4, Strawbridge & Clothier Collection, Hagley.

54. Memo from General Manager, D. M. Yates, November 8, 1924; *Fashions of the Hour*, Christmas Number 1924, 1, Marshall Field's Archives.

55. "The Retailer–Happy as the Bride," *Sales Management* (May 1, 1950), 8.

56. "The Bride's Preference List," *Brides, Grooms, & Carsons*, July 1960, Marshall Field's Archives.

57. *Fashions of the Hour*, Christmas Number 1924, 1, Marshall Field's Archives.

58. "A Wishing Well Helps Brides Receive the Gifts They Want," *Department Store Economist* (August 1944), 34.

59. "A Beautiful Beginning, B. Altman & Co.," *Bride's* (Spring 1954), 7, Store Records, box 91 B, Wanamaker Collection, HSP.

60. *Guide for the Bride* (Fall 1955), 99.

61. Memo from General Manager, D. M. Yates, November 8, 1924; *Fashions of the Hour*, Christmas Number 1924, 1, Marshall Field's Archives.

62. Streeter, *Father of the Bride*, 134, 127, 131, 137.

63. *The Bridal Market: An Authoritative New Study* (October 1958), Preliminary Report Conducted for *Bride's* magazine by National Analysts, Inc., Philadelphia, Penn., 17–18. National Analysts' staff interviewers took a random sample of names and addresses of women from marriage license bureaus in specified urban and rural sampling points. Questionnaires were mailed and then to "eliminate any bias due to non-response, 110 non-respondents were interviewed either in person or by telephone" (1–2).

64. *The Bridal Market: An Authoritative New Study* (October 1958), 18.

65. Letter from Mrs. George Berman, Chicago, in "As Others See Us," *Brides, Grooms, & Carsons* (1960), in-house publication, n.p., Marshall Field's Archives.

66. "Engraved Wedding Cards," *Fashions of the Hour* (Spring 1923), 33. Marshall Field's Archives.

67. "Engraved Wedding Cards," 33; "Time for Bridal Stationery," *Department Store Economist* (January 1952), 136; "Ready for 1,600,000 Weddings?" *Department*

Store Economist (October 1959), 62–64; "The History of the Social Invitation," http://www.ed-it.com/p_histinv.htm, accessed February 1, 2003.

68. "Paper Products Personalized," *Department Store Economist* (August 1952), n.p.

69. "The Wedding Secretary Assists the Bride," *Fashions of the Hour*, School Number 1924, 26, Marshall Field's Archives; "House Notice," June 2, 1924, Wedding Bureau, Marshall Field's Archives.

70. Benson, *Counter Cultures*, 290. The rise of computers or electronic data processing eliminated most manual inventory and accounting tasks, allowing for the elimination of the trained, knowledgeable sales person and conversion to part-time workers. Chains were able to attain a low payroll-to-sales ratio, which in turn allowed them to underprice independents and specialty stores. See Barry Bluestone et al., "The Department Store Industry in New England: An Analysis of Market Transformation, Investment, and Labor," December 27, 1979, Report for the Office of Economic Analysis and Research, Economic Development Administration, U.S. Department of Commerce, conducted at the Harvard-MIT Joint Center for Urban Studies, Cambridge, Mass., 25.

71. Marcus, *Minding the Store*, 55; Dilys E. Blum and H. Kristina Haugland, *Best Dressed: Fashion from the Birth of Couture to Today* (Philadelphia: Philadelphia Museum of Art, 1997), 20; "Women's Ready-to-Wear and Specialty Stores," *Method in Merchandising* (Grand Rapids, Mich.: The Welch-Wilmarth Companies, Assoc., 1922), 29–33; Wendt and Kogan, *Give the Lady What She Wants!* 334–335.

72. In Chicago, Eaton's noted only Marshall Field & Company and Carson, Pirie Scott, and in Richmond, Virginia, Cora Lee Sheppard. Eaton's did not distinguish between specialty stores for women's fashions and department stores in this report on the bridal business, nor did it specify the extent of the services rendered at these stores. January 29, 1942, Report to Mr. J. G. McKee from Wedding Bureau, Merchandise Display Department, 1–2, box 6, Wedding Bureau Promo, 1943, Eaton's Collection.

73. "The Wedding Business," *Life* (June 9, 1952), 127. Blue garters were a wedding tradition at least as early as 1941. See *Fashions of the Hour*, Fall 1941, Marshall Field's Archives; Carson, Pirie Scott & Company, Chicago, *Bride's* (Summer 1939), 15, and (Spring 1939), 15; "How to Marry in Haste and Not Repent in Leisure," *Bride's* (Summer 1942), 62–63; "The Gimbel Bridal Service," Gimbel Brothers, Philadelphia, *Bride's* (Winter 1948), 53.

74. See Sosnick & Thalheimer, Winston-Salem, North Carolina, 1950, and Bonwit Teller, Cleveland, Ohio, 1951, Gottscho-Schleisner Collection, American Memory, Library of Congress. In her study of the meaning of the late twentieth-century wedding gown, Susanne Friese argued that these bridal shop mirrors and large empty spaces aided in the process of "projected appraisal"—a period of self-absorption during which the bride transferred the cultural meaning encoded within the dress into her "personal lived experience." Susanne Friese, "The Wedding Dress: From Use Value to Sacred Object," in *Through the Wardrobe: Women's Relationships with Their Clothes*, ed. Ali Guy, Eileen Green, and Maura Banim (Oxford: Berg, 2001), 60.

75. "Looking Toward June," *Eagle Speaks* (February 1955), 2, Wanamaker Collection, HSP.

76. "The Curtain Lifts on Our New Bride's Shop," *Store Chat* (April–May 1949), 10–11, Strawbridge & Clothier Collection, Hagley; Carson, Pirie Scott & Company, Chicago, *Bride's* (Spring 1939), 15; "Looking Toward June," 2.

77. "The Curtain Lifts on Our New Bride's Shop," 10–12; Gimbel Brothers, Philadelphia, *Bride's* (Winter 1948), 53.

78. John B. Swinney, *Merchandising of Fashions: Policies and Methods of Successful Specialty Stores* (New York: Ronald Press, 1942), 132. For Swinney's definition of a specialty store, see pp. 10–12.

79. "More Brides," *Department Store Economist* (January 1951), 37.

80. "For Richer or Poorer," *Field Glass* (October 8, 1951), 6, Marshall Field's Archives.

81. *Adding Security to Your Future Happiness*, 1939, booklet, Marshall Field's Archives; quotations from *The Bride's Book of Plans*, ca. 1939, Marshall Field's Archives. In the late 1940s, they present her with the Wedding Bureau's bride's book. "Here Comes the Bride," *Field Glass* (June 27, 1947), 4, Wedding Bureau file, Marshall Field's Archives.

82. Interoffice Memo, June 3, 1961, "Publicity Story on Bride's Room and/or Wedding Bureau—Comparison of Field's Services with Those at Carsons and the Fair," Marshall Field's Archives.

83. Strawbridge & Clothier explicitly offered "advisory service only" and did "not attend the wedding." "A Customer Services Directory," November 1964, Strawbridge & Clothier Collection, Hagley; Interoffice Memo, June 3, 1961, "Publicity Story on Bride's Room and/or Wedding Bureau," Marshall Field's Archives.

84. Alderman, "How to Run 40,000 Weddings, Yet Not Get Married," 58. In a 1968 interview, however, J. A. Brockie, who was Claire Dreier's supervisor and former head of the merchandise display department at Eaton's during the 1930s, stated that he didn't think Eaton's had the first wedding bureau and that there were "probably already some in the U.S." Interview with Mr. J. A. Brockie, October 8, 1968. Re: Weddings and Parties, box 38, Merchandise—Wedding Bureau, Eaton's Collection.

85. Claire Dreier, "Talk to Advertising Club," October 7, 1948, 3, F229–151, box 6, #167, Wedding Bureau, 1948, Eaton's Collection.

86. Simpson's, Eaton's rival in Toronto, offered a range of Wedding Bureau services by 1942. Simpson's presented potential customers with a bride's book containing information about the reception and gift suggestions, and also sent out a counterpart for the groom. Their bureau assisted the bride with the selection of her trousseau clothes, which were modeled for the bride and accessorized for her, but unlike Eaton's, Simpson's turned over the catering arrangements to a local business, the Arcadian Court. Services provided by Eaton's when their Wedding Bureau opened are described throughout what became a regular Eaton's publication, *Notebook for the Bride* (1938–1939), F229–151, box 6, #165, Wedding Bureau, 1938–1939, Eaton's Collection. For a summary of Eaton's services in 1948, see "Eaton's: Servant of the Bride," *Brides Book*, Fall and Winter 1948, 4, F229–162-D-1055, box 33, Fashion—Brides Book 1948 (part A), Eaton's Collection. For a summary of Eaton's services that were provided at

least through the 1950s, see *Notebook for the Bride* (1957), 26, F229–72, File: [Series 72], Wedding Bureau Notebooks/Pamphlets [1945]–1977, Eaton's Collection.

87. Joy Parr, *Domestic Goods: The Material, the Moral, and the Economic* (Toronto: University of Toronto Press, 1999); Cynthia Wright, "The Most Prominent *Rendez-vous* of the Feminine Toronto: Eaton's College Street and the Organization of Shopping in Toronto, 1920–1950" (Ph.D. diss., University of Toronto, 1992); Cynthia Wright, "'Feminine Trifles of Vast Importance': Writing Gender into the History of Consumption," in *Gender Conflicts: New Essays in Women's History*, ed. Franca Iacovetta and Mariana Valverde (Toronto: University of Toronto Press, 1992), 239; Donica Belisle, "Toward a Canadian Consumer History," *Labour/Le Travail* 52 (2003), http://www.historycooperative.org.

88. Frances K. Johnson to Miss Dreier, June 30, 1942, box 6, Wedding Bureau Promo, 1943, Eaton's Collection. Claire Dreier, "Talk to Advertising Club"; "Wedding Bureau Holds Series of Meetings," October 12, 1942, newspaper clipping, F229–162–1217, box 38, Merchandise—Wedding Bureau, Eaton's Collection.

89. Laura M. Cummer to *Modern Bride*, February 12, 1954, copy to Eaton's, F229–151, box 1, #19, Bride's Week, 1954–1957, Eaton's Collection.

90. Eaton's had on file a list of telephone numbers for society editors at the *Star*, the *Telegram*, the *Globe & Mail*, and *Saturday Night*. Society Editors, list, F229–151, box 6, #165, Wedding Bureau, 1938–1939, Eaton's Collection; Internal account of wedding for newspaper announcement, 2, F229–151, box 6, #165, Wedding Bureau, 1938–1939, Eaton's Collection. This was the Wedding Bureau's first wedding, as only one wedding was listed for the week ending December 8, 1938; "Comparison Report by Weeks, 1938–40–41," F229-151, box 6, #166, Wedding Bureau Promo, 1943, Eaton's Collection.

91. Internal account of wedding for newspaper announcement, 3, F229–151, box 6, #165, Wedding Bureau, 1938–1939, Eaton's Collection; internal account of wedding for newspaper announcement, 2, F229–151, box 6, #165, Wedding Bureau, 1938–1939, Eaton's Collection.

92. Flower Arrangements Used at the "Ellsworth-Holton" Wedding, internal agenda, F229-151, box 6, #165, Wedding Bureau, 1938–1939, Eaton's Collection; quotes taken from Internal account of wedding for newspaper announcement, 4, F229–151, box 6, #165, Wedding Bureau, 1938–1939, Eaton's Collection.

93. Internal account of wedding for newspaper announcement, 4–5, F229–151, box 6, #165, Wedding Bureau, 1938–1939, Eaton's Collection.

94. Internal agenda, Ellsworth Wedding, Eaton Memorial Church, Dec. 3rd, 1938, at 3:30 P.M., F229-151, box 6, #165, Wedding Bureau, 1938–1939, Eaton's Collection; Internal account of wedding for newspaper announcement, 1–5, F229–151, box 6, #165, Wedding Bureau, 1938–1939, Eaton's Collection. B. Ellsworth to Mr. Brockie, 1938, 1–4, F229-151, box 6, #165, Wedding Bureau, 1938–1939, Eaton's Collection.

95. Internal agenda, J. Foster, Ellsworth Wedding, Eaton Memorial Church, Dec. 3rd, 1938 at 3:30 P.M., F229-151, box 6, #165, Wedding Bureau, 1938–1939, Eaton's Collection. Brockie organized this particular wedding perhaps because of its social

importance or because the Bureau was still in its early stage and the bridal consultant's responsibilities had not yet been fully established.

96. B. Ellsworth to Mr. Brockie, 1938, F229-151, box 6, #165, Wedding Bureau, 1938–1939, Eaton's Collection.

97. Internal agenda, Mr. Brockie, Ellsworth Wedding, Eaton Memorial Church, Dec. 3rd, 1938 at 3:30 P.M., F229-151, box 6, #165, Wedding Bureau, 1938–1939, Eaton's Collection; B. Ellsworth to Mr. Brockie, 1938, 1–4, F229–151, box 6, #165, Wedding Bureau, 1938–1939, Eaton's Collection.

98. "Comparison Report by Weeks, 1938–40–41," F229–151, box 6, #166, Wedding Bureau Promo, 1943, Eaton's Collection; Report to Mr. I. Ford, Re: Catering, August 19, 1939, Merchandise Display Department, F229–151, box 6, #165, Wedding Bureau, 1938–1939, Eaton's Collection.

99. "Bride's Week Meeting, April 23, 1957—9:30 o'clock, Staff Training Room," 2, F229-151, box 1, #19, Bride's Week, 1954–1957, Eaton's Collection.

100. Memo to J. A. Brockie, January 4th, 1955, from Public Relations Office, Re: Bridal Promotion Week, F229-151, box 1, #19, Bride's Week, 1954–1957, Eaton's Collection; "Bride's Week Meeting, October 29th, 1956—9:15 o'clock, Georgian Room," 3, F229-151, box 1, #19, Bride's Week, 1954–1957, Eaton's Collection; "Bridal Week—College Street," January 28, 1954, F229-151, box 1, #19, Bride's Week, 1954–1957, Eaton's Collection.

101. Quote from "Bride's Week Meeting, Wednesday, February 24, 1954, Georgian Room at 9:15 o'clock," 4, F229-151, box 1, #19, Bride's Week, 1954–1957, Eaton's Collection. Cynthia Wright discusses the new Canadian market and the relationship between consumer culture and Canadianization. See "The Most Prominent *Rendezvous* of the Feminine Toronto," 210–215.

102. "Eaton's: Servant of the Bride," *Bride's Book* (Fall and Winter 1948), 4, F229-162-D-1055, box 33, Fashion—Brides Book 1948 (part A), Eaton's Collection.

103. Dreier, "Talk to Advertising Club," 5. Other areas of the store were also engaged in "Canadianizing efforts" through consumption. See Wright, "The Most Prominent *Rendezvous* of the Feminine Toronto," 211–212.

104. Stocktaking September 1941, Wedding Bureau, F229–151, box 6, #165, Wedding Bureau, 1938–1939, Eaton's Collection.

105. Grace Lumpkin, *The Wedding* (New York: Lee Furman, 1939; reprint, Carbondale: Southern Illinois University Press, 1976); "Three Boston Windows Gain Effectiveness Through Individualistic Treatment of Various Themes," *Women's Wear Magazine*, June 21, 1926, 83. Also, see the "Little Bo Peep" look or shepherdess look in wedding gowns of the 1920s in Catalog No. 58339, Wedding dress, Cultural History Catalog, Smithsonian Institution.

106. George Sweet Gibb, *The Whitesmiths of Taunton: A History of Reed & Barton, 1824–1943* (Cambridge, Mass.: Harvard University Press, 1943), 212 (quotation), 318–320.

107. Leach, *Land of Desire*, 26–29; David Monod, *Store Wars: Shopkeepers and the Culture of Mass Marketing, 1890–1939* (Toronto: University of Toronto Press, 1996);

Sarah Elvins, *Sales and Celebrations: Retailing and Regional Identity in Western New York State, 1920–1940* (Athens: Ohio University Press, 2004), 78–79.

108. Fred W. Adams to Clare [*sic*] Dreier, November 8, 1939, F229-151, box 6, #165, Wedding Bureau, 1938–1939, Eaton's Collection; Fred W. Adams to Claire Dreier, November 17, 1939, F229-151, box 6, #165, Wedding Bureau, 1938–1939, Eaton's Collection.

109. Claire Dreier to J. A. Brockie, November 26, 1939, 3, 1, 2, F229-151, box 6, #165, Wedding Bureau, 1938–1939, Eaton's Collection.

110. Transcript, Re: Interview with Mr. Fred Adams, December 5, 1939, 1–4, F229-151, box 6, #165, Wedding Bureau, 1938–1939, Eaton's Collection.

111. Ibid., 3.

112. Conversation between Miss Richardson of the Arcadian Court and Miss Smith of the Wedding Bureau, November 8, 1939, 1–2, F229-151, box 6, #165, Wedding Bureau, 1938–1939, Eaton's Collection. Transcript, Re: Interview with Mr. Fred Adams, 1.

113. Transcript, Re: Interview with Mr. Fred Adams, 4; quote taken from Report, Catering, November 7, 1939, 3, F229-151, box 6, #165, Wedding Bureau, 1938–1939, Eaton's Collection.

114. Conversation between Miss Richardson of the Arcadian Court and Miss Smith of the Wedding Bureau, November 8, 1939, 1–2.

115. Report, Catering, November 9, 1939, 1–6, F229-151, box 6, #165, Wedding Bureau, 1938–1939, Eaton's Collection.

116. Records, Taxi, Caterer, Florist, December 3, 1938, to November 25, 1939, F229-151, box 6, #165, Wedding Bureau, 1938–1939, Eaton's Collection.

117. Wedding Bureau, January 19, 1942, F229-151, box 6, Wedding Bureau Promo, 1943, Eaton's Collection. The records do not calculate profit and provide no numbers for the cost or markup of merchandise. Henderson, "Despite Ailments, Priscilla Still Designs Bridal Gowns."

118. Lyle, *Mademoiselle's Handbook for Bridal Consultants* (New York: Street and Smith Publishers, 1946), 22–23; Interoffice Memo, June 3, 1961, Marshall Field's Archives.

119. "Hudson's, Detroit," *Bride's* (Spring 1948), 83.

120. "A Wanamaker Wedding," *Modern Bride* (Summer 1953), 10; Benson, *Counter Cultures*, 1; Leach, *Land of Desire*, 90.

CHAPTER 5. BRIDAL CONSULTANTS, THE FASHION INDUSTRY,
AND THE BUSINESS OF TRADITION

1. Newsclipping, ca. 1978, box 10, Priscilla of Boston Collection.

2. For example, in 1962 Barbara Howard purchased her long white nylon organza gown for $45 from Herberger's in Ashby, Minnesota. Her reception and wedding costs, including photography, flowers, and church fees, totaled under $100. Receipt, June 21, 1962, Herberger's, material in possession of the author.

3. On the "master of ceremonies" and "necessary arrangements," see Angela

Thompson, "Unveiled: The Emotion Work of Wedding Coordinators in the American Wedding Industry" (Ph.D. diss., Brandeis University, 1998), 71. *Bridal Consultant*, 3rd ed., Entrepreneur Business Guide No. 1330 (Irvine, Calif.: Entrepreneur Magazine Group, 1997), 6; Walter R. Houghton et al., *American Etiquette and Rules of Politeness*, 6th ed., 205–206.

4. "A Woman of Fashion," *Etiquette for Americans*, 107.

5. Grant, "Purveyors to the Bride," 23. The term *wedding director* could also be used for women. "Good Housekeeping Finds Out What a Wedding Director Does," *Good Housekeeping* (March 19, 1942), 36–37; "Wedding Customs and Menus," *Hotel Monthly* (May 1930), 59, 61.

6. The Officiating Clergyman, "Of Weddings and Funerals," *Harper's* (December 1945), 496–497.

7. Streeter, *Father of the Bride*, 141. This stereotype continues in the 1991 remake of *Father of the Bride*, and in a different version, in the reality television show *Queer Eye for the Straight Guy*.

8. Specialty shops were one- or two-person operations and did not have different departments. Specialty stores are defined here as those retailers who used a departmentalized structure (hence the need for a bridal salon within the store), but that sold a limited range of goods. John B. Swinney, *Merchandising of Fashions: Policies and Methods of Successful Specialty Stores* (New York: Ronald Press, 1942), 10.

9. In Catherine Filene, ed., *Careers for Women: New Ideas, New Methods, New Opportunities to Fit a New World* (Cambridge, Mass.: The Riverside Press, 1934), 115. The field was not present in an earlier edition. The first book-length journalistic critique of the wedding industry also described the 1930s as the point of origin for bridal consulting. See Hanson, *For Richer, For Poorer*, 118–119.

10. "Looking Toward June," *Eagle Speaks* (February 1955), 2, Wanamaker Collection, HSP; Filene, *Careers for Women*, 115.

11. "The Wedding Business," *Life* (June 9, 1952), 120–123.

12. Box 29, Store Records. Exec. Div., F31, Wanamaker Collection, HSP; "Looking Toward June," *Eagle Speaks* (February 1955), 2, Wanamaker Collection, HSP; Eaton's Wedding Bureau head, Claire Dreier, also reported to the Merchandising Division head, J. A. Brockie.

13. *Brides, Grooms, & Carsons*, 1960, in-house publication, Marshall Field's Archives.

14. The only letters to bridal services I have found came from mothers of the bride. These happy mothers recommended the Bureau to their friends and praised the Bureau as an efficient, time-saving way to plan a wedding and relieve "a great deal of anxiety." E. V. Neelands to Superintendent's Office, August 4, 1939, F229–151, box 6, #165, Wedding Bureau, 1938–1939, Eaton's Collection. Letter from Mrs. Sidney A. Jones, Jr., Chicago, in "As Others See Us," *Brides, Grooms, & Carsons*, 1960, in-house publication, n.p., Marshall Field's Archives.

15. Claire Dreier, "Talk to Advertising Club," October 7, 1948, 1–11, F229–151, box 6, #167, Wedding Bureau, 1948, Eaton's Collection.

16. Blaszczyk, *Imagining Consumers*, 258; E. Forbes, Bride's Shop, Kaufmann's, to Priscilla Kidder, October 16, 1957, box 13, series 8, disassembled scrapbook contents, Priscilla of Boston Collection.

17. B. Ellsworth to Mr. Brockie, 1938, 1–4, F229–151, box 6, #165, Wedding Bureau, 1938–1939, Eaton's Collection.

18. Grant, "Purveyors to the Bride," 84, 86.

19. Filene, *Careers for Women*, 116.

20. "The Wedding Business," 122.

21. Thompson, "Unveiled," 81.

22. Benson, *Counter Cultures*, 210–215.

23. Julietta Arthur, "Here Comes the Bride's Business," *Independent Woman* 18 (June 1939), 172.

24. "From Our Family Album," *Bride's* (Spring 1940), 51; "Tips to You," *Modern Bride* (Winter 1950–1951), 71.

25. Arthur, "Here Comes the Bride's Business," 172, 183.

26. Margaret Enck to Vicki Howard, March 30, 1998, transcript in possession of the author; The Dayton Company, Minneapolis, *Bride's* (Spring 1940), 44; "A Bride's Best Friend Is Her Bridal Consultant," *Modern Bride* (Fall 1949), 104.

27. Filene, *Careers for Women*, 116.

28. Angel Kwolek-Folland, *Incorporating Women: A History of Women and Business in the United States* (New York: Twayne, 1998), 132–133.

29. Swinney, *Merchandising of Fashions*, 10.

30. Arthur, "Here Comes the Bride's Business," 183–184; Marie Coudert Brennig, *Wedding Embassy Year Book*, 4th ed. (New York: Wedding Embassy, 1937), 43, 39, 19, 50, 84, 93.

31. "Strawbridge & Clothier," *Bride's* (Autumn 1939), 36; Brennig, *Wedding Embassy Year Book*, 1.

32. Filene, *Careers for Women*, 117. On the "good social background" needed, also see Arthur, "Here Comes the Bride's Business," 172. Other bridal consultants included elite introductions and endorsements in their publications. See Jeanne Wright, *The Wedding Book* (New York: Rinehart, 1947).

33. Arthur, "Here Comes the Bride's Business," 183, 184, 171.

34. Ibid., 184; Brennig, *Wedding Embassy Year Book*, 1; Filene, *Careers for Women*, 116.

35. Kwolek-Folland, *Incorporating Women*, 70, 143; Margaretta Byers, *Help Wanted—Female: Careers in the Field of Fashion* (New York: Julian Messner, 1941), 9. Also, see Dorée Smedley and Lura Robinson, *Careers in Business for Women* (New York: E. P. Dutton, 1945), 21–23.

36. Susan Ware, *Holding Their Own: American Women in the 1930s* (Boston: Twayne, 1982), 27.

37. Arthur, "Here Comes the Bride's Business," 170 (quotation); Kwolek-Folland, *Incorporating Women*, 133.

38. Filene, *Careers for Women*, 115; Ruby Robertson, "Adopt Specialty Shop Techniques for Linens," *Department Store Economist* (September 1943), 71.

39. Peg Davies, interview by the author, telephone transcript, June 4, 1999; Peg Davies to Vicki Howard, March 30. 1999, transcript in possession of the author. Also, see Peg Davies' wedding books in the possession of the author: Betty Stuart Rogers and Elizabeth Connelly Pearce, *Altar Bound* (Danville, Ill.: The Interstate, 1955); Sallie Newton, *How to Plan a Beautiful Wedding* (Pittsburgh: Jonasson's Bride Shop, 1939).

40. Ownby, *American Dreams in Mississippi*, 95.

41. "Speaking of People: Bridal Consultant," *Ebony* (December 1951), n.p.; "Speaking of People: Bridal Consultant," *Ebony* (February 1958), 4.

42. "Speaking of People: Bridal Sales Expert," *Ebony* (September 1965), 6.

43. The bridal salon was not named in the *Ebony* piece. Consulting may have been done at her or the bride's home, a practice that was not uncommon for independent consultants. "Bridal Consultant" (December 1951), n.p.; "Bridal Consultant" (February 1958), 4.

44. Bahn, "Changes and Continuities," 57–58.

45. For a discussion of the "whiteness" of the white wedding, see Ingraham, *White Weddings*.

46. Lyle, *Mademoiselle's Handbook for Bridal Consultants*, 1.

47. Otnes and Pleck, *Cinderella Dreams*, 86–87, 92; Nancy Starkey, Weddings Beautiful Worldwide, to Vicki Howard, December 7, 2004, e-mail correspondence, transcript in possession of the author. http://www.nationalbridalservice.com; Christine Maurer and Tara E. Sheets, ed., "Bridal Services," *Encyclopedia of Associations*, 34th ed., vol. 1, National Organizations of the United States, Part 1, 58; *Bridal Consultant*, 3rd ed., 3; "Meet the Other Woman in Your Romance!" National Bridal Service ad, 1957, reprinted in Otnes and Pleck, *Cinderella Dreams*, 88.

48. Http://dmoz.org/Society/Relationships/Weddings/Consultants_and_Coordinators/Profession. Accessed July 10, 2003; http://www.nationalbba.com/html/articles/family.html. Accesssed July 10, 2003.

49. *Bridal Consultant*, 3rd ed., 3; Thompson, "Unveiled."

50. Maurer and Sheets, eds., "Bridal Services," 58.

51. As Angela Thompson has shown, bridal spending is difficult to measure and industry statistics are often self-serving and unreliable. This statistic was unfootnoted, and came from an industry publication. See "Unveiled," 1.

52. Kwolek-Folland, *Incorporating Women*, 90–91.

53. Mary Klemmer, interview by the author, telephone transcript, June 21, 1999. By the 1980s, the three main bridal associations were headed by men. See listings for "Bridal Services" in *Encyclopedia of Associations*, 57–58.

54. Dion Magee, "Family Members Aren't Wedding Consultants," National Black Bridal Association. http://www.nationalbba.com/html/articles/family.html.

55. Peg Davies, interview by the author, telephone transcript, June 4, 1999; Peg Davies to Vicki Howard, March 30, 1999.

56. Letter from Mrs. Sidney A. Jones, Jr., Chicago, Ill., in "As Others See Us," *Brides, Grooms, & Carsons*.

57. Susan M. Prendergast, "American Wedding Costumes, 1600–1900," unpub-

lished manuscript, Summer Institute 1975, Henry Francis du Pont Winterthur Museum, Costume Library, NMAH, 1.

58. Rothman, *Hands and Hearts*, 80.

59. Pleck, *Celebrating the Family*, 207; Ingraham, *White Weddings*, 34; Barbara Tober, *The Bride: A Celebration* (Stamford, Conn.: Longmeadow, 1984), 88.

60. White gowns were labeled as "traditional" in company newsletters by employees at an insurance company, a department store, and a garment factory. Accounts of wedding dresses drew attention to their whiteness and pointed out exceptions. See *Between Ourselves* (January 1936), 28; (September 1938), 172; (September 1939), 241; (December 1939), 255, Provident Mutual Life Insurance Company Collection, Hagley; *Store Chat* (March 1944), 3, 16, 26, *Store Chat* (November 1950), 10, 12, 32, Strawbridge & Clothier Collection; *Jantzen Yarns* (April 1949), 8, Jantzen Collection.

61. Pleck, *Celebrating the Family*, 215; Ingraham, *White Weddings*, 34; Rose C. Feld, "The Bride Wore . . . ," *Collier's* (June 1928), 32 (quotation); Simon Charsley, *Wedding Cakes and Cultural History* (London: Routledge, 1992), 92, 149, 93–94, 67.

62. Gamber, *Female Economy*, 111, 109; Olian, *Wedding Fashions, 1862–1912: 380 Costume Designs from "La Mode Illustrée"* (New York: Dover, 1994), iv–v.

63. Tober, *The Bride*, 88; *Store Chat* (July 15, 1914), 200. Strawbridge & Clothier Collection.

64. "Simple and Definite Rules Govern the Etiquette of the Wedding in Church or House," *Good Housekeeping* (June 1926), 237; Holly Brubach, "In Fashion: For Better or for Worse?" *New Yorker* (July 10, 1989), 86; "Correct Bridal Millinery," *Illustrated Milliner* 2 (June 1901), 31. On the "re-use" of gowns and the gown's importance, see "Ready for the Altar," *Illustrated Milliner* 2 (June 1900), 41.

65. Pleck, *Celebrating the Family*, 226, 228.

66. *Jantzen Yarns* (December 1952), 11, Jantzen Collection. Ruth B. Lenson, "Fashions and Chit Chat," April 15, 1971, newsclipping, box 10, Priscilla of Boston Collection.

67. John Burbidge, interview by author, telephone transcript, July 16, 1998; Anne Hollander, *Sex and Suits* (New York: Alfred A. Knopf, 1995), 169.

68. Gamber, *Female Economy*, 10; Claudia B. Kidwell, *Cutting a Fashionable Fit* (Washington, D.C.: Smithsonian Institution, 1979), 47, 98–99; Olian, *Wedding Fashions*, iv. See personal note, Priscilla Wood, Smithsonian Institution, to Vicki Howard, August 29, 2003. Note in possession of the author.

69. Gamber, *Female Economy*, 99, 113; "Record of Trousseau and Marriage Expenses," Warshaw Collection of Business Americana—Matrimony. Winans purchased the materials for her trousseau and wedding gown, which were made in part by the Rochester dressmakers Karle & Rhines. See Rochester City Directory, 1900.

70. For example, see Margaret Oliver Holmes to Sarah Hawley, box 2, 12, March 11, 1914, Sarah Davis Hawley Papers, Rosenberg Library, Galveston, Texas; Jeanne Sully Smyth Scrapbook, 1911, John Smyth Family Papers, Hill Memorial Library, Louisiana State University, Baton Rouge, Louisiana; Mary Moody Northern, *My Wedding Book*, 1915; Scrapbook, 1913–1915, Moody Mansion, Galveston, Texas; Pauline

Wright to Irby Nichols, May 2, 1918, Irby C. Nichols and Family Papers, Hill Memorial Library; Titcomb-Shepard Wedding Album, 1889, Massachusetts Historical Society, Boston.

71. Elaine Abelson, *When Ladies Go A-Thieving: Middle-Class Shoplifters in the Victorian Department Store* (New York: Oxford University Press, 1989), 35–39; Nan Enstad, *Ladies of Labor, Girls of Adventure: Working Women, Popular Culture, and Labor Politics at the Turn of the Twentieth Century* (New York: Columbia University Press, 1999), 27–29.

72. "Wedding Trousseaux," advertisement in D. B. Loveman & Company, trade catalogue, Spring and Summer 1887, Winterthur Library; Kidwell, *Cutting a Fashionable Fit*, 94, 81.

73. "Record of Trousseau and Marriage Expenses," Warshaw Collection of Business Americana—Matrimony. For a discussion of the millinery industry, see Gamber, *Female Economy*, 177–188; Kidwell, *Cutting a Fashionable Fit*, 98–99; Mamie McFaddin-Ward Diary, April 28, 1919, April 29, 1919, McFaddin-Ward House Museum, Beaumont, Texas.

74. "Effective Costumes and Hats for the Trousseau of the January Bride," January 7, 1911, 4 small scrapbooks of news clippings, series 8, box 76, Strawbridge & Clothier Collection, Hagley. Men's ready-to-wear work clothing appeared much earlier in the 1840s, but gentlemen continued to visit tailors to have their formal-wear clothing custom made. By the 1920s, however, different varieties of ready-made groom's formal wear had already been long available. Gamber, *Female Economy*, 10; Paul H. Nystrom, *Economics of Fashion* (New York: Ronald Press, 1928), 476.

75. Dressmaking and millinery constituted the fourth most important female occupational category in 1870, surpassed only by domestic servants, agricultural workers, and seamstresses. By 1900, dressmaking ranked third and millinery fourteenth among occupations for women. Gamber, *Female Economy*, 7, 12; Kwolek-Folland, *Incorporating Women*, 151, 162.

76. Kidwell, *Cutting a Fashionable Fit*, 90.

77. For descriptions of brides using dressmakers in the 1850s, see Rothman, *Hands and Hearts*, 166. For a description of visiting a milliner on "bridal business" see "Steven Lawrence, Yeoman," *Galaxy* 5 (June 1868), 664 (Online, Cornell University, Making of America). On Carlisle's, see Blaine Workman, interview by the author, telephone transcript, September 22, 1999, transcript in possession of the author.

78. Gamber, *Female Economy*, 223, 226–227, quotations on 226.

79. On Pandora Frocks, see Bernadine Morris, "Wedding Gown Designers Will Flout Traditions," newsclipping, 1967, box 10, folder 4, Priscilla of Boston Collection; Hanson, *For Richer, For Poorer*, 117–119; Ingraham, *White Weddings*, 47; Seligson, *The Eternal Bliss Machine*, 132–136.

80. A 1940 Letty Lynton dress with the puffed, shirred short sleeves like those worn by Joan Crawford in *Letty Lynton* is in the Smithsonian. Accession No. 309930, August 27, 1940, White Wedding Gown, Cultural History Catalog, NMAH.

81. "Gone with the Wind," *Bride's* (Winter 1939–1940), 43, 60; Howard, "American Weddings," 108.

82. Isadore Barmash, "More Fathers of More Brides Are Paying for More Gowns Than Ever," *New York Times* (February 9, 1969), F1, 2; Seligson, *The Eternal Bliss Machine*, 132–136. As gown manufacturers grew in size and as mass discounters appeared on the retail scene, the number of manufacturers began to decline. By 1980, the number of bridal apparel manufacturers had fallen to seventy-five. "News Flash," Fashion Group, Inc., October 2, 1980, 2, box 10, Priscilla of Boston Collection.

83. Elizabeth Hawes, "The Lady Who Marries the Best People," 64, clipping, box 10, folder 3, Priscilla of Boston Collection; *Modern Bride Magazine, A Study of Bridal Market Retail Spending*, 16.

84. Sharon Basco, "Phyllis and Priscilla Have Just the Thing," *The Magazine*, February 26, 1978, clipping, box 10, folder 13, Priscilla of Boston Collection. Phyllis Bianchi's House of Bianchi was also in the top four. "When Fashion Goes to the Wedding," *New York Times* (June 28, 1966), 38, newsclipping, series 8, box 12, folder 6, Priscilla of Boston Collection.

85. Hawes, "The Lady Who Marries the Best People," 64; Basco, "Phyllis and Priscilla Have Just the Thing." Now, Priscilla of Boston is a specialty division of the May Company. http://company.monster.com/priscillab/.

86. Thanks to Priscilla Wood of the Costume Division for the observation that Priscilla Kidder designed for "the masses." Basco, "Phyllis and Priscilla Have Just the Thing." http://www.eagletribune.com/news/stories/20011014/LN_005.htm.

87. Jim Hjelm headed their design team in the 1960s. See catalogue card for Catalog no. 1997, 0329.5, Wedding, designer, 1968, Cultural History Catalog, NMAH.

88. Romola Metzner, "Priscilla Busy with Details of Julie's Wedding," ca. 1969, box 10, Priscilla of Boston Collection; "Priscilla, Queen of the Wedding Business," ca. 1970, box 10, Priscilla of Boston Collection; Priscilla Kidder, interview by the author, telephone transcript, July 23, 1998, transcript in possession of the author.

89. Basco, "Phyllis and Priscilla Have Just the Thing."

90. The Officiating Clergyman, "Of Weddings and Funerals," 496–497.

91. RG 179, War Production Board Office Procedures Work folders, L-85, L-99, box 2, National Archives II, College Park. Also see Hanson, *For Richer, For Poorer*, 114.

92. Ad*Access On-Line Project—Ad# W0162, John W. Hartman Center for Sales, Advertising & Marketing History, Duke University Rare Book, Manuscript, and Special Collections Library. On the BBAA position, see "The Wedding Business," *Life* (June 9, 1952), 124.

93. January 29, 1942, Report to Mr. J. G. McKee from Wedding Bureau, Merchandise Display Dept., 2, box 6, Wedding Bureau Promo, 1943, Eaton's Collection; "100% Increase in Brides Points Up Bridal Shop," 29.

94. "War Brides Find Davison-Paxon Ready," *Department Store Economist* (January 1942), 17. Recently married women looked forward to peacetime to be able "to establish their dream homes." "One Thousand Brides," *Department Store Economist* (July 1944), 36–37.

95. Reeves, "Marriages in New Haven Since 1870," VII-36.

96. Lyle, *Mademoiselle's Handbook for Bridal Consultants*, 66; *Amy Vanderbilt's Complete Book of Etiquette*, 58.

97. "Grandma's Gown Preferred," *Palm Beach Post Times* (April 6, 1969), newsclipping, box 13, folder 2, series 8, Scrapbook Contents, Priscilla of Boston Collection. According to Kidder, "borrowed" dresses were often ill-fitting and looked "absolutely horrible." Randi Henderson, "Despite Ailments, Priscilla Still Designs Bridal Gowns," *Baltimore Sun* (1983), newsclipping, box 10, Priscilla of Boston Collection.

98. Agnes Foster Wright, "To Our Brides," *Bride's* (Summer 1936); "Heirloom Laboratories," *Modern Bride* (Spring 1955), 37; "Here Comes the Bride," *Eagle Speaks* (July–August 1956), 6, Wanamaker Collection, HSP.

99. Newsclipping, ca. 1970, box 10, Priscilla of Boston Collection; Beverly Maurice, "Boston's Priscilla Speaks Out," *Houston Chronicle, Texas Magazine* (1970), newsclipping, box 10, Priscilla of Boston Collection.

100. Keller and Mashon, *TV Weddings*, 76–79, 81–83. For a discussion of the way advertisers appropriated countercultural trends, see Thomas Frank, *Conquest of Cool: Business Culture, Counterculture, and the Rise of Hip Consumerism* (Chicago: University of Chicago Press, 1997).

101. See Lisa McGirr, *Suburban Warriors: The Origins of the New American Right* (Princeton, N.J.: Princeton University Press, 2001), for a discussion of the rise of the middle-class suburburban conservative movement in California in the 1960s. Those in the industry argued against "hippie" weddings, noting that the majority still favored traditional ceremonies. Maurice, "Boston's Priscilla Speaks Out."

102. Hawes, "The Lady Who Marries the Best People," 64; Barmash, "More Fathers of More Brides Are Paying for More Gowns Than Ever."

103. "Brides Say 'I Do' to Ageless Fashion," *USA Today* (March 21, 1983), 3D, newsclipping, box 10, folder 18, Priscilla of Boston Collection; "The Wedding Capital of the World," newsclipping, 1979, box 13, folder 2, series 8, Scrapbook Contents, Priscilla of Boston Collection. See card catalogue description and the Burbidge quote: Catalog No. 1997.0329.2, Wedding, designer, 1979–1980. Also, see Catalog No. 1997.0329.3, Wedding, designer, 1986–1987, Cultural History Catalog, NMAH.

104. Reeves, "Marriages in New Haven," VII-37; Priscilla Wood, interview by the author, transcript, July 23, 1998. Also, see Howard, "American Weddings," 329–330.

105. Henry Boucher Interview, American Life Histories; Vito Cacciola Interview, American Life Histories. Reeves, "Marriages in New Haven," VII-39.

106. Trudy Knicely Henson, *The Wedding Complex: The Social Organization of a Rite of Passage* (Omaha, Neb.: Park Bromwell, 1976), 7, 54.; "News Flash," Fashion Group, Inc., October 2, 1980, 2, box 10, Priscilla of Boston Collection.

CHAPTER 6. CATERING TO THE BRIDE

1. Michel de Certeau, *The Practice of Everyday Life*, trans. Steven Randall (Berkeley: University of California Press, 1984), xix–xx, 31.

2. John Modell, *Into One's Own: From Youth to Adulthood in the United States,*

1920–1975 (Berkeley: University of California Press, 1989), 10; Katherine Jellison, "Getting Married in the Heartland: The Commercialization of Weddings in the Rural Midwest," *Forum* (Fall 1995), 46–47. Expenses for the wedding dress, flowers, and church décor at the Robinson-Via wedding in 1958 in Brandywine, Maryland, totaled $132.60, not including the cost of their double rings, church fees, wedding reception refreshments, pre-printed napkins, or their honeymoon in New England. Box 14, Robinson-Via Family Papers, NMAH.

3. Reeves, "Marriages in New Haven Since 1870," VII-31.

4. Howard, "American Weddings," appendix, tables 1–12.

5. *Jantzen Yarns* (April 1937), 6, Jantzen Collection; for other examples of large home weddings, see *Jantzen Yarns* (July 1932), 11, and (July 1935), 9–10; and *Between Ourselves* (February 1936), 51, Provident Mutual Life Insurance Company Collection, Hagley.

6. *Jantzen Yarns* (July 1950), 14, Jantzen Collection.

7. *Maiden Forum* (June 1959), 7, Maidenform Collection.

8. "Your Wedding at Home," *Wedding Belle* (June 1948), 8–9; Fenwick, *Vogue's Book of Etiquette*, 189; Wade, *Social Usage in America*, 123.

9. At a 1903 Philadelphia church ceremony of a textile teacher and his bride, for example, the groom paid the organist and minister each $15. Martha Campbell Talley Seal, Diary, September 1903, Joseph Downs Collection of Manuscripts and Printed Ephemera, Winterthur; Wright, *The Wedding Book*, 90; "Two Country Weddings," *Vogue* (October 1, 1938), 76–77.

10. "Budget for a Bride," *Fortune* (June 1933), 39; *Elsa Maxwell's Etiquette Book* (New York: Bartholomew House, 1951), 79.

11. Wright, *The Wedding Book*, 90; "From Bachelor Girl to Bride . . . and Back Again?" *Ebony* (June 1947). According to one inflation calculator, $300 translated into $2,702 in 2003 dollars (see http://www.westegg.com/inflation/infl.cgi). Susan Strange's family material (receipts and budget) in possession of the author.

12. Lydia Maria Child, *The American Frugal Housewife*, 12th ed. (Boston: Carter, Hendee, and Co., 1833), 72. For "bridesmaids' luncheons" and "wedding supper" menus, see Sarah Tyson Rorer, *Mrs. Rorer's Every Day Menu Book* (Philadelphia: Arnold and Company, 1905), 271, 237–238.

13. Post, *Etiquette in Society, in Business, in Politics and at Home*, 347, 374; Marvin Dana, *American Encyclopedia of Etiquette and Culture* (New York: Eilert Printing Company, 1922), 32; Kessler-Harris, *Out to Work*, 113; Ethel Frey Cushing, *Culture and Good Manners* (Memphis, Tenn.: Students Educational Publishing Company, 1926), 127 (quotations); Mrs. John Alexander King, *Weddings: Modes, Manners and Customs of Weddings* (New York: Delineator, 1927), 8.

14. "W. H. Barmore," "S & J Davis," box 1, Warshaw Collection of Business Americana—Confectionery; "Geo. M. Helmken, Variety Bakery and Caterer," Savannah, Georgia. vi. *U.S. Census & Business Manual: Containing Official Census Returns for 1880 and 1870* (Richmond: J. Rippey & Co., 1882).

15. Wharton, *Age of Innocence*, 28. As early as 1913, etiquette writers noted that the

caterer "usually supplies all the necessities for the wedding feast, even to china, linen, silver, candelabra, and flowers, should the bride's parents so wish." Edith B. Ordway, *The Etiquette of To-Day*, 3rd ed. (1913; New York: George Sully and Company, 1931), 212. I did not have the first edition from 1913 and was not able to determine whether this reference was from the original early edition or was added in the 1931 version. Wade, *Social Usage in America*, 136.

16. "S & J Davis," box 1, Warshaw Collection of Business Americana—Confectionery.

17. Daniel Kempner Scrapbook 1, 1894–1915, 39–40, 48, Rosenberg Library, Galveston, Texas; Sinclair, *The Jungle*, 9; "A Wonderful Wedding Cake," *Supply World* 11 (November 1902), 26.

18. Penrose Lyly, "Enter the Bride and Groom," *Pictorial Review* (June 1932), 32; Tasha McCready, "The Story of My Wedding," *Woman's Home Companion* (June 1939), 74–75; *Ladies' Home Journal, The Bride* (Philadelphia: Curtis Publishing, 1938), 25–31.

19. Weddings, Emily Post, Speech File, April 11, 1931, 5, Manuscripts Division, Library of Congress, Washington, D.C.; *Amy Vanderbilt's Complete Book of Etiquette*, 84; *The Bride's Book of Etiquette* by the editors of *Bride's* magazine advocated the use of a bridal consultant, assumed a caterer, and provided menus (but not recipes) for the reception. *The Bride's Book of Etiquette* (New York: Brides House, 1948), 19, 91, 138–139.

20. Fenwick, *Vogue's Book of Etiquette*, chapters 28 and 30; Emma Aubert Cole, *The Modern Bride Book of Etiquette and Entertaining* (New York: Ziff Publishing, 1961), chapters 9 and 16; Joan McClure, *McCall's Engagement and Wedding Guide* (New York: Saturday Review Press, 1972), chapter 3.

21. "Above All . . . the Wedding Reception at Sherry's," *Bride's* (Spring 1948), 138.

22. http://www.ifsea.com/history.htm; Ronald Kinton and Victor Ceserani, *The Theory of Catering*, 5th ed. (1964; London: Edward Arnold, 1984); Howard F. Lange, *Catering* (New York: Ahrens, 1955), 38–39.

23. Juliet E. K. Walker, ed., "Catering, Inns, Hotels," in *Encyclopedia of African American Business History* (Westport, Conn.: Greenwood Press, 1999), 128–130.

24. W. E. B. DuBois, *The Philadelphia Negro* (Philadelphia: University of Pennsylvania Press, 1899; reprint, New York: Kraus-Thomson Organization, Ltd., 1973), 32–35. The Florist Telegraphic Delivery Service (FTDS) barred black members as late as 1948. While this hurt African American florists, they countered with the formation of an interracial National Florists Club. "Roses and Carnations Found Favorites with Young Romeos," *Ebony* (November 1948), 52.

25. Walker, "Catering, Inns, Hotels," 132.

26. Ibid.

27. Albert E. Dutrieuille Catering Collection, Balch Institute, Philadelphia, Pennsylvania; "Main Line Caterer," *Ebony* (August 1950), 34–38.

28. "Main Line Caterer," 38, 40.

29. Newsclipping, *Grant County Herald*, Elbow Lake, Minnesota, ca. June 1963, in

the personal collection of the author; Barbara Howard, telephone interview, September 4, 1999, transcript in the possession of the author; "Main Line Caterer," 40. Also, see Katherine Jellison, "Getting Married in the Heartland: The Commercialization of Weddings in the Rural Midwest," *Forum* (Fall 1995), 48.

30. Cile Bellefleur-Burbidge, interview by the author, telephone transcript, July 16, 1998, transcript in possession of the author; Beverly Clark, *Book of Wedding Cakes* (Philadelphia: Running Press, 1999), 34, 37, 123; Kwolek-Folland, *Incorporating Women*, 125–126; E. N. McConnell, advertisement, E. N. McConnell Material, Hagley; Expense Account Book, vol. 1, 1937–1945, E. N. McConnell Material; Doll expense, Business Records, vol. 3, 1955–1956, E. N. McConnell Material; Accounts Receivable, vol. 2, 1955–1956; Business Records, vol. 3, 1955–1956, E. N. McConnell Material, 1937–1956.

31. One or both of these dishes appeared repeatedly in prescribed wedding menus. For example, see *Boston Cooking-School Magazine* (June–July 1906); Post, *Etiquette in Society, in Business, in Politics and at Home*, 365, 368; Shaw, *Etiquette for Everybody* (1952), 242; "The Wedding Reception," *Ebony* (June 1950), 128; Lange, *Catering*, 65; Ronald Kingston and Victor Ceserani, *Theory of Catering*, 355. For a history of Delmonico's see http://www.delmonicosny.com/delmonicosny/.

32. Post, *Etiquette in Society, in Business, in Politics and at Home*, 374. According to an early 1990s equipment rental chart from Ridgewell's Caterers in Bethesda, Maryland, customers rented everything but the kitchen sink, from ashtrays and trash cans, to table lighting and the tables themselves. Nancy Loman Scanlon, *Catering Menu Management* (New York: John Wiley & Sons, 1992), 218–221.

33. H. A. Johnson & Company, Boston, n.d., Confectioners' Supply Catalogue, box 3, Warshaw Collection of Business Americana—Confectionery; *Jaburg Brothers General Catalog for Bakeries, Lunch Rooms, Hotels and Other Institutions*, trade catalogue, 1921 (established 1885), Hagley; Ethel Frey Cushing, *Culture and Good Manners* (Memphis: Students' Educational Publishing, 1926), 127 (quotation).

34. Howard, "American Weddings," 40–41. For a discussion of the evolution of American wedding cakes, see Wendy A. Woloson, *Refined Tastes: Sugar, Confectionery, and Consumers in Nineteenth-Century America* (Baltimore: Johns Hopkins University Press, 2002), 168–178.

35. Wilton graduates who went on to become retail bake shop owners, bakery employees, and hotel chefs were likely mostly male, as represented by a photograph of graduate exercises. Students were also referred to in the masculine. "Wilton Graduates 1,000th Student," *Mid-West Hotel Reporter* 44 (May 1950), 16. By 1970, however, according to one photo of a graduating class, women composed nearly half of a "typical" class. See *Magic for Your Table: Cake and Food Decorating by Wilton* (Chicago: Wilton Enterprises, 1970), 2.

36. Scanlon, *Catering Menu Management*, 85 (quotations), 215.

37. Ibid., 217, 219.

38. Molly Berger, "A House Divided," in *His and Hers: Gender, Consumption, and Technology*, ed. Roger Horowitz and Arwen Mohun (Charlottesville: University Press

of Virginia, 1998), 40–41, 43 (quotation). A popular source argues the opposite, noting that until the Waldorf-Astoria opened, hotels were not considered appropriate places for high society to give balls or dinners. Catherine Donzel, Alexis Gregory, and Marc Walter, *Grand American Hotels* (New York: Vendome Press, 1989), 51.

39. Donzel et al., *Grand American Hotels*, 40.

40. Leach, *Land of Desire*, 19, 114; Lisa Davidson, "Consumption and Efficiency in the 'City Within a City': Commercial Hotel Architecture and the Emergence of Modern American Culture, 1890–1930" (Ph.D. diss., George Washington University, 2003), 2, 14, 124, 13.

41. "A Haven for Newlyweds," *Mid-West Hotel Reporter* (September 27, 1935), 9. For an image of a wedding reception in the Blackstone Hotel, see Donzel et al., *Grand American Hotels*, 31. For the Iowa example, see "A Room for Weddings," *Tavern Talk* (January 2, 1937), 11.

42. Razed in 1929 to make way for the Empire State Building, the hotel moved to a new Art Deco building with a modernistic lobby, though it still had traditional period room banquet halls, including the Basildon Room designed as a replica of an eighteenth-century English salon. Davidson, "Consumption and Efficiency," 5–6, 111; "The Waldorf's Adieu," *Tavern Talk* (May 18, 1929), 6–7. After it was purchased by the Hilton Hotels Corporation in 1949, according to trade literature, the Waldorf-Astoria's character and individuality were to remain unchanged, and the hotel continued to follow its original purposes, among which were "to provide self-contained accommodations for public functions, such as balls, banquets, expositions, conventions, receptions . . . and other large gatherings." See "Hilton Buys Control of the Waldorf-Astoria Corp. for $3,000,000," *Tavern Talk* (October 22, 1949), 4.

43. "Wedding Customs and Menus," *Hotel Monthly* (May 1930), 61; George Sweet Gibb, *The Whitesmiths of Taunton: A History of Reed & Barton, 1824–1943* (Cambridge, Mass.: Harvard University Press, 1943), 239, 327–329, 372.

44. Martha Campbell Talley Seal, Diary, n.d., September 1903, Joseph Downs Collection of Manuscripts and Printed Ephemera, Winterthur.

45. "How to Plan a Wedding Reception," *Wedding Belle* (May 1948), 36; Marie Coudert Brennig, *The Wedding Embassy Year Book* (New York: Wedding Embassy, 1934), 26–27.

46. "Has Unusual 'Title,'" *Tavern Talk* (June 21, 1919), 15. Catering managers and banquet managers were sometimes distinguished from the maitre d'hotel, but not always. "Blackstone's Catering Manager," *Mid-West Hotel Reporter* (September 27, 1935), 9.

47. Davidson, "Consumption and Efficiency," 5, 9; Oscar of the Waldorf, *Setting the Table Correctly* (Sag Harbor, N.Y.: Alvin Manufacturing Company, 1917), trade catalogue, Winterthur.

48. "Wedding Customs and Menus," *Hotel Monthly* (May 1930), 61.

49. "Bridal Promotion Idea," *Tavern Talk* (December 31, 1949), 19.

50. "Above All . . . the Wedding Reception at Sherry's," 138.

51. Post, *Etiquette in Society, in Business, in Politics and at Home*, 375. "Hotel Re-

ceptions," *Bride's* (Summer 1941), 130; "Planning the Reception," *House Beautiful's Guide for the Bride* (Fall 1955), 66–67.

52. Barbara Morrow, "How Much of a Wedding?" *Bride's* (Winter 1946–1947), 110, 154. Employees in my study who had receptions at country clubs were in professional or white-collar positions. For example, see *Store Chat* (November 1953), 35, 9, 11. Clubs are not necessarily commercial venues, coming instead out of social organizations. They often include country clubs or clubs for specific elite groups that limit membership and charge fees. For this reason, I include them with commercial hotels that charge for their services.

53. *Rainbow Reporter* (Winter 1959), 9, Binney & Smith Collection, NMAH; Davidson, "Consumption and Efficiency," 4.

54. Reeves, "Marriages in New Haven," VII-2.

55. Joselit, *Wonders of America*, 27–28, 33–35; John M. Oskison, "Public Halls of the East Side," *University Settlement Society of New York Report* (1899), 39.

56. Joselit, *Wonders of America*, 27–28, 33–35; "Wedding Customs and Menus," *Hotel Monthly* (May 1930), 59, 61 (quotation); Lange, *Catering*, 88–89.

57. Elsewhere in the country, other nonwhite groups, such as the Chinese, were also segregated in hotels in separate sections. See "A Chinese-American Hotel," *Tavern Talk* (May 31, 1919), masthead page.

58. Http://www.state.ky.us/agencies/khc/hotmet.htm. http://www.hotel-online.com/News/PressReleases1999_2nd/June99_AtlantaNABHA.html.

59. "The Arlington to Negroes," *Tavern Talk* (August 10, 1929), 30.

60. "Finest Negro Hotel," *Ebony* (June 1950), 81–86; Federal Writers' Project, *The WPA Guide to New Orleans* (1938; New York: Pantheon Books, 1983), 1. http://special.lib.umn.edu/findaid/html/ymca/yusa0002.phtml.

61. "Finest Negro Hotel," 81, 85. Also, see recent article on the declining fortune of Detroit at http://www.detnews.com/2001/detroit/0111/07/s06-336948.htm.

62. Http://info.detnews.com/history/story/index.cfm?id=174&category=life; Ernest H. Borden, *Detroit's Paradise Valley* (Charleston, S.C.: Arcadia, 2003), 26, 30, 35, 40–41. "Most Fabulous Negro Wedding," *Ebony* (October 1958), 36.

63. Borden, *Detroit's Paradise Valley*, 11; Walker, *Encyclopedia of African American Business History*, 134; http://www.baystatebanner.com/frontpage4.htm; http://www.hotelmotel.com/hotelmotel/article/articleDetail.jsp?id=62445.

64. For example, one Maidenform worker had her ceremony at St. Joseph's Catholic Church and her reception in St. Joseph's Hall. See *Maiden Forum* (September–October 1947), 3, Maidenform Collection. Another employee married at Assumption Church in Bayonne and had her reception in Assumption Hall. See *Maiden Forum* (November 1947), 4. At the New Jewish Community Center in Bayonne, one Maidenform employee had a wedding dinner for 200 guests. *Maiden Forum* (January 1954), 10. Sinclair, *The Jungle*, 20–21; Randy D. McBee, *Dance Hall Days: Intimacy and Leisure Among Working-Class Immigrants in the United States* (New York: New York University Press, 2000), 222.

65. Oskison, "Public Halls of the East Side," 38, 39. Others included the Progress Assembly Rooms, the Apollo, the Golden Rule, the New Atlantic, and Teutonia.

66. http://www.balchfriends.org/bhmap.htm

67. Oskison, "Public Halls of the East Side," 38. For an account of public hall weddings at the turn of the century, see Peiss, *Cheap Amusements*, 90–91.

68. Oskison, "Public Halls of the East Side," 38. Vito Cacciola Interview, American Life Histories.

69. *Store Chat* (April 15, 1916), 1, Strawbridge & Clothier Collection, Hagley; *Maiden Forum* (August–September 1953), 8, Maidenform Collection; *Maiden Forum* (November 1953), 9, Maidenform Collection; *Store Chat* (November 1953), 9, 14, 35; Reeves, "Marriages in New Haven," VII-G3.

70. Hanson, *For Richer, For Poorer*, 48–49, quote on p. 48.

71. *Rainbow Reporter* (Spring 1965), 6, Binney & Smith Collection; *Rainbow Reporter* (Fall 1961), 15; *Rainbow Reporter* (Winter 1963), 14; *Rainbow Reporter* (Winter 1966), 14–15; Hanson, *For Richer, For Poorer*, 66.

72. Howard, "American Weddings," 316, 348; *Jantzen Yarns* (December 1940), 3, Jantzen Collection; *Maiden Forum* (February 1947), 4, Maidenform Collection; *Rainbow Reporter* (Winter 1965), 5, Binney & Smith Collection.

73. Wright, *The Wedding Book*, 93. She did include ballrooms, but I take that to mean more exclusive nightclub venues like the Rainbow Room, and not the ethnic halls or wedding palaces that were also available at the time.

74. Studies of newspaper wedding announcements in Newark, New Jersey, in 1954 linked more expensive choices with higher education levels. Those who chose home, hotel, or club receptions were more likely to have a college background than those who chose a restaurant or hired hall venue. See Wallace H. Sinaiko, "The Symbolic Representation of Social Status in a Newspaper: An Empirical Case Study of Wedding Announcements" (Ph.D. diss., New York University, 1954), table 14.

75. For a Greek-American example of a consciously Americanized wedding, see Cecilia Patrourstsa Interview, American Life Histories, discussed in Howard, "American Weddings," 332–333.

76. Judy Yung, *Unbound Feet: A Social History of Chinese Women in San Francisco* (Berkeley: University of California Press, 1995), 168.

77. Hanson, *For Richer, For Poorer*, 67–68, 85, 90, quote on p. 67; "Be Married in the Wedding Manor!" *Wedding Belle* (May 1948), 36.

78. Hanson, *For Richer, For Poorer*, 67–68, 86; Margaret Gray, "The Lord Fox's Way with the Bride," *Restaurant Management* (March 1960), 92; "Weddings + Champagne: Volume," *Restaurant Management* (May 1961), 90.

79. Gray, "The Lord Fox's Way with the Bride," 164; "Weddings + Champagne: Volume," 91.

80. Gray, "The Lord Fox's Way with the Bride," 93; Thatched Cottage quotes from "Weddings + Champagne: Volume," 90–91; for mention of the "316-year-old wishing well," see "Thatched Cottage" advertisment, *Bride's* (December 1970), 26D.

81. Gray, "The Lord Fox's Way with the Bride," 92–93; "Weddings + Champagne: Volume," 90–91.

82. Gray, "The Lord Fox's Way with the Bride," 92–93, 164 (quotation).

83. Jacobson, *American Marriage and Divorce* (New York: Holt Rinehart and Winston, 1959), 50.

84. "Elkton, Marry-land," *Washington Post* (February 13, 2003), C2.

85. Quote from H. Perry Davis Interview, American Life Histories; *Maiden Forum* (February 1951), 9, Maidenform Collection.

86. *Store Chat* (December 1955), 8, 13, 37, Strawbridge & Clothier Collection, Hagley.

87. *The Bride, by Ladies Home Journal* (New York: Curtis Publishing, 1938), 19; quote taken from "I'd Choose Wedding Bells," *Delineator* (July 1936), 4.

88. Reeves, "Marriage in New Haven," VII-29.

89. In the period 1870–1930, according to one 1938 study, native-born whites, who were likely more economically advantaged, had civil ceremonies less frequently than foreign-born whites or African Americans. Reeves, "Marriage in New Haven," VII-12; On Pocomo City, see Perry Davis Interview, American Life Histories; *Maiden Forum* (February 1951), 9, Maidenform Collection; Modell, *Into One's Own*, 135; Jacobson, *American Marriage and Divorce*, 58–59.

90. Reeves, "Marriages in New Haven," VII-27. Couples had secret weddings for many different reasons, but in the nineteenth century such marriages were attempts "to escape disapproval." Peter Ward, *Courtship, Love and Marriage in Nineteenth-Century English Canada* (Montreal: McGill-Queens University Press, 1990), 110. On blank marriage certificates, see H. Perry Davis Interview, American Life Histories; Jacobson, *American Marriage and Divorce*, 50–52, 57.

91. "Elkton, Marry-land," C2; "Little Wedding Chapel," postcard in possession of the author.

92. http://www.see-tennessee.com/counties/east_counties/sevier/smoky_weddings.htm; http://www.smokycountry.com/PF-Wedding.html; http://gatlinburg.com/hillbillyweddings/.

93. "Wedding chapel. Yuma, Arizona," 1942, photograph, America from the Great Depression to World War II: Photographs from the FSA-OWI, 1935–1945, American Memory, Library of Congress; "Quickie Drive-In Wedding Chapel," *Ebony* (November 1948), 60–61.

94. Youn-Hoon Kim, "The Commodification of a Ritual Process: An Ethnography of the Wedding Industry in Las Vegas" (Ph.D. diss., University of Southern California, 1996), 21, 27–28, 41–44, 125. Bally's, Circus Circus, Ex Caliber, Imperial Palace, MGM, Plaza, Riviera, Tropicana, and Treasure Island had wedding chapels in January 1995. See Kim, "The Commodification of a Ritual Process," 47; interview with Youn-Hoon Kim at http://uscnews.usc.edu/detail.php.recordnum1808.

95. Kim, "The Commodification of a Ritual Process," 38, 121–122, 117, 126.

EPILOGUE

1. Otnes and Pleck, *Cinderella Dreams*, 2, 50; Bernadine Morris, "Bringing the Bride up to Date," *New York Times* (April 14, 1970), 56; William E. Geist, "Weddings Flourishing; For Bridal Merchants, It's a State of Bliss," *New York Times* (May 18, 1982), B2.

2. "The Most Expensive Celebrity Weddings," *National Enquirer* (June 28, 2004); 34–39; "Oxygen and The Knot Get Hitched for Television Miniseries, 'Real Weddings from The Knot,'" http://www.theknot.com/10.21.02.shtml; "Star Jones Says 'I Do' to Wedding Freebies," http://www.usatoday.com/life/people/2004–11–10-star-jones_x.htm. For a good critique of celebrity wedding culture, see Ingraham, *White Weddings*, 105–112.

3. I am using the term *postmodernity* as a way of periodizing a new aesthetic that appeared in different areas of the wedding industry in the 1990s. Postmodernity was characterized by new modes of representation that were often self-referential or ironic. Finding primary expression first in literature, film, and architecture, postmodernity celebrated heterogeneity and accepted instability, fragmentation, and ephemerality as a natural condition of modern (or postmodern) life. David Harvey, *The Condition of Postmodernity: An Enquiry into the Origins of Cultural Change* (Oxford: Basil Blackwell, 1989), 7, 82–83, 98.

4. Harvey, *The Condition of Postmodernity*, 7. Harvey quotes Terry Eagleton's definition of postmodernism here.

5. "Here Comes the Net" (July 9, 2000), http://www.freep.com/money/con sumer/guide9_20000709.htm.

6. "Publisher of *Bride's* Magazine Invests in Weddingchannel.com," press release, CondéNet 2002, http://www.condenet.com; quotation from press release, "*The Knot* Magazine: The First and Only Wedding Shopping Guide Breaks the Mold of Old School Bridal Mags," http://biz.yahoo.com/iw/040908/072283.html; Alice Keim, "The Computer as Wedding Consultant," *New York Times* (October 15, 1998), D10.

7. http://www.theknot.com/au_pressrelease.shtml. "Company Overview," http://www.theknot.com/au_companyoverview.shtml.

8. Tess Ayers and Paul Brown, *The Essential Guide to Lesbian and Gay Weddings* (San Francisco: HarperSanFrancisco, 1994). According to the owner of the Thatched Cottage, the Long Island catering hall discussed in Chapter 6, the demand for gay weddings appeared in the mid-1990s. See Elissa Gootman, "New Specialty at Wedding Expo: Same-Sex Unions," *New York Times* (October 21, 2001), 34; Julie Flaherty, "Freedom to Marry, and to Spend on It," *New York Times* (May 16, 2004). For a discussion of gay weddings, see Otnes and Pleck, *Cinderella Dreams*, 231–237.

9. Aude Lagorce, "The Gay-Marriage Windfall: $16.8 Billion," http://www.forbes.com/2004/04/05; Ethan Jacobs, "Wedding Bells are Ringing" (December 4, 2003), http://baywindows.com. Otnes and Pleck, *Cinderella Dreams*, 235; Bill Werde, "Media; A First at *Bride's Magazine*: A Report on Same-Sex Unions," *New York Times* July 28, 2003.

10. Anne d'Innocenzio, "More Retailers Say 'I Do' to the Gay Marriage Market" (April 17, 2004), http://www.iht.com/articles/515539.html. Gay tourism that thrived in certain resort areas added a wedding industry component after same-sex rulings supporting the right to marry. See "Gay-Marriage Ruling in Massachusetts Brings Boom to Provincetown," *New York Times* (January 21, 2004), A1, A14.

11. "Company Overview"; "Oxygen and The Knot Get Hitched for Television Miniseries."

12. For example, see Zale jewelers at http://www.zalecorp.com/company/company 2.aspx. On Wal-Mart wedding rings, see http://www.diamondblog.com/archives/ 002002.html or http://www.diamondblog.com/archives/cat_jewelry.html.

13. The two magazines are part of the "Condé Nast Bridal Group," which includes seventeen regional magazines. http://www.fairchildmediakit.com/mod/publisher .cfm; "Primedia to Sell Modern Bride Group to Condé Nast," http://www.write news.com/2002/011802_primedia_modernbride_sale.htm. Bridal magazines launched their own Web sites, which provided local information for planning a wedding in any state. http://www.modernbride.com/.

14. Evan L. Schwartz, "Industry View," *New York Times* (June 20, 1999), C4; "Federated & WeddingChannel Agree to Tie the Knot: Federated to Take 20% Stake in Wedding Channel Web Site," http://www.weddingchannel.com (May 25, 1999); "Retailer Prepares to Welcome New Owner," *Daily Oakland Press* (July 11, 2004), http://theoaklandpress.com; Rebecca Mead, "You're Getting Married: The Wal-Martization of the Bridal Business," *The New Yorker* (April 21 & 28, 2003), 86.

15. "The May Department Stores Company and The Knot Announce Marketing Alliance," http://www.theknot.com/02.25.02.shtml.

16. "Press Releases," "Company Overview," http://www.theknot.com; "The Knot Reports Second Quarter and Six Months Results; Company's Online Advertising Revenue up 43%," *Business Wire* (August 12, 2004), http://phx.corporate-ir.net/ phoenix.zhtml?c = 99931&p = irol-newsArticle&t = Regular&id = 603578&; "The May Department Stores Company and The Knot Announce Marketing Alliance."

17. "Retailer Prepares to Welcome New Owner," *Daily Oakland Press* (July 11, 2004), http://theoaklandpress.com; Bob Brown, "May Sees Bliss in Tuxedo Tie-Ins: 3 Chains Become 1 Under Retailer" (February 27, 2004), *Chicago Tribune*, http:// www.siliconinvestor.com.

18. Ads in 2003 for Priscilla of Boston stated only "Simple elegance. A tradition for over 50 years." *Bride's* (November–December 2003), 124–125; Mead, "You're Getting Married," 86; Otnes and Pleck, *Cinderella Dreams*, 101.

19. Mead, "You're Getting Married," 85–86, 78. For a discussion of David's Bridal, also see Otnes and Pleck, *Cinderella Dreams*, 102–104; "Introducing David's Bridal Style Plus," *Bride's* (Summer 2003), advertising insert section; http://www.davids bridal.com. "David's Bridal," *Bride's* (May–June 2003), advertising insert section (quotation).

20. Mead, "You're Getting Married," 78. Wang opened her first luxury salon in 1990. http://weddings.about.com/od/styleandattire/a/VeraWang.htm. One example of an independent discounter is The Bridal Mall, the largest bridal store in Connecticut. Mead, "You're Getting Married," 83.

21. Brown, "May Sees Bliss in Tuxedo Tie-Ins." Slightly different numbers of stores acquired were reported elsewhere. "The May Department Stores Company Announces Purchase of Gingiss Formalwear," December 29, 2003, http://www.for release.com/D20031229/nym095.P1.12292003162905.18269.html.

22. http://www.davidsbridal.com.

23. "Beware of the Bridezilla Syndrome" (August 30, 2002), CBS News, http://www.cbsnews.com; the term *Bridezilla* differs from earlier critiques of wedding consumption and female spending out of control in its self-reflexive awareness. The term is a social critique, but one that pokes fun and then accepts or even embraces the type.

24. Dennis Hall, "Modern and Postmodern Wedding Planners: Emily Post's *Etiquette in Society* (1937) and Blum & Kaiser's *Weddings for Dummies* (1997)," http://pcasacas.org/SPC/spcissues/24.3/Hall.htm.

25. Alice Keim, "The Computer as Wedding Consultant," *New York Times* (October 15, 1998), D10.

26. Otnes and Pleck, *Cinderella Dreams*, 81, 87–88.

27. Editor's Letter, "Style and Substance," *Bride's* (September–October 2003), 26.

28. "Lash Track," *Bride's* (Summer 2003), 16; "Fortunoff.com: Stress Relief for the Bride and Groom," *Bride's* (Summer 2003), advertising insert section.

29. "ClubWedd from Here to Happily," advertising insert section, and "$415,811—Before the Flowers," *Bride's* (May–June 2003), 62; "The Great American Wedding," *Bride's* (November–December 2003), 480–483.

30. "Walking Down the Aisle," *Bride's* (May–June 2003), 114.

31. "A First at *Bride's* Magazine: A Report on Same-Sex Unions," *New York Times* (July 28, 2003), C6; David Toussaint, "Outward Bound," *Bride's* (September–October 2003).

32. Gwynne Morgan, "Designers Woo Mature Brides," 1981, newsclipping, box 10, Priscilla of Boston Collection, NMAH. Otnes and Pleck note that Peggy Post "gave the go-ahead for pregnant brides to wear long, white gowns," though not wedding veils. *Cinderella Dreams*, 243.

33. Regular etiquette features dealt both with modern dilemmas and long-standing concerns. "Etiquette Q&A," *Bride's* (September–October 2003), 198; "Down the Aisle at 20, 30, 40," *Bride's* (Summer 2003), 390–397.

34. "Mori Lee," advertisement, *Bride's* (Summer 2003), 176–177; "Christina Wu," *Bride's* (September–October 2003), advertising insert section; "Vera Wang Talks Tinseltown," *Bride's* (May–June 2003), 52; "Pink Is the New White in Weddings: The Knot Reports Color Is All the Rage for 2004," press release, http://www.theknot.com/06.07.04.shtml.

35. "Vera Wang," *Bridal Guide* (March–April 1997), 17. Over a short period, advertising styles could change dramatically even for the same designer. For example, compare the traditional presentation of bridal fashion in "Reem Acra," *Bridal Guide* (March–April 1997), 31, with the postmodern style of "Reem Acra," *Bride's* (November–December 2003), 2–3.

36. Harvey, *The Condition of Postmodernity*, 7. Harvey quotes Terry Eagleton's definition of postmodernism here.

37. "Reem Acra," *Bride's* (November–December 2003), 2–3.

38. "Aisle View: Past Forward," *Bride's* (November–December 2003), 49–50; Harvey, *The Condition of Postmodernity*, 44, 85.

39. Lyn Mautner, "Reigning Over the Bridal Trade," *New York Times* (January 8,

1989), NJ10. The Bridal Expos Inc., was one of the largest expos during this period, and was featured in twenty-two cities across the United States. Joe Sharkey, "Jersey; Down the Aisle, With Checkbook," *New York Times* (September 28, 1997), 13NJ; Southern California, http://www.weddingbells.com/stores/bs_California.html; Mid-Atlantic Wedding Expo, http://www.mysticproductions.com/wedding/Default.htm.

40. "The Original Wedding Expo," http://www.originalweddingexpo.com./ They have been in operation since 1978; Mid-Atlantic Wedding Expo, http://www.mysticproductions.com/wedding/Default.htm. I also attended several wedding expos in the late 1990s. For example, see Austin's Wedding Showcase poster, October 26, 1997, Austin Convention Center, material in possession of the author.

41. "Vendors," Black & Beautiful Wedding Expo, http://www.blackbeautiful wedding.com/faq.htm; Austin's Wedding Showcase poster, October 26, 1997.

42. A traditional Boston jewelry store, Shreve, Crump & Low, sought the gay market with a recent advertisement for wedding bands that stated "This is love. It's not up for a vote" (http://www.commercialcloset.org); Flaherty, "Freedom to Marry, and to Spend on It," *New York Times* (May 16, 2004).

43. Bloomingdale's held "The Pink Event" in the Lenox Hotel in Boston. Flaherty, "Freedom to Marry, and to Spend on It"; Macy's adopted "spouse" and "registrant" to accommodate same-sex couples, while Filene's planned to keep "bride" and "groom" labels in its wedding registry. Sasha Talcott, "Gays Have Suitors in Wedding Industry: Firms Hope to Cash in as Legal Vows Begin" (May 15, 2004), http://www.boston.com; Tiffany, Williams-Sonoma, and Michael C. Fina made their wedding registries non–gender specific around this time period as well. See d'Innocenzio, "More Retailers Say 'I Do" to Gay Marriage Market."

44. Elissa Gootman, "New Specialty at Wedding Expo: Same-Sex Unions," *New York Times* (October 21, 2001), 34.

45. Talcott, "Gays Have Suitors in Wedding Industry." Also, see Steve Lowery, "Just Another Wedding Expo," *OC Weekly* (July 23–29, 2004), http://www.oc weekly.com.

46. Lowery, "Just Another Wedding Expo"; Christine Hauser, "Top Hats and Two Grooms on a Cake, but No Licenses," *New York Times* (March 21, 2004), 29; Talcott, "Gays Have Suitors in Wedding Industry"; Flaherty, "Freedom to Marry, and to Spend on It."

47. Dianna Marder, "Love" column, *Philadelphia Inquirer*, April 3, 2005.

48. Other protests against the wedding industry in the late twentieth century were directed against the sweatshop labor practices of major wedding gown manufacturers like Alfred Angelo Company in 1997. Ingraham, *White Weddings*, 46–47.

Index

Acknowledgments

From the first day I began thinking about American weddings and the bridal business I have benefited from all of those people who generously shared their wedding memories and experiences with me. I would like to thank all those friends, relatives, students, and even chance acquaintances who have shared their wedding dreams with me, who brought out their wedding albums, or recounted the details of their bridal gown and their ceremony and reception. This book has allowed me to share in one of the most special moments in the lives of these people and has enriched my own life in the process.

Since I began researching weddings in 1997 I have received financial support from several different institutions. I would like to thank the University of Texas at Austin for its University Continuing Fellowship, 1997–1998, which released me from teaching to focus on my dissertation, "American Weddings: Gender, Consumption, and the Business of Brides." I am deeply indebted to the Hagley Museum and Library in Wilmington, Delaware, for helping me complete my dissertation research and begin writing with a Henry Belin du Pont Dissertation fellowship in Business, Technology, and Society in 1999.

Thanks also to the Smithsonian Institution, which generously awarded me both a predoctoral fellowship in 1998 and a postdoctoral fellowship in 2002 to work at the Archives Center in the National Museum of American History in Washington, D.C. The staff of the Archives Center went out of their way to help me with my project, drawing on their expertise to suggest sources and find the diverse wedding-related materials that were spread throughout a number of different collections. Many thanks to archivist Craig Orr for suggesting on my preliminary scouting trip to the Archives Center that my topic was "made for the Smithsonian" and for encouraging me to apply for a predoctoral fellowship. Susan Strange's enthusiasm for my topic meant a lot to me as she continued to keep me abreast of collections and wedding-related material after I left the Archives Center. Thanks also to my mentors during my predoctoral fellowship, curators Charles McGovern and Claudia Brush Kidwell. And during my postdoctoral fellowship, a special thanks to Shelly Foote and Priscilla Wood in Costumes. All four shaped my work in different ways and I feel fortunate to have met them and been able to draw on their immense knowledge and expertise while they were all still at the Smithsonian.

I was fortunate to be awarded a two-year Woodrow Wilson postdoctoral fellowship beginning in 2000, jointly sponsored by Rutgers University-Camden and Hagley Museum and Library. This generous award from the Woodrow Wilson Foundation allowed me to do extensive research beyond the dissertation. At Hagley I found rich archives and a brilliant intellectual community revolving around conversations in the hallways and at the water cooler, brown-bag talks, monthly research seminars and Thai dinners, and regular conferences. This great institution and the terrific people there gave me a second home—providing housing, but also welcoming me into their community while I faced the sometimes isolating time of researching away from home. I cannot thank Roger Horowitz and Philip Scranton enough for all they have done for me. And thanks also to Carol Lockman for all the conversations and to Glen Porter for helping to bring me there in the first place. While a Woodrow Wilson Fellow at Rutgers University-Camden I found another supportive intellectual atmosphere that helped in the completion of this book. Carol Singley was an excellent mentor there in English and American Studies. In the History Department Janet Golden, Howard Gillette, and Philip Scranton welcomed their postdoctoral sojourner like a colleague and made my teaching semesters very rewarding. Dean Margaret Marsh at Rutgers-Camden offered useful critiques of my research, and her work as a historian has influenced my own.

Numerous mentors, friends, and colleagues helped this project come to completion. As a graduate student in the Department of American Studies at the University of Texas at Austin I benefited from the teachings and example of some great American Studies scholars. I would like to express my deep gratitude to my dissertation advisor, Jeffrey Meikle, who encouraged me to take on big subjects and intellectual questions in the manner of a great teacher. In the years since, Jeff has continued to support my career and has always offered good advice when I most needed it. Heartfelt thanks to Janet Davis, who remains a friend and is a role model for me in many ways, both personally and professionally. Janet continued to support my work after I left UT, reading portions of it and providing much needed guidance. Many thanks to Desley Deacon for her helpful reading of the dissertation and crucially important suggestion that I focus on the wedding industry, rather than on weddings as a whole. Thanks also to Mark Smith, who made all the graduate students feel at home in American Studies. And finally, thanks to historian Sally Clarke. Sally is largely responsible for my continued interest in business and consumer culture and I am very glad to have had the opportunity to study under her.

In the course of my research I have met many scholars who were generous with their time and resources, sharing accounts of weddings, image of brides, and other related information that they came across in the course of their own research. There are so many of these individuals that most will have to go unnamed, though I remain very grateful to them all. However, I would like to thank the following friends and colleagues who shared their ideas with me, as well as book titles, references, and wedding-related primary documents: Ann Boylan, Jan Davidson, Lisa Davidson, Debbie Doyle, Paul Erikson, Sandy Howarth, Sarah Johnson, Larry Malone, Sonya Michel, Arwen Mohun, Cindy Ott, Edythe Quinn, Maureen Reed, Colleen and Clayton Rustad, Susan Strange, and Peter Wallace. I would like to thank my friends Leilah Danielson and Dwonna Goldstone for the readings they gave my work at different stages. And I owe a debt to the late Susan Porter Benson, whose work I admire very much. As the original outside reader for my book before she passed away, her constructive criticisms and excellent suggestions on a portion of the book much improved the project overall. Other scholars provided insights on the topics of business, gender, and consumption that helped my own thinking on these issues. Chrys Ingraham offered helpful comments on a paper on ring traditions that I presented at the Berkshires Women's History conference. Numerous conversations with Regina Blaszczyk shaped my approach to business history and consumer culture. Susan Strasser read a portion of my work and gave me excellent advice on finding my voice in writing. And many thanks to my editor, Robert Lockhart, whose editorial pen also did much to benefit the final shape and tone of the manuscript.

I would like to acknowledge all who agreed to be interviewed about their work in the wedding industry or their experiences with it. Thanks to Cile

Bellefleur-Burbidge, John Burbidge, Peg Davies, Margaret Enck, Dorothy Benjamin Holmes, Barbara Howard, Priscilla Kidder, Mary Klemmer, Barbara Tober, Priscilla Wood, and Blaine Workman. A special thanks to the late Wells Drorbaugh, Jr., who graciously provided me with a detailed history of *Bride's* magazine.

There are many personal debts I would like to acknowledge. Thanks to my friends for their support along the way and for all the good times in graduate school and beyond. The enthusiasm and cheer of my dear friend Jennie Golo-boy has meant a lot to me as we kept in touch over the years, talking about research and teaching, our job-search experience, and most recently, the joy of motherhood. Thanks to my good friends Mitch and Michelle Lerner for their contribution to my sanity during graduate school and for opening their house to Sean and myself over many holidays in recent years. Other old friends continued to support my project and encourage me over the years it took to finish: Eric Meeks and Leilah Danielson deserve special mention. Thanks to new friends and colleagues who have read my work or offered useful advice that helped the project get to the final stages, including Mieko Nishida, as well as Lisle Dalton, Dora Dumont, Cherilyn Lacy, and other members of the Susquehanna Research Seminar in Oneonta, New York.

Thanks to my family for all their love and support. My sisters, Valerie Howard Jones and Laurie Howard, and my parents, Barbara and David Howard, have helped me in so many ways, with encouragement but also with information and clippings. Erin Kelley, Alice Horton-Kelley, and Tim and Harriett Kelley have also been incredibly supportive and great cheerleaders from the West Coast. Most important, I want to acknowledge the immense contribution of my historian husband, Sean Michael Kelley. Without him I could not have conceived of, researched, or written this book. Not only has he taken time from his own writing to assist me on research trips, help me with databases, and offer critiques of innumerable versions of conference papers, dissertation chapters, book outlines and chapter drafts, he has done so with the unflagging enthusiasm of a true scholar. And last, my daughter Kathleen Howard-Kelley who arrived at the very end deserves special mention for making everything a lot more fun.